Annie M. P. Smithson
— novelist
— see if mystery
novels.

Gallery Books
Editor Peter Fallon

POETRY, MEMORY AND THE PARTY

Irish Writers + Exile -
Seán Lucy?.

Thomas McCarthy

POETRY, MEMORY AND THE PARTY

Journals 1974-2014

To John,

With gratitude to you
for _buying_ the book —

blessings on your own
work

Tom McCy
2023

Poetry, Memory and the Party
is first published
simultaneously in paperback
and in a clothbound edition
on 4 January 2022.

The Gallery Press
Loughcrew
Oldcastle
County Meath
Ireland

www.gallerypress.com

ISBN 978 1 91133 812 3 *paperback*
     978 1 91133 813 0 *clothbound*

A CIP catalogue record for this book
is available from the British Library.

Poetry, Memory and the Party receives financial assistance
from the Arts Council.

POETRY, MEMORY
AND THE PARTY

1974

January 4th Tonight a westerly wind rattles the shutters of Glenshelane House. Drops of rain skate across the window-panes and our rampant *Superstar* rose moves in the light from the window. This rose is a spectral survivor of 1973, another dreadful year in our land. A sinister time, security forces everywhere. There's talk that Colonel Ghaddafi has sent boats laden with guns into the Republican strongholds around Dungarvan Harbour. The Christmas temporary postman told me that he saw IRA men testing fancy new Libyan equipment in a field near Tooraneena, the birthplace of the poet Pádraig Ó Mileadha. What will become of us all? It's not just Ulster: the whole of Ireland is in the grip of something horrible. These Libya-backed Republican bombers, these history-licensed beasts of anarchy so feared by Yeats, have handed us a destiny that no small country deserves. I think it's time to plan an escape from Ireland. I must get out while I'm still young. I must emigrate; there's just no other way to shed this heavy Republican anarchy that's gripped the country. You'd think you'd be safe from Ulster history this far south in County Waterford.

I was stopped by armed detectives at Lismore Bridge on Christmas Eve. They insisted on opening the carrier box of my motorbike. They found two books within: Lady Anson's memoirs and *A Book about Roses* by Canon Reynolds Hole of Lincoln. Neither publication banned by Liam Cosgrave or Conor Cruise O'Brien, so I was waved on without comment by a bored and grumpy officer. Some good things in the last year, I admit, like Heaney's *Wintering Out* and the Seán Keating painting 'Economic Pressure' that I saw in the Crawford Gallery.

January 6th The Feast of Epiphany There's little enough epiphany in my life. I thrive in the depths of my own loneliness. Here in the kitchen the ten-o-clock pips from the BBC coming from Denis H FitzGerald's (the Brigadier's) old *Hacker* radio are my sole companions. Yet my childhood held a kind of epiphany. When I was born I was given only four hours to live by our local Dr McMahon. I still catch my mother looking at me as if I were her miracle child, as if she expects me not to be here.

January 8th Petrol shortages because of the Middle East oil crisis. The Minister for Education has ordered secondary schools to stay shut for another week. I went to the post office in Cappoquin to complete an Application Form for a petrol ration for the Brigadier and Glenshelane House but Maurice Kelleher has run out of forms.

I finished a poem on Mr Allen of Whitechurch House over Christmas. I will always be grateful to him for passing on my poems to Dervla Murphy.

January 14th English Literature Society meeting in the Kampus Kitchen at lunchtime: I was ready. I had all my notes. Are there any politics more treacherous than the politics of undergraduate life? Even more treacherous because there is so little at stake: perhaps a choice of guest lecturer and a budget of £35. Such power. But it is here, in undergraduate life, that many future politicians first learn their cruel game.

January 27th Terrible storms during the week: the worst continuous winds since the big winds of seventy years ago. Wind gusts of up to 110 miles an hour were recorded at Cork Airport. At Glenshelane the eucalyptus fell down, damaging the electricity wires. A huge rhododendron fell across the path to the garden. At least five other major trees fell. The telephone link was cut. On top of this storm the Government has announced that it is going to introduce new taxes. I sent a letter to the Brigadier with a map of the garden, marking all the damaged and felled trees. I will have to organize tractors and chainsaws.

Dolours Price, the IRA bomber, has gone on Hunger Strike. The British are force-feeding her.

February 13th Handed up my second Archaeology essay. I've been studying Map-Reading and Interpretation and Early Man in East Africa.

March 6th My twentieth birthday. Sick in bed, a flu-like fever. This morning my father came upstairs while I was lying still with a handkerchief over my face. My poor father thought I'd died. He started shouting 'Thomas! Thomas!' in a voice of pure panic. I had to tell him to calm down. Indeed it was not the first time in this life that I had to tell him to calm down — but my copybook was covered with blood. It looked hilarious. I felt like Francis Ledwidge in the trenches.

April 12th I have overdrawn my student overdraft by £25. Already in trouble.

April 30th Yesterday, found a pamphlet in the College library published by the Ulster Museum. It contained an account of river transport on the Blackwater between Youghal and Cappoquin in the 19th century. Fascinating photograph of *The Dartmouth Castle*, a steamer, leaving the quay at Cappoquin in 1910.

June 3rd I would like to have a pamphlet printed in Cork. M has three of my new poems. As she has no interest in me I must get them back.

July 20th The Brigadier came home to Glenshelane today. Full of London stories and Conservative Party gossip from all the business luncheons and Panmure Gordon projects he's involved in. He had no useful literary news. Because he's a partner in Panmure Gordon, the stockbrokers, the circle he moves in is the wrong circle for a poet like me. He spends his time with capitalists, directors and shareholders of publishing houses, rather than with the humble and impoverished editors: it is the salaried and depressed editor sweating on the afternoon Tube rather than the grandee proprietor at Ascot who will determine whether I succeed or fail. He mentioned again the possibility of an office job in Sidgwick & Jackson (he met Lord Longford yet again). Molly Keane has been urging him to find a job for me in London. She has taken a shine to me since I helped her with cuttings from the *Kalmia latifolia*, the calico bush, at Glenshelane. If I could get to London it would, at least, be the beginning of a real literary life. John Montague says I would grow imaginatively, like John Hewitt in Coventry. I think he's right. There are exciting things happening in literary England; there's a terrific new energy in London. There's already a huge contingent of UCC graduates, most of them working in pubs and on building sites. In the last five years Ireland has provided the UK with the most highly educated labourers in history. The other day Montague said, very dramatically, that half the bar managers around Euston Station have degrees in Celtic Studies and that the other half can read sheet music. In the end they will all become rock-band managers or music producers with the big companies.

Reading Heaney and Yeats. In truth there's really no need to read anyone else: well, maybe Kavanagh or MacNeice. Rereading the forty pages of my play 'Local Election' that I wrote into the Brigadier's *Bernard Wardle Company* notebook. Pubs and meetings and grocers' shops; the thing disgusts me. Too much Fianna Fáil, but my character Edward says, 'We have had too much talk. We've had too many lies and too much silence.'

August 2nd I was sitting in the sunshine on the patio at Glen-shelane today reading the Brigadier's back copies of *Lloyds*

Log. As I recited the names out loud the Brigadier filled me in on the background to each Lloyds member. This kind of education is certainly not available in the UCC English Department, or any English Department. It was so strange that I felt I was reading an Anglo-Saxon text, a page from the *Doomsday Book.* The Brigadier is a Lloyds 'name' which means that he has underwritten a level of risk with Lloyds, with his account handled by Bowrings in Tower Bridge Road as well as by Withers, the royal solicitors.The other day I said to him, 'How are you going to keep track of all these things when you retire and you no longer have the services of your secretary at Panmure Gordon?' He went into the house soon after that and came back with files from Bowrings of London, Sedgwick Dineen of Cork, where he's been buying high-yield bonds for his retirement, as well as Robert Flemings and Bank of Scotland in the Channel Islands. He went through letters and accounts for forty or so minutes. Then he looked at me and said: 'No, everything in order, everything in order. Shipshape.' He went off again and came back with a glass of sherry for both of us. (We'd successfully moved the Catalpa tree with its root-bowl intact, so he was pleased with himself.)

Then he went back to looking at a Spink catalogue that had just arrived this morning. There's a beautiful but hugely expensive Jacob Bogdani for sale. It was painted at Hampton Court in the 1600s. I watched him furtively, dying to make a comment, but I could see that the image had begun to overwhelm him. Beauty, beauty is the one thing that intoxicates him. In this he is a little like myself, though the gulf of class between us is enormous. Yet it is strange how sensibility is a personal and intimate thing: the love of beautiful objects, for example, or a love of gardens. It's really not a matter of class at all.

August 5th Lord Dunsany was here at Glenshelane. Many great stories about his father who disliked Yeats so much (the feeling was mutual). Molly Keane, who was also visiting, relaxed in the summer heat of the patio, read my poems for about twenty minutes. She likes the Protestant Church poem as well as 'Shattered Frost'. Again she pointed out a fault in 'Shattered Frost' — the totally unsatisfactory closing couplet. Pat Crotty in UCC pointed out the same weakness. I will have to change that last verse. When it comes to the art of poetry I'm still a child. But how long will this childhood last, I wonder? How long should a poet be apprenticed? In the old Celtic world a poet's apprenticeship lasted seven years. That seems about right. I began to write in earnest at the age of fifteen: my apprenticeship should end at the age of twenty-two.

August 10th Michael Hartnett has decided to write exclusively in Irish. I can understand the politics of his decision, but from the point of view of poetry it is a huge mistake. Paul Durcan thinks he's our greatest Southern poet, more lyrical and beautiful than Kinsella, more disciplined than Kennelly. But why is he is so easily pushed from the podium of his own voice? English poetry offers endless possibilities, and it can embrace even the most eccentric and parochial kinds of Irishness. So why this rush into the Irish language? Is it a spiritual pursuit of Caitlín Maude or an emotional escape from Seamus Heaney? Perhaps the Irish language will be like a second wife to him:

> *. . . As gold-green moss*
> *close to the bark*
> *when the winds toss*
> *my limbs to tragedy and dark.*

But it is sad to lose such a good Munster poet in English. Almost like Ledwidge, but very primary and angry and raw. The delicacy of *Anatomy of a Cliché* is beautiful, poised, elegant. And this is the problem with switching from English to Irish: is his Irish vocabulary equal to all the suffering and pain of human consciousness? Will he be able to carry all that existential grief like Seán Ó Ríordáin? And will he have an audience? Or has he merely committed an act of linguistic piety, thereby creating an imaginative dead end like Daniel Corkery? Corkery's embrace of the Gaelic League marked the end of his career as a serious artist. Middle-aged Irishmen often embrace 'The Language' with the same hopeless abandon that certain English writers embrace Roman Catholicism — and their decision is defined not by what they've embraced but by what they think they've abandoned.

August 15th In *Wintering Out* Seamus Heaney breaks away from the mere material of Ireland like a greyhound out of a trap. He has found an impersonal personal voice and method, something beyond our national, conventional voices. His year in California has changed him, loosened him and enlarged him, though it does make him sound more like Ted Hughes: the Hughes of *Wodwo* and *Crow*. Heaney still hasn't reached Hughes' intensity or precision. The linguistic precision, the calculated emotional weight, in every phrase of Hughes is simply astonishing. There is still too much of pietistic Irish Catholicism and too little of hard Pennine granite in Heaney but, still, he has his own material: he has Ireland, he has Ulster. Heaney is surely the poet of eels as Hughes is the poet of eagles. And, poetically, Hughes is Heaney's great technical rival. I wonder is Hughes, over there in England and making a completely English life, aware of Heaney yet? Does he think of him with fear and contempt, the way Montague does? Or is he unaware of this powerful, un-wavering Irishman, the way Lord Byron was unaware of the real power of Shelley? Can one poet ever really feel the force of another poet's future? A poet can only imagine his own success, never another's.

Montague does feel marooned in UCC, too far away from the poetry action of Belfast. Munster is not a province of England: (how ironic that is, given the success of the Tudor and

Elizabethan plantations of Munster). Nowadays the English establishment treats Ulster poets as if they were all from Bristol. And why not? Legally, isn't Belfast as much a part of the UK as Hull, Bristol or East Anglia? Here in the South we can't have our cake and eat it: we cannot on the one hand resent that British element in Ulster's connections, and politically refute it at every turn, whilst at the same time envying Ulster's connections to the BBC and London publishing. I said to Seán Dunne the other day that we'll never be that lucky in our careers. Seán said, 'I don't give a shite!' Seán is such a wild creature, but I think he does 'give a shite' much more than he's willing to admit. He is as ambitious as any other normal young poet, but he takes great pains to hide this ambition — perhaps, in him, not simply ambition, something more bohemian, a yearning for notoriety. I have no such yearning. Like every McCarthy before me I yearn for a quiet life, a comforting backwater, a shelf somewhere.

October 12th Good lecture from John Montague today about Dryden and Pope. He delighted in talking about the Restoration of the Stuart king. And Dryden's political timing — when the king was brought back from France Dryden tried to bring back French Theatre as well. Also, the echoes of Milton in Dryden, especially in 'Absalom and Achitophel'. J M quotes Hobbes approvingly, 'Imagination is nothing else but sense decaying or weakened by the absence of the object', and then he quoted Blake on 'the object' — 'natural objects deaden and weaken the imagination in me'. Montague told us we should read Ian Jack's *Augustan Satire* and F R Leavis's *Revaluation*.

November 14th Poem in *Aire*. M will type some poems for *The Examiner*. I must send 'Shattered Frost' to *The Irish Times* and more to *Caritas* as well. Gregory O'Donoghue read his poetry last night. He said that Heaney had now become a problem for everyone, that he has created a sort of cult around Ulster poetry, and that things can only get worse. Gregory is completey immersed in Montague's *Tides* and Montague's view of the poetic world. I think Heaney has disturbed something that was once comforting in Irish poetry: in a very real sense his arrival hasn't been properly 'sanctioned' in Dublin circles. As far as Liam Miller and John Montague are concerned Heaney is a man operating without a licence. But who issues these licences to Irish poets? The Dolmen Press? The Irish Academy of Letters? The Royal Irish Academy? The fact is that to become a poet requires no permission from any standing authority. A poet claims territory and ascends his or her own throne without permission. As Wordsworth once observed, a new poet always creates the new taste by which he is to be received. Heaney is creating an entirely new kind of taste in Irish poetry; he's teaching an entire generation to receive his work, right across the world. There is nothing any rival poet can do to prevent the development of this new taste — indeed, I am certain that to complain about this new 'taste' is to intensify the public yearning for it. (M's latest put-down, at which we all nervously laugh: 'Heaney's the Hush-Puppy poet.') But it is impossible to advise or caution poor Montague. When any artist becomes envious or worried about the rising reputation of another artist he becomes utterly irrational, beyond good advice. Montague's argument, though, is that Heaney is not a new taste in poetry, but merely a *réchauffé* Kavanagh. But today I saw Niall MacMonagle, the undergraduate guru of the English Department, carrying copies of two Heaney books into Montague's lecture. I thought: he's delivering nails for John's coffin.

In Munster poetry we should all try to give expression to a looser kind of Irishness. We can reach towards a Protestant meaning of the past in a way that's not open to Ulster Catholics: we can be sanguine and idealistic in a way that no hardened Belfast nationalist can be. It is very difficult to communicate this basic fact to Montague. He doesn't want to hear such talk. For him there's no such thing as a Munster or Southern Irish view of things — and even if he could admit such a viewpoint he would characterize it as deficient, as lacking the Ulster experience, as a mere 'Free State' view of hard history and politics. In this, of course, he shows his Ulster Catholic origins. He won't betray them, not even while safely inside the bourgeois cocoon of UCC. The integrity of the Ulster Catholic experience is a fearsome thing. Despite its integrity Munster poets can still refute it: it is not our experience. We need to be faithful to the kinds of experiences we've had, especially our experiences with Protestants. And Southern Unionists generally.

November 16th Reading Larkin's *The North Ship* and Betjeman's *Collected Poems*. Strange, in Betjeman, those poems of Southern Irish Unionism, such as 'Penniless Irish Peer' and 'The Irish Unionist's Farewell to Greta Hellstrom in 1922'.

Has anyone ever interrogated these Betjeman poems? They capture a unique atmosphere; they are poetic companions to the early 1920s novels of Molly Keane. I find them completely haunting. Does anyone in Ireland even know about them? I doubt it. The Brigadier and my mother are the only two people who will listen to me reciting the Greta Hellstrom poem — two listeners from the opposite ends of society, the one listening because he remembers Betjeman on British television in the early 1960s, the other listening because any mention of Dungarvan transports her back to a blissfully secure Keating Street childhood. For my mother all of the security of life fell apart when she reached Cappoquin.

1975

January 11th Working hard at the garden in Glenshelane. I rotavated the vegetable patch and cleared weeds from the base of the blackcurrants. My mother is very ill. She has had flu and a stomach bug — in bed on and off for nearly four weeks. I did most of the cooking on Christmas Day and St Stephen's Day.

January 18th Mother in hospital in Waterford City. I went to see her on the Express bus. It's terrible that I have no car. I rejoice in poetry. And when I rejoice in my poetry I am merely rejoicing in an alternative self, a self free of origins or, rather, a self of widened origins. Through reading my way into writing I've widened my origins so that my background doesn't explain me. It would be idiotic of anyone to look into my background in order to explain my literary nature. And it's difficult to explain this to people. But Molly Keane really understands this. One day before last Christmas she said to me that her entire soul was in her fiction, that it wasn't anywhere else. I knew instantly what she meant. And she knew that I understood, instantly. The Brigadier, who overheard our conversation, hadn't a clue what she was saying. He is utterly conventional. An Anglo-Irish aristocrat, yes, but a profoundly conventional man. Molly looked at him with pity in her eyes. Then she looked at me, full of pride the pride of recognition. Everything around us became silent: I could see right into the heart of Molly Keane's old novels. I could see their power, the power of *The Rising Tide* and the power of *Two Days in Aragon*. I felt that nobody else alive could go there, into that luminous territory of her books. She is the sole custodian of a land that she alone has imagined and made real.

January 22nd Last week two poems of mine published in *The Cork Examiner*. There's a very succinct introduction to my poems by Gerry Fitzgibbon of UCC's English Department. He's a good man, a man of the theatre now, though I suspect poetry is his first love.

January 25th First meeting next week of the UCC Poetry Workshop that I am supposed to direct.

February 3rd A letter from the Brigadier saying that he'll come over from England to Glenshelane in March, in time for St Patrick's weekend. How wonderfully ordered his life is. It is punctuated by holidays, festivals and commemorations. How I envy him his ordered life, constantly reaffirmed by public and regimental commemorations. As for my life, it is one continuous working-class daze: a kind of twilight of sameness, compounded by the disorientation of undergraduate life. One of the absolutely distinguishing things about our family, the thing that marked us as underprivileged, was the complete lack of response to public events. The poor don't participate in a public realm. A family in poverty is always inward-looking, self-obsessed. I remember as a child coming into our house to tell my parents that John F Kennedy had been assassinated. I had heard it on my grandmother's radio. I was so animated by Kennedy's assassination that they thought one of my schoolteachers had died. That I could be so moved by a public death so far away, by anything in the public domain, amazed my mother and amused my cynical, defeated father. And Fianna Fáil has fed off this Catholic passivity in the manner of Falangists or Peronists. From the point of view of an educated Protestant in Belfast the Irish Republic must sometimes seem to be part of Latin America.

February 6th My Mr Allen poem published by Seán Dunne in the student *Broadsheet*.

February 11th Things are really moving now. My Poetry Workshop idea has taken off. Twenty students attended last week's workshop on campus. UCC is buzzing with young poets. Five poets read their poems and discussed the structures rather than any philosophy behind the work. This is exactly what a workshop should be. Tomorrow I must read more workshop poems. John Montague and Gregory O'Donoghue attended last week's workshop. Montague was uncharacteristically reasonable and co-operative. He says that 'something big' could happen out of the work of our group.

February 19th Charles Haughey has been recalled to the Front Bench of Fianna Fáil. The Party was forced into accepting him back. He has a brilliantly calculating mind; it's just impossible for ordinary mortals to control him. He has become the Fianna Fáil Spokesman on Health. Of course he is a man who can never again be trusted and — in the long term — his reappearance will do untold damage to the Party. It may even lead to the disintegration of Fianna Fáil. But Haughey is so intelligent and competent. Poor George Colley must be furious and Dessie O'Malley must be apoplectic.

Michael said there were terrible tensions at a recent Party meeting in Dungarvan, resulting in a serious fist fight. Who would believe that this kind of thing could go on? It's the politics of the rabble, the uncontrollable property-less rabble, that has been warned against by every piece of Fine Gael election literature since the time of Yeats (the uneducated mob that cannot partake of Parnell's heart). But this recent chaos all stems from the weakness of Jack Lynch.

February 20th Two important English Lit Society meetings within the last ten days. We had Hilary Pyle, a Cambridge post-graduate and a director of The National Gallery, talking about James Stephens. She said that Cambridge refused her a doctorate. They said that Stephens was only worth a Masters. But, even more importantly, we had Michael Hartnett, the bilingual poet, reading his poetry and discussing his ideas. I chaired a discussion on the future of Anglo-Irish poetry between Hartnett, Seán Lucy and John Montague. The whole discussion vacuous, pointless and generally without an ounce of sense.

Dinner in a superb restaurant, The Oyster Tavern, with Hartnett and his wife Rosemary, as well as John Montague and his wife, Evelyn. Montague and I are reconciled again. Wonderful atmosphere in The Oyster with Montague and Hartnett exchanging brilliant snippets of gossip and filling each other's glasses to overflowing with terrific French wine.

March 17th St Patrick's Day The Brigadier reminded me that the Queen Mother presents shamrock to the Irish Guards today. How incongruous that is to almost every Irish person, except those who went through the experiences of the last War with the British. The War created an astonishing bond between everyone who wore a British uniform. Today it would be dangerous for any Irish person to wear an English uniform. Even the Poppy is no longer worn around Cappoquin. Because of the Ulster 'Troubles' nationalist Ireland has closed ranks. To think that in the Oireachtas of 1927 and 1928 more than twenty Deputies and Senators wore the Poppy on Remembrance Day. The other day Michael told me that one of the ——s from Lismore has been a Metropolitan Policeman in England since the mid '60s. He hasn't been able to come home to Lismore since the start of the Troubles in 1969 because IRA lunatics from Helvick would kill him.

March 25th At Glenshelane. We are awaiting the arrival of Adrian FitzGerald, the Brigadier's heir and son of the Knight of Kerry, and two friends, one a Uniacke-FitzGerald of East Cork, all coming from London, all to arrive in time for dinner.

April 8th John B Keane was up at UCC for a lecture to our Society. A very affable man indeed; chatted and joked with us in Jurys Hotel. I gave him the title of his talk *Is the Holy*

Ghost a Kerryman? He said to me that someday he was going to use it as a book title. He is very angry with the Provos, and with the use of violence generally. A humane and sympathetic Kerryman.

April 10th Peter Fallon, Seán Dunne, Gregory O'Donoghue and Theo Dorgan read their poetry. I did the introductions. Talking to Fallon and Montague afterwards in the Millwheel Bar. Fallon very withdrawn and shy.

April 11th Met Peter Fallon again in the Green Room. Spoke with him for three hours, from four o'clock to seven. An incredibly interesting person, very enigmatic and hooded. He spoke about The Gallery Press, its operation and his life.

May 5th A sensational English Literature Society reading. Robert Graves came to visit us from Majorca. I sat beside him and his wife at the Oyster dinner. He said to me that Rupert Brooke was 'the nicest of the Georgians'. He also said that 'of that lot' Winston Churchill was the only gentleman. He said that poetry is no longer being written in England but that he got 'the sense of poetry' when he landed in Ireland. I doubt this statement on poetry in England. Poetry is a natural occurrence in the population, very like a winter virus. England with its vast population must have at least ten times more poets than Ireland. At the reception after his reading he was besieged by people. Very fatigued, with a face the colour of aluminium. He looked at the crush of students, then looked at me, the Auditor of the English Lit, and seemed very frightened. He expected me to do something, to control somehow the adoration of this Irish crowd. I went over, sat beside him, actually held his hand, and talked to him for a while. Then Montague announced that I'll be the first gardener-poet of Ireland. Graves looked up at him, wondering what this statement had to do with anything in the great poet's life. For all his personal anarchy and independence

Montague has a very academic, categorizing mind: he sees himself as the Exile-Poet, Heaney as the Farmer-Poet; and now he wants me, his student, to become the Gardener-Poet. He is happiest once a category has been settled upon. I find such categorizing really tiresome, even annoying. Maybe I'll end up living in brilliant penury, like Michael Hartnett in Inchicore, and become a dark Urban-Poet.

One thing is certain, Robert Graves has never ceased to be the Servant-Poet of the White Goddess: the firmness of his poetic convictions is thrilling. He is exactly as he should be, exactly as his books *The Common Asphodel* and *The White Goddess* announce him: 'The nucleus of every poem worthy of the name is rhythmically formed in the poet's mind, during a trance-like suspension of his normal habits of thought, by the supra-logical reconciliation of conflicting emotional ideas.' When Graves tells us that he's been to heaven several times what he really means is that he has lived frequently in a territory where great poems are formed. At one point in the evening, at dinner, Graves turned to me and said, 'You know, Thomas, I have been to heaven.' I thought he had taken too much drink, until he showed me his box (silver with what looked like an emerald set into the lid), a little box of hallucinogenic mushrooms that had been a gift from Carlos Castaneda. Graves' wife slapped him on the wrist and said, 'You mustn't ruin that young boy with your dirty mushrooms!' He returned his magic mushrooms to his pocket very sheepishly. What an old devil he is, what a pure, irresponsible lyricist of the mid-century! Still, his sanity is recovered every ten years with every new version of his *Collected Poems*.

Later, at the seminar in the English Department, the immortal Graves was asked if he had any advice for budding poets. He answered, 'Poets! If you are budding come into bloom!'

June 13th I met Maurice Riordan in the College Quad and he showed me the new Heaney book, *North*. A beautiful production with a very grand Edward McGuire portrait of the poet on the back cover. This collection is more than a book. It has a magnetic, majestic presence; it is the public announcement of a great arrival, like Yeats's *The Winding Stair* or Kinsella's *Another September*. A real sense now that Heaney has arrived at the zenith of Irish poetry, that he has just staked a huge pioneering claim to vast territories of Irish influence. Mossy agrees that from now on all the older poets will be running themselves ragged in order to catch up with him. In terms of public profile he is now light years ahead of the Irish pack, so far ahead that he doesn't even hear them snapping at his ankles. Heaney's educational programmes on BBC and his Ulster work in teacher training have really created a marvellous new public for his poetry. He has created his own public, this is what's so amazing. He has done this all on his own. No doubt if *North* becomes wildly successful there will be many poets claiming to have 'helped' him or anticipated his success. But I've heard no major Irish poet endorsing him; if anything I've only heard negative rumblings about him from among the elite. In creating his own public he has created himself. He owes nothing to anyone.

June 16th Home to Cappoquin to serious problems. Want and hopelessness and despair. A crushing, fatalistic unhappiness. My mother definitely not well.

June 17th Back in Cork. Up to John Montague's house. At printers, Miros Press in Lavitt's Quay. Theo Dorgan and I stayed at Montagues' for a chat. Discussed the rose garden with Mrs Montague. Will plant ten rose bushes in a plot. Had tea. Later watched the *Pallisers* on TV. After *Pallisers* we listened to a radio interview with John on RTÉ Cork wavelength. He spoke about his Golden Stone Press and Ó Riada. It was wonderful listening to him reading his poem on Ó Riada with all of us, Theo, J M, Evelyn and myself, sitting by the fire. After the interview we discussed Northern Ireland.

John would not commit himself when Theo asked what he would do in the event of a Civil War in the Six Counties.

August 13th My poetry pamphlet *Shattered Frost* is published. Three hundred copies have been printed. Now for the selling part. I gave a copy to Pat Crotty and he said, 'McCarthy, frost doesn't shatter. Ice shatters.' Crotty, always the critic, but nearly always right.

August 14th Getting rid of *Shattered Frost* quickly. Mawe got her Leaving Cert.

October 21st Bought a brilliant book, *The Seventh Man* by John Berger.

October 26th Mr and Mrs Stacy who are caretakers of the Duke of Westminster's flats in Stack House, Ebury Street, the Brigadier's London home, arrived at Glenshelane. They brought me some books as well as a typewriter, a present from the Brigadier. My first typewriter. Fair play to the Brigadier who has given me this, along with Lady Inez FitzGerald's kimono and two Japanese prints. When I phoned London to thank him he replied, 'It is important to mark one's twenty-first birthday.' He feels more strongly about this than I do: I grew up entirely indifferent to birthdays. Today while the Stacys were here at Glenshelane, chatting about life in service and the advantages of working for the aristocracy, I couldn't have been happier. Other possibilities seemed to be opening, possibilities of an entirely different, un-modern kind of life that would suit my temperament.

October 29th Sent a poem sequence to *The Cork Examiner* ('Enclosure', a four poem sequence). Sent poems to *The Irish Press* for the first time in three or four years. No poems left to send to *The Listener*.

November 4th Poetry Workshop at UCC. This is the first meeting of the year. A fine gathering, about thirty or so. One beautiful, fidgety, nervous, bright-eyed girl. I wonder who she is? Now I mustn't go and fall in love with her.

November 5th Thinking of writing a long poem about Hall's house in Villlierstown, a home called 'Bleach House'. I already have one part called 'The Weavers'. It would be excellent if it could be as long as 'Enclosure' but more accomplished, modern and didactic. Words have been accumulating in my head about this for over a week.

November 6th Yesterday, had my first talk with Professor Lucy about my MA (Qualifying) Exam. He said that all poets have lost their nerve; that poets are now afraid of positive statement. I felt that this observation was part of some earlier conversation he'd been having with someone else, probably Bob Welch. But Lucy is like that; he has all of these complex but dislocated monologues and opinions. The other day in Roches Stores I saw an implement called a 'hair-straightener'. There should be a brain-straightener for middle-aged professors. When I met Bob Welch in the College bar the other day he seemed upset by a recent meeting he'd had with Lucy. But, I have to admit, Lucy's *Five Irish Poets* is a very fine Cork anthology.

December 5th Peter Fallon of The Gallery Press down at UCC to read poetry with Gregory O'Donoghue. Greg's book, *Kicking*, is out. It was a small reading. Met O'Donoghue's poor father, Bobby (poor because the poet-father has been eclipsed by the poet-son). Gregory will go places if he widens his range. But where is all the political discussion, all the lust, all the drinking, of Cork in this book? Nothing there, all very orderly, finely edited first by Maurice Riordan and Montague. The awkward bits have been shaved away. Fallon asked me why I didn't try to get my booklet published in Dublin. Told him honestly that I didn't think it was good enough. He said OK, but *still* why didn't you try at least? He is a very rational person and it was a very good question. But my first answer was correct: I'm painfully aware of the limitations of my work. Some of the poems in my pamphlet are truly embarrassing.

December 9th Missed classes in College. My County Council grant not in yet.

December 11th I was looking over Mary B's poems. Showed them to Theo Dorgan. He liked them too. They are filled with a sense of injustice and hatred of mediocrity.

Working on poems today. 'Bleaching Green' has taken too much time. Have these poems in my head — 1. Guards Captain ('Death by Fire'); 2. Uncle Jack ('Feeding Ground'); 3. The Idea of the Breath ('Warm Circle').

1976

January 8th Glad that Christmas is over. It rained and rained and rained. I spent all my time running between Glenshelane House and Shanbally Terrace, Cappoquin; and at Glenshelane, running between the garden and the kitchen.

My own new poems have caused a stir. I didn't tell J M that I had a poem in *The Irish Times*. When I met him again yesterday he wanted to know why I was keeping so secretive about my new work. Seemingly Sr Una, who teaches in the English Department and hates all living poets, told J M about my poem — while Mossy Riordan had kept copies of the poems I published in *The Examiner* while John was away. Truth is I didn't want to tell him about my latest work until I have 8-10 poems published. I had some of the poems I wrote at Christmas in my shoulder bag so I took them out and gave him a quick glance. He didn't have a good opinion of my *Shattered Frost* last year (in truth, it is an effete embarrassment of a booklet) and he has to revise his opinions now. He says he wants us to meet for a serious chat about the poems. He says there's a poet in me for sure, no doubt: 'Begad, McCarthy, you took the opportunity of my absence in America to blossom forth!' What triggered the real poetry? I don't know. Does anyone know why real poetry begins to happen? You spend years and years writing sincere and competent verse, then one day real poetry happens — you realize that everything that's gone before is just embarrassing shit. Does this happen to every poet? It probably does.

January 19th As a special favour to our Fianna Fáil neighbour John Fraher, and to save my poor, ill mother embarrassment every time she passes him on the street in Cappoquin,

I attended the Party Youth Conference in the Burlington Hotel in Dublin. A very impressive affair, carefully managed by the FF Front Bench. The pace was exhausting. Young delegates spoke for 14-16 hours over the two days. Old Joe Brennan gave an after-dinner speech in which he said we must find a compromise between sound and happy free enterprise and socialism. That was a sensible observation; and typically Fianna Fáil, promising both private wealth and public largesse.

Haughey's entrance to the Party Conference was carefully choreographed, calculated to undermine Lynch as he gave his Party Leader's address. Just before Jack Lynch spoke three men rose from their seats at the front of the hall, then three different men marched down the aisle between the crowds of young people and took their places, directly beneath the podium. It was Charles Haughey and two henchmen from the Border counties. It was sensational, like Hitler flanked by Himmler and Goebbels. The entrance created a wave of amazement. All calculated to belittle Jack Lynch. Lynch is easy enough to bully, God help us. Haughey, a strange and dangerous man. But his people are devoted to him.

The Provisional IRA high priests were selling pamphlets at the gates of Trinity and the Maoists were selling books inside the College grounds. I bought from both parties.

The only downside of the weekend was that a photographer from the Fianna Fáil newspaper *Iris* photographed me for publication. The horror of this permanent record stayed with me as the train sped back to Cork. I must admit it: as a poet I have supped with the devil. As far as every intellectual in Ireland is concerned Fianna Fáil really is the devil. Irish intellectual life resides in our Labour Party. It can't be found anywhere else. Truly, the intellectual destiny of Ireland will live or die with the Labour Party.

January 21st Poems in *The Irish Times* and in *The Examiner*'s 'New Poetry' page. 'Grandmother' was broadcast on *RTÉ* last night. What an amazing feeling.

Up at Montagues' again last night. John upset by the review of *A Slow Dance* in *The Irish Times*. Edna Longley's praise comes only at the end of the review within which she calls him a 'fussy' writer. I said, 'John, isn't it better to be called fussy than fuzzy?' I see that William Peskett's book got a review in *The Irish Press*, but not Gregory O'Donoghue's book. Why? Why is everything from the South ignored?

January 29th At Glenshelane. The depth of winter. The countryside always makes one aware of the seasons, especially the season of winter. The house is very cold and damp. I switched on the heating. A piece of glass has fallen from the greenhouse so that it now looks very sad. At least the rabbits haven't eaten the irises, but they've been chewing through the wallflowers. Winter is a dead kingdom.

February 10th John Montague supervised our first Poetry Workshop of this year. We all came to his house on Grattan Hill. A very friendly atmosphere, a sense of occasion. I submitted my poem 'Death by Fire'. Montague liked the poem. He recognized that the Brigadier figured in the poem, and that the poem was a dialogue between the Brigadier's experience of the Battle of Nijmegan and my experience of watching the late butterflies dying in the fire. I'll send the poem to Terence de Vere White at *The Irish Times*.

Reading Wilfrid Owen and Theodore Roethke all week. Read the Bucknell University Press books on Montague and Heaney. Heaney baffles me. His technique and prowess as a poet has amazed the whole English-speaking world. It would be wonderful to have Heaney's craft and Montague's depth of soul. Even as I had this thought Saul Bellow's words came into my head: 'Remarks are not literature.'

May 8th Margaret Drabble spoke about Wordsworth at UCC yesterday. A gifted, fiercely intelligent Englishwoman.

But with an inexplicable shyness. Where does this shyness come from? In someone so vibrantly intelligent, so attractive physically, it is very strange. Niall MacMonagle took care of her during her visit. He shadowed her with all the nervous energy of an ornithologist minding a rare oriole or eagle. His empathy with her was intense.

May 20th Yeats never believed in a little poetry of little people. For him the act of making poems was a mighty act. All poets should continue to honour Yeats for that belief alone.

June 15th Letter from Dolmen Press. Disgusting — dictated by Liam Miller and typed by someone else. Meantime I will have to rewrite 'The First Convention'.

July 28th We had a terrific Glenshelane picnic today by the river under the old Lyre Bridge. Brilliant sunshine. Mrs Merrill of Villierstown Rectory and Molly Keane's great friend Mrs Phyllis Mitchell of Fortwilliam House, Ballyduff, as well as the Brigadier and the Stevensons of Castle Dodard on the high road from Lismore. The Stevensons used to live in North East India and they still have an Imperial aura, an aura of the Raj. Pam Stevenson, a woman in her mid-forties, is spectacularly beautiful, absolutely ravishing. She is like the beautiful Sylvia Simms in *Ice Cold in Alex*. I find it difficult not to stare at her. When she catches my eye she stares back, laughing inside because she knows the effect her looks have on a very young man. Her husband is a real colonial gentleman of the old school, self-possessed, as satisfied as a man who sleeps with a Kimberley diamond on his pillow. Whenever they visit Glenshelane the atmosphere becomes charged with a sexual energy. All the men in the company form a kind of unconscious choreography of Martinis, snacks, cushions offered, coats taken, seats vacated closer to the fire in the drawing room beneath the portrait of the equally beautiful Lady Inez FitzGerald. The Brigadier is always trying to seat her where he can see his mother in the painting and Pam on her fireside perch as he speaks. It is ancient and interesting behaviour, but it is charged sexually, even if all the people involved are over forty and sex must be well beyond them at this stage.

Bill Wall (Liam de Bhál) came yesterday with his girlfriend, Liz, who is a first cousin of the poet Seán Dunne. Bill said that Montague was talking to him about an anthology of Southern poets and that he (Montague) had contacted the Arts Council about it. The Brigadier very impressed by Bill and Liz. 'Are they not the most superior young people, really most charming?' he remarked as they sped way down the avenue. The Brigadier loves good social breeding and Bill Wall and Liz have that in spades. Finished and expanded 'Only Child'. It's now quite a substantial poem.

September 2nd Too much activity at Glenshelane House. I can't write my poems.

September 15th Molly Keane came to stay tonight. We gave her a heated room, luxurious new blankets and an electric fire. Anything else, the Brigadier asked her. 'Oh, yes please. A hot-water bottle, dear.' She brought two volumes of Proust with her because she wanted me to read them. 'A little light reading for you, Thomas. You must read all of Proust, all of him, I tell you.'

September 16th We spoilt Molly Keane by giving her break-fast in bed. She wanted to talk about Proust again. I would like to read more of Proust. I tried the two early volumes of *The Guermantes Way* in the Brigadier's library. But I need to read more Beckett than Proust. And Strindberg: Beckett had seen Strindberg's *Ghost Factory* twice before sitting down to write *Waiting for Godot*.

I spoke to Mrs Keane for a long time about her book *Conversation Piece*, especially the long story 'Pullinstown'. She loved the idea that I had been reading her work very carefully. My questions were unexpected, so much so that when she rose from her bed she was in terrific form. Also, today, an American lawyer called Tyler recommended a book by Leon Uris called *Trinity*. She promised to send me this book which is, according to Molly Keane's arch-enemy, Lady Keane, very 'pro IRA'. At lunch there was a woman called O'Shea who is divorced from the Musical Director of Covent Garden.

December 10th Hugh Leonard at UCC. What an absolutely brilliant man — and brave as hell; he's been roasting the IRA leadership in his newspaper columns. A security man took me aside at UCC and complained that College security staff should have been 'advised' about Hugh Leonard's talk to the English Literature Society. I expressed surprise and he explained that Hugh Leonard was controversial and unpopular in 'certain quarters'. If the English Lit has discomfited 'certain quarters' in UCC I'm only delighted. At the reception in Jurys Leonard insisted on cashing our cheque and buying drinks for everyone. A glamorous Mercedes convertible, a glamorous wife, an urbane manner and a generous heart and, on top of that, an uncanny dramatic skill: that's Hugh Leonard's life. What a fantastic life for an Irish writer. An urbane, sardonic Dubliner; he really is the most attractive person imaginable. And a great advertisement for life in the theatre: such luminous, modern, liberal theatre people shine a bright light into the provincial darkness of Irish life. His brazen magnanimity scatters the pious and the frightened and alarms the dark and evil ghouls of the South Armagh diesel-laundering IRA brigades. Ireland needs a thousand Hugh Leonards, an army of Hugh Leonards, to fight Irish mediocrity and its cowering hypocrisy.

December 15th Cutting wood today with a chainsaw. I had to sling timber from the river with a tractor. I shouldn't have been doing this tree-felling on my own, it is dangerous work. But there's terrific satisfaction in the energy of a chainsaw.

December 22nd I am writing this aboard the B&I Ferry *The Innisfallen*. Two hours from Swansea. Beautiful sleepy day trip. Had lunch. My first meal at sea. A fish dish that tasted like sawdust. I have £314 to spend. That's more than enough.

Christmas Eve Bristol. Went onto the wards with my sister. The poem 'Friends, Voices' or 'Voices, Friends' that I'd hoped to finish in Bristol was left on the damn Cork-Swansea Ferry. So these days are wasted. Nothing has come to me since 'Touch Wood'.

December 31st Home again. Terrible crossing, that dreadful *Innisfallen*. Very ill throughout the crossing, very messy. But the New Year will arrive in less than an hour. I hope that 1977 has less vomit in it.

1977

February 9th Theo was at Glenshelane for the weekend. Had a fascinating time of gossip and wild planning with him. His girlfriend, Mary B, was with him. She is an amazing person. All Theo's women are exceptional; he attracts the most brilliant and lovely people. He really is a very blessed person.

February 10th Long discussion with Theo on his lack of poetry. A very serious discussion. Theo thinks that a stay in an Anglo-Irish house was rather like 'poetry', like the 'poetic life' that we should all aspire to. He said why bother writing down the poems when one is just living within them. I was very confused by this question and couldn't give him a decent answer.

Recently, when we were in Bill Ludgate's pub, Patrick Crotty said that moments in life are fleeting anyway, even the happiest, fullest moments are fleeting. Even in the most perfect Revolutionary society, Crotty said, there would be Death. Even the most loving and kind system in the world will still end with our deaths. We have to accept this ultimate absurdity of the human condition, the nothingness of the grave. Perhaps we construct poems in lieu of an answer to this riddle, this absurdity, at the heart of life. To write a great poem is to spit upon the spitefulness of the grave. I wish I'd been able to recall Crotty's words when I was talking to Theo at Glenshelane. Crotty has been reading a lot of Beckett, most recently *Watt, Molloy* and *Malone Dies*, and this reading has made him very insightful on the big questions of life. Beckett has effected even his speech pattern — he now talks more quickly, but in shorter sentences. He has lost the idleness of 1976, the languid idleness of Leonard Cohen's LPs. I love listening to his conversations with the brilliant Marie Baker, him holding a copy of Beckett or Marcuse and she intensely involved in the *Irish Times* cryptic crossword. They sit together in the Kampus Kitchen and being with them is like sitting in on the rehearsal of a Beckett play. They are two of the cleverest people I know. Marie must be the most brilliant woman ever to pass through the corridors of UCC. To be so bright and so good-looking is an astonishing good fortune; in these things she is the female equal of Theo. I notice that Theo and Marie avoid each other like dominant lions, but very politely, as if they recognize an alpha intensity in the other.

February 17th Talked to Seamus Heaney in College today. My first time meeting him in person, though I feel I know him well from his poetry and his publicity. He had read my pamphlet *Warm Circle* and thought it good— 'accomplished' was the word he used. (Montague must have given it to him, fair play to old Montague.) He said he felt terrific poetic vibes down here in the South, and said he would like to do a Poetry Workshop with us at some time in the future. Terrific. 'Your work is not what I expected,' he said to me, 'Not at all like the work of Patrick Galvin. It's like Ulster stuff,' he repeated this as he read through my pamphlet again. It's funny how the word 'Ulster' has become a byword for excellence, for achievement.

February 19th Poem in *Icarus*. Also got a letter from *Cyphers* saying they would like to use two old poems, 'Chiselled Rock' and 'The First Convention'. Amazing. Two more years of apprenticeship to these quarterlies and I'll be ready for a book.

Feb 21st For the last week I've been reading Doctorow's *Ragtime* and David Jones' *Epoch and Artist*: both brilliant in entirely different ways.

February 26th Tonight I wrote a poem, 'At Frascati'. Today I made myself happy by imagining a first collection of poems, and what it would look like. I wrote out a full list of all my publishable poems. Thirty-six.

March 15th Beginning a poem 'At De Valera's Cottage'

> *I heard you talking*
> *About a country funeral —*

March 17th St Patrick's Day Went to see Dervla Murphy today. She lives in an atmosphere of scholarship and travel: there's a very British 19th-century atmosphere in her library, even more than in the Brigadier's library at Glenshelane House. She has really continued that journey of discovery where W E D Allen and St John Philby and Freya Stark and people like them left off. But she has a less Imperial view of the world. She understands though — like Wilfred Scawen Blunt and T E Lawrence and Laurens van der Post — that the Islamic world between Istanbul and Indonesia is an entirely different place, a charged kingdom as strange and unrelated to us as the planet Mars. One of the great disruptive horrors she fears is the creeping Westernization of these lands. To Westernize the Islamic world would be a disaster of astronomical proportions. Not only would it ruin an entire central Asian civilization but, thinks Dervla, it would bring about the ruin of the West. (She looks forward to the latter event with great sanguinity.)

She hates war, all war and every war, seeing war as something encouraged and funded by the arms industry of the world. She says that the main purpose of the arms industry is to create regional victories that smooth out cultural-legal differences for international capital. In a sense Dervla is a classical communist without the Soviet Marxism. The fact is it is not the West, but Islam, that would survive such a political and military Armageddon. She said that, irony of ironies, it is the Cold War that keeps the irreconcilable forces of Christianity and Islam apart. She says that if the pernicious espionage activities of the American and Russian security priesthood (with their nuclear bombs as tabernacles) fell away then international diplomacy would again return to the assassin's knife and the guerrilla's bullet of the Steppe. The world would return to political first principles as outlined in Mr Allen's *Problems of Turkish Power in the Sixteenth Century* — it would return to a conflict of Continental versus Oceanic powers, a long war between the Steppe and the Atlantic West, between what is Christian and what is Islamic. She said we should be grateful to the Cold War for keeping a lid on these tectonic forces.

As I motorcycled back from Lismore, a damp roadway, a dangerous wind, I thought how in this world murder is just waiting to become an intimate and personal activity once more. After the wholesale corporate slaughter of the Holocaust, Hiroshima, Vietnam, it is difficult to believe that international mass murder could ever become merely personal again. In future all political murders will be like IRA murders: personal, rampant, crazed. There may be no more invasions, just a succession of ambushes, car bombs, improvised devices. Dervla is one of the few people with whom one can have this wide-ranging post-Imperial conversation. Few people I know have read Freya Stark or Wilfrid Scawen Blunt; and only a handful would have heard of St John Philby and W E D Allen. These last two summers, riding my motorbike between Cappoquin and Lismore to talk to Dervla, have become a kind of perpetual political seminar. But what I love most about her is that she doesn't fit in, and she doesn't wish to fit in. Her soul is free. She is like a Buddhist. But even to say that she is like a Buddhist is to limit her, she is freer than that, she's more like a 19th-century Unitarian explorer or bee-keeper.

Easter Monday A poem today. About Daedalus, the maker

of the labyrinth. I need more poems like this. I need at least a dozen for a first full collection.

April 30th The Old Days of the Party: it is the Party of old men, of tobacco-blocks and medallioned watches. Old men who tell the same stories framed by Arthur Guinness. Saturdays, after the last meetings, they weld together in these small rooms in Lismore or at Tallow Bridge.

May 16th My motorbike was stolen from the car park at Fermoy. Helmet, gloves, everything gone. Such rotten luck. This is not my summer. *Outposts* as well as *The Irish Press* have rejected 'Daedalus, the Maker'. Damn. Theo was here over the weekend. The Brigadier got a dog or, at least, a dog appeared in the greenhouse and he has stayed with us. So far nobody's come to collect him.

June 7th My Dad was buried yesterday. He died on Saturday at 1.45 a.m. I had spoken to him that night at nine o'clock: told him about the *Irish Times* poems and the letter on Lord Edward. He hardly noticed. How could he? He was seriously ill, dying. I was desperately sorry that I didn't stay with him at Ardkeen Hospital, but the young doctor said that he would 'come out of it' by tomorrow. He would have liked me to stay. He was frightened, I think. He was always a bundle of nerves. I should have stayed with him and that's that, but I was worrying all the time about the poor Brigadier who was waiting for me in the car park. The Brigadier more upset than myself, mouthing stupid inanities, 'He'll be alright, Thomas. It's just a virus. I'm sure he will be alright.' But all the while I had a proper sense of doom. The whole car park at Ardkeen Hospital was enveloped in doom. I should have trusted my instincts and stayed with my poor father, but I was as worried about the Brigadier who now looked as frightened as a child. At some deep level that he would want to deny he must have sensed that we were close to a death.

We buried Dad's favourite books with him: *Accountancy* by Pickles, my *Shattered Frost* and *The Rise of the Irish Trade Unions*. My father may have been a simple, troubled man but he was an unrepentant socialist of the Old School. Yet, being a casual agricultural labourer after he left the army in 1946, he had no Trade Union protection and absolutely no rights. He and poor men like him were at the beck and call of other men who had land and position. As agricultural labourers my father and his companions like Patey Glenville were legally prevented from leaving Ireland, from emigrating, so that they were no better than slaves. Thanks to Maurice Kelleher's father at Cappoquin post office he then got his first real regular-paying job as a temporary postman. He struggled to rear a family, succumbing to illness and depression by the winter of 1963 or spring of 1964. My brother Michael remembers a time when the family was 'viable' in every sense of that word. But nearly all my memories of family life are memories of his mental deterioration, his agitation, want and suffering. My memory of him must primarily be the memory of his unhappiness and that incredibly pervasive sense of wasted intelligence and frustrated ambition. Irish life made a cynic of him, yet his cynicism maimed him with its morbid self pity. And I know that rural Ireland and urban working-class Irish corporation estates are full of such poor fathers, fathers wallowing in 'nerves' and morbidity. It is tragic. I won't write about him until I am ready. And I may never be ready.

But today I feel utterly bereft and totally alone. Life is shit and I have no one to share my grief. I have the Brigadier's company, of course, and our marvellous conversations at Glenshelane House; but the Brigadier's company is like the companionship of a lovely basset hound. It is very real but very limited.

June 8th A review of *Cyphers* in *The Cork Examiner*. Robert O'Donoghue refers to my two poems and praises my work. I must work on the 'Greatrakes' poem.

June 17th I go blindly through the days. I feel so lost, so sorrowful. My father dead at the age of 55: his entire life a terrible struggle, a series of deep humiliations. Poetry is my only strength; the only light I see is the light coming through its fretwork.

September 24th Worried about my MA Qualifying exam. Must go down to Cork tomorrow to check. Looks like I mightn't even get a 2.1. This is desperately serious. Sr Una Nelly has been bitching about me at English Department meetings. She knows I didn't attend many of her lectures. She also knows I didn't bother submitting any essays on the Metaphysical Poets. (I have to admit: such carelessness is unforgivable in someone who aspires to be a College tutor.)

September 25th Today I applied for a job in Cork City Library. It would mean finally leaving Glenshelane House.

September 26th At the Montagues'. No *official* word about my exam but John says that I got a 2.1. The price of getting the MA Qualifying mark was that I'd get no tutorials, and that I shouldn't ask for them. Sr Una insisted that I was not to be employed by the English Department in any capacity, even sweeping the floors. She is reported to have said to Montague as he pleaded with her: *I don't want him in this English Department, even if he's only sweeping the stairs.* It's not the end of the world but it will make my life much harder. Still, if I spend £15 a week and no more, I'll be fine.

Sr Una Nelly: I'll curse her name until the day I die, her slavish 1940s haut-bourgeois Professor B-Jesus MacCarthy Catholicism, her smirking at me every time we passed on the stairs at Brighton Villas while I climbed to the Yeatsian towers of John Montague and Seán Lucy where the light of true poetry was kept alive: under constant academic siege, I must add, but alive and finding oxygen to survive from the interest of distant American scholars. In some other life, no longer protected by her toxic little bourgeois acolytes from Munster's private schools, Sr Una will burn slowly and miserably with all the other righteous Irish on an auto-da-fé lit by a thousand pagan poets of the Déise Gael. I will stand with my resurrected father and watch her burn until she's a cinder. Christ will wink at us as we watch her soul being reduced to pulp. The poet John Donne will tell St Peter that he never heard of her. There is no end to my hatred of Sr Una Nelly. My hatred of her consumes me.

Of course I could have helped myself if I'd actually submitted a few essays to her. I might have at least tried to show some interest in English as an academic subject. Yes, it would have helped. But still I have decided to hate her, to hate her very name. Of the very few women I hate she is the most hated. She has gone to the top of my hate list.

September 27th Back at Glenshelane. A very colourful girl called Mary de Trafford came with me to my library in the coachman's annex and we talked for a long time. She's the daughter of Countess Michalowski of Skibbereen. She is an intense and fabulous creature — it would be easy to fall in love with her. Though, in this summer of 1977, everybody in the Blackwater Valley has fallen in love with Andrea Jameson who has inherited her grandmother, Joan Jameson's, artistic gifts. Even the Brigadier has become besotted with her, talking about her gracefulness, her good looks and her art constantly.

Spent the day at Claud Cockburn's garden, helping Patricia Cockburn. Difficult to tell which of the two is the more intelligent. Claud is hugely impressive, but I think Patricia is an uncharted mine of ingenius opinions. Gardening with someone brings you very close. I felt very close to Patricia today and she has a lot of time for me. I really like her; she is very fine, both as a woman and an intellectual. She's an East Cork Arbuthnott. That says it all.

October 9th At Cockburns' again, in both Youghal and Ardmore. Their new house was once owned by the Jamesons and the garden studio of the artist Joan Jameson is still there. Patricia will now use it for her shell-craft.

October 15th Terrific news. I've won the Patrick Kavanagh Award! No official notification yet, but a journalist from the *Independent* newspaper offices phoned to tell me. I wish my father were still alive. We would have had such fun going up to Inniskeen together. Heaney and McGahern were on the judging panel: a terrific honour to be chosen by them. But all this attention will ruin the quiet rhythm that was just beginning to develop in my life. I had just perfected a creative rhythm of moving between the garden at Glenshelane and the library in UCC, a life of parson-like quiet. This rhythm suited me, it's the rhythm that's been inside me since I was a child. The entire objective of my life has been to protect this rhythm. I've been trying to protect this quiet space in my life since I was nine years old. It has been the consuming ambition of my life, to be quiet, to find quiet.

Sunday Wonderful piece in *The Sunday Independent* about the Award. Huge publicity. More phone calls to Glenshelane House all day. People wanting to talk to me and, for once, nobody wanting to talk to the Brigadier.

Monday Registered for my MA. Met lots of old friends. Marie Baker, gifted and beautiful as ever. Pat Crotty who was registering for an MA. Afterwards I met Pat and his fabulous girl Bríd Galvin in The Long Valley. Bríd, who has an eye and ear for things, said something startling to me: 'Funny, isn't it, Tom, the way your opinions are now quoted in newspapers, now that you've won something! Surely your opinions were worth as much before.'

'Sure nobody listened to Tom until yesterday!' Marie Baker quipped, mischievous as always. She stared boldly at me with her cheeky, Baker look, a look that she always has when she finishes her *Irish Times* cryptic crossword before everyone else.

But both women were right. We write poetry to be noticed, to become visible. Quite suddenly, I'm visible. My photograph is in every national newspaper. It is unreal.

October 18th The attention goes on and on. I got a letter from Peter Fallon asking about a collection. Now I'm sorry that I sent the poems to Dolmen prematurely. Fallon is a much better publisher: he really cares about the younger poets. Dolmen is a bit of a poetry veterans' hospital.

October 20th Letter from David Marcus. He has accepted two of my poems at last: 'Stranger, Husband' and 'Greatrakes'. I'm sure I sent 'Greatrakes' to him last June and he rejected it at the time.

October 21st On radio last night, the Arts Programme with Eavan Boland. Seamus Heaney was in the studio as well, reading a poem for Lowell. He spoke about Lowell with great affection and sadness. I read 'Daedalus the Maker' and talked about the isolation of Munster poets. My intensity amused the sanguine Eavan Boland. She really is the coolest dude imaginable.

October 27th Letter from the Dolmen Press announcing that they will publish my collection. I replied that I thought a new collection of mine would be submitted by November 15th. So the die of my life is cast. Got a letter from Lady Beit of Russborough asking me to write. She saw my photo in the paper. I must put pen to paper or I'll lose a very loyal supporter. Later a phone call from the President's office in UCC saying that US Ambassador Shannon was arriving in Cork tomorrow and would I like to meet him outside the President's office at 12.45. This could be embarrassing. How will I meet him alone and for how long? Will he have slotted time within his schedule to talk with me.

November 8th Poetry Reading at College.

November 16th John Ennis rang from Waterford asking if I'd do a reading. It should be great fun and a strange experience to be back in Waterford City. The downside: John wants me to read with Seán Dunne. Don't know if I want to do this. I corrected the sequence 'Pauline's Girlhood' about the childhood memories of Mrs Sargent of Cappoquin. I'll never forget her wonderful stories about returning from New York, where she had been a nurse, after the Great War and settling down to a solid bourgeois life in Cappoquin with the larger-than-life Mick Sargent.

November 21st Snow today. Snow everywhere. Anne rang to say she could not make it to Glenshelane. The avenue is packed with snow. So I'll have to cook lunch for the Brigadier and myself. Vegetable pie yet again. Rex was racing around in the snow, eating it, snorting playfully and kicking it in the air.

December 10th I think that all this fuss over the Kavanagh Award has made me quite hysterical and restless. Will I ever be calm again? I feel that I've been married to Glenshelane House for over four years. It's true that I've always tried to work my relationships with others into a timetable around Glenshelane, the house and garden. This has been grossly unfair. I have never given my attention to anyone completely. Glenshelane has been a physical space that is also a metaphor for an inner place, the place where poems get written. Glenshelane, while it makes me incredibly strong as a poet, has also held me back as a person. Because of my attachment to this garden I've lost at least two terrific girlfriends who were too modern and sensible to accept that weird attachment. I must stop wanting to return to the childhood house of my grandmother. That house of plenty that was full of flowers.

December 15th I've got a full-time job with Cork City

Libraries. This is bizarre and unexpected. For a long time I thought that there were no jobs for poets in this country. It is a miracle, truly a miracle. Has the Patrick Kavanagh Award shoved my name to the top of that list of over three hundred candidates for that one job? Or has Montague been speaking to someone? Who knows.

December 18th Theo and Seán Dunne here at Glenshelane for Christmas. This year is coming to an end, a good year poetically. But the death of my father. How can that ever be a good year? This year, Time, that vile and withering element, took him from us. While my father was dying I had poems in *Cyphers, The Honest Ulsterman, Icarus* and *The Stony Thursday Book.*

December 31st The Brigadier home from Château de la Garoupe in Nice. He immediately set out on the road to the Knight of Glin at Glin Castle in County Limerick. It is a long way off and the inland roads between West Waterford and Limerick are treacherous. I cautioned him about setting out on the winter roads but he was adamant that he wanted to visit the Knight and his wife. I told him about my library job and he didn't seem in the least perturbed. *The Irish Times* published my Zen review. A phone call from Liam Miller of the Dolmen Press. He wanted to know if I had manuscript copies of my collection. He wants to enter the collection for the Poetry Book Society Choice. Usually they require an actual letterpress set-up of the work, but he is phoning them to see if a typescript would do. This has to be entered by the end of January.

1978

January-February I miss my father. I miss his intelligent, provocative conversations, his human company, his superstitious atheism, even his political cynicism. His marvellous intelligence was accompanied by a toxic cynicism about Ireland and a disabling pessimism about the future; everyone's future, not just Ireland's. I could never share his pessimism and cynicism. But he was my father.

Days and days and days have gone by: two whole months without record. Extraordinary things have happened to me since December. I was appointed to my City Library job beginning on March 27th or 28th.

March 1st At John Montague's launch of *The Great Cloak* in UCC. John read his entire book at the reading. This was really too much. Evelyn sat beside me, along with Nancy McCarthy, Hedli MacNeice and Professor Seán Lucy. Nancy was vivacious and talkative. She's very fond of me since I read the poem about Frank O'Connor at my own poetry reading. Bobby O'Donoghue was filming the reading, rather ostentaciously, to please John. But at the end of the reading he discovered that he'd forgotten to insert a film cartridge. So the whole exercise was pointless. Somehow this seems a metaphor for Montague's literary life. I walked home alone, all the while trying to understand the force of this metaphor. Filming without recording: it is a metaphor of childhood, or something like that. Yes, it is Montague's lost childhood; the Fellini that never happened.

March 7th Fever went down this morning. 103 degrees. Tonight, a terrible pain in my back. But began to review Joan

Keefe's book for *The Irish Times*. Looked at the one on Roethke.

March 8th A piece in *The Irish Times* today about the Corkery seminar. A more balanced review than that of *The Examiner*. Mary Leland is good, a sound woman.

March 13th Paul Durcan had a lengthy review of *The Stony Thursday Book*. Mentions for the first time a new phrase 'The New Munster Poetry'. I wonder if he is trying deliberately to set up an image of us young poets as a 'school'? It is an interesting notion. Not since the '50s has there been such a large group of poets: Gregory O'Donoghue, Theo Dorgan, Liam de Bhál, Seán Dunne and myself. We may even have our own George Moore in Niall Carey, a Philosophy student who ridicules my poems.

March 15th Letter from Seán Dunne. He is much happier now. Said he saw 'Greatrakes' in *The Irish Press* and liked it. John Ennis praised it too, as did Liam Murphy. That's surprising; I thought it too traditional for the Waterford City poets who are all true believers in the modernism of the Liverpool/Mersey poets.

March 22nd Cearbhall Ó Dálaigh, our former President, has died. A most ill-used, exploited and brilliant scholar-patriot. Life has treated him badly and unfairly. He had just moved into a new house at Sneem, County Kerry. What a beautiful man he was, and talented. He had just begun working on his books after coming out of hospital. As far as I'm concerned all of the best are gone now. He was certainly one of the best in this miserable nation of ours.

March 23rd Busy clearing out my room at Glenshelane House. I put my books together — the ones I need in Cork. Three large *Gouldings* fertilizer sacks full of books. Incredible, the number of books I've accumulated. The three bags I'm taking away hardly make any difference to my library here at Glenshelane. The Brigadier came into Cork with me this morning. We sold the Allen scythe and got a 14-inch chainsaw instead.

Easter Tuesday Anthony Cronin presented a magnificent RTÉ programme on Thomas MacDonagh last night. One of the last pieces of material he used was a letter from Yeats in reply to MacD's request for advice on publishing. Yeats gave his usual courteous, caring and practical reply. He said to MacD, who was a teacher in Kilkenny at the time, that an edition of 300 copies was more than enough for Ireland. An edition of 1,000 was also sufficient for the UK and Ireland. Yeats told MacDonagh that if he wished to go on he should refrain from publishing until he had found his voice. What good advice. No young writer ever takes that advice, of course. Only a mad rush to fame drives the young writer: the sales, the accolades, the honours. All illusions. But Yeats's advice still holds today: 300 copies of a poetry book is more than enough for Ireland and 1,000 seems about right for both Ireland and the UK. Imagine, 300 readers! That's more than enough for any poet.

March 30th Bus Crash. My sister and I were on the Waterford-Cork Expressway bus that crashed outside Cork City. Thirteen passengers killed. I tried to save my sister by telling her to get her head down, that we were crashing. She thought we were merely turning right, off the main toad. I knew the metal seats would offer some protection. I held her down while I held onto the metal seats. Death, mutilation, decapitation. Scenes of absolute chaos. Catastrophe, absolute catastrophe. Like a bomb in Dublin or Belfast. There is no point in describing the chaos of this accident. With my adrenalin still rushing I made a ten-page statement on the accident to the Guards. Thirteen people definitely dead, yet both my sister and I escaped serious harm. My sister detained in St

Finbarr's Hospital for observation. My mother thinks I am lying; she thinks Mary has been killed. It is a miracle that we both survived.

April 29th Sir Philip and Lady de Zulueta came to stay at Glenshelane. Sir Philip was Harold Macmillan's Private Secretary. An affable, interesting and interested man. Involved now in the setting up of a bank in Dublin, Bowmaker or Intercontinental, or some such merchant bank. We talked all the way back in his Jaguar from Cappoquin to Cork. He was fascinated by Cork, the port and the city centre. He thought that Cork City had great unused commercial potential. The conversation oscillated between the unused commercial and consumer, rather than industrial, capacity of the Irish economy and the fiction of Sir Charles Lever. A shrewd Englishman with a great sense of being the citizen of a free world — one gets that sense from almost all the senior ex-Military and wealthy Englishmen who rebuilt Britain and Europe after the War (the friends of the Brigadier). And, as usual, great affection for Germany and the Germans. As Sir Philip's bank is going to be housed in a building once owned by Sir Charles Lever I promised I would keep a lookout for old Lever books in the Cork bookshops. Lady de Zulueta didn't say a word: an indication always, among these people, that her distinguished husband is in information-gathering mode.

May 6th My review of Montague's book in *The Irish Times* today. Trying to think of the poem 'The Single Sparrow'. Is it too early to write hope into my poetry? Should I stick with sorrow, should I continue to explore what my father's influence means? His search?

I am living during the week in a semi-detached house on the edge of Glasheen with five other young people, all students, one medical, one botanist, one engineer, the President of the Students' Union, a Psychology student and Auditor of the Historical Society. Unbelievably good house, neat, tidy, clean, beautiful. The others are marvellous cooks, curries, sweet-and-sour porks, salads. They no longer act like students, but like people who go out to work every day.

May 27th At Glenshelane. Dolmen Press sent me the completed copies of my book. It looks absolutely wonderful. Liam Miller has done an extraordinary design job. Publication date is set for 22nd June. If only I could get some hardback copies. I suppose this is the librarian in me; I always want to see hardback copies. The only ridiculous thing is the huge photograph on the back. It's alright for Seamus Heaney or Hugh MacDiarmid but hardly right for a first book.

May 29th Nancy McCarthy, Frank O'Connor's old love, rang me at the library the other day. She wanted to know if I knew of any letters from Frank O'Connor to Corkery. Macmillan and O'Connor's widow are planning to publish a selection of his letters. Met Montague in The Long Valley. He said I should go barefoot throughout the summer to increase my sensuous perceptions. I showed *The First Convention* to him. He liked it very much, but thought that Dolmen should have lowered the price. John had just had lunch with singer Mary O'Hara. She asked him to write a song for her.

June 4th The City Librarian, Seán Bohan, called me into his office today. I thought I was in trouble. But he wanted to tell me that he has arranged with the Mercier Bookshop in Bridge Street for a launch of *The First Convention*. Extraordinary. What a terrific friend Seán Bohan has become in the last few months. What a great character he is, a librarian of the old, creative and irrepressible school in the tradition of Frank O'Connor and Dermot Foley.

At two exhibitions. Oisín Kelly. And Pauline Bewick in Lavitt's Quay Gallery. Pauline, a lovely unconventional creature. Montague and I spent ages talking to her; John lusting after her, of course, and she not discouraging him.

June 17th Bríd and Paul Durcan came into the library today. Paul is going to Dublin next week to Eiléan Ní Chuilleanáin and Macdara Woods' wedding. Paul says he received a book by Gerald Dawe. Paul says I *must* get a contract from Dolmen Press for my book.

June 20th Yesterday, a middle-aged man, Eamon Corcoran, who was involved in Republican Socialist parties and whose family or friends fought in the Spanish Civil War, came into the library to praise my poetry. He said I am being ignored by the powers that be. He mentioned the new *Poetry Ireland* thing and saw that I wasn't mentioned. I couldn't tell him then that I don't want to be involved in the *politics* of poetry. But it's amazing how people appoint themselves as protectors of one's reputation. If I were a pop singer this man would be called a 'groupie'. Later he handed me a cheque for £5 as a gesture of goodwill towards my writing and my life. His kindness overwhelms me with its purpose and promise.

June 25th The reception for my book was held on Friday evening. Terrific crowds. Claud Cockburn, looking tired and feeble after his operation for throat cancer. Patricia Cockburn wanted to have the poem 'Breaking Garden' (about them moving house) signed. Mrs Merrill from Washington and the Brigadier there, as well as my brothers and John Crowley and Humphrey Moynihan of The Long Valley — and some nuns from Cappoquin Convent who soon scattered when people got drunk and lay on the floor. Seán Bohan and two women there, one who sang sad old Irish ballads but was in high good humour because she had just sold a farm for £120,000. John Montague there, and Evelyn and Seán Lucy and wife. Senator John A Murphy and Donnchadh Ó Corráin (Mr Bohan kept calling him 'Mr Dinny Curran of Killorglin'). Aidan Stanley of RTÉ rang me, wanting to record a poetry reading.

June 30th Had tea in The Long Valley with Derek Mahon. While we were sitting down three different people came in with my books asking for autographs. I felt embarrassed, with such a brilliant poet beside me. I think Mahon was amused by this and he laughed every time it happened. He knows they should be buying his new book if they want to learn anything about poetry. Mahon, who's published with Oxford University Press, is staying with the Montagues and writing an article on Kinsale. He drank coffee and lemonade. He said that he was thinking of heading to the United States to lecture. That would be the beginning of a new kind of life for him. He is restless. Brilliant and restless like Louis Mac-Neice. He really is MacNeice's only successor, another East Belfast genius.

Reading, also, Françoise Gilot's *Life With Picasso*. Beautifully written, ghosted by another writer. As well as the story of this sensuous life, I'm reading the much maligned and misrepresented Yevtushenko. His 'Zima Junction' is superb; as a poem of origins, both humble and assertive, it is unequalled. Western liberals attack Yevtushenko for his lack of bravery, for his failure to dissent, his failure to become a martyr by 'fleeing' to the West. Why should every Russian poet become a martyr just to reassure the anti-Soviet vanities of the CIA and MI6? Yevtushenko is like any well-heeled poet in Western Europe — he is a selfish and self-serving genius. George Bernard Shaw would understand his position completely. Shaw would admire his bold autobiographical gestures, his independence from the moral imperatives served up by Western media interests.

July 8th My sister's wedding. Reception at Ballyrafter House, Lismore. A great day. First time in my memory that the family and friends from the countryside have been to a meal together. I was taking it all in; the power of family when it coheres, despite its poverty. Afterwards, Mary and her husband decided that they wanted to spend their first night in a tent by the Glenshelane River. I had to pitch a tent in semi-darkness with a drunken cousin. But it was a perfectly happy day. And very strange in its happiness because McCarthys usually only come together to share traumas of one kind or another. A perfectly happy day.

Saturday An amazing review of *The First Convention* in *The Irish Times* today by Eavan Boland. Complete with photograph, this is about as good a debut review as any poet could hope to get. But my mind is more full of an account I just read in an early biography of Lord Byron of the Georgian slave-girl who was rescued by Lord Byron and betrayed by one of the Irish gentry, Sir Henry Fletcher. The thirteen-year-old had been captured by Kurdish raiders from her father's sheep farm in the Georgian highlands and sold into the Ottoman slave trade. She was offered for sale in the slave market at Alexandria where Byron saw her and took pity on her. He paid a huge price to have her released to him and learned the story of her life.

August 11th Tried to work on new poems but with little success. The excitement of the book, the first reviews etc, have chased poetry away. Also, most extraordinary and exciting developments in the last few weeks. The US Ambassador, William Shannon, wrote to say I'd got the State Department nomination to the International Writers' Program at Iowa University. The programme is worth $4,000, so I should be able to pay off my bank debts.

I sat beside Seán Ó Faoláin at a formal dinner in the American Embassy last week and we both faced Terence de Vere White and Rosaleen Linehan across the table. Seán Ó Faoláin brought an inscribed book of his short stories for me. He spoke at length about Corkery, about the difficulty of dealing with terms like 'provincial' and 'regional' when dealing with literature. He thought that Corkery's basic position was defensive from the word go — that a lot of his 'closing the ranks' was due to his own need to remain in Cork to care for his mother and sister: 'Remember, Thomas, he was the sole breadwinner in that family.' Ó Faoláin said that all of Corkery's notions about the Renaissance and the Middle Ages and his opinions on the Irish Language were embodiments of that frustrated personal position. 'He was a deeply unhappy man,' said Ó Faoláin.

At the dinner I chatted with Victoria Glendinning who is in love with Terence de Vere White. They have been together for some time. She asked if I was worried about not getting English reviews for *The First Convention* and I said that I was. She spoke incessantly about Terence de V W; thought that now that he had moved out of Dublin he would write a 'sharper' prose. He has a two-year contract with *The Irish Times* to continue reviewing. Victoria is utterly in love with him. He glanced at her occasionally, with a boyish delight and with mischievousness in his eyes. He said that he was delighted for me, for the seeming success of the book. He thought my reviewing style and content is excellent. He had read all my reviews. That made me particularly happy — especially as Paul Durcan thinks that my reviewing style is suspect.

August 30th The sycamore tree at the end of the Glenshelane garden is just reddening. The swifts have left their nest in the barn at the back of my library. Things that migrate are preparing to leave Glenshelane for the winter: just as I am moving. I feel restless with the readiness to go. Bill Wall is moving to Greystones to teach. So our little group is being divided and scattered.

September 2nd America. A first impression: huge queues at JFK Immigration, the fatigue of waiting, endless lines like a supermarket during the Christmas rush. Two Aer Lingus hostesses are trying to calm a very important businessman, small, stocky, balding, in a light blue suit. 'It's always the same, Mr O'Mahoney. It won't be long.' I am waiting my turn patiently, reading the Yeats *Memoirs* that I bought at Shannon Airport. Suddenly there's a great commotion at the Passport barrier. Someone shouts, 'He's our guy. He's ours!' Two officials, a man and a young woman, seem to be pointing at me. Am I going to be arrested? Has someone slipped drugs into my baggage? These things happen to the innocent. The couple race towards me carrying a white paper, perhaps an arrest warrant. The man keeps saying, 'He's ours, he's ours!' When he is about six feet from me, still running, he says, 'Tom McCarthy. Yes? Yes! Welcome to the United States of America!'

'Hello, Mr McCarthy,' the young woman says. She is training in 'Reception' for the International Institute of Education. I hand her a small gift, a Yeats poem printed by the Cuala Press in Dublin. She's very pleased. She insists on going to get my baggage. 'Hey, Tom,' the man says, 'let's go and get a coffee.' We walk very briskly through the security checks and Passport barrier without stopping. This is great. I hold on tightly to my Yeats *Memoirs*. I have two friends already as I walk briskly into America.

September 5th A terrific party at the Engles' house, and wonderful oriental food. The IWP is run by two charismatic figures, Paul Engle and Hualing Nieh, his wife. He is a distinguished poet of fifty years standing, she an ambitious novelist. The house a magnificent, palatial shooting lodge set in woods above the Iowa river. Paul an Olympian character — a sort of American George Bernard Shaw, ebullient, imprecise, joking all the time, but with his pulse on the world: a fierce belief in the redemptive value of literature, a Yeatsian capacity to organize as well as to create. And founder of the greatest writing programme in the world, the legendary Iowa Workshop.

September 7th Sharing a flat with Dimitri Nollas, a Greek short story writer. We are going to get on very well. We are both lazy, blasphemous and corrupted. Today we learned one marvel of American life — the waste-disposal unit.

September 12th This evening I stood on the balcony of the Engles' house and listened to a strange clicking sound. Paul told me that it was the cicada, an insect. So I've heard the cicada at last. There are cicadas in Whitman and Roethke; I've often wondered what they sound like. I must record this sound. Roethke's work is haunted by cicadas.

September 14th Unbelievable heat. I am still wearing clothes that are more suitable for Ireland. It was raining when I left Cork at the end of August. Today I was walking down Dubuque St when I began to see white spots before my eyes. Then I felt faint. When I reached the First National Bank I soon understood why I felt like that: the temperature was 95°F and I was wearing a woollen pullover from Glenshelane.

September 19th Discussing tyranny and literature with Peter Nazareth and Sahar Khalifeh. Peter fled from Uganda, from the pathological politics of Idi Amin. Amin a kind of miniature Hitler.

September 22nd The Sunday newspaper is a great American institution. *The Cedar Rapids Gazette* is our major local newspaper. *The Des Moines Register* is the huge regional newspaper, bulky, voluminous. One could build a nuclear shelter or reinforce a NATO tank with papier-mâché made from this. *The Register* has a massive circulation, almost as good as a national daily at home. Its staff writers have won twelve Pulitzer prizes, an extraordinary record.

September 30th Coming back from a dinner at the Iowa Power Company restaurant Alfred Yuson, the poet from the Philippines, turned to me and said, 'I suppose you're very sad about the death of MacDiarmid.'
MacDiarmid, the great Scottish poet, has died.
This news shocks me; a hole has been left in the world. Patrick Crotty, the great MacDiarmid scholar and advocate

in Ireland, will be devastated. It is a loss to the whole world. The loss of MacDiarmid really diminishes world culture, like the death of Goethe or Yeats.

October 2nd When Claudia left to teach at the University I rambled about the house, made a pot of tea, turned on the radio, then sat down and wrote. I was overwhelmed by memories of Glenshelane during the winter of a few years ago when we were cut off from the outside world for two days. I remembered playing backgammon by candlelight with the Brigadier, heating soup on the oil stove, running through the snow with Rex.

October 8th Couldn't go on a second boat trip down the Mississippi today because I felt sick. Claudia came to the apartment to keep me company. She has been reading John Montague's *A Slow Dance*, a book that I find difficult to understand. She loved the book. She explains the major sequences in terms of Freudian and Jungian myth. It's amazing the insights she has about this book, all because of her training in myth and therapy.

October 10th Thinking of the stupid thing I said to some of Marvin Bell's creative writing students the other day. I said that living in Ireland/Europe gives one an advantage poetically. (I was thinking of my own good luck in having met Mac-Diarmid and having had dinner with Robert Graves in Cork etc.) But the idea that geographical location can give any tyro-poet special advantage is too stupid to contemplate. It may help advance the early career of a poet, but it makes no damn difference to the production of true poetry. A poet comes out of nowhere, out of anywhere, every time. A poet can come from a small town in Iowa, a small town in Waterford or any unimportant suburb in any British city.

October 17th While I was alone in my apartment today I felt the presence of my father. I was also immersed in Paul Engle's novel, *Always the Land*. It is an amazing reconstruction of farming life in Iowa in the pre-industrial age. This book is a tribute to Paul's own father and grandfather, all great horse breeders, livery men and horse trainers. It is a romance ultimately, an Iowa romance frozen in time, very much in the manner of Daniel Corkery's *The Threshold of Quiet*.

There is such integrity in this novel, such complete integrity, that it makes me very fond of Paul Engle. I feel very close to him when we're talking, as if this novel gives me insights that none of his poetry offers. It's true that fiction is a mansion of the self: it gives us a writer's soul complete. Poetry requires an empathetic commentary. But in the vast root network of the novel you can see Paul Engle's Iowa stretched out before you, the integrity of the Bible Belt and the honest decent lives lived inside it, the great heaving abundance of America's breadbasket, and of course the possibilities of love when men and women are young, lustful, life-affirming. Paul has a magic glow for me now, when he stands to speak, when he shuffles into the IWP offices, his arms full of newspapers, journals, manuscripts and letters. I can see in him the handsome all-American boy who left these plains for Oxford in the 1930s, and the poet who returned, full of earnestness and a yearning to give witness and meaning to the Iowa life he'd known as a boy. He has been trying to do this ever since, in anthologies like *Midland* and collections like *American Song* and *West of Midnight*. But even the latter collection already contains the worldwide distractions that would possibly undermine his pure poetic authority — this yearning of Paul to be politically relevant, to be 'international'. I'm thinking of his poems on the Russo-Finnish War, on an RAF pilot killed in the Battle of Britain. In the poem 'America, 1941', with its heroic *abc/abca* rhyme scheme, he writes:

Muse of American summer when days start
Full of vacation laughter, free of the clock

To loaf in hills where the honey locust humms —
How, in a heartless age, can I find heart
To praise the brilliant morning and not mock
The dread of continents when daylight comes
Laying the land bare to the bomber's chart?

The fact is that the poet who feared him, who envied his early reputation and feared his influence, Theodore Roethke, would never lift his eyes into the stratosphere of world politics but would continue to celebrate American summers, mid-Western silences and hidden places. Both were university teachers and administrators of writing programmes, but Paul would feel that compulsion to react directly, as earnest poet, to all those influences, to the literary wounded who washed up on the seashore of the Iowa Writing Program — the Second World War, the Korean War, the Vietnam War, the rise of communism, the rise of consumerism. The weight of the world has placed a fatal strain on the structure of his rhyme, and on his wide personal and artistic life. But I love talking to him every day and I love going on walks around the Iowa campus with him, the only time, when we are alone, that he becomes completely relaxed and full of childhood memories of Cedar Rapids and Iowa City. He talks to me too — I think because I'm a young Irishman — about the curse of drink and the dangers of alcoholism among poets and professors in English Departments. He has a bee in his bonnet about this, he himself having been a martyr to rye whiskey. He sees much less danger in wine and has expressed delight in me that I don't drink spirits of any kind. And this may be the very reason why he keeps dropping hints that I might stay in Iowa and get into its PhD programme. Not a hope. I just want to write and my job in Cork Public Library is perfect for that. Ideally, a poet should either be a librarian or a postman.

It was Peter Nazareth, educated by the Yeats scholar Norman Jeffares in Leeds, who pointed out the Iowa poems of Donald Davie to me, reminding me that this great English poet and scholar of 'The Movement' once touched down on Iowa soil and tried to make sense of what he found here. Peter showed me some work that Davie had written in Iowa in the mid '60s, more than ten years ago.

What he's describing is Iowa farm life, the harshness and want of comfort that Davie supposes must create an inhuman or animal dullness in people. But surely that can't always be the case and Paul Engle's imagined characters in his novel show us a warmer, warm-hearted life, a life human like any other. But Donald Davie, highly civilized, lately from Cambridge and Oxford, couldn't see the value in ordinary Iowa life. In another really intriguing Davie poem, 'Iowa', the poet writes about dying trees in the landscape: 'Dutch elm disease is in town / Carried by worms from the eastern seaboard . . . ' But here the disease is raised to a level of metaphor, a metaphor for race and racism. Today Peter Nazareth and I agreed that Davie has this excellent English academic quality, this English habit of mind that all English poets travelling or sojourning in American academe display — this strenuous impulse to edit experience, to pulverize it intellectually so that it can be absorbed as a real experience. Only through a kind of cerebral response to American material can English academics find a way to live here: only the most excessive English thinking makes America bearable for them. Then it must be a very Irish thing in me, I said to Peter, this wanting to simply embrace America and American ways of being in the world, without having that need to conquer the material intellectually. There are very large fragments of American life in Ireland, and this is even more so the further North you go at home. Presbyterian County Antrim, for example, is practically already a county in New England or North Carolina. Protestant Northern Ireland is almost an annex of America. When travelling here, we Irish Catholics can feel that Ulster quality in American life.

October 18th Hualing Nieh, the new Director of the IWP, is a *hua-chiao*, an exiled Chinese novelist. She came to Iowa City in the early '60s to help set up the Translation Workshop. Almost impossible for me, a Westerner, to gauge her real achievements, even with the help of translations. She comes from a well-to-do Chinese family displaced by the Maoist revolution; therefore her interests are among the landed and bourgeois interests of China rather than the revolutionary China of the Party. Yet she has a great fondness for communist China and its contemporary writers. She's beginning to wield great power at Iowa, yet retains that intensely private, even hermetic, sense of self. She is inscrutable in the way that Paul is not.

October 20th Spent a long time today talking to Parthasarathy about poetry. He has published a book-length poem, *Rough Passage*, a poem about the British Raj. Very like Montague's *The Rough Field*. Partha would like to return to writing in his native language, Tamil. Last week Alfred Yuson told me that he would like to write poems in his native language, Tagalog. I told them about Michael Hartnett's book, *A Farewell to English*. They were amazed by the international coincidence of Hartnett's decision. Spent the whole afternoon talking about the importance of native languages, the cultural strength to be gained from using them.

Liberation theory or nationalist yearning will never undermine this prodigious range of English as a tool for poetry. To decide to write in a smaller language, such as Irish or Tagalog, is a self-limiting decision from a literary point of view. But from the point of liberation or nationhood it makes complete sense. But for us Irish the career of Daniel Corkery exists as a stark warning against merely patriotic decisions in literature: in embracing the Republic above all other things Corkery sabotaged his earlier literary gift, which was a gift rooted in English and Russian regional prose and urban lower-class life. This was Corkery's first genius.

October 25th Everywhere the storm windows have been put up around Iowa. This marks the real end of autumn and the beginning of the winter season.

November 2nd Gave a talk on Eavan Boland and Eiléan Ní Chuilleanáin to a small group of women writers. Mary Jane White, a poet attached to the IWP, already knew about Ní Chuilleanáin and *Cyphers*. They have difficulty pronouncing the name. So I make them say over and over Elain Knee-Quilly-nawn, Elain Knee-Quilly-nawn, Elain Knee-Quilly-nawn. Five minutes later they've already forgotten how to pronounce it. They ask about the main difficulties that face women poets in Ireland. I say, 'What do ye think?' And they reply, 'Being taken seriously. We mean not being taken seriously.' And I reply, 'Exactly . . . Plus that Irish curse, the cult of the macho in Irish political culture and in the Irish Catholic view of the world.'

November 8th Exhausted after another mad party. I think every writer who throws a party tries to emulate the atmosphere of Paul's terrific birthday party in October. Hopeless to try that. But it means that we all end up exhausted, delighted and in love with each other and each other's countries. Houshang Golshiri stood up on a kitchen table and recited Persian poetry in a beautiful singing tone; his recitation competed with the laughter of Eberhard Panitz and Sahar Khalifeh in the corner. I can see now where Desmond O'Grady got his reading style, Desmond who knew Housang during his days in Alexandria.

November 15th Another day of drinking tea at the Nazareths' apartment. Peter and Mary's flat is a kind of drop-in social centre for disorientated writers. Mary has a stock of real *Typhoo* tea and a real tea-maker's ability. It is funny how both of us, coming from old colonial places, Ireland and Uganda, share a taste for English things: tea, Marmite, water biscuits.

November 30th From Washington DC, William Meredith, who had spoken to us at Iowa, phoned to ask me to come to the Library of Congress. He wanted to record some of my poems. I recorded thirteen, six from *The First Convention* and seven from the ones I wrote at the IWP. The poetry room at the Library of Congress is very beautiful: an outer office with two secretaries and an inner chamber for the writers who are guests. Uwe Herms and Bill and I joked about the luxury of it all — the French furniture, carpets and settees. Meredith a gentle person, with an underlying melancholy. After the recording he brought Uwe and me to lunch. He finds the job of Poetry Consultant much more demanding than he had anticipated.

December 2nd Brief stopover in Boston. Light snow on the streets, much grime. Staying in Union Park Street with Robbie Perkins, the artist who sailed with his brother to Cork when I was at college. Robbie works at the Athenaeum. Robbie has a dog with the rotund body of a small pig. Hairs everywhere; my clothes ruined. Last night had a mad time at an Irish pub in South Boston called Foley's. Dancing until 3 a.m. with the same girl. Robbie, a Protestant Boston Brahmin, used my Irish accent as a passport to get into the place. I think he always wanted to go there. He wasn't disappointed; it was as wild as he'd imagined. More than wild. Absolutely insane.

December 13th A long chat with Bill Merwin today. Before he came to Iowa City I read his book *The Carrier of Ladders*. A very Classical talent, sometimes stilted. A very real gift with rhyme, a technical disciple of both Randell Jarrell and Robert Graves. An American with a very strong European underbelly. (He once worked as a tutor to Graves's children.) His newer poems are more playful, adventurous; but his formalism is so strong that it remains the distinct mark of his style. Extremely handsome face and an athletic build, like a young Charlton Heston. He said that he had met Montague in Holland a few years ago. He was interested in Murphy and Heaney. I told him what I knew, and he seemed pleased with the information. A very pleasant, balanced individual. A beautiful Portuguese-Polynesian partner, a woman with the face of Hedy Lamarr. It's terrible that I can't recall her name now, but I was so dazzled by her that I didn't hear a word she said to me.

December 31st Had dinner on Thursday with Paul and Hualing. Paul talked a lot about Ireland. He would like to return there with Hualing. Also discussed the possibility of an IWP poetry reading in Tokyo in 1980. There was so much to say to Paul about his books, his new poems. I grow very fond of older poets. When the jet rose up out of Cedar Rapids Airport Iowa looked very beautiful in the snow. Mary and Peter and Paul and Hualing had come to the Mayflower to see us off. A sad leave-taking. They had become my family.

1979

January 19th Have I made a huge mistake coming back to Ireland? I should have stayed in Iowa, like Peter Nazareth from Uganda and William Murray from County Clare. I could have gone into the University's PhD programme. Both Professor Murray and Paul Engle wanted me to stay, Paul saying he could supply cash to keep me going for a year until I got a Teaching Assistantship in September. He said the fact that I was a Dolmen Press poet, with Dolmen distributed by Humanities Press and Oxford University Press, would mean that I'd easily get an Iowa Teaching Assistantship. This may be the first really serious mistake I've made in my life.

Sunday Talking to the Brigadier while listening to Roy Mason on Ulster. The problem not only of identity but of perspective. Mason confused the issues of the 'rule of law' and the internment issue, the Maze prison.

Tuesday Got a huge sack of books from the USA. Some interesting ones; the poetry of Gregory Orr, letters of Sylvia Plath, biography of Marie Curie, plus all the International Writing Program seminar papers.

February 15th, 16th Two letters from William Shannon. What an extraordinary man. What an American character! Like Paul Engle he knows damn well that the young poet needs very little criticism but a *lot* of financial and social support. Kavanagh knew this, and such knowledge filled him with great pain. Shannon, not only an Ambassador but a writer, knows about the long tunnel that a writer crawls through in order to make his soul pure, his intentions clear.

February 19th Two phone calls today. The first from David Collins about the nomination of Neil Jordan to the Iowa Program. He would also like to see Dan Mulhall's thesis on 'Politics in Literature'. David Collins and his group held their meeting about the Frankfurt School, but it was very bad — too diffuse and disorganized. They want my report on Iowa soon. The second from Project Arts Centre asking me to do a reading.

February 22nd Reading Cecil Woodham-Smith's *The Great Hunger*. 300 pages in two sittings. A very disturbing book, the ultimate prosecution case against the British administration of Ireland.

Reading Thomas Kinsella's *Notes from the Land of the Dead* — a difficult collection, certainly, but extremely challenging poems of process, pain, decay. With Kinsella it is always the process. 'Lips and tongue / wrestle the delicious / life out of you,' as he says in 'A Hand of Solo', *'All is emptiness / and I must spin'* but it all comes back to the 'glittering brain, withering away' as he writes in 'Crab Orchard Sanctuary: Late October'. In 'Good Night' he writes 'What essences, disturbed from what / profounder nothingness . . . // . . . Would you agree, then, we won't find truths, or any certainties . . . ' But, as André Gide wrote so many years ago, one must be certain whether one wishes to write philosophy or literature; and this is Kinsella's great dilemma; this great ambiguity and untidiness that surrounds our own responses to his work. He occupies that difficult middle-ground of a lapsed faithfulness, somewhere between the troubled, uncomfortable temperament of Máirtín Ó Díreáin and the sheer metallic bloody-mindedness of Thom Gunn or the post-War fatalism of Ted Hughes in *Wodwo*.

March 6th Trying desperately to decide about the American Embassy job. I'd like to be in Dublin. But I must think of my Roethke MA in UCC. And Glenshelane House.

Wednesday In Dublin to collect twenty-four copies of *The First Convention*. At Dolmen Press I talked to Liam Miller on the phone because he was phoning into his office from home. He said that by the time Dolmen gets to my third book their distribution will be better. I doubt it. The pattern of a publisher's distribution network is set from the beginning; it hardly ever alters, unless a publisher is taken over by a conglomerate.

Delivered letters to American Embassy and Arts Council. I hope that everything goes OK. I hand-delivered the proofs of the 3rd edition of *The Rough Field* from the Dolmen office to Montague in Cork.

March 16th St Patrick's Eve Very heavy fall of snow today. It's very unusual to have snow so late. I had just planted onions and potatoes. The snow falling steadily outside, even as I write.

St Patrick's Day My mother very depressed today. This depression has been coming on for weeks. I thought that she didn't feel too well — she had a slight redness in her face and nausea. Today she's even lower; shivering limbs, voice almost a whisper, as if she were in shock. Very like her breakdown of two years ago. There was little I could do. I got up early, went to Mass to please her, lit the fire and made breakfast for Michael and Kevin.

March 19th A report on four ethnic groups just published in the United States. The Irish have yet to solve their drinking habits. The survey showed that the Irish (second or third generation) drink too much, that they are most likely to have problems associated with drink. The report stated that one of the main reasons for the alcoholism etc is the harshness of Irish family life.

March 20th My trouble is that I have the courage of my convictions but not the courage of my feelings.

Very interesting and, as usual, affectionate account of Michael Hartnett's poetry reading in today's *Examiner* by Paul Durcan. Hartnett has published a new book in Irish, *Adharca Broic*, at a Conradh na Gaeilge reading. Paul speaks about the 'exhilarating freedom' of the Irish night, the lack of pretentiousness when no American or Englishman could enter. I hate such nationalist chauvinisms. Americans and Englishmen are no less sincere if they love literature. And literature is what we are about, whatever the language. It is not necessary that the world should speak Irish, any more than that all the world should speak Hebrew. There is no moral superiority in any particular ethnic or language group. We are all placed on this earth to breathe and die. That's it. We breathe, we die, we write.

March 25th John Treacy, an old school mate from Cappoquin, has just won the World Cross Country Championship for the second time. Unbelievable scenes of jubilation: girls screaming in excitement and dancing about the racecourse waving the three crowns of the Munster flag. I admire John for his coolness, his self-possession. Never worried or distracted by such adulation, his mind continuously on the distance to be covered rather than the reward. A true artist, I think, and in his calm a real Waterford man.

April 3rd Catastrophe last night. My mother had a cerebral haemorrhage. Priest was called and she was annointed. Doctor could do nothing. She is in Ardkeen Hospital at the moment, still hasn't regained consciousness. Finding it difficult not to scream, not to shout abuse at Creation for erupting in her brain even before she had a chance to taste happiness. All the women of her generation have suffered so much. It is desperately unfair that she should have to endure further suffering.

April 4th My mother died last evening at 6 p.m. Only consolation is that if she had lived she would have been paralysed and, perhaps, unable to speak. A fate worse than death. She was fifty-three. Dear God, the poor do flower early and are soon swept away. Not surprising that she should die inside two years of my father's death. Mutual suffering made them into one being. The rage I feel is unbelievable. I will never be able to write anything that is the equal of this intense rage. I think of all the forces in Irish life that oppressed and ruined her every waking hour. But for the poor there is no evil force as oppressive as the relentless force of poverty itself. Poverty defined her, like the poor mother of Camus in Oran or the exhausted mother of Frank O'Connor in Cork.

April 5th Last night my mother removed from Ardkeen Hospital to the Church. Huge crowds at the funeral. Councillor Aherne of Knockalara there, ever faithful. Yet he is a good man. My mother in her coffin looked very, very old — compressed years of excessive cruelty and hardship. The world of poverty had cut so deep into her life, so furrowed and wrinkled her brow. Her looking so old in death didn't disappoint me. On the contrary, I felt reconciled to the reality of her passing. Her death is horrendous and cruel. For, God, it is an unforgivable thing.

April 7th My mother buried yesterday. No tears from any of her children: we are still too numbed by our father's death. I threw a few daffodils onto her coffin before the gravediggers covered it. We are all heartily sick of grand gestures. After the burial I drove directly to Cork to give a poetry reading with Theo. I needed to get away from Cappoquin, now a place of death. When I stood up to read my poems I set my mind against my mother's death and pretended to read exclusively for those who were young and beautiful in the audience. John Montague was at the reading. He spoke briefly about my mother's death and said that for a writer most of the sorrows of life occur before the age of thirty. He said that

I was getting an unusually strong dose of sorrow and he hoped I would have the strength to endure. He said I should remember that Hemingway's father shot himself outside the front door, that, at least, I had the grace of natural deaths behind me in my family. But more complaints about Heaney. May God give me patience. What J M doesn't realize is that Heaney has achieved a meteoric unsurpassability and to try to 'catch up' with him would expose a lesser talent to the heights of public ridicule.

April 15th Easter Sunday Real warmth in the sunshine. All the daffodils have perked up, roads drying and grass looking good. A vague sense of summer everywhere in the garden. My mother's death still unbelievable.

April 20th In Dungarvan today. I was walking past the County Council Offices near Lawlor's Hotel when I ran into three Fianna Fáil councillors, Ryan, Armstrong and Aherne. They were very pleasant, very eager to shake my hand. Councillor Armstrong, the old Comhairle Dáil Cheantair Chairman of my youth who is a school headmaster in Lismore, said to Ryan, 'You know this man, our own poet, a distinguished poet.' Perhaps encounters like this also happen in the Soviet Union. But they are dangerous. It is dangerous to be recognized by people whose business is power.

April 23/24th Arthur Shackleton from Mount Congreve Gardens came to dinner. Arthur is a grand-nephew of Shackleton the explorer. The Brigadier and Arthur and I did a tour of the garden before dinner. Arthur very impressed by our planting, especially the many semi-hardy plants that survived the winter. Mount Congreve lost many of its plants.

April 24th Spent the last few days in Dublin. I gave a poetry reading in Trinity College, my first poetry reading in Dublin. A small crowd, 20-25 people, but very appreciative. Had a wonderful few days, visiting the Arts Club, meeting Macdara Woods, Eiléan Ní Chuilleanáin and her mother Eilís Dillon. Eilís Dillon a truly beautiful person, full of warmth, welcome and curiosity. She put her arms around me and said, 'Now, don't disappear. Do you hear me, don't disappear!' She lives in Santa Barbara with her second husband, Vivien Mercier, the scholar and teacher.

Bought Isaac Singer's short stories, Doris Lessing's stories and two John McGahern books. Glad to be back at Glenshelane House. Its garden, and the Brigadier's busy coming and going, are now the most settled part of my life. The Glenshelane garden has become a kind of vessel that I live inside.

May 3rd At breakfast the Brigadier was talking about *The Duchess of Duke Street*. He says the sets are so accurate and beautiful, only the BBC could do such a job. Then he told me about a vivid and fascinating dream he had about his old company of stockbrokers, Panmure Gordon. He dreamt that Panmure had merged with a wholesale wildlife company that specialized in capturing wild animals for sale to zoos and parks. The Brigadier was told that he would be at the bottom of the partnership list, a fate he accepted. But he was also told that the partner who took a share in a camel would have a number of privileges. Then all the partners in the merger between Panmure and the wildlife company set off for a Game Reserve that was outside London (but it seemed to be on the Waterford coast in the dream). This dream had all the ingredients of the Brigadier's character: a ridiculous event, a demotion accepted with equanimity and strict procedural accuracy.

Friday Margaret Thatcher has won the General Election for the Conservatives. The first British female Prime Minister. I stayed awake until 4 a.m. listening to the BBC television and radio broadcasts of the first results. Will England change, I wonder?

May 20th Thinking about the number of fellow poets I meet
who are always on the verge of abandoning literature. Theo
suffers from this enormously, sometimes even Patrick Crotty
plays that game with himself. I wish they knew how much
I've tried to halt that conversation in my head. Camus in his
Notebooks gives Gide's reply to a young person who, sending
examples to him of their work, asked if they should give up
writing — *What! You can stop yourself and you hesitate?*

I went to Castledodard in the foothills of the Knockmeal-
downs behind Lismore to have tea with the glamorous Pam
Stevenson. All the tea-talk was about politics and religion.
The Brigadier was telling Pam how much the unity of Ireland
was put back in the last ten years, a great deal of it by the stupidity of the Southern Government. He said that in the '30s
when he was ADC to the General Officer Commanding
Northern Ireland many of the leading people of Ulster were
moving in the direction of a Federation with the South, but
the Irish Declaration of the Republic and the exit from the
Commonwealth ruined the whole thing. The Brigadier while
ADC had to prepare an Army plan for the takeover of Ulster
barracks and facilities by the Free State. Irish unity was a
constant probability in army conversations, but never spoken
of in the company of local politicians, Catholic or Protestant.
In the late '30s, if things got bad in Europe, England had
every intention of abandoning Ulster with the speed at which
it would later abandon Palestine. We always tend to forget
that England has its own core interests and it must always
act in the light of these interests: it would be idiotic for England to do otherwise.

May 22nd Lunch party at Glenshelane today. I sat beside
Dean Mayes who's just returned from a Church of Ireland
Synod in Dublin. We had a long discussion about Catholic
and Protestant marriages, the education of Protestant
children etc. I tried to interest the Dean in André Gide but
he didn't take the bait. Henry Hooth, once Earl Mount-

batten's Kenyan secretary, was there with his wife — they'd just got married. Henry is at least seventy, wife is thirty-ish. Brigadier didn't talk to her. Perhaps he's jealous. He said (about H's wife), 'she's a bit of an ass, really'. The strongest critical words ever spoken by the Brigadier in my presence. Mrs Mitchell of Ballyduff, a friend of Dean Acheson and Lady Bird Johnson, was here, just returned from Washington. She was very angry about Terence de Vere White and Victoria Glendinning. She says that Terence has made a complete fool of himself. This I doubt, but as she was a guest at Glenshelane I didn't argue with her.

May 24th Councillor Aherne came to the door today to look for my vote in the Local Election. His visit reminded about the time on the 'Here and Now' programme on RTÉ Radio when John Kelly TD accused Fianna Fáil of being the Party of the shadows, the Party of the darkness.

May 25th Long conversation with Seán Lucy today about Anglo-Irish literature, Corkery, Irish writers and the clichés of exile and Ulster. He is having a collection of poems launched at the Listowel Writers' Week. Also, he is organizing a Cork Summer School for American and postgraduate students. He's very excited by the prospect of such a Summer School, the excitement of many new discussions with new kinds of people. I told him that going to America (for me) was like bathing in a bowl of treacle, a rich, rich experience. He read some extracts of his from a manuscript collection of essays — one on landscape in the work of Daniel Corkery and another on exile and Irish writers. I began to tell him my ideas on how Irish writers use exile as a weapon, as a technical advantage, when he unearthed another essay from his folder. This essay developed *exactly* the same arguments, the very lines of my own thoughts. It was amazing. He also showed me a play he'd written on yet another Irish mythical god. *That* was where we parted company intellectually:

I can't bear any more plays or texts on stupid Oisíns and stupid Gráinnes. I long for a new drama on real things in Ireland, a live drama like in the work of Hugh Leonard or Neil Simon. Sweet Jesus, no more myths! If I had any other background I would never write about Ireland, a disastrous, maiming, mythical, collapsing country.

June 1st The countryside has suddenly come alive. All flowers and shrubs in full bloom at Glenshelane. The smell of summer is everywhere. Especially in the evening one can taste the floating pollen, the warmed-up grassland, the dry meadowing in the field between the house and the river. On a day like today Glenshelane becomes a place of magic.

June 3rd Countess Michalowski came to Glenshelane to stay for Sir Richard Keane's 70th birthday party. She brought a copy of the Pope's (John Paul II) poems for me. Some very good poems; many of them working out the problems of finding a language to match emotions and beliefs.

The poetry is nearly as good as Vasko Popa, certainly as intellectual. Apart from Hopkins and in some sense Eliot he's the best priest-poet I've ever read. Yet his reported conservatism is a deeply regressive, even frightening, thing. The Countess likes him, of course, not merely because he's Polish but because he's conservative and actively, relentlessly anti-Russian and anti-communist.

June 7th Another useless day in my life. We spent the morning preparing for a large luncheon party. The Brigadier's wines are dreadful. I told him so this morning and I told him he had no instinct for good wine. Not expensive wine, which he would never buy anyway, but just good wines. I often wonder if his War injuries have damaged his sense of taste and smell. The farmer came to extend the cattle grid.

Sentimentalism is the greatest enemy of art and it's my enemy and I damn well know it. It ruins Corkery's *The*

Threshold of Quiet and Ó Faoláin's *Bird Alone*. In Cork, it seems to me, no great novel has emerged because that powerful place sucks each of its artistic children back into its preciousness, its petty bourgeois self-satisfaction. When I look at West Waterford I see it from the remove of Glenshelane House. Despite the Brigadier's poor taste in wine the place has rigorous standards, of behaviour, political viewpoint and Received Pronunciation. This has been my strength, and it's the reason why I haven't left Glenshelane and gone to live in a falling-down cottage behind Mount Melleray Abbey. For what it's worth Glenshelane is my Paris. The Matson Roths of San Francisco said to me the other day that the Brigadier when talking about me at dinner parties — in my absence — implies that he is responsible for my literary work. But the very *opposite* is true: in the true literary sense I invented the Brigadier. I invent him every day and insert him into my life as an antidote to the boring, humdrum life of provincial Ireland.

June 18th My cousin's wife came to Glenshelane today. She calls Southernwood 'Boys Love' and her husband calls Foxglove 'Lady's Fingers'. A crew from RTÉ Television arrived to do a special programme on Dervla Murphy and West Waterford. Dervla had phoned to ask me to participate. She said it would be good publicity for me (a thing she herself has absolutely no interest in) and it was also worth £15. They took shots of Derriheen House, old Dr White's place where Dervla was born. Dervla and I conversed (unconvincingly) about writing and travelling; Dervla trying to ask questions about my stay in America while I insisted that she answer my questions about her more important journeys. It was very funny but I don't think the television people were that amused. I hope they'll make some use of the day's filming. It is supposed to be broadcast in September. Televison is now the point of entry into people's imaginations, rather as theatre was for Yeats's generation after the fall of Parnell. Dangerous, like the theatre. What Irish TV really needs is a William Fay, or the Fay brothers.

June 28th The poet Gillian Bence-Jones, wife of the historian Mark Bence-Jones and great-great-great-great grand-neice of Jane Austen, came to tea with her husband. She had a lovely memory from her mother of a Bloom-like encounter with Irish history. Her mother, or was it her mother's friend, was wife of the British First Secretary at Dublin Castle during colonial times: she was sunning herself on a beach outside Dublin, accompanied by her two-year-old child (and presumably a nurse/nanny), when her parasol blew away in a sudden gust of wind. The parasol was blowing along the sand when a tall gentleman chased after it and retrieved it. He returned the parasol with great chivalry. The mother was extremely impressed and flushed with embarrassment by this dashing gesture. She began to thank the man profusely and to snare him into conversation. After a while, and after some conversation, the man suddenly backed off and said, 'Madam, I'm afraid I must tell you something. I am Parnell. I know who you are. Perhaps your husband would be very upset if he learned that you had engaged me in conversation. Our politics don't allow us to be friends.' The beautiful mother replied, 'Oh, come, let us not fall out over tiresome things. Let's abandon politics for today. I'm sure that you are quite bored by politics all the time.' With that, Parnell lay down beside the beautiful wife of the British First Secretary and played with her two-year-old child, held it in his arms, bounced it about, all the time chatting affectionately. The child later remembered that England-Ireland contact, the warmth of the afternoon, the splendid affection in Parnell's eyes and the fatherly firmness of his hands. As if, indeed, said Gillian, he had held the screaming infant of Ireland.

Mark Bence-Jones himself remembered Cambridge in the 1950s, particularly Ted Hughes and Hughes' very heavy drinking. Bence-Jones says that he had a friend who ruined his academic performance by taking responsibility for getting Hughes to bed when he was drunk — which was virtually every night. This must have been before Sylvia came along.

Wednesday More letters from America. One from Peter Nazareth in Iowa addressed to 'Republic of Ireland, United Kingdom'. How strange, but all part of the hopeless smallness of Ireland. As an Irishman I'll just have to get used to our smallness. It is something that we must be aware of, not that we should be depressed about it in any way. It is said that in the world there are 40 million Irish and Irish exiles, just as there are 40 million Jews. Do the Jews ever complain about being too small a people? They do not. They act as a mighty people.

Jack Lynch addressed the new European Parliament today and was interrupted by the lunatic Ian Paisley. Paisley left the chamber shouting, 'Hypocrite! Hypocrite!' at Mr Lynch who is currently President of the Parliament. I had hoped that a more generous intellectual air of European politics would soothe some of the venomous nature in Paisley.

Saturday In an interview with Mary Holland on RTÉ Television John McGahern said, 'Well, I suppose, Art is a kind of failed religion. Religion abolishes time and establishes eternity, Art abolishes time and establishes memory.'

Announcement in Rome and Dublin that Pope John Paul II is coming to Ireland. Even before I could have a cup of tea the nutcase Ian Paisley was bawling his head off, shouting 'No Pope for Ulster!'

July 30th Back in Cork again, after an idyllic absence of eleven months. I have a bed-sitting room (16ft by 13ft) made pleasant by books that I brought with me — all of Olson's stuff, all of Duncan's poetry, Octavio Paz's essays and Montale's poems.

Friday Came back to Glenshelane House to many letters and four copies of *The Sewanee Review*.

Wednesday At Glenshelane House, wandering about on my own. The Brigadier has gone out to dinner with Colonel Chevasse who lives in old Arland Ussher's house at Cappagh.

Wednesday night / Thursday morning Terrible storms and rain all night. Many of the three hundred yachts taking part in the Fastnet Race off the Irish coast have been damaged or have gone missing. Six yachtsmen dead. Even Edward Heath in *Morning Cloud* has sent out a distress signal. He's supposed to be making for Cork Harbour with a broken rudder. Winds of up to 55 knots.

September 5th More developments from the IRA bombing this morning — a massive State Funeral for Earl Mountbatten. Brigadier and I looked at the television for two hours. Magnificent display of marching and official solemnity. The Royal Navy and Life Guards did the honours; all the Royals, including members of the collapsed royalty of Europe, were there. At least one Irish person, Irish-American that is, Princess Grace, was in attendance.

Very strange night last night. We had dinner at Glenshelane for the Knight of Kerry and Lady FitzGerald and Adrian. When Lord Donoughmore arrived two Special Branch men drove up and leaped out of a car brandishing sub-machine guns. They wanted to know who was at the party, what dignitaries, and who worked in the kitchen. It was strange — but déjà vu strange — to see two men armed to the teeth with magazines of bullets bulging from their pockets, walking around the house and through the gardens. It is sad to think that even after fifty years Ireland still hasn't settled. The matter-of-factness of Lord Donoughmore when I chatted to him struck me; his refusal to be perturbed by the continuous threats to his life. Old habits die hard in this country — I think of Lady Gregory with her blinds drawn or the single-mindedness of Yeats. Such danger is romantic, even exotic, in books, or for those who live in normal countries. But here in Ireland people actually die: it is not the least romantic. Just a few summers ago Lord Donoughmore and his wife Dorothy were kidnapped from Knocklofty House (over the mountains from Cappoquin). The IRA unit that kidnapped them must have been highly disciplined and well led because the Donoughmores were released unharmed after a week. I wonder if money changed hands? I doubt it, but a guerrilla war needs to raise money to keep itself alive. And the IRA, with its leadership drawn from that most calculating bourgeois class of small farmers, builders, carpenters and electricians, must be obsessed with money in that rapacious gombeen way.

The two detectives asked me if I knew of a poet from Tipperary who had been arrested recently. At first he had refused to give his name. One of the Special Branch men said he liked Auden's poetry. So, with a mug of tea in one hand and a machine gun in the other he discussed the merits of 'The Unknown Citizen'. A strange night indeed. Despite the bravado of the Anglo-Irish sitting to dinner in the dining room that the Brigadier and I had so carefully decorated, and the seeming effort at nonchalance by the police, one could feel the tension in the air. I could feel the nervousness of the younger detective who kept locking and unlocking the magazine of twenty bullets from his gun's mechanism. One live bullet fell from the magazine and rolled under the red-hot Aga stove that had been operating on full power for three hours. The young detective was terrified that it would explode, but Anne wouldn't move from the stove as she was in the middle of creating a warm hollandaise sauce from the roux she had prepared earlier. The detective sweated until Anne's sauce was completed and poured into the silver sauce boat with the Geraldine crest from the great house of Carton. After that the young detective scrambled to his knees to fish out the bullet. He could have lost an eye or half of his face if the bullet had exploded, but Anne danced around him as if he were a tiresome child. When she came back from the dining room she reported triumphantly that Lord Donoughmore had said that her sauce was just perfect.

October 11th Letter from Matthew Sweeney asking for poems for *Green River Review* in Michigan. Also, a small cheque from the Dublin Arts Festival. Attended a funeral on behalf of the Library at St Joseph's cemetery. Spent a few minutes at Daniel Corkery's grave. Before the funeral I had a drink in a tiny pub near Clarke's Bridge with Seán Bohan, the City Librarian.

October 12th Had many conversations with John Montague and Seán Dunne in The Long Valley. John is still desperately worried about Seamus H's and Faber's threat to his reputation. Earlier I had supper with Theo and a revolutionary friend of Theo's who was very confident and middle class.

October 15th I searched all the bookshops in Cork today for Seamus Heaney's new book, *Field Work*. Eventually I found it in Easons on Patrick Street. I was walking around the city aimlessley and felt a great sense of excitement and warmth, a sort of rapt anticipation. It really is amazing what an effect a new Heaney book has. It is not just another book, but an event. Surely the only other Irish poet to have such an effect on younger writers was Yeats. And before Yeats you'd have to go back to Byron for such excitement. I love the book. It is an absolutely crowning work, his best.

October 25th Michael Hartnett has been in Cork all week. I keep meeting him in The Long Valley. He's carrying around Linda Pastan's and Roy McFadden's collections. He has to review them for RTÉ Radio.

Theo has taken responsibility for the magazine *The Rebel*, a poorly produced news-sheet. The enmity between *The*

Rebel's core group and the more bourgeois/practical trade
unionists has led to a split in the Cork Anti-Nuclear Movement. It is strange, and terribly familiar, this civil war between
angels. Theo has failed to get tutorial hours at UCC despite
his brilliance as a teacher and his huge popularity.

Seferis, in his *Paris Review* interview, explains how success
and honour are mere accidents within one's literary life. The
real victory is that the life continues within art.

Seán Dunne is settling into the library job with me. It is
wonderful to suddenly work closely with someone who has
been vaguely a friend for years. I learned new things about
him — his extraordinary vanity, not like Theo's which is
gentle and aesthetic, but more like Montagues's, nervous and
quite aggressive.

November 12th Went to tea with Kristin Jameson, the artist,
at Tourin. It was a dull, brown-grey November day. Arthur
Shackleton and Kristin's mother were surveying the garden
when I arrived. Kristin brought me into the library and we
lit the fire and talked. She's as beautiful as her mother must
have been when she was her age. She told me that once, while
a student in Florence, she sat beside Montale at a dinner
party. He turned to her and said, 'I hear you are Irish. What
do you think of Joyce?' Kristin was terrified, afraid to express an opinion for fear of making a fool of herself, so she
asked Montale what *he* thought of Joyce. He then settled into
an hour-long apologia for Joyce's work; rising from the table
eventually, saying what a brilliant girl she was.

November 17th Jean Rhys's autobiography, just terrific. On
the relationship between writing and life she says, 'A novel
has a shape. Life has no shape.'

November 19th A big night in literary Cork last night:
Seamus Heaney read his latest book to a packed auditorium
on the Grand Parade. I queued for forty-five minutes in

freezing temperatures in a large crowd in order to assure myself of a seat. Eventually people had to sit on steps and stairs and others were turned away. Heaney himself seemed much more reticent, even shy, compared to his 1975 visit. I think he felt the pressure of Montague's presence on the platform. After the reading I queued again to have his book signed. So many people there that H exclaimed, 'My wife tells me that an unsigned copy of *Field Work* is very valuable!' Later, at a party in Montague's house (Evelyn looking relaxed and elegant) Heaney came over to me and said that he liked my first book enormously, as did John McGahern. It was a terrific compliment, all the better for having been unsought. He spoke about America. He said he flew into Iowa in snow-covered February to read at Grinnell College. I told Heaney about my visit to Robert Duncan in San Francisco and he said he remembered my poem 'Poet in the City' in *The Irish Times*. This astonished me. This man has total recall. He said that Duncan 'certainly likes to make a lot of space for himself'. It is a brilliant expression and perfectly describes the easeful kingdom of Duncan's self-contained San Francisco life.

At the Montague party, the fine Limerick bard, Michael Hartnett. Very drunk, and making passes at Mary Leland. He has managed to get a job as a nightwatchman with CMP Dairies. Strange, the way life shines differently on different poets of equal talent. Hartnett is about the same age as Heaney, yet Heaney is Head of an English Department at Carysfort Teachers' College, commercially successful etc, while Michael (who has published the same number of books as Seamus H) walks from factory to factory looking for a job as a labourer. I am very sad for Michael; sad because although there is no jealousy in his nature I feel quite sure that he is disappointed with his life so far. He must be disappointed when he sees how beautifully Heaney's life is flowering. The difference may simply be a relationship with alcohol, the one true debilitating curse of Irish poets; but, in truth, it is also the difference between literary Ulster and literary Munster. It really is the destiny of Munster poets never to be wildly famous. Hartnett accepts this, however sadly.

November 24th Gave a reading last night in Skibbereen. Very large audience. People very pleasant and respectful. Staying with Countess Michalowski who organized the whole affair. Beautiful house situated on the edge of a bog between the mountains and the sea. Situation typical: a large clump of old trees, mainly deciduous, forming a canopy over the lesser laurels; the laurels forming a windbreak for ceanothus and camellias: finally, add a clump of carefully 'informal' heather and then the large lean-to greenhouse with stepped platforms for flowers, trained wires for grapevine, whitewashed walls and solid iron pipes; and finally, finally, the house itself — the front entrance, the carpeted, massive hallway and beautiful rooms. All very impressive, tidy, fruitful, a true 'high chair cushioned with down', as Montague has written, describing a proper place for poets. At a large dinner party last night I met an old woman who acted with Sybil Thorndike; also an old woman (was it Sheila Grant-Duff?) who was in the colonial service; a sculptor, her son, very retiring and quiet who clutched a pint of Guinness. There was also a man there who had attended the Clare County Convention of Fianna Fáil that nominated Éamon de Valera to the Dáil Elections. He had been a very young man — eighteen-years-old — when de Valera approached him and handed him a slip of paper with a motion written upon it: this motion stated that members of FF who were also members of the Knights of Columbanus would have to renounce their oaths of loyalty to the K of C if elected, or leave Fianna Fáil. This is a very interesting insight into the fears that Dev had of Catholic organizations. This same man (at dinner) attacked Seán McBride in a most vicious manner. He said that McBride was a murderer who turned from the fanaticism of guns to the fanaticism of Law. He said that McB had a manic self-obsession, an obsession with his own glory. He said that McBride, 'like Conor Cruise O'Brien', was a political fool because he had no sympathy with the plain people of Ireland. He said that McBride was a single-minded and dangerous elitist. I have never encountered such venom against another politician. But this man at dinner said that he once had a meeting with McBride and the IRA in the 1930s and he looked straight into McBride's eyes and found hatred there: no human empathy, no fullness of love, but empty hatred. I told him that, like most Irish intellectuals, I idolized McBride. The man threw his eyes up to heaven, he just couldn't understand my admiration for McBride, but I wouldn't give way, even when Countess Michalowski interrupted her own conversation to listen to our heated argument. I thought it important, in this particular aristocratic company, that Seán McBride's good name should be defended.

Sunday Brigadier set off this morning for London on his way to Antibes for Christmas. He gave me a Sotheby's Art Diary for Christmas, full of fascinating details about the art world, and Sotheby Parke-Bernet. (This is, of course, merely a recycled present: he had received it free as a customer of Sotheby's.)

December 23rd At Seán Dunne's wedding: it was a beautiful crisp evening at the Honan Chapel in UCC. All the old friends had gathered: Dan Mulhall, who's going to the Embassy in India, Aengus Collins the cartoonist, and the poets Greg Delanty, Pat Crotty and Theo wearing a theatrical cravat. All the O'Donoghues, Pádraigín, Máirín and Eamon. Fr Brendan O'Mahony, the philosopher, married the couple. After the Communion Seán read a piece of MacDiarmid's poetry and I read part of a poem 'Maple Syrup' by Donald Hall. The reception was held forty miles from the city in a cottage on Owenahincha Strand. When we arrived a wind got up and spray drenched the cottage. One could hear the waves breaking viciously in the distance. Much drinking and merrymaking. The party went on until eight o'clock the following morning. A small group of us slipped into the kitchen and held an impromptu poetry reading. We stood on a chair and recited our pieces. Fr Brendan O'Mahony came across the room to me and whispered, 'You know, I envy poets! I envy the world they live in, that sense of purpose and unworldly warmth.'

December 24th At home for Christmas, my time divided between Glenshelane and Shanbally Terrace. Glenshelane was very damp so I put on the heating system to its maximum. Cut down some ash trees by the river with a small chainsaw.

Christmas Day A dinner party at John Fraher's house in Shanbally Terrace, Cappoquin, locus of the *First Convention* poems. John, in his late-fifties, is now married and a father. His house, as usual, full of every possible convenience, two TVs, cameras, stereos, dishwashers, two showers, multitudes of heating systems. Marguerite, his wife, made a magnificent dinner. John took me aside and showed me a file of letters from Jackie Fahey TD, the new Minister for State at Environment. The letters also contained photostats of papers from the National HQ of the Party enquiring about the financial state of the Waterford Party at Constituency and Electoral Area level. Fianna Fáil has got a bad name in the Waterford constituency. This is what worries the Paliamentary Party. We have now truly entered the Haughey era. John agreed with me that, with Charlie Haughey aboard, the coming Fianna Fáil years will be an era of nightmares.

December 30th Reading Robert Payne's *Life and Death of Trotsky*. He ends the biography by saying 'Lenin and Trotsky failed, and Stalin failed more miserably. All the works of revolution must begin again.' The optimism of the true revolutionary.

December 31st Long discussion with Seán Dunne about publishing a book of poems and photographs about Waterford: perhaps ten poems each and old photographs of ships and streets. Within ten minutes of the discussion Seán said, 'But I don't want to play second fiddle to you. We must do it as equals.' Always when I discuss poetry with Seán he mentions the fact that he deserves as much 'recognition' as I. I can't understand what he understands as 'recognition'. I feel that nobody ever treats me as a poet whereas, when Seán enters a pub or room people instantly light up and exclaim, 'Ah, poet!' Seán has so many more practical notions of a literary life than Theo that my minimal success pains him. And John Montague makes things worse by teasing him. In The Long Valley the other day Montague caught Seán by the shoulder and exclaimed, 'Watch Tom McCarthy! Learn from him! He is so political!' A two-edged knife: it insults me and upsets Seán. However, we have decided to go ahead with the book, whoever pays plays the fiddle.

It is January now, ships hooting in the harbour and people out on the streets banging bin lids. A new decade begins. I am alone in my bedsit. I left a crowd of young poets, writers and musicians, mistresses and lovers, all dancing and singing in The Long Valley. The great richness of bohemian Cork. I try to consider the decade that's coming. I have achieved little in 1979. Both my parents are now dead, unimaginable. Unimaginable. In truth, I have gone backwards, and I have nobody in my life. But to hell with it.

1980

Our whole life is spent in sketching an in-eradicable portrait of ourselves ... We recount our lives and lie to ourselves, but our life will not lie; it will recount our soul, which will stand before God in its usual posture.
— André Gide, *Journals*, 3 Jan 1892

January 16th The Cork Review is published with a selection of my poems from *The Sorrow Garden*. Very bad misprints in Dev poem and in 'Listening to Novelists'. Read a poem on RTÉ Radio Cork as part of their coverage of the publication of the *Review*. Reading *Poetics of Reverie* by Bachelard; by now my bible. No book contains so many important flights of genius. Reading even a few pages relaxes my mind and makes my confidence in humanity grow. I've been reading Enno Stephan's book *Spies in Ireland*, also Stanley Kunitz.

Walking through Glenshelane Wood I kept thinking about the death of Lady Brabourne. The Provisional IRA have destroyed us. And the part of us that they haven't destroyed they've cheapened. We live in our vulgar selves, in this paradigm of self-regarding nationalist cruelty. Their religious piety sickens me. It is the piety of a bloodstained Mafia. There is blood on every green tie they wear.

January 17th Small note today from Paul and Hualing in Iowa. Paul seems not to have fulfilled his two book Houghton Mifflin contract. Also, a little calendar from Goza and Marilia. The idea of an essay on peace in Ireland is uppermost in my mind.

Sunday Went to see Claud Cockburn to try to persuade him to write an essay for *The Cork Review*. Success. Claud agreed to write a 1,000 word essay on his move, 'his exile', from Brooke House in Youghal to Rock House in Ardmore. When I walked into the drawing room overlooking the ocean I met Claud sitting on a couch with copies of *The Irish Times* and the *Guardian* on his lap and an old sheepdog by his side. He roared with laughter when I told him that *The Cork Review* hoped not to have too many advertisements. He said that I reminded him of the old editor of *Private Eye* who must have been the only editor to falsify his circulation figures downwards in the hope that people wouldn't bring so many libel suits against him. Also, he talked about his cancer; he said there was no pain. But the most extraordinary thing was the after-effect of the treatment, an overpowering melancholia. Often, while sitting in the garden, if a cloud appeared on the horizon it would trigger hours of deepest melancholy and a sense of abandonment. This must have been a particularly frightening experience for someone like Claud who knows nothing of melancholy, but is always sparkling and exuberant. He was very interested in the Iowa International Writing Program and was impressed when I said that I'd lived for two weeks with Faiz Ahmad Faiz, winner of the Lenin Prize.

January 21st Made a wonderful discovery this week: found Stendhal's early *Journals* in the store of the City Library. They had been removed from the public shelves years ago because of their tentative eroticism.

January 22nd Posted letters to *Outposts*, Kristin Jameson, Terence de Vere White, Padraic Fiacc and Sorley MacLean. Have so many letters to write; never wrote that letter with poems to Seamus Heaney for his edition of *Ploughshares*. Montague says it is now too late. While marching on a huge Trade Union demonstration against excessive income tax I met Theo on Parliament Bridge. He was selling copies of *The*

Rebel, the revolutionary group paper. He has really become a European intellectual of the Left. That is a very fine thing to be, but it may ruin his poetry. At some point he will have to make a choice.

Wednesday Back at Glenshelane. An image of time passing: I was looking through the Brigadier's address book for Adrian's address when I noticed that some of the names were crossed out. As people die the Brigadier puts a line through the name. He doesn't bother cancelling the address, just the name. One of the names crossed out was Doreen, Lady Brabourne. Murdered by the IRA. Her crossed-out name filled me with an incredible sense of melancholy all day.

February 6th Sitting in the sitting room of Adrian's house in Clareville Street SW7, listening to a recital on Radio 3 as well as the sound of someone practising on the piano at the school next door — a peaceful and even privileged London situation. Adrian told me about an interesting new organization, The British-Irish Association. One of the leaders of this new group is Lady Dufferin.

February 10th On Thursday I went to the Royal Academy to see the Post-Impressionist exhibition. Endless rooms of the most beautiful work. AE called the 1912 exhibition 'a second childhood of man' and I can appreciate his sentiment — the Post-Impressionist love of light, of dotted lines, of dot-clusters of colour, colour punctuated by intervals of light; all conspire to form a rumour of the first summers of one's childhood. The Irish world was represented by Jack Yeats and Roderic O'Conor. On Thursday evening also I went to a reading by Longley, Kennelly, Morrow and William Trevor at the Poetry Centre. Huge crowd, all good-humoured and friendly. Had a long chat with Kennelly and Peter Fallon. Saw Gavin Ewart. Also chatted with Derek Mahon who now works for the BBC.

Friday, Saturday. Spent two days in Bristol with Mary and Martin. They are extremely happy. Went to a late night film at the Arnolfini, the Bristol Arts Centre: *Images,* by Altman. A film about alter and ego, past and present, male and female, all fluctuating within and without the lens, with Japanese Bugaku-like music as a backdrop. Visited with Mary on the wards. She is in charge of perhaps 20-30 old men.

Sunday Went to a Service with Adrian at St Mary's in Bourne Street, a very high-Anglican service ('Mass' would probably be a better description of it). Even the Rosary was recited. It reminded me of the Catholic Mass before Vatican II — the Catholicism of my very early childhood. The singing was magnificent. The English take religion so seriously. In Ireland it is impossible to have a religious feeling without its attendant political reverberation. Here at St Mary's there's a yearning for religious experience just for its own sake — a yearning that has been unimaginable in Ireland for at least four centuries.

February 14th Went to the Poetry Society reading last night. An astonishing line-up: Francis Stuart, Bryan Guinness (Lord Moyne), Denis Johnston and Liam O'Flaherty were reading. Francis Stuart, aided by his faithful lieutenant Paul Durcan, read a contemporary version of a biblical theme. Bryan Guinness read some painfully bad poems — Pat Cooke passed a note to me during the reading, 'An aristocrat in search of poetry — the unspeakable in search of the *unspeakable.*' Denis Johnston read an hilarious extract from his autobiography *Nine Rivers from Jordan,* about searching for a bordello during the Second World War. But Liam O'Flaherty was the sensation of the evening. He sat down while reading he was so frail, and read a very early primeval story that had an electrifying effect on the English audience. His voice is pure and unspoilt, as if the voice was still connected with the pure Aran soul. None of the social success of his middle age had spoilt the voice. It was like listening to a Native American chief reciting a legend of the Plains, or a seanachie in Ballyferriter or Ring telling a ghost story. I would think that no other event in *The Sense of Ireland* will bring the English audience closer to the smell of the turf, or the peculiar, seriously tilted, genius of the Irish.

When Andrew Carpenter with his fine Oxonian accent thanked O'Flaherty for reading O'Flaherty replied, 'Yer welcome, Sir. Yer welcome, Sir', just like an old fisherman on the quay at Inishmore. The audience laughed to hear such Irishisms. And I smiled, happy to know that one can be successful while retaining the primary connectedness of one's first rural milieu. His elderly Galway accent had the authority of a personal signature; it was a judgement upon us all.

February 15th Last night I read at the Poetry Society in Earl's Court with Paul Durcan, Seán Ó Tuama and John Montague. Huge crowd; the reading was sold out and people sat on the stairways and in the library next door where a public address system had been installed. Adrian FitzGerald and the Brigadier came to hear me read, with a party of sixteen Anglo-Irish gentlefolk. John Montague was presented with The Alice Hunt Bartlett Prize. Later he gave a superb introduction as I stood up to read. He said, 'Now I introduce a young poet in whose achievements I am intensely proud. He was, I consider, the most brilliant student to pass through my hands. One should watch him because things keep happening to him.' Afterwards a young woman came up to me and introduced herself — she was Patricia McCarthy, the poet. Francis Stuart came up to me and shook my hand. Also, there was a fascinating girl who, when John M asked what she thought of his reading, said, 'Twas alright. Nothing great.' It turned out that she was John's neice.

A great party at Adrian's house in Clareville Street; all Catholics and Anglo-Catholics. Earlier, at Countess Michalowski's, I met the man whose father directed the British O'Meara Opera Company that toured Ireland in the '30s.

Also, I met Jill and Geoffrey Chapman, the publishers of
religious books. Both very anti-Irish, mainly because of the
perceived insider-dealing between the Vatican authorities and
the Mercier Press in Cork. Mercier Press constantly beats
Geoffrey Chapman to English language rights of Vatican publications. Cork's timeless Franciscan-Capuchin connection
with Rome works in Mercier's favour, despite the best efforts
of socially well-connected English nobles in the Vatican
who work on Chapman's behalf. This is only right and
proper — after all, Ireland suffered for centuries because of
its attachment to Rome. It should now be given its little re-
wards (in this world, as opposed to the next).

At lunchtime I met Matthew Sweeney and Eddie Linden
in the Churchill Arms pub. Linden is a frail creature with a
Scottish accent like a sledgehammer. He was full of enthusiasm
for Southern Irish Poetry. He had acquired a kind of stylish
bitterness about the neglect of Southern Irish poetry in England.
I didn't agree with this but I didn't want to start an argument
with someone who wishes to be friendly towards Southern
Irish things. I tried to explain to Eddie that Ulster poetry is
part of British poetry as well as Irish poetry. It is uniquely
placed politically, and the sooner people accept this the better.
As a Munsterman, I must admit, I enjoyed listening to Linden's
savage words of vilification against Ulster poetry. But, still,
Eddie's championing Southern Irish poetry had an unhinged
quality to it. Upon reflection I am right and Eddie Linden is
wrong. What's the point in worrying about these things?
In Munster we just need to write good work; and the same
applies to all Southern Irish poetry. And these are cyclical
matters: in the 1960s when Ulsterman John Montague won
a poetry prize he was announced as 'a Dublin poet' because
all editors assumed that poetry only came from Dolmen
Press and Dublin. So now it is Belfast's turn, and why not?
The wheels of poetry turn; some of the time they turn with
us, but most of the time they turn against us. This is every
poet's lot.

February 23rd Reading Thomas Jones' *Whitehall Diary*, the volume on Ireland. The sorrow of Ireland is endless, endless, endless. And the mis-application of British administration is equally tenacious. What is really amazing in this volume is the very real affection of the Imperial Cabinet for Cosgrave's Government. No such affection for Irish governments exists in the British Cabinet now; nothing but a feeling that oscillates between indifference and contempt.

April 9th A perfect weekend at Glenshelane. The sun shone brilliantly for four days, temperature in greenhouse rose to 100°F. The soil dried up completely while I ploughed so that I felt that I walked through the middle of July. The weather lifted my heart so much, and lifted the Brigadier's spirits too, so that we kept bumping into each other while working and exclaimed each time, 'Isn't it wonderful! Isn't it incredible!'

Adrian, the Knight of Kerry's son, was here for a few days. He and I went to a Benediction Service at Mount Melleray Abbey. Fears in the drawing rooms at Glenshelane and Cappoquin House that he may become a Roman Catholic.

My finances are, as usual, presenting problems. My weekly library pay after tax and health insurance is £52 and my recurring expenses are £44. So I live on £8 a week.

April 15th Just heard on BBC that Jean-Paul Sartre has died.

Five hundred bombers attacked Britain today in a 'mock battle' or war game. As Sartre dies the war games begin again in Europe. The insanity of it all.

April 30th A period of lunatic frenzy, lots of poetry readings for the Arts Council, readings in Cork, too many late nights. Too much socializing. Problems with John Montague. He has fallen into a state of deep depression, almost despair. His doctor thinks that this is due to his determined but unsupervised withdrawal from alcohol. Last week I met John on the street and we went into a pub, The Ivy Leaf, for a quick chat.

We were inside for less than ten minutes but in that time John had three whiskeys and two beers. After that I had to help him home. His depression is certainly connected with this drink problem, a fear of ageing, a fear of the power of Seamus Heaney (Heaney's ascendancy is still blamed for everything: Kinsella's illness, Murphy's darkness, Mahon's drinking) and the difficulties of writing *The Dead Kingdom*, particularly 'The Black Pig' sequence.

I feel incapable of helping him when he gets into this King Lear mood. Nobody can help while he's raging against all these imaginary storms of the literary world.

May 1st Spent an evening with Dervla Murphy. She was also very depressed. Her book *A Place Apart* should have done much better. Her publisher in America is a huge disappointment — she has made only $300 instead of $3,000+ from the work. But her *Wheels Within Wheels* is being published by Ticknor and Fields, the sub-company of Houghton Mifflin. Dervla may still make some money from her autobiography.

May 18th Extraordinary, beautiful weather. Temperature reaching 75°F, and 100°F in our unventilated greenhouse. Day too beautiful to stay indoors and write. Instead the Brigadier and I walked through the grounds to admire the fabulous, pastel-shaded azaleas, gifts from Patricia Cockburn that we had planted on a rainy day in the winter; light pinks, orange tints, pale reds, and the exquisite pale green of young leaves. Everywhere the light is a dappled blaze through the trees.

May 23rd Last Monday at dinner in Dervla Murphy's I met a Hungarian who was a professor of English at a college in Philadelphia — we were talking about Anglo-American culture and cosmopolitanism when he broke in with a marvellous statement: that the writer is engaged in a conversation with his own family, and only his own family. It struck me as a very relevant remark, having just read Walt Whitman and his conversations with his American family. Moving on from that statement we discussed how a writer's cosmopolitanism, his or her internationalism (concepts with a false centre), form only a part of our ability to eavesdrop into those intimate family conversations within nations, cultures, cities, histories. Thus I feel that we eavesdrop into Borges' intimate conversations with the people of Buenos Aires, or we listen to Isaac Bashevis Singer's private dialogue with the old learned Yiddish men of the New York cafés. As readers we are not being addressed directly, but we overhear the conversations: this is how literature works.

When rewriting *The Solitude of the Party* I must remember Willa Cather's phrase: 'Description is revelation.'

Yesterday I made Theo laugh when I told him about Standish O'Grady's original plan for Yeats and his circle. O'Grady, the old dreamer, had hoped to assemble a body of Irishmen who would be so brilliant that they would move into the highest echelons of British administration and gradually take over the reins of Government in England. In this way, O'Grady hoped, Ireland would control the British Empire while England would get the blame. The fact is, it wasn't the Irish but the educated Scottish who ended up controlling the Empire.

I went to GBS's *John Bull's Other Island* in the Opera House. A packed house to see Cyril Cusack. The play might have been written last weekend. Shaw is always contemporary; it's a proof of his genius. He is unquestionably our greatest national genius: the breadth of his vision and his capacity for work makes him unique among Irishmen. Only Beckett can touch him, but Beckett doesn't have the same sense of national purpose. Indeed, to have no purpose was Beckett's purpose. Shaw was never happy with the mere choreography and music of theatre: he wished to also make a speech, a theatrical purpose that Beckett would find repulsive.

Monday Met Des Hogan at lunchtime in The Long Valley.

He had come to Cork for a reading in the Arts Centre (poorly attended, I heard, only twenty people). We had a long talk about America, about the freedom of 'going way', the freedom of exile.

Tuesday I borrowed £2 from John Montague in The Long Valley. He had been on a reading tour of the North of England with Michael Longley. He was excited about his meeting with Basil Bunting who had been thrown out of his home by his wife. Bunting refused to share the quart of whiskey that Montague had brought him, so instead they had to drink the inferior Scottish stuff that Bunting already had in his cupboard. John spent two days in the Lake District and was stunned by the landscape that diminishes even Killarney. He was so moved by that part of England that he began to have visions — or so he says. He had a vision in which a tree spoke to him and advised him to give up alcohol. As if to sustain the veracity of this Mercian vision he was drinking nothing but coffee. I expected the wooden round table of The Long Valley to start speaking at any minute, in the voice of Geoffrey Hill, telling him to take up the drinking again.

May 30th The greatest upset in political things for some time has occurred with the publication of an article in *Magill* magazine about the Arms Trial in 1970. The article shows the weakness of Jack Lynch and how foolishly he allowed the Cabinet to become involved in irresponsible activities — like the importation of arms and collusion with the IRA. Did Fianna Fáil create the Provisional IRA? This will be a key question in the history classrooms of the future, as depressing as the question of whether de Valera single-handedly caused the Civil War.

June 8th Spent a marvellous evening at Mark Bence-Jones' house in Glenville. Before dinner I walked through the huge wild garden with Mark, masses of rhododendrons in full bloom, and one excellent specimen of *Embothrium* in a blaze of red. After dinner his wife Jill read many of her poems, reclining on a seat under what looked like two faded Bogdanis. Many poems on their visit to India and Nepal last spring — the best she has written so far. Later Mark turned to Jill and asked if she remembered having lunch with Seán Ó Ríordáin in a restaurant in Cork years ago. A priest-friend of the Bence-Joneses (Fr Tadhg Ó Murchú, probably), who had written a book on Carrignavar, arranged the lunch with Ó Ríordáin who was then working as Clerical Officer in Cork Corporation. The Bence-Joneses were astonished by Ó Ríordáin's shyness and embarrassment. Whenever Jill or Mark asked him a question he would wait for the priest to translate the question into Irish, then he would reply in Irish and the priest would translate the answer for the Bence-Joneses. The funny thing about all of this was that the priest and Ó Ríordáin carried on their own hilarious conversation in English. Mark felt that Ó Ríordáin used Irish as a filter or a crutch through which he overcame his shyness. I can imagine Jill's overpowering effect on Ó Ríordáin — after all, she's very much the John Wayne of Suffolk poetry while he is the easily bruised Ungaretti of Ireland.

Thursday Rereading an essay on Yeats's Ascendancy poetry in *The Sewanee Review*. That lovely image of Stephen Gwynn gardening during the Civil War: I feel that image belongs to my poetry. I've been gardening right through the Troubles. Ulster Catholics couldn't possibly trust me because of this love of flowers. Roses are Protestant things, they belong to the MacCreadys and the Balmoral Show.

The Brigadier has had a letter from Christie's admitting that they've lost the painting that we shipped to them before Christmas. The matter is very serious. Christie's are usually so reliable. The Brigadier is going to meet the Knight of Glin on Sunday to see what they are going to do about this.

Saturday The Brigadier sat beside the Queen Mother at a formal dinner in London last week. Although she's over eighty her heartiness and her bright remarks throughout dinner amazed him. But what really wins him over is the fact that she's taken to the Irish Guards in a big way. She is officially Colonel of another regiment, but she has begun a tradition of having an equerry, or ADC, from the Irish Guards always at her side. This is a tradition that she's developed completely of her own volition. Under the great string of pearls she had incongruously but affectionately pinned a little gold shamrock that had been a present from the Regiment. When the Brigadier asked her if she'd have a second (large) glass of port she said 'No' at first, but when the carafe was being handed back along the table she stopped the movement and said, 'You know, I'll have another glass, it's such a great party!' Then she turned to the Brigadier and whispered, 'I often wondered why my equerry looked so bleary-eyed the morning after the Regimental Dinner, now I know why!' When it was time to go she stood up and said, 'Colonel, I think I'll take a little snake around the tables.' With that she went off on a tour of all the tables that lasted the best part of an hour. At that stage even the younger officers were too tired to move, yet this lady of eighty years kept going. The Brigadier loves that quality of going-on. Going-on, never giving up, an aristocratic quality.

June 21st My poem, 'A Meeting with Parnell' in *The Irish Times* today.

On Thursday I had lunch with Seán Dunne who explained the saga of John Montague's latest fall. Seemingly John went on a terrible 'batter' while I was on leave last week. He turned on Seán, saying, 'None of you Munster poets will succeed! You're finished before you start! No good publishers!' And then he kept repeating that Heaney would win the Nobel Prize. This has now become a new fixation with him. He really believes that Heaney is going to be awarded the Nobel

Prize. This new absurdity is doing the rounds among the older poets. It tortures John. I don't know where he's picked up this mad idea. Some wag in Dublin teasing him, no doubt.

June 30th Yesterday I went to see my aunt in Dungarvan who is dying of cancer. She is very weak but still manages to smoke a cigarette, one of the very things that have killed her. In a whisper she said to me, 'I have suffered so much but your generation have a wonderful chance to do things, to achieve things.' She pressed her scarred, knarled hand to mine and said, 'We had nothing. It was all such a struggle to exist, just to hold on to life was an effort. You can't understand how we had to suffer.'

Wednesday First full day of the Listowel Writers' Week. Last night I met John B Keane, Bryan MacMahon, who was full of stories about William Boyd and Paul Engle at Iowa, and President Hillery. The President spoke about the loneliness of the writer and the importance of a week like Listowel in which writers emerge from the forest to reassure each other with their presence. Paddy Hillery is a lot smarter than people think.

At breakfast this morning I sat with Mary Leland who has won a short story competition and Brian Fallon who gossiped about John Broderick's and Kate O'Brien's homosexuality (he had also lost his Delacroix journals and was fretting in the way only Brian Fallon can fret). Also met the poet Eavan Boland. Eavan: quiet, like a fish out of water in a place like Listowel, keeping her counsel. She has a lot to say but she certainly wasn't going to waste her words in the company of provincial males. She belongs to Dublin; she has no concept of the countryside, except as a repository of Famine memory and women's victimhood. I never met such an urban person as Eavan Boland; even her privacy and self-possession is a snobbish city thing, no doubt inherited from her distinguished father. And she is so remote from us provincial mortals that she is not even aware of her snobbery. In her snobbery she is definitely her father's daughter.

Later I spent the morning swopping epigrams with Brendan Kennelly who has become infected with Michael Hartnett's epigram disease. Then Captain Feehan of Mercier Press brought me to Glin Castle to meet the Knight of Glin, Desmond FitzGerald.

Thursday Held the first two workshops in my Creative Writing series. In the morning Bryan MacMahon arrived to welcome my class to Listowel. He presented me with a gold *Cross* pen with my name engraved upon it. He spoke about Paul Engle's vision for the University of Iowa writing programme and said that that experience had been the reason why he and John B Keane started a series of workshops at Listowel Writers' Week. That link between Iowa and Listowel should be celebrated.

In the morning I felt quite nervous and unsure of myself. My workshop is so large — about 25 persons of all ages and backgrounds. In the afternoon we workshopped a short story. Very poor, and typical *Irish Press* material: about an old country couple who've inherited a farm. O modern Ireland, where art thou?

Went to John B Keane's pub and was entertained by the *Irish Press* cartoonist, DOLL, who sang Irish songs from West Waterford.

Sunday Home from Writers' Week. I shared a room with Neil Jordan in the Listowel Arms Hotel before setting off on my adventures with a girl who is a marvellous poet. Jordan is a very handsome, yet very private person. Lying on our respective beds, we chatted about women, relationships and writing. He is much wiser than I am on these matters. I told him about my meeting with Robert Duncan, and about Duncan's terrific relationship with Jess Collins. Then Neil described his encounters with Christopher Isherwood in Los

Angeles and Isherwood's superb relationship with his boy-friend. We concluded that the reason homosexual relation-ships endure is because of the special bond that develops between partners who are united not just by their affections but by their sense of belonging to a community of threatened outsiders. I then recommended Bachelard to Neil, as he was already reading Barthes and Proust. If he reads Bachelard after having absorbed Barthes and Proust his mind will be ruined. He won't be able to move on, either emotionally or aesthetically. He will be like Proust, stuck to his bed. This is a real danger. But his interest in films might very well save his fiction. So many literary people, both young and old, have invested all their hopes in Jordan's anticipated spectacular future. My guess is that this weighs heavily on him. He may yet have to leave the country to escape from this burden, though working in film is really a way of mentally leaving Ireland. The discipline of 35mm film controls the more garrulous, mawkish aspects of Irish discourse in a way that mere writing never could. Jordan has that advantage over all of us.

Ciaran Carty of the *Sunday Independent*, a generous, gentle, intelligent man, asked me for my Post-Impressionist poem for the *Indo*. Michael Longley bought me a drink. An extremely civilized man, an Ulsterman to the core with a fierce pride in Ulster's loyalty to its own self.

July 8th Saw a lovely painting by Camille Souter that I would love to have as the cover of *The Sorrow Garden*. Called, I think, 'My Father's Vegetable Patch'. It was part of the *Sense of Ireland* exhibit in Cork. While I was in Listowel my aunt died.

July 14th I suppose I am full of death. Looking through the liturgy for some appropriate quote in my prayer at Bríd and Pat's wedding. I found this gem for *The Sorrow Garden*:

> *Isaac loved Rebekah, and so he was consoled for the*
> *loss of his mother.*
> — *Gen 24: 48-51*

July 21st An unbelievably busy week in which I attended Pat Crotty and Bríd Galvin's wedding, made a new friendship, reviewed Norman MacCaig, Jon Silkin and Jean Valentine for *The Irish Times*, and received an interesting and hopeful letter from Morgan Smith in America. I feel my life has been speeded up to such a pace that my poetry is completely overrun. The Crotty-Galvin wedding was a huge affair, a great country-style wedding with over 250 guests and vast numbers of priests. Pat was married by a splendid priest, Pat Hannon, who is a lecturer in Fundamental Moral Theology at Maynooth. I read one of the prayers and inserted a little piece from MacDiarmid's 'Island Funeral'.

Late on Tuesday night, after the wedding, we returned to Theo Dorgan's flat off Military Road for a chat and tea. I don't think there was any drink on the premises, though Seán Dunne may have brought supplies. Seán, who was very drunk, attacked Pat Hannon, the theologian, and challenged him to 'throw off his clerical collar' and 'be a *fokine* man'. The drink had made him very aggressive. I resolved there and then never to drink alcohol except at mealtimes as we Celts are incapable of being civilized while holding alcohol. But I soon forgot about this theological fracas because I became involved in a curious courtship with an artist-photographer called Catherine Coakley, a sister of Pat Crotty's St Colman's College friends, the Coakley brothers. She is one of the new generation of artists and photographers just out of the Crawford Art College. She has work in an exhibition in the Triskel Arts Cenre. This conversation with Ms Coakley went on right through the night. An absolutely bizarre encounter. Afterwards I just wouldn't let Catherine out of my sight. Something blazed as she spoke. She is like a female William Blake, very strange, with strange depths and hesitations, but fabulous beyond belief.

Thursday. Last night I met Catherine Coakley again. We talked a little but she remains a complete mystery. I saw her beautiful photographs; exquisite pieces in black and white, all of the human form made to look like stone, and of stones made to look like human torsos. As an artist she knows exactly what she's doing, but a lot of mischievous humour; a soul very hidden or hooded by impeccable technique. She has made incredible efforts to hide her own hidden splendour, but I could see through her camouflage to that hooded energy beneath.

The fact is that these last few years in my life have been full of death, death everywhere. I am obsessed with death. I have buried both my parents and five aunts and uncles so that the wet earth of St Declan's Cemetery, Cappoquin, is in my blood. When Catherine's talking to me she probably knows that she's talking to someone full of death. She can see the death inside me, but it may be the death in me that draws her in. Things damaged have a fatal attraction for her. In my own life these years have been so troubled and turbulent that she may be just one more passing turbulence. She may evaporate as quickly as she materialized, leaving me with trustworthy Death for a companion. She is a kind of Emily Dickinson, intense and intelligent.

Mary Leland came into the library today and we had a long chat about Márquez and shrub roses. She has ordered yet more shrub roses from Mr White in Maylor Street. Mr White is really the last of the great plantsmen who once dominated the retail trade in Patrick Street. He knows absolutely everything about plants.

Great preparations at Glenshelane for tomorrow's picnic for the Robert Lees from Washington, DC. Lee had been a member of Kennedy's press staff. Several rich Americans, supporters of the Republican Party, have refused to come to the picnic and this has delighted the Brigadier. Like Molly Keane he loves feuding rich people, especially feuding Americans. He chuckled like a boy as he told me the names of the Americans who'd refused to come to Glenshelane, including the Cornells of Headborough House and the Paynes of Tipperary who have bought 'Eddy' Sackville-West's house.

Wednesday Picnic at Glenshelane today for the Lees. Everybody good-humoured despite the indifferent weather and shortage of wine. The Lees gave me a gift of President Johnson's speeches, which had been a gift to them, with a letter from James Jones at the White House attached. After the picnic I read letters from Iowa, letters from the two Ulster women who were in my workshop and Bachelard's essay on 'roundness' as well as a small essay by Borges in which he says, 'It is doubtful that the world has a meaning; it is even more doubtful that it has a double or a triple meaning.' I like the firmness of that statement. We must remain doubtful, simple and doubtful.

After the Lees and the Mitchells had gone away I went up to my bedroom and worked on a new poem 'The Phenomenology of Stones'. Catherine Coakley is at the heart of it, and her photographs, and the things that define her: the sea, stone, coloured bottles, the immensities of tides and waves and bird-chatter in the surf. These are the defining things, the parameters of her mental being. Not that they limit her, they actually make her limitless. Her mind has the luminous quality of a conch shell, or certainly something thrown up onto the sand by the sea's turbulence. Her conversations are never far from the sea. This poem is a sign from God. She's the one. The stars above my head are pointing at her. The evening sunlight blazed through the bedroom window and flooded the room with light. There was such force in this poem, such a dense centre of gravity, that my notebook seemed to eat up all the light there was.

Theo and I are planning a broadsheet to honour the publication of Patrick Galvin's *Selected Poems*. We'll call it *The Patrick Galvin Broadsheet*. As usual Theo is doing most of the work while I am trying to source the money. Michael

Hartnett has promised me a poem about Derek Mahon's overcoat and £35 for the Galvin publication.

August 3rd Received a letter from the Arts Council confirming my suspicions that I failed to get a Council bursary to work on *The Solitude of the Party*. The five stories that I sent to them were in such a bad state I am not surprised that I failed.

August 6th The Arts Council Awards are announced: Paul Durcan got £5,000, which pleases me. Also, John Banville and Desmond Hogan are going to Iowa. This will make Iowa terrific for me in November. I will be able to discuss stories with Des Hogan and have a real conversation with Banville who is without doubt a genius.

Bought a car for £800. I borrowed the money from the Brigadier. Got a letter from Catherine. So she's thinking of me.

September 4th This evening Pat Crotty, who's still doing an MA on Hugh MacDiarmid, and I went to see Claud Cockburn at Ardmore. Claud was delighted to see us, welcomed us with outstretched arms, bottles of beer and glasses of gin. He was very healthy, very sprightly, for a man who has had cancer, a stroke and double pneumonia within the last two years. He was of little use to Pat because Pat's research deals with the early '30s rather than the early '40s when Claud encountered MacDiarmid.

Claud has a new book of reminiscences coming out with Quartet, and he's also hoping to do a book with Ticknor and Fields. We talked about the demise of *Hibernia*. The new Sunday journal that will replace it is only an 'upmarket' news-sheet. It is expected that there will only be a small literary section. Claud was also contrasting the prices paid for reviews in Dublin and London. I said, 'Yes, Ireland is really only a province of the London publishing world.' Claud immediately corrected my statement, and restored me to a correct perception when he said, 'No, Thomas, you must not say that Irish Letters is a province of London Letters just because one cannot earn a decent living writing for Irish papers. Whether it is a province or not does not depend on its financial resources, but on its ability to have a focus within itself.'

Monday 13th Wrote a letter to Paul Engle. Spent the morning in idleness. Reading a memoir of Gide by George Painter, with lots of good photographs. Mary O'Sullivan, who's now got a job in a London casino, sent me the David Hockney catalogue from London. Drawings very poor, but waifishly beautiful.

October 16th Last night Catherine and I went to dinner at the Montagues. Driving from the Montagues at midnight I was stopped by the Gardaí who are still searching for the murderers of a detective in Wexford. The thought of a murdered detective in Wexford really depressed me all day. The Provos are dogs. They will destroy Ireland. How does Ireland breed such beasts? They shame us before the world. The policemen on Wellington Road looked fed up, depressed. I don't blame them. They must be sick of being policemen in such a dysfunctional country.

I bought two copies of the paperback of Stratis Haviaras's *When the Tree Sings*; one copy for Dimitri Nollas in Athens. Amazing, beautiful narrative, a poet's novel.

October 23rd Eiléan Ní Chuilleanáin gave a reading at UCC. She asked me for some poems for *Cyphers*.

Sunday Throughout the weekend I've found myself humming old jazz tunes. I think of the Ella Fitzgerald concert in the Opera House. It was an extraordinary experience.

October 29th Breakfast this morning with the American

Ambassador at the Arbutus Lodge. He has put on weight since I last saw him, but still terrifically friendly and relaxed. We breakfasted for an hour, discussed Charles Haughey. He felt that I had too high an opinion of Haughey and added that Haughey is surrounded by men in his Party who'd 'love to cut his throat'. He wanted to know my feelings about the H-Block issue. I said that now that seven men have gone on hunger strike for their rights the situation has changed. A hunger strike has huge emotional repercussions in Irish politics, particularly if it is a hunger strike against British prison services.

November 7th Back in Iowa City for the last few days — back at the International Writing Program. John Banville is also here. Wonderful to talk with him, though he answers questions, even questions asked in private conversation, with the pithy reluctance of a Detective Inspector. This is a trait of Wexford people. Anthony Cronin is the same. Had dinner last night with Bian Zhilin (Pien Chih-lin) and Ai Qing, two very old Chinese poets. Bian talked endlessly about Irish writing, about Yeats, Joyce, Lady Gregory and Synge. He translated Joyce's story 'Eveline' into Chinese in the early '30s when he himself was only twenty-three. Bian spent a year in London in the late '40s as a guest of the British Council. He remembered the shortages and food coupons, but particularly the search for cigarettes in those years after the Second World War. In China Bian is known as 'the poet of Peking' because he has made the streets and atmospheres of that city into his own personal myth. He had a wonderful story about one word in Joyce's *Dubliners*. He translated 'chisellers' as 'workers in wood', so that the mothers were calling home their workers in wood in the story 'Eveline'. It was years before he discovered that the word 'chiseller' had nothing to do with carpentry, but was a Dublin slang word for 'child'.

Ai Qing spoke through an interpreter. Hualing Nieh introduced us and we embraced. Hualing was very pleased and proud that I embraced Ai Qing. Ai Qing looked quite different from Bian because Bian dresses in a European style, in a navy-blue business suit, while Ai Qing is still dressed in the simple grey Maoist uniform of the revolutionary period. Ai Qing looked serene, but tired, eyes darting from side to side, trying to take in all the trappings of the American scene. He played continuously with a gold cigarette lighter that had obviously been given to him as a gift. Once, after the evening had begun to drag on and Bian began to nod off to sleep, Ai Qing started to flick the cigarette lighter on and off in front of Bian's dozing face to startle him awake. Both Bian and Ai Qing smoked incessantly, more out of curiosity with American cigarettes and lighters than for the physical pleasure. Meeting Ai Qing was like spending time with Tagore or Yeats. I am supposed to travel with him as far as Chicago.

November 30th Only one more day left in Iowa City. I've wasted this last week, eating, sleeping and dreaming. Now — as in 1978 — I am struck by the weight of national heritage and baggage that presses down on writers. Each of us carries our history on our backs, and we discuss the problems of the national past as if we had the power to change regimes or to undo a pogrom.

Sunday One of the most pleasant interludes at Iowa has been meetings with Jane Cooper. She invited me to dinner last week, along with Peter Jay, the poet and publisher, and a Writing Fellow called Chalmers. It was a very simple meal, over-cooked meat and spinach pie, but good wine. Jane was really interested in Seamus Heaney. A group of writing professors from Iowa are going to Notre Dame to hear Heaney in the spring. Marvin Bell says Iowa couldn't afford his fees. (I find this hard to believe: what it really means is that Iowa is confident enough to refuse to pay the exorbitant fees of a New York lecture agency.) Jane also wanted to know about de Valera because her father, an aviation lawyer, had flown around Ireland with Lindbergh in the '30s, and had met Dev. Lindbergh and Cooper were trying to establish the best location for the trans-Atlantic flights stopover. When they met Dev in his office Mr Cooper discovered that he had a book of poems on his desk by a favourite 19th-century American poet (Whitman, I'm sure). This particular book had been the favourite volume of Jane Cooper's mother — Jane's father mentioned this to Dev and he replied, 'Ah, yes, I've carried that book with me throughout the wars.'

Jane was very worried because Grace Paley and students from Sarah Lawrence College had gone to the Pentagon as part of a protest. Paley had trespassed on Federal property so that she was now in danger of being charged with a felony. Frantic phone calls between Jane and the president of Sarah Lawrence. Jane's collection *Maps & Windows* contains an astonishing essay on being a woman writer, on being excluded from important public events; on being forcibly 'domesticated'. It reminds me of Máire Mhac an tSaoi's fabulous, tiny poem 'Cré na Mná Tí' — the same sentiments and perceptions. Jane's essay is called 'Nothing Has Been Used in the Manufacture of This Poetry That Could Have Been Used in the Manufacture of Bread'. I've already photocopied it and sent it back to Ireland. It contains urgent insights about women as poets, really crucial, empowering insights that could stiffen the resolve of women poets in Cork. The important thing is to get this text to them before their confidence is destroyed by the provincial masculinities, the pathetic masculinities, of influential poets operating locally. This essay and Levertov's *The Poet in the World* could be massively empowering texts for women in my workshops, especially at Listowel.

December 13th Back in Ireland. When I unpacked my suitcases I discovered that three quarters of my luggage was books! Work by Barthes, the Murphy biography of JBY, Seferis, Ritsos, dozens of books that I'll carry around for months and years, maybe until they've lost their sun-drenched American smell.

December 14th While I waited at the International Arrivals lounge at Shannon I met Thomas Kinsella, our best poet. He was as surprised as I was by the encounter, and equally amazed to find a poetry enthusiast at Shannon at 8 a.m. He didn't know who I was, even after I had told him that Dolmen Press published my first book. 'Oh, yes, yes,' he said apologetically, 'Of course. You published a novel, or was it a book of short stories?' He thought I was Neil Jordan or Des Hogan. He was incredibly tired and couldn't even recall the *Sense of Ireland* festival in London last February. He hadn't heard of Jane Cooper or Marvin Bell which makes me feel that his mind never leaves Ireland although he spends six months of every year in Philadelphia at Temple University. When I said that I knew John Montague he said, 'Ah, John and I cut our teeth on each other in the early '60s.' He discussed the difficulty of publishing in Ireland; and the souring of his relationship with Alfred Knopf. We lamented the need to work in order to earn a living and he discussed his time as an Administrative Officer in the Civil Service. A very pleasant encounter; the first interesting person I've ever met at an airport.

December 30th Brigadier home today from the South of France. He was in a very jolly mood when I met him at Cork Airport. His face seemed tanned and his gait firm. It's really important that he gets a few weeks of strong sunshine every year. The indifferent sun of Ireland isn't enough. Later I discovered why he was so cheerful. Christie's had just auctioned the painting from the master bedroom for an enormous sum. The painting had been bought from a street trader in Dublin in the 1960s as a canvas rolled up and tied with binder twine. The painting is a lost Guercino (Giovanni Francesco Barbieri), titled 'Amnon and Tamar', a work commissioned by Aurelia Zanoletti of Reggio, but sold by the artist to Girolamo Bavosi on 28th January, 1650. The Knight of Glin at Christie's had discovered not only the date of the painting but the date of its commissioning. Bavosi sent the picture to Venice where it was subsequently sold by the French art agent, Pierre Berton, to William Fauquier in 1742. The Brigadier wouldn't tell me how much it got at auction but we chatted about what he should do with this windfall which he absolutely does not need. He says he'll try to buy another Bogdani. In 1981 he will keep a vigil over the Christie's, Bonhams and Spink catalogues that come through the door from London. I should have really asked him for a loan to buy an even better car, but to have asked for money for myself just then would have spoiled the moment.

1981

January 7th Letter from Ambassador Shannon. He'll be staying on for a few months, even after Reagan comes into office. He wants me to come to Dublin to stay at the Ambassador's residence for a few days.

January 8th-9th Sore throat has turned into flu. All last night I sweated with fever. How horrible it must be to be chronically ill, to be an invalid. Sickness takes one back to the world of the body. I could read Sylvia Plath or Anne Sexton right now. They are all body.

Winter sunlight shining into my room: always when I'm ill I get winter sunlight, that strong white sheen on the glass unlike the yellowness of summer. Light like ice. I want to read Gide's or Stendhal's diaries, but I must get some sleep. Both authors are lying at my bedside. I'm like a child who has to have his favourite toy soldiers or train set in full view before going to sleep.

January 10th Seán Ó Tuama said to me that Heaney is now leaving Ireland to teach at Harvard for four years. Heaney is forty-one or forty-two years old, time to spread his wings, to test himself against huge competition in the biggest poetry amphitheatre on earth, the American campus. It's sad but perhaps inevitable that Ireland would lose Heaney to American academe, and it's also inevitable that Heaney should choose to go West where fame and wealth await him. As Anthony Cronin said, Nothing succeeds at home like the rumour of success abroad. Heaney's fame in Ireland will only be increased by our hearing of his victories in Harvard, New York and Notre Dame. He was born for this, this great fame that's already brewing around his work. He is becoming more Greek as the days go by, I think, more like Seferis in his mixture of social distinction and national purpose. He carries himself already like the patient plenipotentiary of some as yet undeclared Republic, like the Seferis of 'Last Stop' — 'And if I talk to you in fables and parables / it's because it's more gentle for you that way; and horror / really can't be talked about because it's alive, / because it's mute and goes on growing . . . ' Yes, Heaney is definitely our Seferis.

Sunday Catherine phoned. She is going to the Michael Hartnett/ Eiléan Ní Chuilleanáin reading in Mallow. I'd hoped that she would come to visit me.

January 19th We stayed in bed until 11 a.m. We bought wellies. Catherine has a funny blue pair. She spent all the afternoon jumping into puddles (with a great sense of purpose). Catherine and Una and Seán Dunne and Maurice Riordan went to Limerick to give a reading. Eamon O'Donoghue has borrowed £5 from me, Seán Dunne has borrowed £2. In the last two weeks I've frittered away the £80 I was carrying around to put into the bank.

Claud Cockburn had a mild stroke. It has affected his eyes, but Patricia says that he is in great spirits. His life is a victory over the body. I hope he doesn't die before May Day when I intend to organize a committee of trade unionists and poets to visit him.

Molly Keane's new book should be out soon from André Deutsch. They seem very excited about it. I hope it's a triumph: after twenty-five years of silence. The Brigadier says that it's better than any book Molly has ever written, better than *The Rising Tide* or *Two Days in Aragon*. Everyone's so excited for her, excited and terrified. If this book isn't well received it'll be a crushing blow for her. It will kill her, I'm sure of it. I can't imagine a writer being silent for twenty-five years, except in death. John Banville's new book on Kepler has been getting fantastic reviews in the English papers, as well as in the new *Sunday Tribune*.

February 11th Spent the whole evening working on *The Sorrow Garden*. All of this work done in response to two letters from Anvil Press. I had hoped to work on a story. Beginning to get worried about *The Solitude of the Party* until I found this statement in Camus: 'It is in order to shine sooner that authors refuse to re-write. Despicable. Begin again.' Camus was twenty-six when he wrote this.

Rev Ian Paisley was suspended from the House of Commons. He called the Northern Ireland Secretary a liar. In the Dáil Mr Haughey suggested that Ireland was shifting from its position of pure neutrality. Great worries now that Ireland may drift into a Western Power Bloc position.

February 19th John Jordan was in Cork for a lecture on Patrick Kavanagh. As usual he didn't want to return to Dublin afterwards and spent two days in Moore's Hotel. His lecture was superb, much better than in 1976. He himself looked twenty years younger. I met him again on Wednesday at noon in The Long Valley; he had already been drinking in Moore's Hotel and Canty's. Even Seán Dunne was astonished by his capacity for drink. I sat with him for two hours but had to return to the library at around 3 p.m. When I took leave of Seán and Jordan they had managed to get as far as Crowley's pub on Bridge Street, beside the Triskel Arts Centre, where Tina Nealon, the editor of *The Cork Review*, had arranged to meet them. Jordan was full of scandalous stories about most writers. He affected an interest in all homosexual affairs all the time and he began to rub my forehead and my arm. All of which made Seán Dunne squirm in terror. But he was just being playful, I thought, and what harm could come of it. I was ecstatic about the Heaney poem, 'The Names of the Hare'. Jordan seemed very worried about Katherine Kavanagh also, who, he confided in me most pointedly, may have had a hysterectomy. She has been ill for some time, stricken down and worn out, Jordan said, 'by the insane jealousy of her brother-in-law'. John was delighted when I produced copies of the old *Poetry Ireland* series. He read out the lines from Kavanagh:

> *Nae gane, nae gane, nae fram us tarn*
> *But taking a rest like John Jordan.*

That was in Number One, and he said that he had gained immortality by being mentioned by Kavanagh in a poem. 'Even as a living young man I was made immortal.' Then I showed him the issue with Heaney's 'Valediction', 'End of a Naturalist' and he said forcibly, 'I was the first to give him the international audience.' Indeed. Success has many fathers. Why shouldn't John Jordan feel that he was one of Heaney's fathers?

Seán came into the library tonight looking exhausted and shattered. 'He left at eight o'clock last night. Or I left him. He's not in here, is he?' Seán was afraid that he mightn't have taken the Dublin train. 'Even Montague couldn't keep up with that guy's drinking,' said Seán in desperation.

Friday John Jordan is still in Cork. When I arrived at the Triskel Arts Centre today I asked (jokingly) if John Jordan was still around — the reply was a resounding, 'Yes!' I met Seán this evening and he had stuck his head nervously into The Long Valley just in case Jordan was there.

Found these statements in Camus' *Diaries*, both mean the same thing: 'One must encounter love before having encountered ethics' and 'I chose creation to escape crime.'

February 28th A very pleasant evening when I met John Montague in The Long Valley. He seemed so crestfallen with news of the Heaney tour of America (its success, etc) that I offered to walk home with him.

March 6th Charles Haughey has announced an extraordinary scheme for writers and artists whereby artists would have a guaranteed income of £4,000 per annum. It's like the ancient Gaelic tribal scheme of supporting poets. It's unlikely that I'll qualify. But many poets down to the age level of Paul Durcan might qualify. Fair play to Haughey. I never trusted him politically as I came from the Jack Lynch/George Colley wing of the Party, but there's no doubt he can think thoughts at the highest level. He has caused a sensation in arts circles but all the writers in Cork are playing it ultra cool. Evelyn Montague was in a high state of excitement when she rang me about the scheme. She insisted that I would benefit while I protested vigorously that I am too young to qualify. But I loved her for insisting that I'd qualify for this scheme: it's just that she wants me to qualify. She is French and is determined that things shall be as she insists they are. Derek Mahon and Peter Fallon read at Triskel Arts Centre. Mahon was terrific. The mantle of Louis MacNeice has slipped quite unobtrusively but indisputedly onto his shoulders. He referred to the new Artists' Scheme as 'The Haughey Dole'.

Sunday Large luncheon at Glenshelane. Molly Keane was there looking very contented and healthy despite her seventy-five years. André Deutsch are publishing her new novel in September. It's called *Good Behaviour*. It's about the Anglo-Irish, but with a rare angle in that it views the Anglo-Irish from the inside with an intense sense of the claustrophobia of that world. Knowing Molly in recent years there will be a fair amount of satire and sharpness in this book. She said to me the other day that as she grew older she had fewer and fewer delusions about people. She said this bitterly. She hates Sir Richard, she feared W E D Allen and she is always on the point of having a fight with the intellectual Cockburns. (She calls the Cockburn household 'Communist' but what she means is 'Intellectual'. For her, these are interchangeable words.) She really doesn't like most people. Her Anglo-Irish neighbours either bore or frighten her. The residents of a number of Big Houses around Cappoquin are bracing themselves for the arrival of this new book. The Brigadier said that there will be 'holy murder' because of the number of persons who are libelled. The connections of the Godfrey sisters in Lismore are already in correspondence with their solicitors in Dungarvan (the Godfrey sisters appear as 'the Crowhurst twins' in the novel).

Mr Madden from Ulster was also here (is this the Captain Madden who rammed a Tiger tank of the Waffen-SS with his little Irish Guards tank during the Battle of the Falaise Pocket?). He went to the school in Wales where Evelyn Waugh taught English. He had Waugh for Second Form English. Each time he submitted an essay it would be returned with lots of horned devils with tails drawn around the essay title. Waugh spent a good deal of time discussing the merits of motorbikes and often rose at 5 a.m. to give his own machine a speed test on a length of straight road.

St.Patrick's Day Read four poems on the radio, 'A Neutral State', 'A Meeting with Parnell', 'Her Blindness' and 'The Poet of the Mountains'.

April 1st Here in Skibbereen on a Poetry Ireland tour with John Liddy. John is a very pleasant fellow. He has written a poem on Emmet Dalton. Last night we stayed with Alexander Sokolov and his girlfriend. Alex has some beautiful new pieces. I commissioned a bas-relief of James Joyce for the Joyce Centenary; hopefully to have it displayed in the City Library. Castlehaven has magnificent wild gardens, so wild and yet intimate.

April 2nd In Kenmare where we gave a reading to a literary group organized by a retired schoolmaster and a Church of Ireland canon.

April 4th I keep thinking of John Liddy's story about the old Gaelic poets: how when all inspiration failed they lay down in their cells with a stone on their stomachs. They believed that the 'idea' or the poem would concentrate upon the stone and would enter their bodies through the stone.

Wednesday Peter Jay rang yesterday to say that Raven Arts Books wanted 1,000 copies of *The Sorrow Garden* for Irish distribution. Reading Alexander Sokolov's manuscript 'Stoned'. He told me that he wrote it in response to Seamus Murphy's *Stone Mad* because Murphy 'gives nothing away'. Sokolov uses the word 'auto chthonic' to describe his aesthetic — chthonic meaning earthy and dark spirited, as opposed to 'celestial visions'. He tries to get back to the primary subconscious forces, to that first moment when a stone sheds a tear. He tries to sculpt as if man had just walked out of stone.

May 2nd Bobby Sands is in a coma. His hunger strike has opened up many of the emotional aspects of our dealings with England. I feel that one should be able to write as powerfully as Bobby Sands dies. How can a poet lay down his life for a poem? Once again the IRA scuppers literature with their ability to make a deeper sacrifice. The fact is that Bobby Sands doesn't represent me. Out of Ulster, Seamus Heaney and Michael Longley, the givers of life, represent me.

May 8th Proofs of *The Sorrow Garden* arrived. Very well produced, the usual mistakes.

May 14th This morning Catherine and I motored to the Inniscarra Dam and waterworks. On the way back we stopped at the cottage of the dead poet, Seán Ó Ríordáin — a desolate and inexcusably neglected site. If he had been a French writer the state would have stepped in by now to preserve his home; but because he wrote in Irish he is forgotten.

Friday Called on Theo this morning. He is very much involved with the H-Block protests. He wanted to discuss the proofs of *The Sorrow Garden*. I left his flat after only a few minutes because I had to return to the Mobile Library. Like Claud Cockburn or Hugh MacDiarmid Theo doesn't believe that writing can be above politics; he believes that to write is a fundamentally political act. I don't disagree with him, but I think that politics comes *after* the fact of writing: it is politics that accommodates itself to the life of imagination, not the other way round. I am always the weary and disillusioned Essenin while Theo is always the energetic Neruda. He makes me think of Goethe's words: 'Youth is drunkenness without wine.' The other day Evelyn Montague said, 'Oh, Theo, he is a thoughtful girl's honey trap.' Evelyn is so perceptive, so insightful, about people — especially writers and the sex lives of writers. There is certainly something of Weimar in Theo, something of Goethe's quality. Like the young Goethe he is forever midnight-riding through the woods of Sessenheim to meet his Friederike Brion. As my clairvoyant mother once said of Theo, there's an awful lot written in his tea leaves.

Sunday The Brigadier is worried about the IRA's latest campaign of burning down the houses of the aristocracy. He thinks they may burn down Glenshelane House if more hunger strikers die. It's the first time that I have seen him afraid — perhaps because he is growing old. He is not as irresponsible as Lady Gregory because now all the shutters in the drawing room, sitting room and kitchen at Glenshelane are closed at night. Closing them before he listens to Radio Four News at 10 p.m. has become a new ritual; he sits shuttered inside this Home Service world while Helvick Republican killers and kidnappers prowl the West Waterford hills around his house. He now keeps his double-barrelled *Purdy* shotgun by his bedside, and a box of cartridges. He is determind that if an IRA unit bursts into his bedroom he will kill two of them before they get him. From these two IRA corpses, he says, the Irish Special Branch will be able to determine which IRA unit targeted him. Even in death he would want to be of use to the authorities, North and South.

Wednesday Met Theo who is very upset about the death of another IRA hunger striker. He was wearing a black tie. I held my tongue. I was far more upset about the prospect of the IRA burning down Glenshelane House and killing an elderly man, the direct descendant of Lord Edward FitzGerald who had fought Fascism in Europe for five long years so that all Irish nationalists, including the Provos of Dungarvan and Old Parish, could sleep easy in their beds.

Thursday At the American Embassy; a reception to say goodbye to the Shannons. I met Ben Kiely who took me under his wing for the whole evening. I couldn't shake him off. He talked about having two new novels at the '60,000 word stage' but finding it impossible to go on. While under Ben Kiely's wing I met Val Mulkerns, F X Martin (the brilliant historian), Donal McCartney and Kevin B Nowlan. I gave Bill Shannon a bottle of poteen to take home to America. It was in a bottle marked 'Lourdes Water'. A man from Macroom, a faithful library borrower, had given it to me last week. Now the American Ambassador will have to buy a greyhound so that he can dope it with poteen.

Last night Richard Murphy read in Cork. A large crowd. He read new poems about money and Dublin. He explained his move to Dublin (from the solitude of the West) by saying that he could no longer live in the past (the past of his ascendancy ancestors, and the past of his previous achievements and relationships, such as the relationship with Tony White). In order to escape from the past he moved to a place that would challenge his personality, a place that he loathes and fears: Dublin.

Saturday Another large luncheon party at Glenshelane. Andrea Jameson, whose painting we use on the cover of *The Sorrow Garden,* was there. I embarrassed her by hugging her too wildly in the hall. A young writer from England, Simon Blow, told interesting stories. He freelances for the *Guardian* and *The Telegraph* — an unusual combination. He has been commissioned to write a history of the Tennant family, and he has a novel up his sleeve, both destined for The Bodley Head. What was most interesting about him was that his first assignment was to interview Henry Green (whose books I'd just bought for Catherine). Henry Green had become a recluse, living in the back room of his house in Knightsbridge, studying the backs of his long elegant fingers. Green first tried to dictate the interview, saying things about himself in the third person i.e. 'Mr Green gave up writing twenty years ago, a decision which — judged by the excellence of his work — I feel to be most regrettable.' Simon said that Green was so buoyed by his English success in the late '40s that he went to New York personally to negotiate an American deal, accompanied by his solicitor. The delusions of writers are always pitiful and, no doubt, I also suffer from these delusions.

Thursday Poetry reading with Patrick Galvin at the Café Lorca. Galvin's stuff very well made, full of the excellent technical devices of a good dramatist. His words seem inevitable, immortal. Seán Lucy was there, and Anthony Blinco — Blinco, now a small businessman, looked totally out of place with his light grey suit and umbrella. He looked like a businessman who had strayed into a corrupt poker school and longed to get out before he was recognized by his best customers. Seán Lucy has taken to wearing a cravat, the result of his year in Chicago, no doubt. But he's such a gentle person, and so learned. He astonishes me with his learning, and his prodigious actor's memory. Anthony Blinco has bought a mobile home by the sea at Fountainstown. He told me that he intends to divide his writing year between the family business in Patrick Street and this mobile home: he paints a picture of an idyllic provincial life. It is like the life of Roger Martin du Gard that André Gide so envied.

June 11th Polling Day. A spectacular summer's day. I spoke on the radio yesterday about Frank O'Connor with Seán Lucy and Nancy McCarthy. Nancy still full of life and full of love for Michael/Frank. She spoke about the time O'Connor had a fight with Yeats because WBY wouldn't accept that the word 'beggar' existed in Irish in a poetic context. WBY made O'Connor change 'beggar' to 'stranger' in his Valentin Brown translation. Said O'Connor to Nancy, 'That fella would ruin all my translations if I let him.'

June 15th Spent the weekend at Glenshelane. Everything overgrown and weedy. Impossible to work the vegetable patch because of incessant rain. In the last six weeks we've had at least four-and-a-half inches of rain. Little time for poetry. I keep thinking of the poem on Ó Ríordáin.

June 21st Beautiful summer's day at Glenshelane, the sun splitting the stones, everything erect and cheerful in the heat. I tried to do some weeding but was driven away from the vegetable patch by the intense heat of the sun.

Met Gerald Dawe yesterday in The Long Valley. He was taken aback when he discovered that Catherine, a member of his workshop, was my girlfriend. He wants me to give a reading in Belfast in the Spring.

Earlier we had met Gregory O'Donoghue and his poet father, Robert, with John O'Donoghue. Montague was 'eyeing' us very cagily — as if he expected his two young poets, his pupils, to throw punches at him.

September 12th Last night BBC Radio 4 announced that Molly Keane's book has been shortlisted for the Booker Prize. The turnaround in her career has convinced me that anything of real value, like *Good Behavior*, will be justly treated in the end. A writer or poet identifies all the usual enemies — bad publishers, poor distributors, demanding friends, personal exhaustion — in an effort to explain the neglect of work, only to discover that the main enemy is within oneself, a tendency merely to vegetate. Success changes one's image of a writer. I always thought of Molly Keane as an old lady, terribly bothered and slightly tipsy, asking me if her chihuahua, 'Hero', could sleep with her in her bedroom at Glenshelane. I always thought of her battered old Morris Minor, later an old Renault 4, setting off in the rain to go back to the loneliness of Ardmore. Then, when I learned that first Collins in London and then Mercier Press in Cork had turned down early drafts of her new novel, I felt that she was finished, a spent force. But, now, how her image has brightened! Every day she's in the newspapers, blazing with a new authority. Her life has been renewed in old age but she has also been renewed in my mind's eye, even in memory. And, among the resident Ascendancy families in the Blackwater Valley, she has been reborn: even they are quickly scrambling to revise their memories of her. Yet her strength as a novelist comes from her own capacity to retain the frail image, the image of decayed women and impoverished old men. Being true to the catalogue of her own depressions and frailties she has transformed herself into a major talent.

September 16th Read a few pages of the new book on Ted Hughes. A troubled and complex man, not violent but enduring through violence in the order of things. For an Irish poet, like Heaney or Montague, all violence is political, but an English poet has no such luxury. An English poet has to understand violence as part of a personal realm. This is the true angst of English poetry, brought to life dramatically in the new work of Hughes and Thom Gunn. Hughes and Gunn in their inimitable English way remind us to stand on our own two feet, not to be constantly relying on forms of political rescue. For the mature English writer there is absolutely no solace in politics. We Irish, on the other hand, console ourselves with constant, familiar politics. The desolate personal isolation of the average, educated English writer is simply unimaginable from an Irish point of view.

September 26th-October 5th A great week. *The Sorrow Garden*, beautifully produced, was published at a huge party in Triskel Arts Centre. Over 100 people came along. 80 copies sold. Peter Jay came over from London with his former girlfriend, Alison, who has edited Spender's essays for Fontana. Jay was amazed that we sold so many books. He said that when one holds a reception in London everybody expects to get free copies. The Brigadier came along and seemed very proud, while Catherine blossomed in the swim of people. She is such a strong, benign presence in my life. Molly Keane's daughter, Sally, also came along, as well as all the lovely Burtons from Lismore Castle. Montague arrived from Dublin, too late to launch my book. He is hopeless, just hopeless. But he was so apologetic and sheepish that it was impossible to be angry with him. Drink, Dublin and missed early trains: the story of his life. The story of most poets' lives, if the truth be told. Despite everything I'm fond of Montague.

October 25th In Dublin with Catherine for her Hennessy Fiction Award. It was great to watch her having to sit for publicity pictures. She is such a reluctant public figure. Terence de Vere White was there. No Heinrich Böll, though; Heinrich Böll who said that Catherine 'could really turn a yarn' (a phrase that Seán Dunne keeps repeating to Catherine when they meet on the stairs at Sidney Place). Terence de Vere White was full of jokes and good will. He apologized for not meeting me in London last year but explained that he was depressed at having been left out of the whole *Sense of Ireland* festival. Dublin looked dreary and run-down, just as Peter Jay said in his letter.

November 4th Having spent the weekend with the Brigadier and having looked again at Yeats's *Memoirs* I can understand how the literary impulse can be traced back to the need for a pure, non-critiqued memory. This was what Aidan Higgins meant in his RTÉ interview when he denied being a writer of fiction and said, 'I'm only a memorizer.'

Seán Dunne's review of *The Sorrow Garden* was published in *The Examiner* on Tuesday. No photograph. A good cautious review, a brave review in fact. No amount of negative commentary can upset me when I have Heaney's comments ringing in my brain as a mighty buffer. Heaney and Vozneshensky are reading in Dublin tonight. They have been reading together across America, for prodigious sums of money, Theo says. Heaney may as well make hay while the sun shines on him.

November 19th Each day when I come home to our flat from work I hear Seán pounding away on his typewriter, his radio going full blast and his little son muttering and chuckling by his side. His life, his home life, seems to be a fountain of fruitful activity. I worry that I am not able to get down to work so easily. I mope around, willing to find *any* excuse to evade the responsibility of the blank page. But Seán, sober for many months, is now driven by a fabulous industriousness. He has become frightening in his intensity.

November 26th At Glenshelane. The Brigadier and I were digging drains, or rather clearing them of leaves and brambles, to make everything ready for a contracter who is coming tomorrow to tarmac the avenue. The Brigadier very troubled about Paisley, and mostly astonished with his 'Blueshirt' style parades which remind him of the Fascist parades of the '30s.

December 4th Review of *The Sorrow Garden* in *The Irish Times* by Brendan Kennelly. A splendid notice, full of quotes and the best kind of praise. I read the review over and over and over again all day. Catherine and I had gone shopping in

Cork, the streets teeming with people in from the suburbs and the countryside because this is the first Saturday in December. The Christmas lights in the city look marvellous and festive. The good review combined with the general air of happiness, of having Catherine by my side, all caused a sense of ridiculous joy.

December 14th Terrible weather. On the way home to Glenshelane I ran into six floods. The Brigadier, on his way to lunch with the Cornells at Headborough House, had to abandon his car in three feet of floodwater. In the middle of the storm I went off into the upper Glenshelane woods with Rex to cut down a Christmas tree for Seán. A wonderful sensation, that: the rain pouring down and squalls blowing against my face while I strode through the woods — like a poacher of my father's generation, with my saw tucked beneath my raincoat.

December 19th Today Catherine and I became engaged. What a fabulous day and what a fabulous woman. We spent the day idly wandering through the Christmas shops and feeling happy. Catherine had worn her ring for no more than twenty minutes when she fell on the stairs and injured her ring-finger.

December 21st A review of *The Sorrow Garden* in *The Sunday Tribune*, as well as a 'Book of the Year' choice from Brendan Kennelly in the same paper. Today I got a letter from Peter Jay saying that the National Poetry Centre in London has run out of money — would I do my reading for nothing? I wonder if Elytis will be asked to read for nothing. I suppose I should do the reading, but the poverty of the Poetry Society is a pitiful thing. It saddens me to think of it. Is the wealth of London falling, I wonder? Is cultural London declining?

Christmas Day After a crowded and fabulously happy Christmas Eve with Catherine in Cork I'm back at Glenshelane. With Rex, washing my clothes and watching 'Gone with the Wind'. Christmas belongs to the city, the great festival of surplus wealth and riotous merriment. Theo came to lunch yesterday, Seán also wobbled in the door, and Catherine's sister, who's been delivering Christmas hampers to her Community Welfare clients, arrived at my flat exhausted and bewildered. I bought an old copy of *Diary of a Nobody* and a history of the Jewish community in London. I gave Theo a notebook with inscriptions from Stendhal.

1982

July 27th France. In the park of the Promenade des Anglais in Nice. All morning Catherine and I basked in the hot Mediterranean sun. Yesterday we lunched in the Luxembourg Gardens, Gide's Paris.

August 1st Back in Paris with Catherine. The city left to the mercy of tourists because all self-respecting Parisians have left for their holiday in the South. Yesterday more than ten million people took to the roads of France.

Everywhere the bookshop windows are filled with the face of Camus; all part of a huge promotion by Gallimard of the 50th anniversary of the Pléiade editions. I've found it impossible to get the French language versions of Stendhal, Camus or Gide. Many, many lavishly illustrated biographies of the authors, but no books with their very own secrets.

August 6th Many of the good bookshops of St Germain and Montparnasse have been closed for the August holiday. But in the street stalls of the Pont Neuf and St Michel I bought Gallimard texts of *L'Étranger* and *La chute* — as well as Gide's *Les Nourritures terrestres, Retour de l'URSS* and *Si le grain ne meurt*. The latter text has kept me happy for hours on end, now that I have Gide's own words. With the help of Dorothy Bussy's translation I intend to read a page or two a day. At Shakespeare and Company I bought the American edition of Harold Nicholson's *Diaries and Letters*. An impossible shop with no order on the shelves and no access to the higher bookshelves. I chatted with George Whitman who was running the shop on his own; a frail, emaciated figure with a beard that even looks anaemic! He spoke to me when I mentioned Anthony Cronin's name and thawed completely when he realized I was Irish. We talked about the English diarists and Irish poets, and on leaving he shouted after me, 'It's great to have an Irishman calling here. Come back again!' His raised voice startled all the young American tourists who were browsing and courting among the nooks and crannies of the shop.

August 18th Last month the Brigadier had dinner with Harold Macmillan at Sir Philip de Zulueta's house. When he came home to Ireland he was still peppering with admiration for Macmillan. All four guests had assembled at de Zulueta's house when Mac arrived in a chauffeur-driven car (always provided by the family publishing house when Mac is in London). The Brigadier felt that he was still a bright and intelligent man, even witty. Much of the talk at dinner dealt with the Falklands' crisis. When the crisis first broke Mrs Thatcher asked to see Macmillan, not so much to get his opinion as to get his blessing, and therefore his moral authority. Mac saw the Falklands' crisis as more than a mere post-Empire bother. He said that eventually the Russians will overrun Europe as far as Holland or Paris. Because of this, said Macmillan, lonely outposts such as the Falkland Islands will come into their own, strategically speaking, as places where western forces will be able to assemble and regroup. Even to the Brigadier, an ex-Director of Plans at the War Office, this all seemed very far-fetched. But this does tie in with the continental-oceanic historical view of conservative historians and MI6 advisors such as W E D Allen of Whitechurch House.

At 10 p.m. precisely Macmillan sat up and said to the company, 'I must go now.' Sure enough the same limousine drove up outside the Zuluetas. Mac was returning to his country house. But not by limousine, or at least not all the way. He was being chauffeured to Victoria Station where, with the help of his chauffeur and some West Indian porters who knew him, he would board a train for Gerrards Cross. He would travel free by train because he possessed a 'golden ticket' as a former Director of the transport company. At the other end of his journey yet another chauffeur and limousine would be waiting to pick him up.

I record this dinner now, nearly two months after it happened, because the Brigadier was intent upon telling me about it when he arrived back at Cappoquin from London. He was excited by every detail of the encounter. I could see the immense pride he had in Macmillan, the huge respect he felt for the old statesman.

August 30th Last week saw John Montague's return to Cork — for the opening of a play by Gerry Fitzgibbon, based on Montague's political stories and poems. On Friday night last John came alone to my flat with the typescript of *The Dead Kingdom*. Seán Dunne and I spent three hours looking over it, analysing and criticizing it, section by section. Some very beautiful poems, poignant, delicate, even tightly rhymed — typical of the Montague tone. But if the book has a weakness it's in the urgency to tell yet another 'great story'. Sometimes in his poetry the underlying brain-work behind good poem-making gets swamped or diminished in that overriding concern of Montague to make yet another 'big gesture'. Though this criticism could also be levelled against MacDiarmid: it's the weakness of genius, rather than lyricists like myself who like to operate in 'water-tight compartments'. Negative criticism of myself in *Cyphers* and *The Anglo-Welsh Review* force me to retreat to the well-made poem. Montague, on the other hand, is never diminished by harsh criticism. His hard Northern edge is challenged and he readies himself for a determined act of revenge against the reviewer. We are too passive in the South: John says there should be consequences for people when they attack you in print. But what can you do? You can't go around shooting critics.

At about 2 a.m. I accompanied John on his homeward trek

to Grattan Hill. He insisted that I come inside to read Robin Skelton's rave review of his *Selected Poems* in *The Malahat Review*. After I'd read the review John confided in me his fears that Seamus Heaney would win the Nobel Prize. He said that many people, especially Americans who are impressed by Heaney's success at Harvard, had mentioned this possibility to him. He said that Faber was now grooming Heaney for the Prize. I told John that that kind of talk was foolish, that Kinsella as an isolated, commercially unsuccessful poet, and senior Irish poet, would surely get it long before Heaney. And what about Máire Mhac an tSaoi, the doyenne of Irish poetry? But John refused to be comforted or consoled by my reassurances that this won't happen. Indeed just mentioning Kinsella's name made things worse between us as it reminded John of earlier humiliations at the hand of Kinsella in the 1950s.

Wednesday Princess Grace of Monaco has died — this morning when I was driving my brother Michael to the airport I switched on the BBC to hear the news. There were tears in my eyes, not just for the death of a Princess, but for the death of an Irish-American dream: the temporary good luck of the Irish that began in 1923 with Cumann na nGael and ended in 1963 with the murder of our own Irish prince, John Fitzgerald Kennedy.

Friday Spent last evening with Theo who has just returned from Crete. Most of the time we discussed his new idea for an MA. He is overwhelmed by his close reading of Robert Graves. Montague encourages him in this reading, a sort of quest for an aesthetic of carnal love; an annihilation of the Self through service to the White Goddess. It's not that Montague will supervise Theo through this MA, but that Theo will have to control Montague. The other day in The Long Valley Theo read sections of Graves' *The Common Asphodel* to me, from an essay entitled 'Modernist Poetry and the Plain Reader's Rights'. The essay was a response to e e cummings' 'Sunset'. It was a thrilling analysis, charting the territory between 'necessary' and 'unnecessary' poetry. It should be required reading in every poetry workshop on earth. Theo was so enthralling on Graves that I forgot to eat my huge Long Valley sandwich. I had to leave it there on the table and go back to the library.

October 17th In England for some poetry readings. On Thursday I gave the Alice Hunt Bartlett Reading at the Poetry Society with Carol Rumens. We were introduced by the poet Hugo Williams who looked about nineteen-years-old in his 'Teddy Boy' outfit. He was on his way to a rock 'n' roll concert. Pamela Clunies-Ross and Brian Mitchell were there, as well as old friends like Bill Crowder and the Derry poet, Robert Greacen. I felt that I didn't give of my best because I had so little practice. I hadn't even decided on the best sequence of poems. Carol Rumens, on the other hand, was brilliantly prepared and accomplished. She joked and cajoled and offered up a rich bowl of witty poems to the audience. On Friday I went to see Matthew Sweeney in his new flat in Dombey Street. He jokingly refers to it as 'next to Faber and Faber'. Matthew keeps a detective's eye on the poetic comings and goings in Russell Square. He knows everybody and he's already writing better poems than any poet of his generation. He may yet end up inside Faber. I hope he does.

October 19th Staying at Hertford College, Oxford, after a poetry reading. Over forty people, mainly female. Very attentive and silent, but very curious about the 'stone' and 'photographic' imagery of my love poems. Their questioning made me realize how deeply Catherine has affected my imagination. I found myself talking at length about her when introducing my poems. After the reading we returned to the common room to see Molly Keane being interviewed on the BBC *Bookshelf* programme. I was amazed that none of the students had heard of Molly, despite her book being on the Booker shortlist.

Earlier today while Adrian and I were shopping near Gloucester Road we literally bumped into Rosamund Lehmann. Adrian introduced me and she was quite genuinely amazed that I knew about her work. I had read her *A Swan At Evening* only last month. 'Oh, you've made my day! You've made my day! An Irish poet knows about me!' she exclaimed and she held my hand all the while as Adrian and she chatted. We walked with her to her house in Clareville Grove (directly across from Adrian's) and she screamed, 'Damn blast it! Blast it!' when she saw that a traffic warden had slapped a parking ticket on her car door. Then she began to complain to Adrian about parking problems in South Kensington. Adrian had to stand and listen and smile because he is on the local Council.

But back here in Hertford College it's after midnight. The yards around us are finally growing quiet. Since eleven o'clock a lot of noise seemed to come from All Souls, but that too has stopped. Everywhere one finds images of prosperity and comfort, in the streets, in the College yards, even in the student rooms I visited. The students who took me to dinner seemed very mature and confident products of a Public School education. They are immensely proud of their own colleges. One is doing History at Balliol while another is a Second Year English undergraduate at New College. Most significantly of all they are aware of the ethos and physical environment of their Colleges. They point out a particularly beautiful tree or a colourful herbaceous border or a particularly beautiful courtyard. Unlike Irish scholars who wander around like zombies these Oxford undergraduates are sharpening the teeth of their taste, their sensibility, on the local environment. They are already mapping the world so that they may command it.

October 23rd Reading Stephen Spender's *World Within World*. I came across this fascinating passage from July 1929:

'I have no character or will power outside my work . . . and have no opinions of my own. Therefore I must develop that side of me which is independent of other people. I must live and mature in my writing.'

October 29th This week, two great occasions of joy — Gabriel García Márquez has been awarded the Nobel Prize in Literature and Seamus Heaney has been given a huge American award.

November 6th On Thursday, a reading at Queen's University. My journey north had a twilit, dreamlike quality, beginning at 4.30 a.m. in Cork and ending forty-eight hours later with the most biblical red sky I've ever seen. At Connolly Station I switched trains to the blue wagons of the Northern Ireland Railways where conductors and engineers were wearing poppies for Remembrance Day. As the train gathered speed at the Border we passed a large contingent of British soldiers guarding a small railway bridge. Most of the soldiers were armed to the teeth, but a few hundred yards up the line there was a little group who were resting in a circle, drinking tea or coffee. One particularly poignant image: a young soldier was playing with his bomb-disposal Labrador. Soldier and dog rolled down a grassy embankment that was peppered with fallen sycamore leaves. As the train pulled away towards Belfast I felt that the effect of the leaves on the grass was like that of paprika scattered over a pie. Beyond Portadown the train came to a standstill, then crawled along for ten minutes while a British Army helicopter flew up and down the line. As much as I believe in the homogeneity of the Irish world and the integrity of this island I felt that between Portadown and Belfast the train sped through a different country — a Larkinesque or Audenesque country of quietened chimney stacks and windowless North of England factories. Certainly I was not in Ireland.

When I arrived at Belfast Central Michael Longley was

waiting for me. Aidan Carl Mathews, the poet and godson of President Cearbhall Ó Dálaigh, who had journeyed from Dublin, was also there. Michael Longley becomes more and more like Orson Welles, while Aidan M looked slightly ridiculous in a Sherlock Holmes cap and holding a huge barrister's briefcase. But when Mathews speaks he does so with all the force and erudition of his intense, Joycean Jesuit education. He talks as I imagine Stephen Dedalus talked, and when his accent settles down it reveals not so much an Etonian affectation as a real Dublin upper-class baritone, rather like that of Norman Jeffares or Conor Cruise O'Brien. From the station we motored through 'The Markets' area, now mostly disused and ignored by all except the youths, the ghetto cruisers, from whom the Provos and the UVF get their cadets. Frightened clusters of British soldiers. The University area of Belfast is almost wholly untouched by the Troubles, with long uninterrupted lines of trees and late Victorian houses. At the University Aidan and I were met by Edna Longley, the scholar and wife of Michael. Edna has an incredibly shy and retiring demeanour. But she has a brain like a wood-chipper and many an Irish poet has been reduced to fragments by her critical blades.

At the reading Gerry Dawe introduced me and announced his *Anthology of Younger Irish Poets*. I was first to read; read all the new 'Party' poems and love poems like 'Waking' and 'Luxembourg Gardens'. I got a shock when I looked up from my poems and saw the front row of the audience — it included Paul Muldoon, Ciaran Carson, Robert Johnstone. Medbh McGuckian, and even the doyen of Ulster poets, John Hewitt. I was followed by Aidan Mathews who read poems that were filled with familial piety and Jesuit scholasticism. Then Frank Ormsby read. His first poem was a random selection of names and addresses from the *Yellow Pages*. His whole manner of delivery is very funny; and he exaggerates the stockiness of his body while he reads — in order to make a point he buries his head deep into his high collar and looks at the audience from the top of his glasses. This is a visual trick, tortoise-like, but very effective.

After the reading I spoke to John Hewitt about Coventry and libraries, and about Medbh McGuckian — whose poetry he just can't understand. 'But I want to understand her!' he yells at me, straining to be heard over this Belfast literary crowd, the noisiest crowd on earth. Then I met Medbh herself. Even here in Belfast the ghost (or should I say *spirit*?) of Seamus Heaney is a dominant theme of conversation. Just as the poets in Munster feel on the periphery of the literary world, so these Belfast poets, even Michael Longley, feel pushed sideways by the enormous centrality of Heaney's reputation. The centre of Irish writing is wherever Heaney is at that moment. Again I find myself stifling my admiration of Heaney in order not to give offence to the sensibilities of these Ulstermen. But Aidan Mathews was quite uncompromising in his public affirmation: he explained at length to Michael and Edna Longley why Heaney is in the central poetic line of Ronsard, Eliot, Lowell. I tried to veer Aidan away from a discussion of Heaney but only succeeded in getting him on to religion — on which subject he asked Michael and Edna if they believed in baptising children. What a strange question to ask in a city of sectarian murders, where baptised Christian murders baptised Christian. The Longleys are not atheists by any means, they are more like Unitarians, 19th-century scholar-Unitarians. The red-brick of the English Midlands and industrial North is the atmosphere that surrounds the Longleys — it is an atmosphere of massive integrity, embracing the integrity of the evangelical United Kingdom that envelops Ulster Protestant life. It does exclude Irish nationalist experience and perspectives, but with great honesty and integrity. I like this viewpoint, I admire it, mainly because it isn't my point of view — but its very difference makes the island of Ireland more plural and interesting. British Ulster doesn't in any way offend me. I hope it endures. I want it to endure, because it is living proof that a civilization can endure in unpromising borderlands. In this I suppose I am a very weird Irish Catholic. Yes, I am weird politically, but I can't un-weird myself.

Michael drove us from Belfast to Dublin. At Newry we had to slow down because of military traffic. The Army garrison building is an horrific sight, entirely grey and windowless with a huge convoy of grey military vehicles always at the ready. When we reached Dublin we were held up by the funerals of the Irish UN soldiers and the Union leader Michael Mullen. At the funeral of the soldiers we saw the Provo leader Seán Mac Stíofáin wearing a grey morning suit and carrying a large black umbrella. My blood boils to think that a rotten creature like Mac Stíofáin can walk ceremoniously through Dublin while the victims of his Republican murder gangs have to die without ceremony and without honour in the ditches and backstreets of Ulster. I absolutely hate the Provos and I hate almost as much the thinking that creates them, both in Ireland and in America. Such thought processes as theirs give brutal murder an Irish legitimacy.

November 12th After my visit to Belfast the post brings good news: a poetry book from Medbh McGuckian, a card from Aidan Mathews asking for two poems for an American magazine edited by Robert Creeley, and a card from Seamus Heaney thanking me for my note of congratulations on his American Award. He says, 'The award creates odd kinds of pressures and what you did was a good shot in the arm, or gut or wherever.' I think I'd correctly judged that the Award would make him feel more rather than less isolated in Ireland. In literature, as in the theatre, envy is first cousin of imagination. The crowd that waits for Heaney to stumble grows and grows.

November 27th This last week has seen the collapse of Charles Haughey's Government. Charlie's demise has become more apparent as the weeks dragged on. He even began to accuse

Garret FitzGerald of 'collaboration' with the British over Ulster policy and went as far as accusing the Duke of Norfolk of spying on behalf of England. Witty, intelligent and with a genuine respect for poets and artists, Haughey has many qualities. But a sense of reality is not one of them. In this he is most like the artists he admires.

At Glenshelane my uncle Jasper has cut down half a maple tree for the Brigadier. Last week I planted a weeping birch and replanted a rare Bourbon rose that we got from Patricia Cockburn. As the Brigadier and I walked about in the rain, lifting trees, mulching shrubs, examining camellias for buds (at Glenshelane camellias are about to flower after eight years) I felt an immense concentration of happiness. The garden at Glenshelane was my first and best university.

December 18th The other day I took the Brigadier to the airport, on his way to a Christmas sojourn in Château de la Garoupe near Nice. I forgot to lend him Noel Coward's *Diaries* which contain two references to Molly Keane — one to a breakfast with her in the South of France and the other to the atrocious fatal production of her last play directed by John Gielgud.

December 20th When Catherine and I woke this morning the city was covered with snow. The brilliantly white roofscape was really beautiful. It was a small snowfall, perhaps two inches, but the whole city became silly with the enchantment of the thing. The Mobile Library couldn't be delivered until noon so I spent the morning standing in the snow in Mayfield to greet our readers as they arrived. During the day I went to the Coal Quay to buy a Christmas tree and some holly for my mother-in-law. The place was in total chaos, with raggedly dressed old women walking up and down in the snow trying to peddle their wares. They charged exorbitant prices for tiny sprigs of holly. They shouted abuse at those who protested and screamed with anxiety at any motorist who dared to park near their stalls and obscure their business. This time of year in Cork, on the Coal Quay especially, reminds me of Frank O'Connor's delicate mother, who surrendered to the delights of Christmas despite the terror of poverty and the poverty of a useless husband.

Catherine and Seán Dunne and Sara and I went out to Diarmuid Hurley's house in Blackrock to listen to Frank O'Connor's taped lecture on Joyce's *Portrait* and *Finnegans Wake*. What fascinated us was not O'Connor's genius but his voice, so elegant and strong, so unlike the weakly boy of 'An Only Child'. Diarmuid had a copy of a rare book of Irish poetry translated into Hebrew. A selection of Ó Ríordáin was included, 'Adhlacadh Mo Mháthar' being the most adventurous translation. Seán Dunne's admiration for Catherine is immense, he idolizes and idealizes her. I have to admit sometimes this really annoys me, but I hide my jealousy from Catherine.

December 22nd The postman brought a welcome parcel of books from Henry Sotheran's of Sackville Street, including Bill Allen's *History of the Georgian People*, published in the early '30s while he was still a New Party MP and a Gollanz edition of *The Private Diaries of Stendhal*, translated by Robert Sage.

December 27th Here in the kitchen of a cottage in Ballyferriter; a turf fire blazing and the old wall clock ticking in the background. Catherine and her brothers and sister and Pat and Bríd Crotty have gone for a walk to Ballydavid. I suppose I should have gone with Catherine to share her obvious happiness at being in Kerry.

December 29th Pat Crotty came down to breakfast this morning and cursed Robert Graves while holding Martin Seymour-Smith's book open. Pat condemned Graves for his jealousies, his envy and his English snobbery. What sort of a

man, said Pat, would hold a celebration dinner on the death
of Yeats? But three hours later, after we'd walked along the
cliffs by Clogher and watched huge waves pounding the
pathetic coast and while we sat around a table full of rich
pints and hot whiskeys in Kruger's Pub in Dunquin, Pat
announced that Graves would be one of the three poets of the
20th century to survive. All assembled in Kruger Kavanagh's
pub agreed that Graves never published a bad poem. And
Patrick Crotty, literary star of St Colman's College, Fermoy,
was pleased with this and drank his pints in peace. Outside the
rain lashed against Kruger's windows as if the entire Blasket
Sound was emptying itself over the roof of the pub. The penetrating rain came down the chimney, the pathetic turf fire in
the grate hissed and spluttered as we considered Crotty's
words of wisdom.

1983

January 16th In Evelyn Waugh's diary for 22nd May 1940 there's an entry describing a lecture by a surviving officer of the Norway campaign — a FitzGerald who came off the *Curacoa*. I wonder if this officer was the Brigadier? Or was it his cousin, the Knight of Kerry, who also served in the Norway campaign. (Probably not the Brigadier, he was on the *Chobry*.)

Reading Nicholas Mosley's irreverent biography of his father, the Blackshirt: the book is an act of revenge. Nicholas was disinherited by his father who explained that his son was 'not my sort of person'. Good for the son. There's one reference to Bill Allen of Whitechurch who left the Unionist Conservative Party to join the New Party. Mr Allen has been appearing all over the place at the moment: in Dervla Murphy's *Irish Times* reviews, in Laurens van der Post's latest book, and now in this Mosley biography.

When I showed the Mosley book to Humphrey Moynihan, owner of The Long Valley, he told me about an incident with The Irish Youth Movement (not to be confused with the Blueshirts). A huge display of IYM uniforms took place in a clothes shop window in Winthrop Street (probably Vignoles). Eoin Neeson, the RTÉ broadcaster, complained about their display to the Fascist community in Cork and was promptly assaulted. The Irish Youth Movement couldn't pay for the uniforms so the German Embassy in Dublin finally paid out the cash.

Friday evening Medbh McGuckian telephoned from Belfast to ask me to give a reading with Paul Muldoon on February 25th. Problems with the library — I think I've only got one-and-a-half days' leave left, and I need a day off for Una Coakley's wedding.

February 4th Still reading Skidelsky's biography of Mosley and surprised to find therein many references to W E D Allen. The more I learn about that man the more I feel honoured to have known him. How could I, a Cappoquin poet of seventeen years, have known what an important person W E D Allen was? How could I have known the way history touched him? A Unionist Conservative MP for West Belfast at an appalling time in Irish history, he had travelled in and studied Georgia before it became Sovietized. He had known and befriended Kim Philby at Ankara (well, thereby hangs a tale, including the whole Volkov affair and Philby's obvious negligence). He had married four beautiful women and known many more. For Allen, Mosley the Fascist was 'an aristocrat reborn, an Elizabethan adventurer'. Like Yeats he was magnetized by what was grand and vigorous.

Whenever Dervla Murphy talks about Allen she talks about his disappointment in life, his loneliness.

February 7th Letters from Matthew Sweeney and Molly Keane. Matthew still beavering away. He has succeeded in getting a £300 advance from Allison and Busby for his second book of poems — an amazing figure, if one thinks that a publisher is certain to lose money on a book of poems.

February 20th Last week there was an article in the *Observer* about the happy state of poetry publishing in England. It seems that the activity can be profitable. People like James Fenton and Craig Raine can sell 10,000 copies of each collection. The new *Penguin Book of Contemporary Verse* has sold 15,000 copies in the six months since its publication. Publishers have become wise to the fact that their poets can sell as if they were popular novelists.

February 27th Back in Cork after a two-day stint in Belfast, a return poetry reading with Paul Muldoon sponsored by Poetry Ireland. Muldoon wore a marvellous, expensive lounge suit that caused a lot of comment. Ciaran Carson made caustic comments about it and Frank Ormsby did his best to spill beer over its waistcoat.

Coming home on the train I listened to Charles Haughey's speech at the Fianna Fáil Ard Fheis. After the reality of Belfast I could only see its flaccid unreality, its callous underestimation of the resolve of Ulster to fight everything that isn't Ulster. Hatred and loss have given them a memory tougher than our Southern numerical strength. I see a bleak war coming, like Lincoln's war in the US. Bought a copy of Hughes' *The Hawk in the Rain*. Medbh McGuckian gave me her copy of Mahon's beautiful book, *The Hunt by Night*. She disliked it intensely. I was astounded when she expressed this opinion. Then I remembered the cruel and unnecessary review of her book in *The New Statesman* where Mahon is the Poetry Editor. I'm sure she blames Mahon for that.

March 27th In bed with a sore throat. My voice is gone after a hectic weekend. Medbh McGuckian and Gabriel Rosenstock stayed with us after the Poetry Ireland reading on Saturday night. Absolute chaos.

March 28th A flood of visitors to my bedside which means that I can't rest and get better. Theo came here yesterday and brought a copy of Robert Graves' letters (edited by Paul O'Prey). He saw that I was reading a 1947 edition of *La Porte étroite*. I made him read the first few pages, then made him listen to Robert Frost reading 'After Apple Picking'. All of these mere schemes devised by me to save my throat. Greg Delanty then came along with a copy of his unpublished poems. Seán Dunne arrived with a cup of tea. Then Suzanne, Captain Kelly's daughter, now Theo's girlfriend, arrived with a large bottle of lemonade. We talked about Kevin Boland and Haughey and the Party. She says that she is seriously thinking of joining Fianna Fáil. I didn't discourage her but it could be an unwise move for someone who wants to make a life in professional circles in provincial Ireland. Fine Gael would be a better bet for her if she wanted to make a life as a Tax Accountant. But she is her father's daughter; she suffers from a fatal sincerity. I wanted to tell her that this notion of joining Fianna Fáil will be her ruination but I was too ill to start a deep discussion. But she must be acutely aware how socially damaging an attachment to Fianna Fáil can be for a person who wants a professional, client-based life in Ireland. The educated upper class in the Irish Republic are either Fine Gael or Labour Party. The whole point of Fianna Fáil is that it's for people of no background, people of the industrial 1960s in Cork and Dublin, the intelligent and ambitious poor. They are not the kind of people who need accountants; indeed, not keeping accounts at all might be a distinctive trait of this class. That, and a passion for Gaelic games. The rugby-following class that needs accountants lives entirely within Fine Gael: I wanted to make Suzanne aware of that. I fear that Theo will give her bad advice and that out of love she'll act upon it and ruin her prospects in life, ruin her parents' hope that she might mature into a wealthy professional.

April 7th In general Ireland has been an ideal culture within which to grow hatred, and grow it abundantly. But what makes West Waterford so different from every other part of Ireland is that it has produced an inclusive, an integrated, rather than an exclusive society. Protestants here talk to Catholics, the Anglo-Irish actually converse with their Catholic neighbours. Last week Lady Keane walked around Cappoquin to deliver invitations to every Catholic household for a concert in the Protestant Cathedral of Lismore. The Redmondite nature of County Waterford remains absolutely intact, and it gives Waterford life a non-sectarian ease. I don't underestimate the power of politics, and the corrosive effect of the Helvick IRA, but I think West Waterford life contains non-sectarian impera-tives that defy Irish politics. The atmosphere of my childhood in Cappoquin would be utterly unimaginable in Belfast.

Wednesday Molly Keane was on television last night being interviewed by Paddy Gallagher. Ever since the shortlisting of *Good Behaviour* for the Booker Prize Molly's life has been an incessant round of interviews and broadcasts. This new situation leaves her exhausted and thrilled. She mentioned my name in passing and this has thrown everyone into a paroxysm of interest in me. Old ladies came into the library today and spoke to me and ogled as if I'd won the Irish Sweepstakes. The power of television is incredible, almost daemonic. Just to have one's name mentioned. God almighty.

Rereading Kresh's peculiar biography of Isaac Bashevis Singer. For *Satan in Goray* Singer received the princely sum of $90, for *In My Father's Court* he received $300, the equivalent of what I got for my last book of poems. He says to Kresh that he couldn't have made it as a writer if his wife Alma hadn't held down a permanent job as a sales clerk. But he adds, and I'm convinced of his sincerity, 'When I began to write I was fifteen and I never heard of anybody making a living from writing . . . I was brought up with the idea that the Torah is not to be used as a means of livelihood and that spiritual work is its own reward.'

Friday Spoke to Paul Durcan on the phone. I asked him if he would be one of my sponsors for an Arts Council application. He agreed and talked for a long time about Molly Keane's interview on RTÉ. No mention of Russia where he has lately been with Anthony Cronin. Paul said that I should emphasize the fact that I work every day — that I am, as Máirtín Ó Díreáin said to Paul, 'chained to my civil service desk'.

April 17th The desperate need to write is with me every day.

'Take rest,' Ovid says, 'a rested field gives up a beautiful crop.' But Pasternak says, 'Everywhere in the world one has to pay for the right to live on one's own naked spiritual reserves.'

The price I pay is tiredness and a perpetual agitation. But this agitation is like a perpetual companionship — it's the tiredness I find difficult and frightening.

April 18th I arrived a Glenshelane too late for lunch today but in time to meet the Duke and Duchess of Leinster and a Mr Brennan from Wexford (a very friendly man) who writes reviews and books under the pseudonym John Welcome. The Duke was smaller, older and less friendly than I'd expected (from the Brigadier's descriptions), but he had a kind face with lots of mischievous character, very like the face of Lord Longford. The Brigadier says they live a very simple life for a Duke and Duchess. He works as a manager of an airport and they go to a caravan camp in France for their summer vacation. To think that his predecessors had a choice of Kilkea Castle, Johnstown Castle, Carton House and Leinster House. But I can't be grieving for the collapse of an aristocracy; yet there is something poignant about the destiny of the Leinster FitzGeralds. They tried to create prosperity for every tenant-farmer of their vast 75,000 acres, and many such farmers are the leading families of County Kildare today — people who could now buy and sell the poor Duke. The Leinster Fitz-Geralds did nothing to deserve such a decline: nothing but ill-luck and another Duke's gambling brought them down.

Typewriters have been banned in Hungary. The Hungarian Government has ordered that everyone who owns a typewriter must register with the Government and that no ex-criminal can own a typewriter. With every day that passes Koestler's fiction of communism become more believable.

April 21st Mary Leland came into the Mobile Library today, brandishing a rejection slip from Heinemann for her novel, as well as a copy of the reader's report. Mary didn't appear too worried about the rejection: she's already working on a new novel. The amazing thing was that if this reader's report had been published as a review in a newspaper Mary would have been delighted with it. Yet in the same breath the novel is rejected. How can this happen? What the hell do editors want?

May 6th At a very well attended launch of a 'Poetry Introductions' book published by Raven Arts Press of Finglas.
The book was launched in Cork because it included Seán
Dunne and Aidan Murphy. One of the largest crowds I've
ever seen in Cork for a poetry reading, perhaps 150 people;
certainly the largest crowd since Seamus Heaney's reading.
Paul Durcan presided while Theo had done the organizing.
Seán read very well, without nervousness and with convic-
tion. People really love Seán Dunne, women adore him, even
children run to him. He is magnetic.

Dermot Bolger had a great story about the Irish soccer
team's visit to Moscow for an international match. At the
match (which was won by the Russians) the Irish supporters
were outnumbered 300 to 99,700, so after the match the massive
Russian crowd stood up and applauded the little colony of 300
Irishmen. All was very diplomatic and friendly until one of
the Irish supporters fell in love with a Russian girl.

May 12th On Monday evening Rory Brennan rang from
Dublin to ask if I would take over from John Jordan as Editor
of *Poetry Ireland Review*.

Catherine and I went to a concert given by Charles Lynch.
It was introduced by Sheila Goldberg, looking really beautiful in a black gown with a tight string of pearls acting as a
sort of neckband or choker. Lynch, when he entered the hall,
looked frail and old, shuffling slowly across the floor. But
when he began to play he played beautifully, like a thirty-
year-old genius. He played Beethoven, Arnold Bax and Ravel.
There was wild and loud applause when he finished, except
from me — I was too worried about being forty minutes late
back to the library after lunch. I am completely intimidated
by the new woman in charge of my Lending section. She will
go places.

May 16th This morning in Patrick Street I was struggling
through the rain with three bags of groceries when I was

stopped by the old British soldier, Michael O'Callaghan. I curse the day I recognized his regimental tie in the library. He now lurks in street corners and reading rooms to destroy my peaceful moments. He has too much time on his hands while I have very little. I firmly believe that he suffers from schizophrenia. He has a wild persecution complex; he has delusions of grandeur; he is obsessed with the idea of a religious apocalypse. I suppose he's not unlike a number of Irish poets. Today he said that a group of Irishmen, or else a group of Fianna Fáil men, had tried to suffocate him with ether while he slept —

'Why should they want to kill you?' I asked, exasperated and drenched with rain.

'Because I know too much.'

'What do you know?'

'I know about Michael Collins. I know Collins was killed with the help of de Valera and the British.'

'Nobody knows who killed Michael Collins,' I say.

'The answer to Collins' murder is known in five places.'

'Name them so.'

'The answer to the riddle of Collins' death can be found in Trinity College, UCD, in Dublin Castle, in Whitehall and in Scotland.'

'What's Scotland got to do with it?' I ask.

'It was a Scot who killed Collins. And I don't mean McPeake.'

He went on to explain that de Valera came back from the US with trunks full of cash, that Dev went around Ireland buying drinks for every Tom, Dick and Harry, all the while discrediting Collins' name. ('That fellow's at the gates of Hell this very minute, a Machiavelli for power.') He then tells me that Dev sends Collins to London so that Collins would get killed — the oldest pub-lie in Irish history.

'I have my sources,' he says, and then he adds, 'How's the Brigadier? I suppose he thinks I'm insignificant.'

After fifteen minutes in the rain I try to escape but he continues to talk about various obsessions. He mentions (again) the honesty of the British while admitting that 'they played a few tricks in Ireland, like the Collins' job'. Then he gets on to his second pet subject: the conversion of Russia to Christianity and the eternal damnation of the anti-Christ, Marx. Mr O'Callaghan prays every day to Our Lady of Fatima and believes that in 1985 all the nations of the earth will come together as Our Lady foretold. 'Where,' he asks, 'is the most important shrine to Our Lady?'

I admit that I don't know.

'In Moscow,' Mr O'Callaghan says, 'in the Kremlin, the very core of the Communist regime, there's a little patch of green grass left where the great shrine to Our Lady once stood. The Communists burn the spot with chemicals, they pour tar and concrete on it; but the grass continues to flourish and won't go away. This is because the Kremlin is really a Holy Place. Our Lady still lives in that green patch of grass in Moscow. She awaits the return of the Holy Faith and the rebuilding of her shrine. Our Lady is the Queen of All the Russias.'

I'm impressed by this fantastic story and while he tells it I think of all the newspaper photos of Solzhenitsyn who was in London last week to receive a prize for helping Russian Christianity. The Russian novelist was photographed with Margaret Thatcher. What a wild, anti-Soviet trio they make — Mrs Thatcher, Solzhenitsyn and Michael O'Callaghan, the old Irish Guardsman. As I escape from him into the dingy Cork traffic he shouts, 'I have my sources! Remember that, young man!' It struck me that in saying this he was like a poet: all of his sources are inside his own head.

May 30th Last Friday night Catherine prevented a man from committing suicide by drowning. We had been out walking near the Coal Quay when Catherine noticed a young man sitting on the Quay wall near some deep water. Catherine said, 'He's very depressed looking. I know he's going to drown himself.' We couldn't make up our minds whether to go to him and persuade him to come away or not. We decided to sit behind him and talk loudly so that the sound of human company might break his alienation. But our ploy didn't work. Within five minutes the man had hurled himself into the filthy river. Immediately I bolted towards the Bridewell to alert the Gardaí. Catherine ran to the quayside to shout at the suicidal victim. Within sixty seconds a young Guard had thrown a lifebuoy to the man in the water and missed. The man went under for a second time, then the lifebuoy caught the young man's chin and he was dragged to the side, unconscious and, I thought, dead. At that stage — it was only a matter of two or three minutes — a Fire Brigade engine and at least six motorcycled Gardaí were at the scene. The young man was taken away. I got *The Examiner* on Saturday morning to see if the man was really dead. In fact he survived by about a minute and he was recuperating in the Regional Hospital. Whether he is grateful to us or not for supervising his attempted suicide and raising the alarm is something I don't want to know. He's probably incredibly annoyed with us. But he's alive — which means he has options.

June 8th A letter from Medbh McGuckian, containing a poem on Sylvia Plath. I had lent her Plath's *Letters Home* and now they've depressed Medbh very much. Medbh fears for the safety of her husband and her children.

At a protest reading in the Quay Co-Op in support of Nicky Kelly who was wrongly imprisoned and who's now on hunger strike. Both Seán Dunne and John Montague refused to take part. Seán says the reading would be no good and anyway he doesn't want to 'overexpose' himself. Oh, for God's sake, the vanity of poets is insufferable. Montague says he won't read because the reading is pointless. I read, not just for Nicky Kelly, who is dying on hunger strike, but for the committee who organized the protest — perhaps someday I will need the support of such a committee of idealists.

June 9th Chrissie Ahern of Blackrock, one of the senior councillors on Cork Corporation and a member of the Library Committee, came into the Mobile Library today. She wanted to talk to me. She was very upset after having failed to become Lord Mayor. She had been promised a Mayoralty by the Fianna Fáil Group in the Corporation — the Mayoralty was in Fianna Fáil's gift because of the rotation agreement between the three main parties. But when the voting had finished Chrissie got only her own vote, plus her nominator's vote. A secret deal had been worked out among the men. She was deeply shocked and embarrassed. She is very bitter now and said to me: 'I used to go to Mass and Communion every day, but now I just can't face the Eucharist because of the bitterness in my heart.' I felt for her deeply. She is a simple, but faithful person, devoted to Fianna Fáil's interests in Cork.

June 22nd Much bitterness among the young poets of Cork — Theo, Seán Dunne, Gerry Murphy and Greg Delanty all received Arts Council rejections in reply to their Bursary applications. Louis de Paor, a brilliant young Irish language poet, and I are still waiting for news. Most people think that we've got an award, but I doubt this.

June 29th Letter from Lar Cassidy on Monday to say that the Arts Council have given me a Bursary, a whopping £4,000. This should be enough to keep me going for a year. But the project I have in mind will take only six months. The most important aspect of this will be the completion of the second draft of *The Solitude of the Party*. In order to finish the first draft I would love to complete a chapter a week.

July 3rd Spent all of last Friday night with The Montague and Seán Lucy. We were going through the proof pages of John's *The Dead Kingdom*, a very substantial collection. The more I see of it the more faith I have in its possible success. A letter from Peter Jay saying that *The Sorrow Garden* has nearly sold out. A note also from Morgan Smith in America who makes tentative enquiries about the same collection. Now there's the prospect of a second edition as well as an American edition.

July 19th Yesterday went down to Glenshelane to check on the Brigadier and the garden. We had a long chat over tea. He's decided that he wants to be buried at Kilkea in Kildare, beside the castle where he spent the happiest days of his childhood. His aunts and uncles are buried in the small private chapel which was a marriage gift from his grandfather to his grandmother. There was great happiness in his face as he re-called his memories of Kilkea Castle, his memory of walking to chapel with his aunts and uncles while the sound of a hymn ('Faraway Hills'?) being played on the chapel bells resounded through the tall shrubs and trees. He remembered the chapel jammed with tenant farmers imported by his ancestors and planted in Kildare, the Campbells, the Shackletons, the Greenes. All of the congregation stood to attention when the Duke and the Ladies FitzGerald entered. That sense of timeless feudal security, it is still deep in his bones. It is the world of *The Leopard* by the Prince of Lampedusa. The power of his family, the Leinster FitzGeralds, came back to him with a vengeance last week because he attended the funeral of an old tenant farmer, a Greene — now established at Kilkea as a dis-tinguished Anglo-Irish family — and he was also reading the Christie's catalogue of paintings from Carton being sold by Desmond FitzGerald, Knight of Glin. He had hoped to bid for a charcoal drawing of his grandfather, the Duke, and his cousin skating on the lake at Carton, but the drawing went for an outrageous price.

Filled with the euphoria of dukes and paintings and con-versations with the Brigadier I returned to Cork to a small financial crisis. Catherine and I had discovered that if we went out for a meal to celebrate our first anniversary we wouldn't have enough money to cover the monthly repayment for our car. We had just discovered this when Seán Dunne came into our kitchen looking absolutely ill and distraught. The ESB have threatened to cut off his electricity supply tomorrow if he doesn't pay them the £60 that he owes. He asked Catherine if we could lend him the money. Catherine and I looked at each other and, without exchanging a word with me, she said, 'Yes!' Thereby the prospect of our dinner disappeared, but at least a poet will have some light by which to write. What an absurd world, what a perverted moral system we live under that allows one artist to become so destitute that he cannot pay for fuel for himself, his wife and child, while £30,000 changes hands for an obscure and minor drawing of a duke. This world is absolutely unjust.

July 28th At Paul Durcan's last night with Catherine. Paul a little surprised and depressed that Edna Longley's edition of his poems has sold very badly.

Diarmuid Hurley came into the library today. A very happy man because his daughter, Emma, has become a doctor at the Regional Hospital. She's just 22 years old. We talked about the RTÉ interview with Gerald Goldberg, the former Lord Mayor. Both of us were sickened when Gerald described his experiences with Alfred O'Rahilly, the old Registrar of UCC. Alfie told Gerald that he couldn't do both Arts and Law 'because he was a Jew'. This anti-Semitism was typical of Irish Catholicism in the 1930s; and it survives among the haut bourgeois of Ireland to this day.

August 6th 'He who has not absolute faith in History does not belong to the Party rank.' And 'The Party's warm, breathing body appeared to him to be covered with sores — festering sores, bleeding stigmata. When and where in history had there been such defective saints?' Both quotes are from Koestler's *Darkness at Noon*. A copy of this is in Paul Durcan's library. I've read it at three sittings. The hero, Rubashov, and the interrogator, Gletkin, are the most real characters I've encountred in a long time.

August 31st For Pasternak *Doctor Zhivago* was an extension of, rather than a departure from, the work of poetry. He thought of the novel as a long narrative poem (*poema*), submitting to poetic intuition which was more capable than anything else of expressing 'the atmosphere of life'. In fact the novel was a deepening of poetry.

September 2nd Went to Paul Durcan's house last night to deliver Mr Allen's three books on Georgia. Each time I go there Paul needs to hear again the story of Mr Allen's life — How a rich Ulsterman, a scholar, is elected an MP for West Belfast, joins the Secret Service, joins the Fascists, writes British Fascist Union propaganda, writes novels, marries two Russian women, fights in Abyssinia, befriends Kim Philby and chaperones him in Ireland for MI6, breeds dogs, restores icons.

But Paul is still upset by the collapse in sales of his *Selected Poems*. Still fewer than 300 copies sold out of a 1000 printing. Does this mean that Blackstaff have no distribution in England and no representation in the English book trade? If so, that is really disappointing: it means they haven't learned to exploit the real advantage of being from Ulster, of being able to belong to two quite distinct markets.

September 3rd If ever I write a major work of prose it will be *The Last Geraldine Officer*, with its Anglo-Irish background, its nationalist perspective, its frustrations with English and Irish society, but most especially its frustration with the political narrowness of Ireland at a time when Fascism might have overwhelmed Europe.

September 5th A letter from Seamus Heaney in *The Irish Times* about the absurd anti-abortion referendum, which will do nothing to prevent abortion but will do everything to reassert the special position of the Catholic Church in Ireland. Heaney says that if the referendum is passed he will be ashamed to be an Irishman. I can't imagine him ever being ashamed of being Irish, his entire poetic being is attached to his Irishness.

September 21st A copy of *APR* arrived today with a huge cover photo of John Ashbery and a poem by Heaney spread across the back cover.

September 26th Vincent Buckley phoned this evening. He is coming to Cork next week and wants Theo to meet him at the train. He sounded tired and confused on the phone.

September 27th Fr Denis Faul on the television: he pleads with the IRA leaders not to take their new 'anti-supergrass' campaign onto the streets. Fr Faul says simply and honestly, 'The RUC and the British Army are bad people. We mustn't allow the poor Catholics of the ghettos to have their brains blown out yet again. This has already happened during the Civil Rights marches, and later during the H-Block protests.'

October 5th A letter in my postbox from Seamus Heaney today with three new poems, 'The Underground', 'Sloe Gin' and a sonnet from the 'Station Island' sequence. He says that he sent four poems to *APR* and wished that they'd not used the 'Spike' poem. Between Seamus H, James J McAuley and John F Deane's contributions I have the makings of a very strong *PIR*.

October 8th Vincent Buckley came to stay until next Thursday.

October 12th Vincent Buckley left yesterday for Limerick where he is to give a reading, before moving on to Kilkenny for the Australian Festival there.

October 19th Tonight the BBC broadcast a beautiful programme on Elizabeth Bowen; they played recordings of Molly Keane, Charles Ritchie and Elizabeth Bowen herself, as well as two Bowen biographers, Victoria Glendinning and

Hermione Lee. Molly Keane sounded great. Her way of speaking belongs to the late 19th century; it is slow, clear and pensive with only a hint of Irishness in it — just enough to make her authentic. She spoke about the 'presence' of Bowen, her lack of beauty but her immense attractiveness. The last time Mrs Keane met EB was in an expensive restaurant in Kinsale in 1972. Bowen spent most of the lunchtime discussing the pros and cons of wearing a wig (she was undergoing chemotherapy). What came across most clearly was that the world of prose, the world of prose fiction, belongs most naturally to those cool and articulate Anglo-Irish women. The talent of the native Irish lies in our lyricism, our song, our poetry.

October 24th The Late Unionist World. I'd like to write an essay on Molly Keane's two novels and their accuracy in depicting the second period of Free State Southern Unionism. The Keanes of Cappoquin were a typical such family. But my own *The Last Geraldine Officer* is a book that's ten years away, at least.

November 11th Yesterday's *Irish Times* carried a report on the released MI5 files in which Mr Allen is mentioned. Lord Ravensdale, Mosley's son, believes that Bill Allen was MI5's main contact in the BFU. I think it was common knowledge among the Anglo-Irish of West Waterford that Bill Allen worked for either MI5 or MI6. In inviting Kim Philby to become his secretary/assistant for six months in 1956 Mr Allen was merely 'housekeeping' the spy for British Intelligence. Whatever about Mr Allen's shady past he was the best sort of Ulster Unionist, a scholar and a gentleman. What's more, through Terence de Vere White he put Dervla Murphy and myself on the road as writers. His extremely benign and cosmopolitan Loyalism also had a deeper effect — it created a whole circle of anglophiles in West Waterford.

Gerry Dawe has sent me Heaney's *Sweeney Astray* for

review. It seems that the only way to ingest Irish myth is to render it into English. In handling 'Sweeney' Heaney has discovered that a poet's true importance lies in inward, downward journeying. The outward journey towards fame might have ruined his talent through too much exposure and too much self-explanation. The *dinnseanchas*, or place lore, of 'Sweeney' is also an important aspect of the book. It gives Heaney's talent yet another source, a myth-kitty, that is older than the more modern Ulster Troubles.

November 15th Went to Glenshelane on Monday to discover that the Brigadier was disabled by gout. His right foot was badly swollen and very painful. I tried not to make light of it with jokes that gout is a disease of the aristocracy. But I could sense the ill-ease that he felt at being immobilized. Apart from injuries during the War he has never had a burdensome illness. The death of Paud O'Donoghue at the Glenshelane gate lodge has also dampened the atmosphere. Paud had been at the gate lodge since the Brigadier bought Glenshelane. He was the brother-in-law of Molly Keane's old gardener at Belleville House. He had been a chronic alcoholic and a marvellous singer. Only three weeks ago I'd walked with him from the lodge into Cappoquin. He was full of talk about the old days, full of gossip and full of dismissive comments about the new petty-bourgeoisie who've built bungalows on the Melleray Road beside Cappoquin. He had lately come into an inheritance. It was this inheritance and the social duties adhering to it (drink) that killed him. Last Thursday he was sitting between two old buddies in the Tavern Bar when he stood up, took a large swig from a pint of porter, sang two verses of 'The Galtee Mountain Lad' (his favourite song), then sat down and died. What a perfect way to end one's life.

November 21st Last night a group of gunmen — calling themselves The Catholic Reaction Force — stormed into a Protestant prayer meeting and sprayed the congregation with machine-gun fire. They were probably members of the INLA, a Left-wing anarchist group. It's a long time since we had a vicious massacre like this, a massacre perpetrated after great deliberation rather than mere anger, calculated to bring about a Protestant reaction and further sectarian murders. It is endless, this cruelty of Ireland is endless.

November 23rd Tonight Greg Delanty told me that he won the Patrick Kavanagh Award. He was immensely excited and disorientated by the news. He's the first Cork poet to win the prize. At last some attention is coming South.

December 13th This morning Seán Dunne showed me a long letter written by David Marcus. Seán had written to Marcus about Teresa Deavy. She had been one of Marcus's youthful heroes. Marcus was worried about possible embarrassing openness in the letters.

December 15th Yesterday the Mobile Library was parked beside a little encampment of Travellers. They had halted in the suburb of Blackrock to sell Christmas trees. Two itinerant children, a boy and a girl aged about eight and eleven, came into the library to get some warmth and dryness. It was bitterly cold outside with an easterly wind blowing, bringing with it a sharp and icy rain. The children sat against the heaters and looked at the books. The only books that interested them were ones with large illustrations of horses, caravans, tents or cowboys. The little boy spent at least an hour looking at a large Boy Scout annual. He was fascinated by the pictures of scout camps and tents. His sister brought a book to my desk and asked if 'it was about tinkers, sir'. The book was about the wagon trains of the American West. After about two hours had gone by I heard an adult shouting their names, Pauline and Tommy. Later Pauline came back to the library to ask me if I had any books on 'Dallas', the American TV series.

December 22nd I've nearly finished reading Molly K's *Time After Time*. It's a picture of tired reactionary landscapes and therefore limited in importance. But her skill as a writer is amazing. There are beautiful prose-portraits of childhood places and domestic interiors, as well as blistering and bitching dialogues. Molly's skill depresses me even further. She really is a genius.

December 30th The US has decided to pull out of UNESCO, a typical Reaganite gesture of short-sighted arrogance. Reagan has pulled out because this world body has a Third World bias. Unbelievable.

1984

To deny politics to a writer is to deny him part of his humanity.
　　　　　　　— Cyril Connolly, *Enemies of Promise*

Thus all my past is there pressing, urgent, imperious,
but its meanings and the orders which it gives me
I choose by the very project of my end . . . Thus the
urgency of the past comes from the future.
　　　　　　　— Sartre, *Being and Doing*

January 1st Finished Chapter 20 of *The Solitude of the Party*. At the beginning of the year I expected that I'd have the entire first draft finished. I'm eight chapters short but if all goes well I shall have the full thing first-drafted by the end of February.

January 5th In his autobiography Graham Greene says that novels, unlike poems, are a matter of characterization and drama. Words, individual words, their weight and colour and ambience, are of secondary importance. This is why it's difficult to concentrate on a novel while trying to make new poems.

January 15th Heavy snow for four hours this morning, the heaviest continuous snow for a very long time. The atmosphere was spoilt by sudden piercing sunlight. But — wait — it's becoming dark again as I write.
　　This is from Stendhal's second notebook: 'All men on earth are seeking the things that will benefit them, the poet alone is in quest of nothing but our happiness, Divina poeta!' and ' . . . in order to write sublime works, you must live for your

genius, form it, cultivate it, correct it'.

February 29th We launched *Poetry Ireland Review* with a
reading by Greg Delanty and Seán Lucy. Nancy McCarthy
was there, and John Montague turned up late. Theo became
very insulting and offensive to Montague. I tried to intervene
on Montague's behalf and Theo shouted at me, 'You have a
very short memory!' Meaning, of course, that I'd often criticized Montague for his competitiveness and insecurity. But
I think at that moment Theo was thinking mainly about
Montague's unreliability.

March 23rd Pat Crotty phoned this morning to ask if I would
publish three uncollected poems of Hugh MacDiarmid in
PIR. I said I would provided that the note accompanying
them wasn't too long. Pat said that he would limit his ex-
planatory note to five hundred words. Crotty also talked
about some influences within MacDiarmid's communism; on
his relationship with his father and how this may have given
rise to his scientific but compassionate socialism.

March 26th Last Friday the Civic Guards raided the Quay
Co-Op, a café and bookshop run by a friendly society of
vegetarians. The police claimed that the place was being used
as a centre for subversive activities. The only 'subversive'
activity in which the Co-Op engages is vegetarian cooking.
The Guards took away registers of members of the Co-Op,
but these registers are already on view in the Department
responsible for friendly societies. It is typical of the idiocy of
our authorities that they would create a great commotion,
and great public relations problems for themselves, when
they could easily have inspected the registers in the relevant
Government Department. Though it has occurred to me just
now that the Guards, all second sons of strong farmers,
would do anything to harass vegetarians, and all such enemies
of the Irish meat industry. In Ireland enemies of the beef

industry are even more suspect than terrorists. The power of the Irish meat industry, that great mafia of Meath and Westmeath ranchers, cattle dealers and live-cattle shippers, came home to me the other day when I read this shipping Cobh (Cove of Cork) log from 1847, the year of the Great Famine. 'In July of that year, while two million Irish peasants starved, the ship *Ajax* steamed out of Cork bound for Bristol, carrying 236 lambs, 60 boxes of salmon, 200 sacks of wheat, 276 boxes of eggs, 5 casks of ham, 25 bales of bacon, 296 sheep and 55 kegs of butter. Nothing would be allowed to interfere with the rights of the big grain and meat merchants to export their property. As the *Ajax* sailed away her crew might have noticed the inbound *Iona* from Philadelphia, a ship carrying 121 barrels of Indian corn for the starving Irish.' How disgusting is that fact from our shipping history? The starving would not be allowed to interrupt our lucrative food business, even if it saved their lives. The same interests, the big rancher interest, propelled us into the Common Market of Europe, a community that has destroyed working-class life in Cork Harbour by closing all our native industries. Ah, but it's been good for farming. In Ireland, truly, that's all that matters. Europe has left our working-class life in ruins. In Cork the once vibrant Marina Industrial Park is now a silent quarter of rusting machinery.

April 16th Yesterday Cathy and I went to a 'workshop' performance of a play by Hugo Meenan. We sat beside Tom Murphy, the playwright, and in front of Hugo who was bubbling with joy at the huge audience. The play was about a young Catholic couple in Derry and their involvement in the Republican movement. In many ways it was a 'Sticky' play, very anti-Provo, particularly in some of the longer speeches. A good performance. Afterwards Tom Murphy directed a discussion of the play. He workshopped the characterization and the sequencing of the drama, the 'structure of the happenings' as he called them. It was terrific to listen to him, dissecting — gently but absolutely firmly — both the structure and language of the piece.

Cathy and I bought a painting by Julie Kelleher for £380. We couldn't afford it but that has never prevented me from buying things in the past.

May 1st One thing I'm sure of and it's this: poverty robbed me of my childhood. When I write poems of memory I refer to a childhood I should have had. I had no such childhood. From the age of seven or eight I was too worried about the tensions within our family, about the alcoholism of my uncles, the blindness of my grandmother, the loneliness of my Aunt Maggie whose husband had gone to live and work in England, about the improvidence and the dreaminess of my father, about my mother's interminable struggle with shopkeepers and rent collectors. Such an unnatural burden at such an early age turned me into a solitary child. A solitary child doesn't have a childhood, certainly not in the normal way. I listen to people talking about their happy childhood memories — it's like listening to people who've visited a far-off planet.

May 2nd The Report of the New Ireland Forum is published. Another dead duck. This one was thought up by the SDLP to give them some authority in the face of the continuing electoral victories of Provisional Sinn Féin. Tonight on the television John Hume and Ian Paisley are arguing. They are so far apart they are hardly arguing: they are carrying on two separate monologues.

May 5th The other day Gay Byrne announced the death of Seamus Heaney in Seattle. He meant to say *Joe* Heaney, the distinguished singer from Donegal. What a bizarre error by our own Gay Byrne.

May 13th I wonder when I first seriously considered writing prose as well as poetry? When I was at university I had no time for novelists — I considered them to be mere story-tellers, narrators, without an aesthetic. The whole impetus of life at UCC was towards poetry. This was because our influential lecturers were poets, Montague, Lucy. Most of our tutors also wrote serious poetry (Crotty, O'Donoghue, Riordan): poets all. Apart from the novels of Molly Keane I must have been twenty-three before I read a novel completely. Before that I'd 'dipped' into Joyce, Faulkner, Hardy. I half-read more novels than anyone I know. There was Michael Ayrton's *The Maze Maker*, a brilliant novel, but I loved it because the author was a sculptor, not a novelist. At that time I didn't know that William Trevor was also a sculptor. When I was at college sculptors were 'hot' just as poets became 'hot' later — we lived in an atmosphere of John Behan, Moore, Epstein, Hepworth; they seemed like confirmations of the genius in John Hogan and Séamus Murphy. But it was the work of Márquez and Patrick White that convinced me that a novel could be a work of art. Both *The Tree of Man* and *One Hundred Years of Solitude* were the first entire books I accepted as works of art, achievements as great as poetry, books that could be considered 'verbal objects' to be apprehended in an aesthetic mode like poems.

May 18th An astonishing letter from William Shannon of the American-Irish Foundation. He tells me that I've won the Foundation's Literary Award. The prospect of sharing the same pedestal as Heaney, Dervla Murphy, Richard Murphy and Banville is not an easy one. But I am grateful to Bill Shannon who has always taken a great interest in my work.

June 16th Our sixth day in Greece. On Tuesday we had coffee with Dimitri Nollas in a café near Omonia Square. Earlier we visited the Acropolis and its museum: an amazing structure. On our first day in Greece we watched workers from the Communist Party, KKK, making preparations for a massive rally. Athens, like Dublin, is mutilated by developers.

Whole streets have been destroyed and the noise of rebuilding is everywhere. And in this atmosphere the twin smells of hot asphalt and dried, powdered concrete.

On the island of Crete, also, there is mutilation and decay. Especially in Iraklion where huge apartment blocks (that can't be more than 50 years old) with their beautiful wrought-iron balconies are boarded up or partially demolished. It's as if a whole race had disappeared — emigrated to America or Germany — and a new, more restless, race had taken its place.

Today we visited the tomb of the great Kazantzakis, a lavish garden set on a hill over his native city, and a simple wooden cross rising out of six massive slabs of rock.

June 21st Our last few days in Crete. On Monday we walked through the Gorge of Samaria in Western Crete. It was an exhausting hike of fifteen miles in intense heat. We emerged from the Gorge at a tiny village, Agia Roumeli, on the Libyan Sea. Cathy went for a swim after walking over a red-hot shingle beach. From this beach we took a caique to a village called Loutrón, then steamed on to Chora Sfakion. The spectacular clarity of the sea: one could see to the bottom even while the ship was moving into Chora Sfakion, the town from which we took a bus back to Iraklion.

Today visited Knossos and Heraklion Museum. A morning of amethyst, lapis luzuli, ivory, filigree gold, black stoneware — an immense cocktail of high style. Artefacts that Yeats would delightedly misinterpret.

June 24th Last week in Athens the playwright Hugh Leonard 'led' a classical tour of the city on behalf of Budget Travel. By all accounts the tour was a disaster. Leonard had no interest in the venture: the intense heat, too much ouzo went straight to his head making him petulant, moody and impatient with his clients. But there was one old lady in Hugh Leonard's group, a Mrs Grace from Tipperary, who provided some light relief. Having reached the summit of the Acropolis and having surveyed the magnificent ruins someone asked her what she thought of the whole wonderful scene. She replied, with an air of terrible pity, 'That whole bloody Acropolis is a ruin. Wasn't de Valera great to keep us out of the War?'

July 9th Spent most of the day at Mount Melleray Abbey where I went to collect Seán Dunne who was writing an article for *The Irish Press*. Had a long chat with Brother John, a very erudite and sensitive man.

July 21st At Molly Keane's 80th birthday party with Catherine. The Brigadier was there, David Keane, Sir Richard's son, Lady Katherine Dawnay, Baron de Breffny, and a horde of wealthy Americans. Molly was overcome with excitement; genuinely overcome. She was genuinely moved by the universal adulation, but also by the atmosphere created by a good cocktail party — such an atmosphere propels her back to her youth in the Roaring Twenties. I read a poem I'd composed about life at Belleville House and I proposed a toast to her health, and this pleased the Brigadier. Afterwards we sat in the living room of Sally's mother-in-law's house and chatted. Catherine huddled in a corner with her and came away delighted because Molly said to her that writing was hell, that she hated it, that it depressed her enormously to have to face the blank page every day. I think this gives Catherine the confidence to go on.

July 24th This morning brought a good post — the proofs of *The Non-Aligned Storyteller* as well as the small collection, *The Wishbone*, by Paul Muldoon from The Gallery Press. Peter Jay seems genuinely excited about the new book, feeling that it is as strong as *The Sorrow Garden*. This means more to me than anything else. Peter also very happy because the Anvil poet Peter Levi has been elected Professor of Poetry at Oxford.

July 26th Spent last evening at Dervla Murphy's house with Catherine. Patricia Cockburn was there, and Rachel, Dervla's daughter. Dervla was very excited about a new book she's doing on the African and Asian communities in Britain.

Patricia Cockburn told me a great anecdote about Sir John Keane — an old friend of his, Lady X, was terminally ill with cancer in the Bons Secours Hospital in Cork. At the time Sir John was a Senator in Dublin. The woman's family had been very careful to conceal her imminent death. Despite this the Lady received a letter from Sir John which went like this: 'Darling X, I hear you are dying. How awful! I should like to come and say goodbye to you because you are one of my dearest friends, but a complication has arisen which, when I explain it to you, I'm sure you'll understand. At the moment I'm following 'Mrs Dale's Diary' on the radio. I find that I cannot get down to Cork from Dublin without missing an episode of the serial. This is why I am writing to you to say goodbye. I know you will understand! Your dear friend, Jack Keane.'

August 12th Spent the weekend at Patricia Cockburn's house in Ardmore. And I spent most of the time in Claud's study weeding through his massive political library. Most of the books have been allowed to fall into a terrible condition; dust, cobwebs, dampness and grey mould on many volumes. Only the garden and the view over Ardmore Bay are magnificent. This was the library of a thinker, a polemicist, a man who didn't fetishize books, but saw books for what they are — information-instruments, collections of thoughts.

Last night a Catholic street protester was murdered by the RUC. More than thirty million people throughout the US saw the incident on network TV — an RUC officer firing a plastic bullet at point-blank range into the chest of a Catholic. Ulster, it's a bloody disaster.

August 25th I gave a reading with Seamus Heaney at the Yeats Summer School. A packed house, and a very select audience too, that included Donald Davie and Helen Vendler. Knowing that they had all come to listen to Heaney I read quickly and nervously. I gave a very bad account of myself. On my journey home from Sligo I visited Thoor Ballylee near Gort. A beautiful, peaceful place, with the bees still building in the masonry in the upper part of the tower. I saved some beech nuts and apple seeds from the Tower garden. I hope they'll germinate and grow.

September 3rd At Glenshelane today. The first signs of autumn, a cool breeze and the first red tinges on the leaves of the sugar maple. The Brigadier is in very good form but Anne was in a furious mood. His tightness with money has begun to annoy her. He is continuously trying to find ways to save money, even ways to make money which he doesn't need. Anne is at the end of her tether and I'm afraid that she may leave. If she does leave she will disgrace the Brigadier. It's such a disappointment to me that the Brigadier is so anxious about money: it means that he is not permitting himself to have a comfortable and indulgent old age. He can well afford any comfort; only last week he asked me to file away his latest spreadsheet from Panmure Gordon, his portfolio of common shares listed upon it, shares worth a great deal of money. He has many high-income bonds and the same again in investment trusts. I had a heated argument with him, telling him that he'll never be poor like the old gambling Duke of Leinster who lost everything in Monte Carlo. He told me that when he left the Army he had no money. I know for a fact that that isn't quite true, because at the outbreak of War when there was a threat of invasion he converted his holdings in English companies into American Depository Receipts. But he has worked hard in London and provided for himself, covering every eventuality. He has enough savings to cover even round-the-clock nursing if he had a stroke or heart attack. But he says tax and inflation is eating into everything, that he needs to be cautious as taxation in Ireland will get worse, not better. He sounded tortured as he said this, knowing that I didn't quite believe him. He absolutely hates not to be believed. He can't understand that any normal person would welcome such tax problems: such tax problems imply a very high income. But it is impossible to get through to him. I left the house having made him feel miserable and consequently I felt very miserable while driving back to Cork.

September 4th This morning, a really funny, gossipy letter from James Simmons. He has bounced back to life after years of personal troubles. Also, a letter from Aidan Mathews inviting me to stay with him when I get to Dublin.

September 14th A happy, momentous day in our lives. Catherine went to the Erinville Hospital to have an ultrasound scan. We saw our baby in her womb, its little hands and its heart pumping. To see a real baby, with its own heart and independent vascular system, was a powerfully reassuring thing. The radiographer, a Mrs McCarthy, was wonderfully enthusiastic and motherly. Please God everything will develop normally and without incident. There are twenty-six long weeks still to go.

September 20th Finished typing *The Solitude of the Party (Without Power)*. Tonight I typed out the dedication (to the Brigadier) and put the manuscript in an old envelope. It is finished. I don't care what happens to it from here on. I have kept my word. I have proved my fidelity to the past.

October 12th Listened to a marvellous BBC programme on Heaney, a really high-powered encomium with Edna Longley, Muldoon and Blake Morrison. As Peter Porter said in Cork last week Heaney is now the number one poet in the English language. Heaney himself was interviewed and said that he was now more committed to his private world and his poetic craft, rather than to the external world of politics and Ulster terror. But he emphasized that one can't escape the disturbed politics of Ireland. As if to prove this the IRA blew up a hotel in Brighton last night, killing four delegates to the Conservative Party conference and seriously injuring two Ministers. Mrs Thatcher, who was working on official papers until 3 a.m., had a narrow escape.

October 15th Cathy has begun to feel the baby moving in her womb. Yesterday it made one really terrific jump, taking her by surprise. I have never seen Cathy so happy or so full of wellbeing — it's as if the whole of the future had opened up and revealed its happiness to her. She had doubted the future so much.

November 1st Our neighbour, who was in his second year of studying for the priesthood in Maynooth Seminary, got a summer job in Killarney last year working in a restaurant. One night he was asleep in his bed when the young wife of the absent restaurant owner appeared at his bedside. When he was fully awake she removed her clothes slowly, saying, 'Look at me. This is what you're going to miss if you become a priest. Feel my breasts!' Our poor saintly young neighbour, who had never before seen bare breasts, not to speak of full female nakedness, began to scream with fright. The others who worked in the restaurant ran to his room and howled with laughter when they saw his predicament. The wife of the proprietor couldn't resist the temptation of a young priest-to-be. The next morning he hightailed it out of Killarney. A few months later he decided to leave the seminary. I met him the other day and he said to me that his curiosity had been aroused: 'Tom, I don't have the resolve of St Thomas Aquinas.'

November 24th The Non-Aligned Storyteller published last week. A fairly decent crowd at the launch party, including the Brigadier who braved a dangerous fog. Seán Lucy came, and Nancy McCarthy, Frank O'Connor's belovèd. Patricia Cockburn was there, and Sally Phipps, Molly Keane's daughter (they had both braved the same fog to get here). Montague gave a very good and generous speech. Everyone sang dirty songs until four in the morning. Mary Leland told me that Hamish Hamilton have accepted her first novel. She was on top of the world. This could be the beginning of a huge career for her. I hope it is.

November 26th Last Friday we went to dinner with Sally and George Phipps. George's ninety-year-old mother was there, as well as Ken Thompson and his wonderful wife. Sally has begun to write a novel. Words must be in her blood. Old Mrs Phipps spent the period 1914-1918 in London where her young husband worked at the War Office. She says she can remember air raids vividly; the memory of them still fills her with fright. Once, she looked out her bedroom window and saw a Zeppelin trapped between two searchlights. 'The most exciting image of my life,' she said. She remembers Queen Alexandra at Lismore early in the century. Listening to her one could easily feel that nothing had changed: that the British Empire still stood triumphant. 'I remember a Lady Butler,' she went on, 'who was out walking in her garden in Kenya when a hive of bees fell on top of her head. The Lady died that evening. A Mr Andrew has told me that there is nothing un-usual in this, for Kenya is full of bees . . . Well, there you are.' The conversation inevitably drifted towards politics, at the mention of which Mrs Phipps excused herself and left the table. Everybody, Irish and Anglo-Irish, in despair over the Summit meeting between Garret FitzGerald and Mrs Thatcher. The whole of Ireland is still trying to recover wind after Mrs T's pro-Unionist blows. Everyone agrees that there will be no movement while she is British Prime Minister.

December 5th In London for the launch of *The Non-Aligned Storyteller*. A packed reading at the Poetry Society, not for me but for Paul Muldoon with whom I was reading. Anthony Cronin there (after having had a conversation at Faber about his new novel), as well as Desmond Hogan, depressed about the sales of his novel, *A Curious Street*. In came Eddie Linden leading the tall and blind John Heath-Stubbs. After the Poetry Society I left for a reading at Oxford, held in a depressing place called The Old Fire Station. I read in a room that looked like the cloakroom of a public toilet. Fewer than twenty people in the audience, and five of those were officers of the Oxford University Poetry Society. Only Seamus Heaney can pull in the crowds in England (and Muldoon, his pulling power can't be denied). The students are all besotted by Heaney and wish to hear nothing from Ireland except what 'Mr Heaney' says and does. All in all a depressing day in Oxford. It helped to show me that Anvil Press Poetry and I, even when working together, have absolutely no pulling power and absolutely no ability to promote a book. At the Poetry Society I bought John Ashbery's *A Wave* and *Houseboat Days*. And in a new shop in Gloucester Road I found Stendhal's *The Life of Henry Brulard*. This has made my whole trip to England worthwhile. I cradled my precious Stendhal all the way from Piccadilly to Heathrow.

December 26th St Stephen's Day Yesterday when we had sat down for dinner it began to snow. It was a real snowstorm, heavy and persistent. Even my parents-in-law, who are in their sixties, were amazed by this huge blanket of snow. They couldn't recall such a perfectly white Christmas. Snow is a permanent source of enchantment because it is so rare here in the South.

December 28th Reading Hermione Lee's book on Elizabeth Bowen. Hermione L recognizes the ambivalent nature of the Anglo-Irish: their very ambivalence is the root of much of their fame and their reason for survival. It is impossible for history to eliminate what it cannot define. But this Anglo-

Irish ambivalance has led to much playacting and hypocrisy. I think there is a great deal of fiendishness and hypocrisy in Molly Keane — when she talks about 'our Army, our Navy, our Government' she means the English Army, English Navy, English Government etc. Yet when she goes to England she talks about her Irishness, her homeland etc.

December 29th Today a postcard from Bernard O'Donoghue, the Cork poet at Magdalen College, Oxford. He says that there was a terrifically positive reaction to my reading at the terrible Old Fire Station. Also, a frenetic note from Dervla Murphy (sent Christmas Eve) saying that she had just been opening her mail received in the last six weeks. She had been trying to finish her book so that all correspondence was ignored. 'The distraction of the daily intrusion from the outside world increases the amount of concentration needed to get on with what one is doing.' I wish I had Dervla's ability to say no, that singleminded determination to cut everything out of one's life so that one could finish a book.

December 31st I wrote fewer poems this year than any other year since I began to write. And this — despite the fact that I had a whole year free from the City Library! But I finished *The Solitude of the Party* and published *The Non-Aligned Storyteller.*

1985

January 2nd

> *I think that only heroes deserve a real biography, but that the history of a poet is not to be presented in such a form . . . The poet gives his whole life such a voluntarily steep incline that it is impossible for it to exist in the vertical line of biography where we expect to meet it.*
> — Pasternak, *Safe Conduct*

January 10th On RTÉ Radio's *Appraisal* programme, recording from the Union Quay studios. This morning a letter from America with $2,000 from the American-Irish Foundation. God bless their noble hearts, and God bless the triumphant dollar.

January 27th An unenthusiastic review of *The Non-Aligned Storyteller* in today's *Sunday Tribune*. The reviewer dismisses the Party poems as too vague to be of use. This poor review, coupled with Bill Wall's forthcoming bad review for *The Connacht Tribune* really depresses me. I have worked for years to construct this metaphor of the Party — to *construct* the Party as a possible metaphor, the way Roethke constructed his greenhouses. Yet two reviewers have failed to go beyond the image of politics to see it all as a *metaphor*. All they can see is the politics, the rhetoric. Depressing.

February 5th Phone call from John Montague who has been asked to edit a book of Cork writing for the 'Cork800' celebrations. Also a strange phone call from a film-maker called Sé Merry Doyle who wants to make a film on my work, but

particularly on my poem 'The Phenomenology of Stones'. I
treated this call as a hoax. Yet another phone call from the
Brigadier who had told Molly Keane about *The Solitude of
the Party* — Molly said that she wanted to see the novel
immediately. Yesterday a note from Peter Jay to tell me that
Richard Cohen (of Hodder & Stoughton) had moved to
Century publishers. This editor is bringing *The Solitude of
the Party* along with him. If Century publish me I'll be on
the pig's back — though not critically.

March 1st I saved letters from Theo and the Brigadier. Someday these letters might form the basis of a work of fiction,
possibly *A Child of Camus*.

March 17th Today Seán Dunne told me that there was a good
review of my book in *The Observer*. The other day I learned
that there are good reviews coming up in *Studies* and in *The
Irish Literary Supplement*; so that all is not lost. *The Non-
Aligned Storyteller* may yet bring me some joy.

March 28th Today a long and detailed letter from Richard
Cohen about *The Solitude of the Party (Without Power)*. He
is interested in the novel but he has discovered very serious
flaws in characterization and structure. I will probably have
to rewrite the entire first half of the book; more than 40,000
words. The prospect of having to do this all over again really
depresses me. But I understand that it is in the rewriting that
a writer is made. I *must* begin again.

Reading Eliot's 'Four Quartets' and Ashbery's *Self-Portrait
in a Convex Mirror*. It is in those 'Four Quartets' that Eliot
establishes the primacy of his American-ness. He may have
become an Englishman socially, but he couldn't shed the
wide adventurous intellectualism of his American education.

April 29th Still no writing done. The last two chapters of
Parables of Happiness still remain unwritten.

May 18th A wonderful review of *The Non-Aligned Story-teller* by Bernard O'Donoghue in *The Poetry Review*.

May 30th Yesterday I took Thomas Tranströmer, the Swedish poet, to Mallow station so that he could get a train to Tralee. He had given a reading in Cork the previous night — a reading attended by only twelve people and constantly interrupted by noises from a hotel kitchen and a Salvation Army recital. Tranströmer took all these vicissitudes with good humour. Afterwards, when John Montague remarked that he expected all Swedes to be depressive and dour, Tranströmer replied: 'You've been watching too much Bergman.' He is an immensely warm man, always self-deprecating, and his seriousness is tinged with irony. He looks like a retired tennis coach, or a very bookish naval officer on leave. His latest collection has been published in an edition of twenty thousand copies in Sweden, yet from his manner one would think that he had just published a single pamphlet late in life. He says that his main literary gift is patience: he writes only five poems a year.

While I drove him and his wife to Mallow we had a long, deep, searching chat. He was anxious to know about the tensions between various major poets in Ireland; between Heaney, Kinsella, Montague and Murphy. He wanted to know what I thought of their reputations and their poetry. (I wonder is he a member of the Swedish Academy, or is he preparing a report for that Academy?) He then asked for news of the young poets who had attended his reading. 'Are all these poets very ambitious? Do they hate each other?' When I said that we all seemed to get along he was pleased. He said he had a great longing to return to the days before he became a well-known poet: then he might enjoy friendships with fellow Swedish poets. Today, however, he has few friends among Swedish poets, he said. He has done nothing wrong but some invisible force connected with literary reputations has crept in and driven the middle-aged writers apart.

It happens in every country, in every literary culture, he said. At Mallow he boarded a filthy, rickety train without a dining car. A beautiful man: physically beautiful and emotionally sublime. Today at 10.40 p.m. I finished the final chapter of *P of H*. Much work to be done, but the story is told. I feel an immense sense of relief.

June 3rd

> *The whole early part of my life was poisoned with egotism, a reverse egotism, of course, beginning with self-consciousness. And then gradually I began to lose it.*
> — Steinbeck, *Letters* (1935)

June 15th The other day I heard that Peadar O'Donnell was staying in a guest house near my flat. He was in Cork on Irish Academy of Letters business with John Montague. I went to see him while he was having breakfast in bed. Very frail, a peculiar elderly face like the face of an old woman. 'Hand me my teeth,' he said when I sat by his bedside. 'I can't talk without my teeth.' He was delighted when I told him that I knew Claud Cockburn. He said that Claud was a man he had always wanted to meet. He was saddened when I told him that Claud had died. Then we spoke about his own novels. He said that *The Big Windows* was one of his favourites. The germ of the book had been in his head for over twenty years. He first got the idea while he was on the run during the Civil War. He was sheltering in a house in a valley in Donegal and noted that the house had very big windows. He was told that the young wife in the cottage was from the islands and she had been depressed by the lack of light when she came into the mainland. Immediately he understood her need for big windows — he was from the islands himself and knew that an islander would miss the light of the islands above everything else. What also struck him about the house was the fact that the young wife and her mother-in-law seemed to get on very well together. He said it was the first cottage he'd ever lived in where two women lived in harmony. Those two ideas: the big windows and the loving in-laws, stayed in his mind and became a novel. I gave him a copy of *The Non-Aligned Storyteller* because of the Claud poem. Yet I know I'll not reprint that poem. Claud was a Stalinist, an unrepentant propagandist during the Spanish Civil War. The whole poem is a lie because it sets Claud up as a metaphor for the truth-teller, the chivalrous journalist etc. All untrue.

July 10th Today, an appointment with Malcolm Tyrrell of Cohalan Downing and Associates of South Mall. Our first move toward a house of our own.

July 24th Another radio interview today, the second discussion on poetry in a week. Next month I read at the Kilkenny Arts Festival. All these public activities yet not one copy of my poetry book in any bookshop in Ireland. Paul Durcan's new book has been chosen as the Winter Choice of the Poetry Book Society. At last he has had some luck after going through a long personal purgatory. Today, also, there's an essay on the poetry scene in Ireland by Eavan Boland in *The Irish Times*. She says of my new book: 'particularly eloquent and original in its approach. He canvasses the whole subject of collective pressure, the idea of the dehumanizing effects of loyalty to a Party, to the State. His is a new and important voice in Irish poetry.'

July 26th Cathy met Molly Keane's daughter, Sally, in Oliver Plunkett Street. Sally said that Patricia Cockburn is walking ten feet tall at the moment because she has just received a fan letter from Graham Greene about her autobiography.

July 28th Meet Seán Dunne at Mount Melleray Abbey at 7 p.m.

July 31st At Cohalan Downing, a deposit of £3,200 for a house. The money thanks entirely to the American-Irish Foundation. Well, they can always say, 'we housed an Irish poet.'

August 19th Thousands of people have been flocking to a Marian Shrine near Kinsale where a statue of Our Lady has been seen moving. Elsewhere in Ireland other statues have been moving. There was a report in *The Irish Times* this week about Yeats's vasectomy operation. He thought that this surgery would help him to have an erection but it did nothing physically for him. Admittedly, after the operation Yeats's poetry enjoyed a permanent erection!

August 23rd RTÉ Radio, *Liam Nolan Show* at 2 p.m.

August 24th At Kilkenny Arts Week. My reading was at 10.30 p.m, an ungodly hour to listen to a poet.

August 28th Seán Dunne at Mount Melleray Abbey. John Montague after dinner, and Theo on the way home. Deposit for our house, £3,707. Tim and Kitty Coakley, my parents-in-law, have offered to help us get over the line on our deposit. No offers of help from the Brigadier. I thought he might help me at this critical moment. No such luck. He absolutely dreads parting with money. Is this a trait born of historic Anglo-Irish insecurity?

Sept 28th In England for the last week — on a poetry tour to promote Seán Dunne's Munster anthology: Oriel Gallery, Cardiff, Battersea Arts Centre, Bolton Institute, Lancashire, a pub in Bracknell, Berkshire. By now exhaustion has set in. Seán and Paddy Galvin want to take a flight home from London and not wait for the boat. The tour has been a 'minor' success. We've had quite respectable audiences, with the exception of Cardiff. Even Battersea Arts Centre has turned out for us. And this trip has given us a chance to see England, to appreciate the vastness of the place and the intense nature of each individual English life. When we journeyed from Manchester to Bolton we all felt that we were voyaging on another planet — the train moved through a grey and black landscape of factory roofs, billowing power stations, endless vein-like railway tracks and disused cotton mills. The cotton mills are built of red brick but this has become blackened with pollution and general decay. 'Imagine travelling to work every day in that,' Paddy Galvin remarked. 'I'd commit suicide. You'd have to commit suicide.' Yet Bolton is a place of culture. They've had a series of literary readings here for many years. This week they had us, next week Maeve Binchy and Bernard MacLaverty. We took the 'Flying Scotsman' to Newcastle to read at the Morden Tower. A good audience, but a more laid-back and cynical one. Newcastle poetry lovers have seen poets come and go so that we had to fight for their attention. In Newcastle, also, I read a one-line review of *The Non-Aligned Storyteller* in *Stand* by Terry Eagleton. *Stand* seems to specialize in one-liners.

At Greenwich there was a literary party to celebrate the anthology. The usual Irish crowd: Desmond Hogan (very friendly, very inquisitive) with a new companion, Anthony Cronin and Anne Haverty, Richard Holmes and Blake Morrison and a host of Anvil poets. I had hoped that Richard Cohen of Century would turn up, but he didn't. This is disappointing because it may mean that he has lost interest in my novel. Century has bought Hutchinson and moved from Greek St. They are now ex-Directory. Met Gregory O'Donoghue, Mossy Riordan and Matthew Sweeney. Matthew looked worried and tense whereas Gregory O'D seemed more relaxed and whole than I ever remembered him. Gregory talks of 'a big book of really international poetry'.

The tiredness and loneliness of Paddy Galvin prevailed so that we didn't wait for the abominable *Sealink* ferry from Fishguard. We took a flight from Heathrow. It was Seán

Dunne's first flight. He was as excited as a little boy. After we had booked in and paid for our tickets I said to Seán, 'We'd better go to the check-in desk and get our boarding cards.' Seán answered, 'Will we have to pay more money there?' Paddy Galvin nearly missed the flight because a part of the Underground was closed off after a night of rioting in Brixton.

October 2nd Nuala Ní Dhomhnaill wasn't very impressed by Peter Jay and the rest of the Anvil crowd. They were too quiet to satisfy her marvellous gregariousness. She complained thus to Seán Dunne, but Seán replied that Peter was 'reserved'.

'Reserved for who?' asked Nuala in a flash. And in Peter's copy of *The Munster Poets* Nuala had written 'Go dtuga Dia ciall duit' — 'May God give you sense.'

Met Theo on Patrick Street. He was planning to sue a playwright who had insulted him on television. The things Theo does with his energy. I could have shaken him.

The other day a man came into the library to tell me about the Éamon de Valera Forest in Israel. In 1966 the Irish-Jewish community collected funds to plant ten thousand trees near Kafr Kanna in Galilee, beside the village where Jesus performed his miracle of water and wine. Ten years ago six saplings from the new Israeli forest were brought back to Ireland and, after quarantine in the Botanic Gardens in Glasnevin, they were planted in the grounds of Áras an Uachtaráin. I wonder have they survived the Irish climate, are they still growing there? I'd love to go to Israel and see this de Valera Forest. I'd love to visit Israel for many reasons, not least to experience the cosmopolitan atmosphere of Tel Aviv, now a beautiful, lively ocean city of the Levant.

October 6th Captain Kelly, of the Arms Trial, a member of the Fianna Fáil National Executive, came to see me last night. A quiet man, totally dominated by his fiercely intelligent wife

— or maybe he just happens to be completely in love with her. He says that nothing will come of the Anglo-Irish discussions because Charlie Haughey will scuttle them after the next election. He wants to run for the Senate. Yet he doesn't know which panel to run on. He doesn't have any clear-cut policies. I told him that he should concentrate on (a) employment and (b) emigration. He won't achieve anything if he doesn't concentrate his efforts. But I suspect that he has had enough, he has little ambition left. After the vile and treacherous way our Government and nation has treated him he would really prefer a quiet life. His relationship with the Army is ruined, and all of the companionship and friendship of other Army officers and their wives, and the powerful Army officer social networks in Irish life, have been closed to him and his children. If this were the nineteenth century, a man as gifted as he, victim of a *cause célèbre*, would go to America and become editor of a prosperous New York or Washington newspaper (and write brilliant and immortal memoirs in exile). In old age he would be the honoured guest at a hundred Irish-American dinners. However, we live in a mean time. While he was in our flat I felt touched by history; I felt that I was in the presence of the betrayed Captain Dreyfus: I had encountered a man of the most profound honour, a man whose entire being is the product of excellent Irish Army officer training. Will Captain Kelly ever be exonerated? Probably not, because to exonerate him fully and offer him compensation the authorities would have to admit that both a Government minister and an Army Colonel committed perjury at a sworn State Tribunal. So a brilliant Captain of unimpeachable honour is sacrificed, and even a seat in the Senate wouldn't save him now because the State has its permanent interests. These interests can't be undermined, and certainly not for the sake of something as trivial as one person's honour and good name.

Robert Graves has died. News agency reports refer to him as 'the author of the two biographies of Claudius who also wrote poems'. This would disgust poor Graves who saw himself as the quintessential poet, the poet-savant. It is over ten years since I dined with him in The Oyster Tavern. Even then he was becoming senile. He spent the last few years of his life copying out his old poems into blank notebooks. A fate worse than death — so that death, in coming, was a kindness.

And Philip Larkin died last week. Larkin paraded as the anti-savant, the ordinary man's poet. The poet Seamus Deane when asked why Larkin 'buried himself in a library in Hull' replied, 'Well, he was a Librarian; that means his life was a form of research into lower middle-class squalor.' John Montague phoned yesterday. He has just returned from a stint in Albany, NY. He says that all the poets of America are angry about something, except Gary Snyder who retains a kind of courteous curiosity about the rest of the world. Snyder I imagine as a Buddhist who lives among wolves in the forests of the American West. But Montague is deeply suspicious of such sanctities.

December 15th Delivered the Brigadier to the airport for his annual pilgrimage to Antibes. And later, a poetry reading at Kilcrone House near Cloyne.

December 27th Mossy Riordan, home from London, called and brought news of Paul Durcan's great success in England. With *The Berlin Wall Café* as a PBS Choice his tour of poetry societies are well attended. It's ironic that Paul's new-found fame should have sprung from a great personal unhappiness. *The BWC* is without doubt his best work; all of the zany perceptions, surreal images and Bob Dylan-ish phrases so discordantly assembled in his previous books have now been perfectly orchestrated. Like Heaney he has achieved a very unique personal technique. So now one can say with certainty that Ireland has two irreplaceable poetic voices: compared to Heaney and Durcan all of the other poets blur into one mediocre iambic haystack.

December 28th In his *Paris Review* interview Carlos Fuentes says that it was the poets who delineated the South American tradition, and it was the poets, also, who fed the language with their radicalism. It could be said that the poetic radicalism of Heaney and Durcan is the greatest achievement of our contemporary literary scene. Again, it is the poets who have led the way.

1986

January 26th Last week there were traffic jams in the city as over 3,000 people flocked into town to join Des O'Malley's Progressive Democrats Party. The disgruntled middle-class of Fianna Fáil have risen up. I have never seen so many Jaguars parked on Wellington Road.

March 17th Spent two days in Galway where I gave a poetry reading. A small crowd, about fifteen people. I was disappointed with this until I attended the reading given by Gerry Dawe and Douglas Dunn — they had an audience of only eleven souls. Where has the Galway poetry audience gone, for Chrissake?

I had breakfast with Sorley MacLean, one of the most genial poets now alive. Sorley has hopes that the Irish Academy of Letters might nominate him for the Nobel Prize. I think he's meeting a group of Celtic scholars at the Institute for Advanced Studies to advance his Nobel cause. After breakfast I took Douglas Dunn and his wife, Lesley, to Coole Park and Thoor Ballylee. Dunn himself carries visible signs of having endured a great agony. He has become totally grey, wizened and even stooped like an old man. His new wife is several inches taller than he and she looks like a young girl out of a convent school as they walk together. Hopefully she will nurse him out of grief and back to full vigour. Yeats's tower was closed but I managed to gather some beech nuts from his garden so that she could plant them in Scotland. At Coole Park Dunn wanted to see the lake where the swans had inspired WBY. We found it, a disappointing bleak body of water. But Coole is very well maintained, with barbed wire protecting Lady Gregory's famous tree, and very impressive lawns and high walls. It was indeed a home of the high gentry. The house is gone, of course, allowed to be knocked down by the de Valera government in an act of appalling vengefulness against a Cumann na nGael Big House.

March 29th Yesterday at Glenshelane with Catherine and Kate Inez. The Brigadier tells me that John Welcome, the novelist and sports writer and bosom companion of the Duke of Leinster, is planning to write a biographical novel on Lord Edward FitzGerald. This annoyed me. I had felt that the Geraldines (at least the *Leinster* Geraldines) were a cordoned-off part of my imaginative territory.

April 19th Charles Haughey gave a brilliant Presidential speech to the Fianna Fáil AGM. He was confident, relaxed and in control. It has taken him a decade to come in from the cold, but he has triumphed. His speech was spectacularly Nationalist and hostile to the Anglo-Irish Agreement. If FF gets back into office the SDLP will be completely isolated and Sinn Féin will triumph in the North. In *The New York Times Review of Books* Conor Cruise O'Brien has a vitriolic anti-Nationalist tirade disguised as a review of Captain Feehan's biography of Bobby Sands. Cruise O'Brien is out of control, although I admire his crazed dissent. It's so like my own sense of detachment from Ireland and Irish establishment values. But there's something unhinged about him, as if he was writing while he was drunk. I wonder does he drink a lot?

April 29th The Brigadier came to tea the other day. He's horrified by Reagan's bombing of Libya. He was the Assistant Director of Plans at the War Office when Anthony Eden had the madcap idea to take the Suez Canal from Nasser. The Brigadier thinks Reagan is obsessed with Gaddafi just as Eden was obsessed with Nasser. The invasion of Suez led to the complete decline of British influence in the Middle East.

What worries the Brigadier is that the whole Arab world will now unite against the US. He thinks that squandering Arab friendship will be the single greatest mistake ever made by the Americans, and that they'll live to regret it as Eden did. 'The U.S. has been the oldest friend of the Arab world,' said the Brigadier, 'what a disaster to damage that relationship.'

June 2nd In Dublin six Loreto nuns were burned to death in a convent fire. Horrific scenes; charred ruins, pathetically small body bags. Like an event in the mind of Gerard Manley Hopkins.

June 6th At Listowel Writers' Week for a day. Met Montague who is giving the short-story workshop. He had a very funny story about a visit that he and Michael Hartnett made to Amsterdam. They were both wearing leather jackets — Hartnett had borrowed his from his wife. They strolled through the red-light district and finally went into a seedy restaurant for coffee. They were seated for about ten minutes, chatting away, when the proprietor of the establishment came over and asked, 'You are enjoying your honeymoon, yes?'

June 12th A visit to Dublin to record some scripts for radio. Met Rory Brennan and John F Deane and Hugo Williams. The two Irish poets were furious with Paul Muldoon's new anthology of contemporary Irish poetry. But I admire Muldoon for publishing only what he likes, even if what he likes excludes me. I like that: Muldoon admires very few poets, and none among our Southern generation. He has high standards for himself and he only publishes to those standards. John F wants to publish my next collection under the Dedalus imprint. Hugo was perplexed and exhausted by our literary politics. At the end of the evening he turned to me and said, 'This really is a different country, isn't it? It really is foreign?' He meant Ireland. Until he came to Dublin he saw Ireland as a part of the United Kingdom, as a sort of troublesome

English rural district far out to the west. It is always a shock for an educated English person to suddenly come upon the atmosphere of Ireland, to come upon Ireland's English-speaking but awkward and garrulous distinctiveness.

June 14th At dinner with Mark Bence-Jones and his poet wife, Jill. Walked round the garden to see the magnificent stand of rhododendrons. One species of rh. in particular was fascinating, a variety called 'Empress of India' that was developed at Glenville by Henry Hudson. An incredible fragrance, very like narcissi. Mark fears that this rhododendron is dying and wondered if I would take some cuttings.

After dinner we looked through an album of photographs that belonged to Elizabeth Bowen's cousin, Noreen Butler of Kilkenny. Fascinating snaps of parties at Bowenscourt in the 1930s. Group photos that included Stuart Hampshire, Eudora Welty, Iris Murdoch, 'Eddy' Sackville-West and Evelyn Waugh. One page of photos in particular took my fancy — shots of a boating trip on the Blackwater near Cappoquin and one of a shopping trip in Cappoquin (Molly Keane and Eliz Bowen outside either Mansfield's or Russell's shop).

July 2nd It is now four days since the Government's Divorce Referendum was defeated. A chilling, extraordinary victory for the New Right. Most of the people I know, most intellectuals and all Southern Protestants, are utterly depressed. The Catholic Church and its moral Gestapo has returned with a vengeance. Many intellectuals are talking about leaving the country. This week the Australian Embassy released details of more relaxed immigration requirements — a fine piece of witty Aussie timing. This defeat of the referendum (and the cynicism of Charles Haughey during its debates) has sent a chill of fear down the spine of everyone who believes in a pluralist society.

July 20th A report in the *Daily Telegraph* the other day about

Philip Larkin's will. Larkin directed that all his manuscripts, diaries, unpublished poems etc, be burned after his death. This request very much in keeping with Larkin's sardonic isolation, yet a scandalous, selfish request from a poet who was also a librarian, a man who even published an essay on the difficulty that British university librarians have in getting authors' manuscripts. Larkin left over £250,000 in his estate, extraordinary wealth for a poet. If one compares this with the poverty of a great poet like Seán Ó Ríordáin one soon understands that there is no justice in this world.

September 25th At a launch party in the Metropole Hotel for David Marcus's new novel, *A Land Not Theirs*. Jack Lynch, the former Taoiseach, launched the book. Jack has hardly changed over the years: his eyes weak and watery, his language woolly, ungrammatical and imprecise. The occasion was loaded with emotional power for David — the last time he spoke to a public gathering in Cork was when he said goodbye to Jewish and Gentile friends thirty-two years ago. Today, all the literati there: Bryan MacMahon, Seán Lucy, Mary Leland, Tim Cramer of *The Cork Examiner*, Seán Dunne, Emma Cooke etc. But also TV cameras, photographers and reporters. The entire event surging with emotion and love for old Jewish Cork.

September 30th Met Costa-Gavras, the Greek film director. A surprisingly unglamorous man. I had expected a great giant of a man, like Zorba, but Costa-Gavras is small and neat with very conventional clothes. He is very apologetic about his new film, 'Family Council', made in French and very funny. He told me that people expect him to be serious and political at all times. 'Family Council' is only one aspect of his character, but it is a genuine aspect. At the Film Festival I also met another Greek Director, Olga Panagopoulou. She knew Dimitris Nollas in Athens. It is a small world, this Greek world. So like the Irish world.

December 1st I don't think Sebastian Barry will ever be for-given for creating his new anthology, *The Inherited Bound-aries*. It is a selection of work from the younger poets of the Irish Republic. All the Ulster poets, or should I say poets of *Northern Ireland,* are excluded. The Ulster poet, Matthew Sweeney, is included because he's from Donegal, in Ulster but also in the Irish Republic. It is a curiously thrilling book, with a terrific selection of my own work, though no Irish language poets — which is a great pity. Any selection of Irish poetry nowadays that doesn't include, for example, Nuala Ní Dhomhnaill, Liam Ó Muirthile and the young Louis de Paor is a deficient book. But its exclusion of Belfast poets has created outrage, and this outrage will kill the book be-cause our Ulster poets now control both Dublin and British commentary on all Irish literary projects. The other day Paddy Galvin called it 'The *Blueshirt* Anthology', and Theo agreed with him. Both Paddy and Theo are devotees of Ulster republicanism. But it is a beautiful book. And to see my poems printed on strong off-white paper in clear, crisp Gallimard type is wonderful.

December 10th At RTÉ in Dublin yesterday to record a dis-cussion on 'poets' language' organized by Rory Brennan. Anthony Cronin, Julie O' Callaghan and I were on the panel. A woolly discussion full of completely inadequate quotations and statements like 'Humour is a marginal thing in poetry' (my statement) and 'There's poetry in everything in life' (Cronin's statement). In the foyer of the studio we bumped into Seamus and Marie Heaney. They were rushing to do a special Christmas recording. H looked tired and slightly bothered, Marie beautiful and relaxed.

Afterwards we went to Cronin's flat, a small bachelor's pad in the centre of Dublin. The flat a complete mess; the sink full of greasy dishes, the sideboard and table uncleaned, the floor littered with week-old papers, all the chairs covered with books and letters: the epitome of domestic chaos. Long political discussion about Fianna Fáil and Charlie Haughey. Cronin a great admirer of Charlie, but not of Charlie's political viewpoint so much as Charlie's energy and ambition. He says that Haughey is an outsider, hated by 'Dublin society' — that politics for him is a form of over-compensation, as poetry is for weaker souls. This connection between art and politics fascinates Cronin. He says that Charlie will abolish the Ministry of Arts — that that Department was only created to give Fine Gael's Ted Nealon a higher profile in his constituency, thereby creating a chance of winning a third Dáil seat there. Cronin thinks Charlie will turn Arts into a Department of Technology.

The talk soon turned to Cork poets, to Patrick Galvin whom Cronin admires, and to Seán Lucy and John Montague. Cronin's distaste for Montague knows no bounds. It must be a UCD thing, a legacy issue since their student-poet days. Out of politeness I allowed him to go on too long about the megalomania of J M — I should have been more loyal, less provincial, in my acquiescence to the metropolitan view. Cronin said that both Montague and Lucy have an exaggerated view of themselves. He cited as an example what happened to Noel Pearson's plan to give poets who wrote elegies for the composer Ó Riada a three-minute spot on his Dublin theatre show. Heaney was very pleased with this; but Montague and Lucy wrote a joint letter to Pearson protesting that they required a much greater 'input' into the Ó Riada project as they knew Ó Riada so intimately. Pearson's reaction was to cancel the whole idea, so that all poets lost a chance of massive exposure. Cronin says that this behaviour is typical of provincial writers. They lack a sense of proportion because they don't come into frequent contact with other established names. A poet who lives in Dublin soon learns to accept that he is one among many talents. When he spoke thus I thought of Daniel Corkery's defensiveness and lack of proportion. It was the fear of that kind of arrogance that drove Ó Faoláin and O'Connor out of Cork. I must guard against this, this Cork danger. It is important to stay engaged in a national conversation, to have a national perspective; not to slide into a doleful, provincial arrogance.

December 30th Harold Macmillan has died. He was a compassionate Conservative, patriotic, flamboyant, slightly sentimental — in other words, the best kind of Englishman. There was a lunchtime discussion about him on BBC Radio while I collected the Brigadier at the airport: the Brigadier, tanned and relaxed after Christmas on the Riviera, was moved by Macmillan's death. Mac embodied so much of what was good in English life. The Brigadier's generation, those who were youngish officers in the War, had their heyday too when Macmillan was in his political prime. They were the generation who 'never had it so good'.

1987

January 30th Had a long conversation with Theo about Anthony Cronin's *Irish Times* articles. It is very true that Cronin is the only literary intellectual in Ireland right now: an intellectual in the French sense, in that he is interested in the play of ideas and their connection with political action. Whatever intellectual education we got as poets came from reading Cronin week after week in *The Irish Times*. His *Viewpoint* became our viewpoint. Our respect for Cronin is so absolute that our reading of other poets is filtered, some-how, through Cronin's commentary. And Cronin's closeness to bad-boy Charles Haughey only raises his prestige in Theo's eyes. But Cronin and Edward McGuire are strange bedfellows for a Peronist politician like Haughey. In another era and in a more cosmopolitan land Anthony Cronin would be a famous Goncourt. He would be both Goncourt brothers, combined into one.

February 1st Theo and Suzanne came to lunch. Theo wants a handwritten poem for Amnesty International.

My new friend, Pat Neville, who is an ESB technician, is probably Ireland's greatest living wine expert.

February 7th Reading at Collins Bookshop in Carey's Lane. I wonder if Seán Lucy will go to America? What a fool he was to separate from Pat, the one person in the world who could drive sense into him, the one woman who loved him unconditionally, for all his flaws, vanities and shortcomings. What a fool he is to give up everything in UCC's English Department. Being Chair of an English Department can be unbearable, all that testosterone and oestrogen of young lecturers from the best families of Munster competing for honour and attention, but it can't be as unbearable as becoming entirely disconnected from academic life. Seán is, first and foremost, a teacher. For him, *not* to teach would be a kind of death. Montague, on the other hand, could take it or leave it.

March 10th Frank O'Connor's twenty-first anniversary. A reading at Triskel Arts Centre.

March 26th London. Visited Justerini & Brooks and Christopher's Wine Shops. Queen Mary's Rose Garden in Regent's Park. Elizabeth Bowen and Charles Ritchie in my thoughts everywhere I go.

May 11th As a favour to Molly Keane I visited Mrs Pegge, Sir Richard Keane's sister, for a long discussion about her poetry. She lives in a dilapidated fisherman's cottage in Mount Rivers, near Cappoquin. She has been dismissed by the Keane family since she married a Catholic English poet years ago. From a poetry point of view the Keanes got it absolutely right. Bad aristocratic poets should never be encouraged and Mrs Pegge is really bad.

May Paris. Michel Deguy's lecture at the Pompidou Centre 'C'est vrai que la modernité n'existe pas — La modernité existe pour le critique, mais n'exist pas pour la poète.'

June 15th Catherine's Listowel Fiction Prize: I was more excited about it than herself. For me it was a vindication of how I feel about her work. But she needs to write more stories. She needs to do this as urgently as possible.

November 4th Last night, the launch of John Montague's novella *The Lost Notebook*. As Pat Crotty said to me, it should have remained lost. A large crowd at Triskel, with Francis Stuart doing the introductions. Barry Callaghan, the ebullient

Canadian also present. No bad vibes: everybody extremely happy. Seán Lucy took Seán Dunne and me aside to tell us that he had sold papers, including some of our letters, to Buffalo University. Seán Dunne was shocked to hear that somebody had sold his private letters. I said to Lucy that it was ironic that he should get money for letters that were definitely begging letters from us young poets.

December 14th A night ago, a farewell dinner for Theo at the Triskel Arts Centre. He is going to live in Dublin after Christmas.

December 28th Reading the autobiography *The Village of Longing* by George O'Brien and *The Island of the White Cow* by Deborah Tall. Both books are extremely well written. O'Brien's book — he's a Professor at Georgetown University — is an account of growing up in Lismore, very literary, gifted and perfectly honest. Deborah Tall, a young American poet, now a Professor back in her native America, went to live on Inishbofin with Tom Mac Intyre in the 1960s. Her book is the most wonderful of all the island books that I've read. It has created a stir in Dublin literary circles. Whenever life is recorded accurately in Ireland it creates a scandal — we are so unaccustomed to honesty, particularly honesty in literary and interpersonal matters. What is it about us in Ireland that we fear these memoirs and diaries? We react to published memoirs as if they were all written as deliberate betrayals. You meet no person more outraged in Ireland than someone who's been remembered in a published book or diary. Why are we like this? Is it some deep peasant mistrust of openness, a horror of someone educated divulging tribal secrets? Is it our Catholic obsession with the secrecy of the confessional? Deborah Tall is now hated among the middle-aged men of literary Dublin. How lucky, and wise, she was to escape from them. She has dared to speak her mind. She has dared to apply her American sense of freedom to the repressed confidences of Irish life. Today I am all for Deborah Tall and her *Island of the White Cow*. I salute her today because I too believe in keeping a record. Bless you, lovely Deborah Tall.

1988

An intellectual? Yes. And never deny it. An intellectual is someone whose mind watches itself. I like this, because I am happy to be both halves, the watcher and the watched.
— Camus, *Notebooks 1935-1951*

March 25th I spent St Patrick's Day with Montague. He is very frustrated and is doing his damnedest to get out of Cork. 'Ah, well, it's too late, too late for so many things,' he says ruefully.

May 17th At Glenshelane. A glorious day, temperatures in the region of 75°F. Anne full of hilarious stories about 'The Mission' given by a young ('and so handsome') Redemptorist in Cappoquin.

'There are more lunatics per square mile in Ireland than in any other country in the world,' was his opening remark. He condemned the hysteria of the crowds who've been flocking to the site of the apparitions of the Virgin at Mount Melleray. At one stage the 'Mission' priest said that he had been told that the Blessèd Virgin had spoken to one of the children. 'What did Our Lady say to you?' he asked the child.

'Our Lady said that Ballyduff would win the next County Final,' the girl replied, in all sincerity.

But the young girl couldn't say whether it was Ballyduff Upper or Ballyduff Lower. There is something profoundly ironic in that heavenly imprecision, but the young priest didn't seem to understand the irony of this.

June 3rd The other day a priest came into the Mayfield

Library and we began to chat about good novels and good writers. After a while he revealed his identity. He was Fr Walter Hegarty, the author of a very successful novel, *The Price of Chips*, and other fairly successful books. He said that he had stopped writing when he became a Redemptorist priest. 'It's difficult to keep two spiritual lives going. Writing is an obsession; it has to be obsessive like the life of a contemplative priest.' He said he lived in Howth with his wife and children when he began to write. His wife became incapacitated with cancer and he gave up work to look after her. As he was housebound he decided to write in order to make money! 'I wrote only for the money,' he laughed. I was amazed to hear this: that one could actually make money from a first novel. He said he made £25,000 and that the book was still bringing in a small income. This now creates problems for him as he's a Dominican with a vow of poverty. When he left the library I started to read one of his books, a brilliant novel set in the Dublin slums — about a girl suffering from catatonic schizophrenia.

And today in the library, when I was having a tea break, I was called out to the desk. 'Are you Thomas McCarthy?' a tall girl with a West Cork accent addressed me. 'I am.' She had a copy of *The First Convention* for me to sign. After ten years I haven't earned a penny from that book. I don't even know how many copies Dolmen sold, either in Ireland or through Humanities Press in the US.

June 30th The library organizes a 'Story Train' that leaves Glanmire Station at 12.30 and returns from Fota at 5.30.

July 12th A quiet day in Ulster.

July 13th Today at 2.50 p.m. Cathy gave birth to a baby boy, Neil Patrick — the first male of the new generation of my family. Catherine held out at home until the pains became unbearable. We didn't get to the hospital until quarter to one.

Neil was born two hours later. When I left Catherine this evening she was in pain but she was radiant and looking more beautiful than ever before. Our cup of happiness is full to the brim. When I think of how far I've travelled in life I am amazed. Alone at Glenshelane a few years ago, working intensely on my poems and with absolutely nothing else in my life, I could never have imagined that at thirty-four I'd be the father of two children. Parenthood is always a shock. It is always, strange to say, unexpected.

July 22nd Phone call from Seán Dunne. He and Sara have finally separated, an absolutely tragic bust-up. Seán always full of love and tolerance towards Sara, and he adores his children. *Krino* are publishing a long poem by him in the Spring. He kept telling me this as if it would mitigate his intense personal pain.

Later, a phone call from Greg Delanty in Caherdaniel, County Kerry. Greg depressed because all the poems he sent out (to *Krino*, *Irish Review*, *Poetry Ireland Review*) have been rejected. Greg doubly depressed when he learned that *Krino* is publishing Seán D's long poem. Catherine met Montague in town. He was depressed also.

So much depression among the poets of Cork. I wonder are the poets in Iowa City as depressed today? They probably are. What can we do with ourselves? It seems to be the poetic condition. Most poets seem destined to drift in and out of depression. The great danger, the great curse, is to start drinking to lessen this depression. Alcohol actually deepens the depression. Sourness becomes embedded through drink.

July 29th A first visit to the new Waterstone's in Patrick Street. A huge selection of books and massive space. I wonder if it can survive? I hope so. Only the death of a writer is more tragic than the failure of a bookstore. I bought two books. One for Kate, and a catalogue of the Seán Ó Ríordáin exhibition at University College, Dublin. In it he writes ' . . . tá leabhar nua agam le scrí inti i nGaeilge na Mumhan. Tá daoine in Éireann a dearfadh nach Gaeilge in aon chur mo Ghaeilge-sa.'

And that entry is dated '1960' after he had published the great masterpiece *Eireaball Spideoige*.

August 6th At Montague's house last night to discuss John's selection of his love poems for Exile Editions in Toronto. Allesandro Gentili, a translator from Florence, was there. John went to the phone (he loves the phone) to talk to Seamus Heaney whose American publisher wants $900 for two of Heaney's poems for the *Bitter Harvest* anthology. This amount is nearly one third of the total cash available for the entire anthology rights. After the phone call John decided to use a Heaney poem just published in *The Irish Times* and therefore not yet owned by his American publisher.

A phone call from the editor of *Fortnight* asking if I'd review the new MacNeice books by the two Longleys.

August 26th At Greg Delanty's wedding, to a lovely Portuguese-American girl. Seán Lucy and Desmond O'Grady there. O'Grady attacking Heaney constantly — comparing him unfavourably with Miłosz, the recent Nobel laureate. 'Heaney's a peasant, you can't give the Nobel Prize to a peasant.' I am beginning to think of Heaney as a real outsider, a man from beyond the Pale. His success has made him as hated as Camus or Seferis. And O'Grady's attitude is disappointing. It is snobbish: we all can't have Harvard PhDs or Italian *principessa*s for girlfriends. Literary envy, of course, and sour grapes. Literary envy is such a toxic thing, it unhinges even good people like dear Desmondo.

September 25th John Montague called into the library on his way home from the Mayfield Swimming pool. He has come back to Ireland from the South of France for two weeks to sort out his papers at UCC. After Christmas he goes to

Albany in America as a Writer-in-Residence. Today he was
in good form, cheery and domesticated. He had just been to
Derry for the opening night of the new Field Day play.
A glamorous evening, he said, with all the distinguished
members of the Ulster uber-Catholic community there,
including John Hume and numerous Bishops.

September 27th Last night I helped Montague to pack his
books at UCC's Brighton Villas. We brought ten large boxes,
but there are so many books and papers left we will need
eight or nine further boxes. It was an emotional moment for
John — at times he stood back from the shelves and asked,
'What am I doing? Am I doing the right thing?' The books,
only a fraction of his personal library, with their annotations
and bulging reviews of the period, create a sort of *mystique*
of Montague's life. Apart from his work they constitute the
best description of his nature. Among the papers were cards
and love-notes from old girlfriends (mainly American),
manuscripts of some poems, a letter that he'd never opened
from Oxford University Press offering £250 for a story,
letters from several young Dublin poets, old French postal
wrappers from his fastidious first wife, timetables, lists of students' names for seminars, a note from Evelyn, dated January
1987, saying that she couldn't collect him because her car was
snowed in, souvenirs from the Rotterdam Festival 1973, a
catalogue of a sculpture exhibition with an introduction by
Ezra Pound. All of this is just a partial list, a selection from
the life of a successful international academic poet. Of course,
it was his 'office', his teaching library, so that the selection of
books was painfully academic and pedantic. There wasn't
even one book on flowers or gardens or show business;
nothing even remotely erotic or kept for pleasure.

Coming away at 11 p.m., locking the steel gates of this
UCC English Department on Western Road, John was speech-
less with emotion ('What can I say? What is there to say?')
and depressed. He had closed the chapter of his life that had

lasted for over fifteen years, the fifteen most creative years of his life. I suspect that he feels he's come to the wrong end of a creative curve. I borrowed *The Letters of Flaubert*: 'What a number of the dead we carry in our hearts. Each of us bears his cemetery within.' (Letter to George Sand, 12/13 Nov 1866).

September 30th RTÉ Cork. Review of David Marcus's new novel.

October 7th At Nancy McCarthy's funeral in Douglas Church. I touched the coffin as it went by. She was beautiful; the best kind of a McCarthy woman, lively and stoical, generous and coquettish. She used to come to my poetry readings. She bought my three collections and lent them with enthusiasm. Her nephew, Henry, told me that *The First Convention* was kept on her bedside bookshelf.

November 24th Today Theo phoned from the Poetry Ireland offices in Dublin to say that Vincent Buckley has died. The world of poetry is one good man down.

November 28th In *The Observer*, a brilliant review of a Catherine Cookson book by Anita Brookner: with this interesting insight —

> *Autobiography is traditionally a genre peculiar to the upwardly mobile, the socially insecure, those who have no context to explain them. Its purpose is to expunge pain, but more than this, to create a life myth, an alternative support system.*

And in *The Sunday Tribune* a review of Thomas Kinsella's new collection, *Blood and Family*. Our greatest living poet, he may still come back to the land of the famous.

Last night a new book by Montague was launched, *Mount Eagle*, John's first book with The Gallery Press. John was in one of his peculiar moods: a mixture of humility and arrogance, both lacking in confidence and argumentative. He was drunk, and yet he sensed that the audience was too quiet. Peter Fallon has faith in him and high hopes for his future.

1989

January 29th In Theodora FitzGibbon's autobiography there is a note on Maxim Gorky, standing naked in front of the mirror in Capri, saying, 'Ten books, one play, twenty-seven women, fifty-five years old. Not bad, not bad.'

February 5th Three poets reading today at 3 p.m.: Rosemary Canavan, Máire Bradshaw, Bonnie Cotter. I read at Collins Bookshop on Saturday.

March 10th Reading. St Patrick's College, Drumcondra.

March 21st Almost a year of no good poems, more than eight months of sleepless nights and a missed deadline for *Seven Winters in Paris*. Only good news on the horizon is that Matthew Sweeney's new book has become a Poetry Book Society Choice and Seán Dunne has succeeded in selling the rights of a long poem to RTÉ.

April 23rd Finished typing the manuscript of *Seven Winters in Paris*. A phone call at the library from Molly Keane to ask me if I'll come to her Honorary Doctorate conferring at UCC. She was feeling uncharacteristically positive, full of ambition to write an autobiography. She says she's just read V S Pritchett's *Chekhov* and thinks it's brilliant. Then I asked her about Daphne du Maurier who died last week. She said that as a writer du Maurier was a 'bit too creamy for me, I'm afraid'. I was amazed when she said that she's sometimes afraid to read really good writers in case she would begin to copy their style.

May 9th At the conferring of an Honorary DLitt to Molly Keane. A really sunny afternoon in Cork with the grounds of UCC looking particularly beautiful. I was sitting outside the Aula Maxima when Molly and Sally arrived in Charles Keane's Volvo. Molly was a bundle of nerves but Sally, who was there to help her, was even worse. I opened the door for Sally and when she saw me she exclaimed, 'Oh, Mummy, we'll be all right! Thomas is here! Thomas, won't you stay with us? You won't leave us?' Molly went in slowly, having been deposited quickly into a waiting wheelchair. I didn't think she'd survive the ordeal: all the fanfare of academic gowns, hats, scarlet finery, trumpet fanfares, and the 'cúpla focal' of Latin. But she survived, barely. Afterwards, she seemed thrilled with herself in her Doctoral robes: she was chirpy, friendly and unconcerned. Like someone who'd survived a visit to the dentist.

At the reception afterwards I met James Aidan Walsh, a lovely man, chairman of Waterford County Council. He told me that he had cycled to Cork from Cappoquin in 1943 to be at his wife's conferring. He is an extremely warm person. Why is it that all the politicians I like personally are in Fine Gael while those I support politically are in The Workers' Party or Fianna Fáil?

June 7th Seamus Heaney has been elected to the Professorship of Poetry in Oxford. What a meteoric career he has had — his picture is in all the Irish papers and in many of the English Sunday papers. His victory creates more excitement in some quarters than the General Election now being fought.

On the day the Election was announced I decided to write a poem every day to counteract the shit that would be fired at me daily until Polling Day (June 15th). So far I've succeeded in keeping up my spiritual exercise. Isaac Bashevis Singer lives at 209, West 8th Street in New York. I *must* write to him to tell him how much I love his work.

July 10th Woke up this morning to Brendan Kennelly's voice on the radio. He was talking about God. He has just published a group of translations of poems on The Blessèd Virgin. He has now done poetry books on Cromwell, God, the Blessèd Virgin and the Ten Commandments.

July 29th I introduced Patrick Galvin at a reading to launch his new book, *Folktales for the General*. A smallish crowd in the Triskel Café, and none of his contemporaries. There is no doubt in my mind that a true poet belongs to no city and no one generation. The poet should have no loyalty greater than his loyalty to the world of imagination, to what this world sends him in codes and what it demands of him. It is because of his integrity as a poet that Galvin has outlasted Blinco, Lucy and Bobby O'Donoghue. His work reveals an astonishing world of working-class heroes; it is especially a world of heroic women, the 'Madwoman of Cork', the wife in 'Plaisir d'Amour' and the mother of 'Woman Who Washed Linen' published in this latest book. He is a radical feminist. He has created more veritable feminist heroes than any other radical poet I know. He is the only Brecht that Munster will ever produce. I love him. There are very few poets that I could love, but I love him.

August 4th Two days ago the newspapers and the radio carried news of the Arts Council Awards. Eavan Boland and Matthew Sweeney also got money. John Banville won the Martin Toonder Prize. Both *The Cork Examiner* and *The Irish Independent* give some emphasis to my name. *The Examiner* even printed a photograph. This has caused a stir locally. It occurs to me that only a local 'stir' is worthwhile. I mean, what good is it if you create a 'stir' elsewhere, a 'stir' you can't see?

Reading, yet again, Seferis' poems, especially the magisterial 'Thrush' and 'The King of Asine'. Each time I read Seferis I am reminded of how like Ireland Greece appears to be — I mean as a body of myth, as a metaphor of both noble and embarrassing suffering. Greece is a much more powerful country than Ireland, of course. It is a huge trading and naval power and a seminal cultural influence on the whole of Western society. Yet there is something tragic about the Greek condition in the way that Ireland can be tragic. There is the impossible religio-cultural problem of Cyprus, so like our own Ulster problem, and the bitter Civil War when Greek brother fought against Greek brother. And the impossibility of solving all these things on one's own. The difficulty too of dealing with national problems that involve a stronger and aggressive neighbour. Yet there is nothing sectarian or oligarchic about Seferis' view. His pain is distinctly Greek but his expression of this pain is both universal and Classical. He is also a constant exile within his own metaphors, his mind engaging with the material like a sailor making slow progress through a mighty archipelago.

August 8th Today Edna Longley mentions my work in *The Irish Times*. In discussing literature and poetry she says, 'I have certainly learned more about the culture of the North from Seamus Heaney's poetry and more about "the political culture" of the Republic from Paul Durcan's or Thomas McCarthy's.'

In the train at Heuston Station. After a hectic rush through Dublin traffic to catch the 3 p.m. train I had to wait for two-and-a-half hours for the present one. At RTÉ in Donnybrook I recorded two short programmes for Seamus Hosey. While in the studio canteen I met Aidan Carl Mathews.

October 20th The Guildford Four released from an English prison. Scenes of jubiliation and hysterical happiness. It seems that the British police concocted evidence against them. Paul Hill was kept in solitary confinement for nearly fifteen years. The viciousness of British treatment of Irish prisoners is something that non-Irish people can never understand. And out of all this chaos and cruelty the only winners are the Provos. Today Provisional Sinn Féin have scored a massive propaganda victory.

October 25th The other night a phone call from John Banville to say that he liked 'Helena', the poem that he is publishing in *The Irish Times* on Saturday. He wanted to know why he hadn't received a copy of the book for review. This is a big week in Banville's life — tomorrow is Booker Prize night and his *Book of Evidence* is on the shortlist.

October 30th Kazuo Ishiguro has won the Booker Prize for *The Remains of the Day* — another one of those 'scent of old vines' novels so loved by the English and so despised by Arthur Koestler. But 'Isch' is an exquisite writer. His *An Artist of the Floating World* is a perfect piece of prose; really a prose-poem.

November 11th Tonight my thoughts are with Eberhard Panitz in East Berlin. The Berlin Wall is being dismantled by the East German authorities. A momentous event, with Berlin in a state of hysterical happiness for the last forty-eight hours. Thousands of cars are streaming across the barriers and young West Germans are throwing bottles of champagne at the border guards. I wonder what Eberhard thinks of this? An innately conservative man, he may think that the whole thing has gone too far. One GDR Government official said, 'Life has intervened.' I thought it an absolutely brilliant comment. John Montague going around on crutches. He has broken his ankle. Paul Durcan to stay. I must get John to phone Paul before Thursday re reading.

December 26th St Stephen's Day The radio reports that Samuel Beckett died on Friday 22nd. He was buried at a private funeral in Paris yesterday. So there it is. The humorous nihilist who was born on the anniversary of Christ's crucifixion was buried on the anniversary of His birth. Very little sadness in my heart — Beckett had an absolutely complete and good life. He served France with dignity during the Occupation (secretly receiving both the Croix de Guerre and the Médaille de la Résistance) and he became the living symbol of Ireland's love of France. He would have been given a hero's funeral if his body had been returned to Ireland, yet he chose France as his final resting place. France that not only gave him love but a new language to go with that love, and an escape from the ambiguities of being an Irish Protestant. His Irish Presbyterianism is always overlooked yet it is an absolutely defining trait of his character and his invented characters. In the end few writers have had his good luck. He was born with a silver spoon in his mouth and a mother on horseback, but he always had an Irish Presbyterian contempt for grandeur and social folly. In this he is so like Derek Mahon. He makes so many Irish Catholic writers look like buffoons and simpletons, yet that was never his intention. But, as in the case of André Gide or Sartre, in revealing his superior nature his life exposed the painful limitations of others.

Rumblings from the Thatcher government against the wisdom of German unity. Mrs Thatcher thinks that a united Germany will be too strong, that it will dominate Europe. She may be right. But the Irish government is fighting tooth and nail in Europe for acceptance of full German unity. For us in Ireland that very word 'unity' has a powerful, magic resonance. And then there is that emotional, historic link between Ireland and Germany — the political fact that the Germans were the first to accept Sir Roger Casement as the plenipotentiary of a sovereign Irish nation. In the Irish corridors of power that noble German gesture of 1916 will never be forgotten.

1990

February 16th Reading at St Maries of the Isle. Sr Benedict says that my 'Sorrow Garden' is quoted by Professor Enda McDonagh in his book *Small Hours of Belief*.

March 16th Eating a burger and chips in Augsburg College in Minneapolis. A generous college set in a deprived area of the city that looks both colourful and hostile. Staying in Guest Room A: from its window I look down on a parking lot where a man has just been murdered.

March 23rd Murphy's Restaurant with Jim Rogers of the Irish American Cultural Institute. On Sunday, 2 p.m., dinner with Pat and Mary McQuillan of W Minnehaha. McQuillan a great, prosperous middle-class Catholic Ulster name, an SDLP name.

March 29th Leaving Albany after a day with John Montague at SUNY Writers Institute. Spent all the morning discussing John's poems. He is perfectly landed in America, a wonderful job, superb salary and conditions. I met Stanley Kunitz briefly at Albany station, a man of eighty-eight but still alert and powerful. We talked about Theodore Roethke. He was amazed that I had read all of his essays on Roethke. 'It's a small world,' I joked. 'It sure is,' he replied, though not sincerely. A man of his grand age has no concept of how small the world has become. In his mind the Europe of Seferis and of the Princess Caetani is still weeks away by passenger steamer. To reach Athens, in his mind, a shipment of *Partisan Review*s would take the long sea route from Marseilles to Piraeus. But it was lovely, and so utterly unexpected, to stand for a while with this American immortal on the freezing, windswept platform, this immortal soul who has worked at the heart of American poetry with the patience of an Einstein.

It struck me, as I worked on John's poems about his adolescence and growth, that it is the lives of others that fascinate me, and I feel that I have been given the lives of others to work with. John thinks I should be more humorous. This is true. But being humorous is self-consciously wanting to create an effect, to make a splash. I have absolutely no urge to make a splash; I'm after something else, something that draws together the years as they pass inexorably into my work. This is impossible to explain to John, though I did try to explain myself as we sat in his office, an office that seemed somehow an unhappy, very temporary place. But it is time that I want to draw into my own poems. By drawing time into me I will also draw a small audience — over time, that is. And this could be a particularly deep audience, a group of deep readers, a band of fairly private partisans. It is impossible to share this kind of thinking with J M: for John everything, including literary success, is primarily social; and, for John, it needs to be immediate and huge. In this he is very French.

April 2nd Sitting at a table in Scooters Café in the College of St Thomas in St Paul, Minnesota. Momentarily, I am the Hemingway of Summit Avenue, a coffee on my table and a bad review of my book in my hand. The bad review is by Robert Nye, from the (London) *Times*. Nye is a snobbish and pretentious shit, even if he is a half-decent novelist. He says that one can excuse the doggerel because I am a gentleman who writes 'modest meditations'. Catherine phoned me earlier and told me that there is another bad review in *The Independent on Sunday*, a brilliant London paper. So this book is going to be another depressing collector of bad English reviews. But the Nye review annoys me. He should have been more welcoming, but then again he is unbelievably precious and snobbish about his own artistic process. Because he is a 'modernist' he thinks he's special. He bloody well is not. As Peter Jay says there will always be people who just don't like me and that's that. My Southern Irish voice offends them, my very being offends them.

Thursday College of St Thomas. A huge crowd at my poetry reading here last night, perhaps three to four hundred people. The room was packed with people standing while others stood crushing into the doorway. No one more surprised by this than myself. In fact I headed for a room at the other side of the corridor, thinking that the packed room was for some major event. The other room, with five students in it, was actually a German class. The major event, therefore, was my own reading. That was bizarre. Such a crowd was a timely boost to my ego. Will I ever again draw such a crowd in America? It is all the result of Tom Redshaw's propaganda in his Minnesota Irish-American circles. Tom must be the most influential Protestant in Catholic Minnesota.

April 10th Two more bad reviews of my book arrive from home — the one from *The Independent on Sunday* is hilariously abusive and the one from *The Sunday Times* does say that 'my best pieces are the inventive, more directly political ruminations', but only says this after demolishing all my poems on love, family and illness. The presence of 'The Dáil' really gets me into a lot of trouble, though respect is shown for the 'political' stuff.

April 20th English Majors' Conference in Macalester. 'Eliot Under Siege' and 'Terry Eagleton's Political Criticism'.
Yesterday I went to Haskell's Liquor Store with John Bernstein and his wife, Cindy. Cindy is an absolute darling woman in every way. I bought two bottles of Mayacamas, a bottle of Rieussec and a 1985 bottle of Léoville Barton. John, a Professor at Macalester, bought three cases of wine, all first rate stuff. John is amazing, a typical Macalester Professor of

the older generation: stylish, well travelled, intense, agitated, an Anglophile in Scottish tweeds, a socialist. These six weeks have taught me that I enjoy teaching, especially when I profess poetry. My faith in poetry does seem to get across to the young Americans. On Wednesday night Jack Nemo, the Kavanagh scholar and Dean at University of St Thomas, offered me a job. I doubt if he's discussed this with the English Department staff — always a mistake as English professors hate when someone is parachuted into a department. I said to Jack that I would enjoy teaching. What I didn't say was that I feared they may not be able to offer me a substantial salary. With all our debts and loans in Ireland I would need to earn a huge salary to make a long sojourn in America feasible. But I will always be grateful to Jack Nemo, bless him. Any man who offers a poet a job and a living wage is a saint and a true prince among men. God bless you, Jack Nemo: your name will be blessed wherever I go.

This is the second time that a job offer has come to me out of the blue from America. The first time was from Ambassador Shannon at the Dublin Embassy. As I come from a family of landless casual labourers it is a deeply moving experience to be offered permanent work (and 'in out of the rain' as my mother would say). Even Seamus Heaney, a strong farmer's son, describes the dignity of blue-collar work so well in 'Digging' — even Heaney was conscious of how lucky he was to be offered a fine professorship in America. The dignity of this cannot be overstated. I do bless Jack Nemo for this. I will tell Heaney about this offer from St Thomas; hearing about it would move him greatly, and he should know it so that he'll praise the University of St Thomas in his own extensive travels across America.

A letter from Ireland. Poolbeg Press is going to publish *The Solitude of the Party* next March. It is now called *Without Power*. As is usual with me my mind is racing on already into novel number three — *The Little Soviet by the River* or *LSBTR*. The *LSBTR* will be different in that it will be first person narrative.

Cardinal Ó Fiaich is dead. A great scholar and lover of poetry. At the funeral Gerry Adams took Holy Communion. Let's hope he has turned towards the light of Christ.

May 19th Revised and typed first chapter of *Parables of Happiness* (*Asya and Christine*). The style almost too traditional and plodding. The flaw of the novel (yet again) is the flaw of having too many voices. Can't wait to escape from the first two novels. My mind has matured by at least ten years since they were conceived.

Saturday The face of a middle-aged Romanian man begging in Bridge Street, Cork, yesterday. The look of absolute fear in the faces of his older children, the look of despair in his wife's face, the hopeless situation of his three-week-old infant. I gave him £3. Half an hour later, trying to write in Catherine's studio on Paul Street, I couldn't put him out of my mind. I went to the bank and took out £60 to give to him. But he was gone. I cruised around the city for two hours looking for him. Nowhere to be found. How can five or six people disappear like that?

May 28th Another review of *Seven Winters in Paris*. This time a good one, from the *TLS*. William Scammell has reservations but praises the book, its 'sober craftsmanship' etc. And this evening a phone call from Mícheál Ó Siadhail in Dublin — he wanted to warn me about a hostile review in *Poetry Ireland Review*. Impossible to insulate oneself from the stinging annoyance of bad reviews, but the *Guardian* and the *TLS* reviews have now given me great fortitude.

June 17th Yesterday, went with John Montague and the American publisher, Dillon Johnston, and his wife, Guinn, to see Seán Ó Ríordáin's cottage at Inniscarra. The cottage now dilapidated and the entrance covered in brambles and wild roses. We were all indignant at the state of this place, the home of the 20th-century's most important Gaelic poet. It was only afterwards — when Montague's fine indignation and Guinn's real sadness had abated — that I thought, Well, what's so tragic about it? Maybe there are too many holy places in Ireland, too many shrines that weigh down upon our literary imagination and prevent us from taking flight. After all, it is art, not the life from which it springs, that yearns for immortality. I'm sure there are half a dozen young Irish scholars in UCC or UCD or Galway or Queen's who know Ó Ríordáin's work very well. Their knowledge is the only monument a poet needs.

June 29th In the library today, showing a young American scholar the old volumes of *The Bell, The Dublin Magazine, Cyphers* etc, when I came across a review of my *Non-Aligned Storyteller* by Maurice Harmon in the *Irish University Review.* I was amazed that I never saw it before as it was published five years ago. It is the best reading of my poems that I've ever seen.

Also in the library I found the current issue of *Fortnight* magazine. It contains a very good review of *Seven Winters in Paris* by James Simmons.

July 25th Yesterday spent a morning in Portlaoise Prison with IRA prisoners. A lively, useful discussion on literature and politics. I felt that the IRA men took to me because of my satirical, lyrical stuff: they loved the poems like 'Shopkeepers at a Party Meeting' and 'Question Time'. They were positively filled with glee when I read a poem about Charlie Haughey, comparing his face with the fake 'Turin Shroud'. Seven prisoners in the workshop, held in an oppressive, stuffy room in a third-floor cage. I took to Pat Arthurs, the CO of the Provisional Wing; a fit-looking, tanned, gentle-voiced man in his thirties to early forties. He gives the impression of great strength, great moral strength. Each of the prisoners speaks quietly, without arrogance or defensiveness. They have all the confidence of a religious sect — the session was full of private jokes, elbow-nudging and embarrassed laughter. I read Hemingway's story 'On the Quai at Smyrna' and a Seferis poem. I workshopped three of the prisoners' work. They listen to criticism keenly, not passively. They are constantly judging, searching one's face for something: for a clue, possibly, to some flaw of character or lack of sincerity. I'll be meeting them again at the end of next month. Portlaoise is a sinister place. The prison is a series of cages, huge cages that contain rooms and corridors — and the place crawling with prison officers (many of them friendly, not suspicious or touchy as at Spike Island). Even in the room where I did the workshop there was an officer in a separate cage, listening. I had the distinct feeling that everything we said was either taped or written down in shorthand. Coming out of the prison I felt an unexpected sympathy for the IRA men. They may see themselves as POWs, national heroes, but they cannot escape from the role of victim, the role of the Ulster Catholic.

My sympathy for the Provos has lasted all of twenty-four hours, until this morning's news on the radio. The IRA in Armagh have murdered a young nun, a Sister of Santa Lucia, and three RUC officers. One of the officers has a five-year-old and an eleven-month-old child. It is ironic that while half an IRA unit was learning about poetry with me the other half was planting a murderous landmine in South Armagh. Yet I know it isn't fair to think that literature is just one of the games that terrorists play.

September 16th The proofs of *Without Power* arrived by courier from Dublin yesterday, on the same day that we received notice from the EBS that the Bank of Ireland had bounced our mortgage cheque. It's six weeks before I go back to work and our financial situation is absolutely dire. I underestimated how much money I would need for my leave.

Nothing left in the bank.

The proofs of the novel lifted my spirits a little. The type-face is large and beautiful, making the book into a substantial 270-page novel. I'm full of hope for its commercial success though I've no illusions about the critical reception it might get. It will probably be rubbished by those who hate Fianna Fáil. Six weeks of impoverished freedom left. I must work my ass off to make *The Summer of Asya and Christine* into a really decent book.

September 30th Decided to sell part of my library to help us get through the next month. I'll try to sell at least 150 good books. From my best bookshelves I've removed *The Art of Delivering Written Speech* (1745), Smith's *History of Waterford* (1749) and first editions of *Poems* by Yeats, *A Book of Irish Verse*, edited by Yeats, Corkery's *The Threshold of Quiet*, *The Living Torch*, a selection of AE by Monk Gibbon, *The States Through Irish Eyes* by E Somerville, *The Silver Fox* by Somerville and Ross, *Seven Winters* by Elizabeth Bowen, *The Green Fool* by Patrick Kavanagh and *Seven Pillars of Wisdom* by T E Lawrence (a magnificent quarto-sized illustrated book — I hate to part with it). I've always warned people against selling their books. One never gets the true value from a bookseller (how can you, a bookseller may hold a rare book for five years before getting his money back). Selling books privately is always an act of desperation. It's the times we live in.

October 2nd Sold my books, except Corkery's *Hidden Ireland*. I got £100 for them, plus a credit-note for £30, from Adrian Connolly in Paul Street. I might have got a better deal from Ger McSweeney in Lee Bookstore but the humiliation of taking the four boxes away and traipsing through the city centre made me stay put. The Lawrence *Seven Pillars of Wisdom* and Smith's *Waterford* were probably worth more than £100 each, but beggars can't be choosers. Strangely enough I don't feel any sense of loss. Since we had children my attachment to books has lessened. The urge to sell even more books is upon me, although the £100 will keep us going until Catherine is paid in ten days. Catherine's story, 'Christy Rides', is published in *Stet* magazine. It looks terrific and reads very well — excellent, witty dialogue and really perceptive descriptions. Certainly four years in Art College is the best training for a writer.

October 3rd While weeding out my books for sale I came across my critical books on Theodore Roethke. Read again about the 'Lost Son' and the greenhouse poems. It was Roethke who gave me an approach to the central theme of all my poems — the theme of the fatherless place: his greenhouse became my 'Party' and his 'Lost Son' became my absent father. Metaphors all.

October 5th Already the £100 I got for my books is gone. It lasted three days.

October 14th Yesterday I did my last two workshops with the IRA in Portlaoise Prison. When I was leaving they presented me with a hand-tooled leather wallet. Coming home through Laois and Tipperary the weather was foul and menacing, rather like the prison itself. The IRA men won my sympathy at a human level — there is something very vulnerable and desolate about them. They live desolately in jail like driftwood thrown up by a storm, the storm of history. They try to keep up morale with workshops and political discussion groups. They responded very strongly, very positively, to my sympathetic ear and were delighted with my interest in history. I explained to them that I couldn't sympathize with their activities because I was a citizen of Dáil Éireann, and there could only be one army and one Parliament of Irish national interests. They refute my 'Free State' attitude completely. They try to defend themselves — many arguments quite valid and impressive. But I wasn't in the least moved by their arguments. Their murderous actions are despicable and anti-democratic. The Dáil of our 'Free State' is now as established and legitimate as the American House of Congress. There is no denying this. The Provos, in reality, are really just Croatian Fascists abandoned by history and marooned by historic values that were roundly defeated in 1922. There is absolutely no escape from this. The majority of Irishmen voted for the Treaty with England in 1922 and Dáil Éireann is the embodiment of that referendum. There are now two forms of viable Irish political being — civic life under the Dáil and civic life under a Stormont Parliament. The idea that Southern Ireland could annex the six counties as if Ulster were a Sudetenland is a complete absurdity. We may see the forces of Unionism weakened or displaced occasionally, but these forces never really diminish; their moral core is too strong. It is almost impossible to get Nationalists to see this. Even Anthony Cronin, the most sophisticated and highly educated of Irishmen, would never concede the rights of Unionism and its political/historical validity. In Anthony's scenario Ulster can never be allowed to get away. Cronin's quip that 'a few Lambeg drums does not a culture make' is often quoted by other poets in the South. But this is to miss the point: Protestant Ulster never left us precisely because it was never part of us. Why can't they see that? Political Ulster was always 'apart', even in the time of The Great O'Neill, but its 'apartness' was completed by the Unionist agitation of the early twentieth century, by Unionism's refusal to be 'annexed' by a Catholic version of unitary Irish history. Protestant Ulster belongs more to Ontario or North Carolina than to Ireland. Will Irish nationalism ever understand this? In this Irish context I really am a dissident poet. My mind was formed in opposition to the national consensus. I can see why dissidents get themselves killed. Our tribal history makes what I might say seem intolerable. I must be the only true dissident since Conor Cruise O'Brien. He and I should be placed in a pea-green boat and made to sail away for a year and a day. Yet I don't think I'm as unhinged as Conor Cruise. I'm trying to think rationally, reasonably, about Ireland, but about all of Ireland. People will hate me for having these thoughts, but hatred is no substitute for hard thinking. Reading Günter Grass in the *Guardian* on the unification of Germany. He turns it into a depressing scenario. Then again writers are not the best judges of a political situation. They can be humane and faithful archivists, but not good analysts.

Met Montague yesterday at the Harvest Festival at St Luke's Church of Ireland. He says he earns £8,000 a year from his writing alone. I was going to ask him for a loan to keep me going until 15th Nov when I'll receive my first Corporation pay check. We went for a drink to the Country Club Hotel overlooking the city. Rain lashed against the windows. I kept thinking of poor Daniel Corkery who lived and taught school in this area for years. What a lonely man Corkery was. And John Montague beside me, wearing an expensive and colourful new jumper; John who at least fights against personal loneliness. Corkery's life in this parish of St Patrick's was certainly the more unbearable one. Though John always refers to our bailiwick as 'The St Luke's Parish' because he goes to the Protestant church with Evelyn and the children. I have to give credit to John: he has transformed his life into something absolutely fascinating. Through his poetry and his capacity to earn money from poetry in America he has created an expensive, artisan-woollen Irish bohemia for himself and for those who love him. His is a good life, though he won't admit it. The fact is Evelyn has created a wonderful life for him to live within. He has thrived in the ether she created.

October 30th An amazing week in Irish politics has just passed by. Possibly the most sensational week since the Arms Trial of the 1970s. Brian Lenihan, the Fianna Fáil dead-cert for President (polling day next week), has been 'stung' by a young researcher who taped him telling lies. The poor fellow.

He is undone. Politics is so cruel. 'Upon mature reflection' or is it 'Upon mature recollection'? These phrases will haunt Irish political discourse for years to come. I can already hear the Fine Gael PR consultants and RTÉ's satirical writers at work. Sometimes I think they are the same people, or at least they've been to the same dinner party in Ranelagh.

1991

*From our remote standpoint it may be said that life
no sooner started than it swarmed.*
— Teilhard de Chardin, 'Le Phénomène humain', 1955

February 3rd Sunday Catherine's story 'Rembrandt and
Escher' is published in *The Sunday Tribune*. The story and a
beautiful photograph of Cathy takes up nearly a whole page
of the newspaper. And the text itself reads very well, the
prose controlled and paced like in a really good poem. I
bought two copies of *The Sunday Tribune* in O'Brien's shop
in Montenotte. I couldn't resist the temptation to say to
people in the shop, 'My wife Catherine has a story in this.
That's why I'm buying two copies.' Catherine would be so
enbarrassed. But to hell with people, they need to know.

February 16th Night at Glenshelane. The Brigadier heading
for England.

February 19th Yesterday, a small luncheon party in Cappoquin House, Sir Richard Keane's home overlooking Cappoquin. Molly Keane was there; not as ill-looking as in recent
months, and in good spirits. Mary Pegge, the Cappoquin
poet, and formerly Adela Keane before her marriage and
conversion to Catholicism, was there too. Molly was impressed by the dustjacket of *Without Power*. She said that I
must send the published novel to Gina Pollinger to see if an
American publisher could be found. There's a lot of the actress
in Molly — she tends to be gushy ('darling, you're wonderful!'),
just like Nancy McCarthy. This is a style born of theatre
people.

After lunch we sat in the booklined study. A dusty Mainie
Jellett painting hanging above the chimney piece. Mrs Pegge
told me that she used to sit by the same fireplace eighty years
ago while her father, the famous Senator Sir John Keane,
recited poetry, especially Shelley, to her. Later she stopped
under the lovely staircase and told me that she'd fallen off
the banisters and banged her head. I asked Lady Keane to
explain a strange looking contraption in the hallway, a box-
like thing covered in baize cloth. She told me that it was a
sedan chair used by an older Lady Keane when shopping in
Dublin in the 1920s. 'Dublin was so dirty in the old days,'
explained Lady Keane, 'one had to be carried.' Wasn't life
grand for some, I said in my own mind.

I drove away slowly from Cappoquin House. A spectacular
view. From the avenue everything seemed so very close that
I could almost touch it, even the River Blackwater. And
Cappoquin looked so small, so vulnerable, in the evening
light. That place held such terrors for me as a child, such
enormous sinister tensions from the threats of the dysfunctional adult world around me. Yet writing has ensured my
release from this mental serfdom. I doubt if wealth or social
success would have released me from the nightmares of rural
poverty in the way that art has done. Looking at the little
town, a troubled pile in a beautiful setting, I felt that I could
pick it all up and place it in the palm of my hand. How
strange, and strangely deliberate, that I've been trying to
recreate that place as the world of the Party, the world of
Deputy Glenville and his fictional family.

March 21st One of the good weeks in my writing life.
On Tuesday a huge article praising my novel in *The Irish
Independent* — by one of the paper's leading writers, Tom
O'Dea. The article has set a whole series of furious phone-
calls in motion, two from TV producers and two from
Dublin radio. An interview is coming up in *The Irish Times*.
I am on television tonight, and scheduled to appear tomorrow

night as well. At lunchtime on Sunday I'll be a guest on the Sunday radio show. The novel is being pushed by a veritable blitz of publicity — but more than this, people who've read the novel (I mean ordinary punters) like it. If this continues word-of-mouth will turn the book into a bestseller. Life is full of wonders, not least of which is popular success.

Today I was at Waterstone's to arrange for a launch reception. I notice that the Blackstaff edition of Daniel Corkery's stories has been remaindered. My book, on the other hand, enjoys a window display and a full front-of-shop dump-bin. Life is strange. Literature is strange. Why, for example, does Gide continue to sell in paperback in Waterstone's of Cork while Corkery is remaindered? Is Gide remaindered in French bookshops?

March 23rd *Sunday Show* on RTÉ. Dan Collins on Kerry Radio.

Another leading article about my novel in the *Independent*, this time by Conor Cruise O'Brien, praising me to the stars. In many intellectual circles, of course, O'Brien's embrace is like a kiss of death. He uses my novel as the basis for a savagely emotional attack on Fianna Fáil. This aspect of the thing is disturbing, and extremely risky for me. But it's fair to say that I knew these risks even before I began to use political material. The only alternative was not to write fiction and poetry about the Party, to suppress myself. How could I do that? Yes, I am a coward when it comes to Fianna Fáil material — but I'm not a complete coward. It's just that I know that most of my friends, whether UCC graduates, journalists or poets, are instinctively left wing. They despise the Peronist populism of Fianna Fáil and they will despise any work that contains these materials. I can't win this battle, it's an impossible one. That imaginative fatalism has made me into seeming like a public coward. But, imaginatively, Fianna Fáil cannot be defended: it is tainted material.

226

March 25th A phone call from Philip McDermott of Poolbeg Press. He doesn't want a launch of the novel at the Triskel Arts Centre: 'Why not, Philip?' I ask. 'I might sell one hundred copies of the novel.'
   'OK. One hundred copies of your novel. That's good. But you might send out the wrong kind of signal to the book distributors.'
   'What signal?'
   'Arty-farty, you know. People might think it's just a *literary* book.'
   I didn't know whether to laugh or cry. But I love him for having that anxiety. It is typical of Philip, who is a populist to the core and thinks that every Poolbeg paperback should sell at least 10,000 copies in Ireland. I would be perfectly happy with sales of 1,000-1,500 copies, but Philip would consider that a complete failure.

April 13th There is a powerfully accurate review of *Without Power* by George O'Brien in *The Irish Times*. He praises the book as documentary, but sees the gaping flaw, the lack of plot interest. With uncanny intuition he sees the wider issues, but especially 'the culture of poverty' from which Fianna Fáil gains power. *The Cork Examiner* on the other hand has a brilliant review by Seán Dunne, complete with photograph.
   Today I thought of bringing Julie Phelan back from Brussels in the final Party novel, making her a contemporary MEP, an ambitious, fast-talking and bitching fifty-three-year-old with a boyfriend in his late 30s or early 40s (a German with a PhD in Celtic Studies from UCD).

April 19th Seán Dunne and Trish Edelstein to dinner.

May 16th A letter from the Irish American Cultural Institute in St Paul to say that I'd been awarded the O'Shaughnessy Poetry Prize for 1991. The $5,000 will be a godsend in September. We will be able to buy kitchen furniture and replace the fireplace in the sitting room.

At the Awards ceremony (a DLitt for Montague) in UCC. Met the College President, Michael Mortell and Garret FitzGerald, the ex-Taoiseach. Garret greeted me warmly. It seems that Fine Gael people really enjoyed *Without Power*. Garret certainly enjoyed it. He said that the novel made him laugh out loud, he said that nobody before had ever chronicled so well the absurdity of Fianna Fáil delusions and yearnings. His enthusiasm worries me — in the way Conor Cruise O'Brien's enthusiasm worried me. But there's no avoiding the politics of the thing. I can't keep denying what I've done, although I want to keep denying it for the sake of my poetry.

A phone call from Philip McDermott. The novel is being reprinted.

My fellow poets have become heartily sick of me and these awards.There is a certain nobility in accumulating a good body of work that is not perforated in any way by awards. Patrick Kavanagh Award in 1977, Alice Hunt Bartlett Award in 1981, AIF Annual Literary Award in 1984 and O'Shaughnessy in 1991: at least there's been a decent interval since this last award, seven years. But I think it's time for Seán Dunne, Theo Dorgan and Liam de Bhál to start receiving awards too.

May 20th At Glenshelane. Lunch on the veranda in sweltering heat. My arrival caused a stir. Anne was busy preparing for a big luncheon party on Wednesday so that there was nothing ready for lunch. An extensive search of fridge and larder uncovered some bacon and leek pancakes as well as a rhubarb fool. An extraordinary thing that the Brigadier learned about his uncle, Lord Walter FitzGerald. Walter used to research an enormous number of local history items for the Kildare Historical Society, but he then employed 'front men' to deliver the lectures. The lecturers were like actors who performed his script while he sat in the audience.

May 25th National Corncrake Day.

June 6th Launch in the Douglas Hyde Gallery of Gerald Dawe's *New Younger Irish Poets.*

June 8th Dinner at Mark Bence-Jones's.

June 11th A tribute night to John Montague, with a small introduction from me. Dear God, how many tributes does this man need? His need for praise is insatiable.

June 17th John McGahern and Mario Vargas Llosa at Waterstone's.

June 26th In Dublin for the launch of *The Great Book of Ireland.* Theo's project. Charlie Haughey and Brendan Kennelly launched the book. Stayed at the Clarence Hotel — an extravagance that I can't possibly afford. Met Heaney and Marie and a plethora of other poets. Spent much of the evening talking to Anthony Cronin. Always an extremely clever man, articulate, sardonic, anecdotal. When I told Cronin that I was writing a prequel to *Without Power* he said, 'A prequel. Good, good! It means that you've learned something about your characters from the fictional characters themselves.' It was an incredibly clever perception, and typical of Cronin.

July 28th Just to deepen my depression I work on the *Stet* poetry submissions in bed. So far I've written about sixty letters of rejection, mainly to poets in Dublin. Sixty rejected poets. You couldn't have a more depressing statistic. I feel like I've stabbed sixty Dublin people in the heart. A phone call from the Brigadier. He said that he may join a committee to restore Maynooth Castle as a Geraldine Museum.

September 23rd A teenager searching for information in

the library. 'Tom, I've looked up all the Henrys, Henry the Navigator, Henry the VIII, but there's nothing on shaggin' Henry Ford.'

September 24th At the Casa de Mateus, Vila Real, Portugal. Astonishing. Beautiful. We met Valente de Oliveira, the Minister for Planning, who was canvassing in the General Election. He had hilarious stories about Pádraig Flynn.

October 6th Ivy Day. We all still live in the shadow of Parnell.

December 15th Going home on the Belfast train after a pleasant day at The Poets' House, a literary centre located in a coastguard's cottage at Portmuck on the northern edge of Belfast Lough. I might have been in Scotland. Workshopping and reading poems. The house run by James Simmons and his wife, Janice Fitzpatrick. A beautiful, delicate child called Ben wandering around the house with his bow and arrows. The Robin Hood of Portmuck. His half-sister Anna (age 9) stops him on the stairs and says, 'Only the Pope shoots arrows at people.' This expression surprises me until I realize that Simmons' world (its axis) is East Belfast and Larne, the Protestant heartland. It is a kind of reverse Gaeltacht. Simmons, as always, pleasant, companionable, liberal, enlightened. Janice, a jewel of a woman, sensuous and devoted to the Boss. I really like Simmons, a sceptical Darwinian in the manner of John Hewitt. Only Ulster could have produced such a man and it is proof of the distinctiveness of Ulster that it does constantly produce persons of Simmons' and Hewitt's cast of mind. Such minds couldn't be created in Southern Ireland, and to deny this is a form of Balkanized Fenian idiocy.

1992

January 27th A poetry reading and workshop in the prison on Spike Island. Mainly teenagers, joyriders and pickpockets. I did my best. A very strange atmosphere, not so much among the prisoners but among the staff. Spike is a kind of dangerous high school.

Oscar Wilde lectured in the Opera House in St Paul on 16th and 17th March, 1882.

February 1st Eoghan Harris's long and complicated phone call at the library. Two hours, at least. 'I would like to embark upon this material for television. We haven't had a television series that shows the development of modern Ireland, from the end of the Civil War to the accession of Mary Robinson.' Eoghan advises me to write out an entire storyline in one sitting, perhaps only five pages: 'Write it in one sitting, carry the reader along.' He says that I must write immediately to David Blake-Knox of RTÉ Television, that I should write a good covering letter and the five-page treatment that tells the story of the rise to power of the Waterford Glenvilles and the eventual decline of Fianna Fáil. This phone call exhausted me and sent my head into a spin.

March 26th Alan Murgatroyd in Lismore, working on the script for the 'Lismore Experience' audio visual. Murgatroyd staying at Richmond House, Cappoquin.

April 14th Rochestown College, 'Book Night' at 7.30 p.m.

April 16th The incomparable Ronan Guilfoyle (friend of Marchioness of Mateus from Hot Club, Lisbon) playing at the Triskel Arts Centre.

April 22nd Reading again Lowell's 'Waking Early Sunday Morning' and 'Fourth of July in Maine'. Both poems are heavily dependent on Marvell's 'Horatian Ode on Cromwell's Return from Ireland'. Jonathan Raban compares Lowell to Marvell: 'Lowell's poetry hunts, like Marvell's, for the private men behind the public faces. It shares the same equivocal obsession with heroes and heroic action. It comes to the same tortured and ambiguous conclusions about the final virtue of privacy.'

The trouble is that all poetry which touches upon politics must arrive at conclusions that are both 'tortured' and 'ambiguous'. It is not possible for a poem to have credibility if it deals only with 'heroic' events. Heroic events are not personal and it is through the personal that one arrives at a state of poetry. Or should I say that it is only through the 'personal' that one can verify the poet's signature in the given world.

But the personal element need not be the autobiographical element. This is what really confuses critics and makes them personally hostile to a poet of politics.

August 16th At Glenshelane today. Arrived just in time to have stuffed yellow tomatoes and cold potatoes on the veranda. Adrian FitzGerald was just finishing lunch and heading off to Tralee to do research on the Kerry FitzGeralds, work that he's been doing for nearly ten years. I told him he should apply to do a PhD on the vast amount of Geraldine research he has already done. He didn't think I was being serious, but I was. Why shouldn't he get a PhD for this work?

The garden looked beautiful and only serves to remind me how inferior my own garden at Montenotte has become. This year has been one of total neglect. Before tea the Brigadier showed me the contents of a trunk left to him by his sister-in-law, Elizabeth. She died in peculiar circumstances last

winter. The trunk contained the most beautiful photographs
of journeys taken during the 1930s, '40s and '50s in Europe
and Ireland: photographs of almost heartbreaking loveliness.
Also, the complete unpublished manuscript of a biography
of Henry Fielding by Brian, the Brigadier's brother, and the
manuscript of another book, *Lord Kildare's Grand Tour* by
Elizabeth FitzGerald. Finally, just for a few magic minutes,
we looked through the journal kept by Brian and Elizabeth
through the 1940s and '50s. On just one page there was a
detailed account of a visit to Dublin in the late '40s during
the period of the Inter-Party Government: conversations
with Donal Nevin of the Trade Union movement as well as
contacts with Erskine Childers, the former President.

September 27th Today at a workshop in Nenagh, County
Tipperary — a beautiful, prosperous town.

Extraordinary phone call on Thursday from Eoghan Harris
who's currently working on a bio-pic of Michael Collins.
Again he wants me to submit a scenario of my novels to RTÉ
under the new Script Development Unit. He was full of
enthusiasm for *Asya and Christine* especially. Harris sees the
entire Glenville story in 6 x 50-minute slots or 3 x 100-minute
dramatic slots.

October 23rd Yesterday, Kevin's conferring at UCC. He is
now a McCarthy PhD — the first Doctor in our McCarthy
clan in recorded history. A triumph of Free Education and
the socialist belief in improving the life chances of the poor.
The ceremony was very moving because Kevin was the only
Doctor conferred on the day. The President of the College
addressed Kevin as he stood alone, speaking to him in Latin
and admitting him as a Doctor of the University. When he
walked to the podium to collect his PhD there was pro-
longed, enthusiastic applause from the assembled BEs, BComms
and MScs. I yelled his name in a momentary act of family
chauvinism. Also, at UCC yesterday, I met Eoghan Harris

for an hour. Eoghan, dressed in Trotskyite black, was standing bareheaded in the rain. His unbelievably troubled face, wounded by the world, too intelligent. A firm handshake. We pushed our way downstairs into the Boole Library basement and eventually found a spare table. Eoghan immediately launched into his reading of the 'Party' story for television. He has a broader view of Deputy Glenville, a more violent view — he will alter the novels into something unrecognizable. He spoke about a dramatic opening to the story such as a botched murder, blood and guts. He had a very good concept of a beginning to the story, but no concept of the most important thing: how Fianna Fáil has held power, how it has made the Dáil its instrument. Not by the gun at all but by the blunt instrument of the ballot box.

November 7th A phone call from John Waters (of *Irish Times* and *Jiving at the Crossroads* fame). We had a long conversation at the Lending desk while a queue of irate borrowers looked on. He has read *Without Power* and some of the poems. Strangely the poem he most remembers is 'At De Valera's Cottage' from *The Sorrow Garden*. He wants to meet me next Monday to take part in a BBC Radio 4 interview on Irish identity.

November 11th Yesterday, a long day. John Waters of the *The Irish Times* and Gweneth, a woman from the BBC Radio 4, called to the library to interview me about 'Politics and Identity' in Ireland. Waters an extremely decent man, very concerned and really fearful about Irish society. He thought I was a little cynical, and a little too sanguine, about the hypocrisies of our society. But I tried to convince him that hypocrisy was a way of life in Ireland, that we were (and are) brilliant at coping with problems by not addressing them. The woman from the BBC wanted me to read the poem on Dev's cottage, but I also read the poem I wrote yesterday! After work I took John and Gweneth to a reception at The

Firkin Crane Centre in Shandon. There we met the City Librarian and Vincent McDonnell, the writer.

Later I went to UCC where Nuala Ní Dhomhnaill was giving a 'Gala Poetry Reading' as UCC's first Writer-in-Residence. Saw John Montague and Patrick Galvin. Ní Dhomhnaill's reading went very well. She is a genius, and I use the word 'genius' deliberately. There is nobody like her, or as important as her, in contemporary Irish poetry after Heaney. She dominates Irish circles with a Russian literary authority.

November 14th The November Election Campaign continues. Today (lunchtime) there's a discussion between Alan Dukes, Proinsias De Rossa and Charlie McCreevy, chaired by Rodney Rice. The discussion is about mortgage interest relief and Albert Reynolds' arrogance over the Northern Ireland talks.

November 16th Driving through Lismore the rain began to fall. Across from the Castle gates, on the new grass margin developed by the County Council, there was a large hoarding advertising the PD candidate Martin Cullen: Cullen smiling face on one side while Dessie O'Malley was on the flip-side facing Cappoquin. At Cappoquin the town was bare and naked and washed clean by the rain. Only Sinn Féin and Democratic Left had bothered to put up posters.

1993

February 12th On the Dublin train, returning to Cork after an appearance on RTÉ's Bibi Baskin show — my first appearance on a chat show. I was on a panel with Rosaleen Linehan, the brilliant actress and comedienne who comes from a Donegal Fine Gael family, and Patricia Scanlan the novelist. Bibi is a wonderful creature, effervescent, intelligent and immensely attractive. I bored her and she could barely hide her boredom with me. I am not a TV person, unfortunately.

March 1st My father born this day in 1923.

June 10th Collected the Brigadier at the airport at 5 p.m. He had spent ten days in London. One of the days was spent at Wellington Barracks where he had to go over old photograph albums that had been sent to the Regiment by the relatives of dead officers. It was a strange task. The Brigadier is one of the few survivors of the Irish Guards in the late '20s and '30s so he could identify many of those dead companions. While at Wellington Barracks he met a young Sergeant who said, 'Did I hear you mention Cappoquin, Sir?' The Brigadier was delighted to discover that the young Guards Sergeant had camped below Glenshelane House when he was a member of the Ballincollig Boy Scouts.

I had to return quickly to Cork to introduce Michael D Higgins at the launch of his new collection of poems. A sensitive soul, still in touch with the real world despite his job as a Minister. One of the few intellectuals ever to make it into Government.

July 27th In County Kerry. Thursday. On our way back from

Gallarus Oratory we went to see a beautiful ruined Geraldine castle overlooking Smerwick Harbour.

September 13th Bumped into John Montague at the traffic lights outside Waterstone's. We went to the Harlequin Café in Paul Street for a cup of coffee — but not before John inspected the magazine rack in Waterstone's to see if there were any reviews of his latest book, *Time in Armagh*. We found a review in the *Steeple*, Pat Cotter's magazine. John says that there's a review coming up in *The Irish Times* on Saturday. J M seemed tired and at the same time agitated. He says they'll have to sell their Ballydehob house because it is too expensive to run two homes. He spoke about the farewell party for Seamus Deane who's heading to Notre Dame to run an Irish Studies Institute at which party Deane became increasingly depressed and unsociable. No doubt the shadow of Heaney's fame has depressed that entire older generation of poets in Ireland: this fame won't ebb so they'll all just have to develop tougher coping mechanisms.

There's a great deal of laziness in Montague. Living off one's reputation is a catastrophe. One's reputation belongs to the decade when it is formed. It cannot be constantly drawn upon like a deposit of cash. Rather, every ten years a writer must remake himself. Montague has been smug for nearly twenty years. But the thing about John is he has immense qualities and capacities. He could remake himself in increasingly magnificent ways — but he is like me, he is inert. He thinks that success and fame will seek him out, that fame will discover him while he drinks quietly in the snug of Henchy's or The Long Valley. But this isn't the way fame works; it is something that has to be sown, harrowed and harvested methodically, as Seamus Heaney has demonstrated. After Heaney no poet can claim that he or she hasn't been warned about this fact of life: fame is not passive. But for John being a poet has been a kind of entitlement rather than any kind of responsibility. And he would be quick to admit this if I challenged him.

October Weekend Went to Dublin to interview Gerry Adams of Sinn Féin for *Stet*. A depressing experience. Adams an attractive, soft-spoken, handsome man but utterly intransigent in terms of politics. He unashamedly believes in the 'Republican cause' — he counters criticism of the narrow view of his fiction (*The Street* and *Cage Eleven*) with the statement that enough people attack the Republican viewpoint so why shouldn't one person (himself) defend that view? His fiction is written to amuse the foot soldiers of the IRA, to cheer up the mothers of IRA men: in other words, it is written specifically to further the 'cause' by raising the morale of the IRA. How can this be literature? One thing is absolutely clear from talking to him: there is really no difference between the current Sinn Féin and the IRA. The idea that there is a 'political wing' and a 'military wing' is rubbish — it is all just one revolutionary movement. The Army Council is everything. It has to be everything.

When I arrived back home to Cork on the 8 o'clock train another drama began. A phone call from John Montague. He was looking for a place to stay. He arrived at the door like a street urchin, exhausted and without possessions. But he wasn't alone. We couldn't refuse him (and therefore them) a bed for the night. Chaos. It is always chaos with John. Chaos. Chaos.

October 29th Last night we evicted Montague and his young love. It was an amicable enough eviction — no RIC men, no battering rams. Just a parting cup of tea from the landlords (ourselves) and a ride for the unwelcome tenants to their new Congested District Board cottage (The Glencora B&B). John had become unbearable. Having come for a weekend he had stayed six nights — and had every intention of staying on. He kept walking around the house, moaning, 'I'm too generous, too generous' at Catherine and me, then eventually at the children.

'He's a poet,' I explain to Catherine. 'An important poet.' There was silence after that. I didn't want to talk about him anymore as it would only lead to tension in the house.

Meanwhile the greatest political drama of twenty years is unfolding in the world outside. The Taoiseach has met with the British Prime Minister in Brussels; the killings in the North go on; the process of bringing Gerry Adams in from the cold goes on. I hope and pray that the politicians succeed.

November 8th Just finished typing the Gerry Adams' interview for *Stet* magazine.

November 10th Spent nearly an hour this evening looking over my most recent poems. I've accumulated about sixty pages of poetry, enough for a new collection. At one time I thought of calling such a book *Honeymoon Portrait*, then changed it to a more provocative *Polling Districts* or *The Waiting Deputies*. But now I'm very taken by the sequence I wrote in the summer — so I imagine a new book of poems called *The Lost Province of Alsace*. What surprises me is that there are so few poems about the children. Almost every waking moment of the last five years has been spent thinking about Kate Inez and Neil. They are absolutely the core of my being, yet none of this has been written down. Why didn't I write these thoughts down? Something to do with privacy, I think; respecting their privacy, becoming aware of the privacy of their lives.

Sunday, later Reading again Seferis's account in his *Journal* (July, 1950) of a visit to his home town of Smyrna, then a part of Turkey. He had returned as Greek Ambassador to Ankara. 'Then, little by little from within, the city so well-known to memory, and so strange now, returns to my mind,' he writes as he walks the familiar walls of his Greek childhood, now in hostile territory. Then the diplomat accompanying him says these fateful words: 'The Greeks say it was the Turks who burned down Smyrna. The Turks say it was the Greeks. Who will discover the truth?' These words were used as an epigraph to Montague's *The Rough Field*, with the additional telling words, 'The important thing is who will redeem it?'

How like Irish history Greek history is; a history of burnings, local betrayals, civil war, fragmentation and exile. And beneath this bitter modern history, something else, an older, classical history, barely perceptible like a sunken wreck visible at low tide.

9 p.m. Just read Seán Dunne's introductory essay to *The Cork Anthology*. He writes about UCC in the '70s, 'Thomas McCarthy seemed to have *The Collected Poems* of Yeats glued to his hand.' That memory of me is half true. It wasn't Yeats's *Poems* that I was reading at all, but Norman Jeffares' masterpiece, *A Commentary on the Collected Poems of W B Yeats*. It was much more romantic than Yeats's hard poems — I found Jeffares' commentaries absolutely riveting; they gave me an almost physical pleasure. It was through Jeffares' commentary, not through Yeats's poetry, that I discovered the narcotic quality of a poet's life.

December 8th In Belfast for the weekend at the Poets' House for a reading and a seminar. Both went well, I thought, except that I've become a little embarrassed by the repetitive nature of my talks. It is always either Gaston Bachelard or George Seferis! Jimmy and Janice Simmons still in trouble with the NI Arts Council, the Blackstaff establishment and the Queen's University circle. In short, they are almost completely alienated from Ulster's cultural life.

While at breakfast this morning we watched the News about Israeli settlers in the Occupied Territories shooting Palestinians. The Simmons' Protestant neighbour whom I met on the road to Portmagee — the kindest, mildest woman imaginable — said to me, 'They say we should be more like the Israelis, give the Nationalists an eye for an eye.' I was taken aback by the strength of her feelings. And last night, in north Belfast, two Catholics were killed by the UVF. So it

goes on. May God have mercy on Ulster. But which God?
The Protestant God or the Catholic God? Greg Delanty is
home from America. My interview with Gerry Adams is
published. At the weekend the IRA killed two RUC men.
They are sick, absolutely sick. Ireland is sick. No, Ulster is sick,
this sectarian hatred is a peculiarly Ulster thing. It doesn't
exist in the South because the circumstances that created such
pervasive sectarian hatred never existed in the South. But it
is not Ulster's fault, it is the fault of successful Plantation.

December 22nd Chaos on the London Underground this
morning as the IRA shows its capacity to disrupt British life.
Bomb warnings have shut down two Underground lines and
caused chaos in the British Rail system south of London.
Whose nerve is the London IRA brigade testing, I wonder?
Is their message intended for John Major or Gerry Adams?
What an appalling risk the Irish Government has taken by
inviting Sinn Féin into the peace forum. Without doubt it's
John Hume who bears responsibility for all of this. I hope
that Hume is proved correct. These days are tense with anticipation. If the IRA war is really over and the internment
camps of the Maze and Portlaoise are thrown open then
poetry will be allowed to settle back into something like its
'natural state', a kind of human unease above and beyond
politics. Irish poetry will be restored to its ordinary unhappiness. We will all end up writing like Thomas Kinsella rather
than Seamus Heaney.

1994

April 3rd This day, at 6 p.m. in 1979, my mother died.

May 29th Poetry Ireland meeting. Dublin Castle.

June 4th My father died this day in 1977.

June 5th Listowel Writers' Week.

June 10th A poetry reading in Glanmire House. They want poems on Memory and Childhood.

June 13th A phone call from Jacqueline Simms of Oxford University Press. She is very interested in my next collection. She was wondering would I move to Oxford. But it is all very complicated because of personal things with Peter Jay.

August 28th Our first week in St Paul, Minnesota.
A long year stretches ahead of us. We don't know what the months ahead will bring. Everything is different. Even the air we breathe is different.
If it wasn't for John and Cindy's kindness we'd be in complete despair. They collected us at the airport and prepared our house, even stocked the fridge. We keep their friendship as close to us as possible, and wear it like a spacesuit.

August 30th A day at the English Department, getting orientated. I have an office that was occupied by Jack Patnode, a Macalester Professor who died recently. His books still cover all the shelves. They have a beautiful smell, that distinct American smell that comes from different glue and bindings.

At John and Cindy's house in tree-lined Vernon Street. Here also a relaxed, cosmopolitan atmosphere. Intensity of reading, good wine, handsome looks, a flair for life. Yes, I am at home in this blessed corner of Snelling and St Clair.

September 1st Today to the Minnehaha Falls, a deep glen cut into a wooded grove between St Paul and Minneapolis. This place reminds me of Killarney, of the Torc waterfall and the romance of Victorian places. Tourism is such a false activity, but the need for it is not false. There is great irony in journeying to places where the imagination has already been. The happiest journeys are the ones that confirm our dream life.

September 3rd To the State Fair. Intense heat, but the constant threat of a thunderstorm. A huge event, thousands of people shepherded through turnstiles, foodstalls and advertising booths. On the way home the bus conductor was asked about a stop in St Paul, 'Heck, I don't know these parts,' he said (rather too proudly, I thought), 'I'm from Minneapolis. I only drive over here during the State Fair.'

Monday 5th Labour Day Went to Stillwater on the St Croix River with our old friend Tom Redshaw, the editor of *Éire-Ireland* and scholar of all things Irish.

September 15th This morning I spent reading Tom Paulin's essay on Yeats's 'Meditations in Time of Civil War'. Paulin is always good on the broad view, putting Yeats's timing of publication into perspective.

The first teaching week. The English Department like the foyer of the Listowel Arms during Writers' Week. Professors and students with papers and timetables rushing about. 'Could you sign this?' 'Can I join your Monday class?' 'I need to do another senior seminar, could I join yours, Professor, please?' It is absolutely impossible for me to say no to such pleadings. Now I think my classes will be overloaded. Interesting young writers in the Poetry Workshop: Mike Dawson from an Irish farming community in North East Iowa. Names that make their mark: Julie Liu, Debbie Siegal. My office takes on the character of a raft in a stormy ocean. More and more students come in, all in a state of panic, wanting to join my class. Not because they admire me, God help us, no; but because they need me and my class credit.

September 20th Today I was talking to a group of students about Irish Modernism. They find it difficult to accept that it exists, yet all of them have read Joyce and Beckett. I showed them Coffey's 'Missouri Sequence' and Denis Devlin's 'Lough Derg'. Without much success, I think. They really want more of Kavanagh, more of Heaney, more of the cluttered story-telling Irish material. But it is a mistake to force them to be Modernist, to make them want to follow Devlin instead of Heaney, particularly when, in every way, I belong to the Kavanagh-Heaney camp.

September 22nd Reading the Brigadier's letter from Glenshelane House. Everything OK in West Waterford, my brother Michael in good form. But he writes that they've had forty-two inches of rainfall in the garden already this year — more than the whole of last year.

October 1st One of my favourite places in St Paul is the intersection of Snelling and University Avenues. The other day my Poetry and Politics class opened out into a general discussion on immigration and racism. The students were surprised that I felt so much at home in America. Why wouldn't I feel at home? A good deal of American life has been 'formatted' (to use a computer term) so that most Irishmen slot in very easily. Our stay here in Minnesota is not exile, it is more like a long commute.

October 10th Columbus Day A day no longer celebrated in

America, but passed over in embarrassment, like the 1916 Rising at home.

October 13th More work today on Auden's social world. I'm not giving the students my best. I know I can teach better than this. It's not that I haven't prepared classes, it's really a matter of paying attention to the students. Are they really getting all these English references? Do they understand the feel of the landscapes? I mean the feel of Auden? I've been trying to get across the idea of Auden's search for a personal landscape. As a poet one of his first agendas was to escape the incoherent waste land of Eliot.

October 12th We took a paddle-steamer on the Mississippi River. As the boat churned through the water I felt a terrific sense of unreality. A tedious journey, despite everything. I hate things that move slowly. Nothing in the world outside books is so compelling that one has to move forward at only five miles an hour.

October 17th Very cold. Walked to SuperAmerica on St Clair to get a bar of chocolate and drinks for the kids. Also, to clear my head after tonight's poetry workshop. My head not so much cleared as anaesthetised by the chilling still air. It is lovely to walk up St Clair towards Mississippi River Boulevard on nights like this. During the day the College is like any busy place, but at night the whole Macalester quarter takes on a distinctive American neighbourhood atmosphere. The hermetic quiet of American suburbs. Two highway patrol cars were parked at the filling station. Three cops chatting beside the coffee machine, their radios crackling, their coffee cups steaming. A young Asian behind the counter, Korean, impeccably dressed and efficient. He breaks into a smile when he sees me. I am one of his late evening regulars. We chat about the weather in a very un-American way. I think it is a comfort to both of us. At this time of the day America is overwhelming. There is really very little else. The non-American world doesn't even seem like a possibility until midnight when National Public Radio rebroadcasts the BBC World Service and *The New York Times* confirms the existence of Europe with its foreign news reports. All through the night, otherwise, every night, there is only America. Elsewhere just doesn't exist. You need to be a settled resident in America to understand this extraordinary sense of Mid-West self-possession.

October 25th Today was a truly wasted day. In class we worked on Auden's interview in *The Paris Review* as well as the aphorisms. I tried to get volunteers to read Spender's *World Within World* so that we could have a general discussion on the mindset of an educated English liberal. There were no takers, but much avoidance of the Professor's eyes. Fall Break is upon us, and with it comes a sense of fatigue among students.

October 26th Talking with Catherine is one of the best things about America. Why can't we have this kind of time at home in Ireland? Do all College Professors in Ireland have this kind of opportunity to talk to the people in their lives? It's not that I don't work hard at teaching. I do. But for the first time in twenty years I feel I have the power to manage each day.

October 28th The terrible political seriousness of Charles Donnelly and John Cornford. Spender, at least, honours Cornford at every turn. Donnelly, a County Tyrone man, was part of the Connolly Column which in turn was part of the Lincoln Brigade. He died on the Jarama Front in February 1937. In his 'Poem' he actually defines the difference between the professional poet and the poet of action. What defines them both is 'simple action'. Only the moment of commitment, what he honestly describes as 'Simple and unclear moment', only that moment divides the two kinds of poet.

It is the moral reticence of Charles Donnelly that makes

him interesting. Sacrifice has not spent all his intellectual resources. He challenges Auden in a way that Pearse could never challenge Yeats or Bobby Sands could challenge Heaney.

October 30th Halloween One of the most magical nights we've spent since coming to America. Kate and Neil, dressed up as a witch and a Power Ranger, did the rounds of houses in Vernon Street and Macalester Street to mark Halloween.

November 1st The days turning colder. Minnesota's winter needle is gradually inserted into our consciousness. When the snow comes we will have already gone under this anaesthetic of cold.

November 3rd Catherine's birthday. We went to a brilliant restaurant, Chez Colette, with John and Cindy. But, first, to 219 Vernon Street for champagne.

November 8th A disastrous election night for the Democrats. Ann Wynia threw away the election for Governor of Minnesota, with the help of almost every socialist and gay supporter of the Democratic party. The Liberals betrayed Wynia with a well rehearsed chorus of extremist fringe interventions at almost every public opportunity. By the time we went to Congressman Bruce Vento's party in a palatial mansion the pennies were already rolling in: one group was having a hostile encounter with another. The blame was being apportioned over the wine and cheese. We drove to downtown Minneapolis where a party that was more like a state funeral was taking place. Everybody saying that Bill Clinton is a disaster, a President who has betrayed every liberal promise. *Plus ça change*.

The lights of the St Clair Broiler still blinking at 2 a.m. when I return home to Macalester Street. One expects Dashiell Hammett or Raymond Chandler to emerge from its lobby. Eternal America. And, in the distance, the sound of a train coming up over the bluffs. At this time of night it could be the *Empire Builder* en route to Chicago. Witnessing a political disaster is so exciting that I can't sleep. What a disastrous night for the Democrats. It is like being at home in Ireland.

November 15th A long conversation with Tom Redshaw on the phone about Nuala Ní Dhomhnaill's poetry. Tom is trying to come to terms with the Muldoon translations, alarmed, I think, by the literal meanings and the Muldoon 'equivilances' in the English language. I often wonder myself about those texts, but I've less Irish than Muldoon, an Irish-language graduate of Queen's who lived in the Kerry Gaeltacht after he left the BBC in Belfast. There is pure and simple mischief in some of the translations: 'Tagann an traein dubh / isteach sa stáisiún' becomes, in Muldoon, 'As surely as the Headless Horseman came to Ichabod Crane'.

Why does he link the Black Train with 'The Legend of Sleepy Hollow' by Washington Irving? Then again, he does something like turning 'bordálann siad / an traein cheanna' into 'they all will mount / the gangway of the Windigo'. This appears to be self-indulgent Muldoon until one realizes that the word 'gangway' is like the German word 'Ausgang' or 'exit'. At the end of this poem there are cattle wagons, Dachau and Belsen. None of these words is in the original Irish text of Ní Dhomhnaill. What Muldoon is doing is spectacular: he is creating a third text, not a version in English. But this third text, neither Muldoon nor Ní Dhomhnaill, is probably closer to the subliminal, voyage-of-the-psyche stuff that Nuala has been creating in Irish. It's not a question of knowing the Irish language. It's really a question of knowing how a poem creates its own distinctive dialect. The students at Macalester were amazed by this process when I pointed it out. The sophistication of Muldoon as translator thrilled them, so that they left the classroom full of excitement. That's a unique moment in a teaching day — when the students feel that they've been party to something intensely private, amazing, and exclusively literary. Muldoon and Ní Dhomhnaill between them have created a kind of new rhetoric of Irish genius; their translation-encounter has been the great event of the 1990s in Irish writing.

November 18th Two weeks of Lowell. Difficult to isolate *Notebook* in the way I had hoped. One can't talk about the political Lowell without reading widely into the two early worlds of religion and family. With Lowell America is personal. For Mary McCarthy, Daniel Berrigan, Bob Dylan, Denise Levertov and others the Vietnam conflict was an issue of political and moral dishonour. But with Lowell it was always personal; the world couldn't be apprehended by him unless it had personal resonances. Lowell's impulse is psychotic, always psychotic, and too unhinged to be merely self-serving. He was the victim of his own tortuous impulses, so that it wasn't America. It was him.

At a book launch in the University Club at Summit Avenue. I drove there in our Dodge Omni, braving St Paul traffic for a few hundred yards. I overshot the Club and almost got lost in the dark streets while trying to turn around. I felt like a character in a Scott Fitzgerald novel as I wandered through the foyer of the warm Victorian building. A mighty crowd had assembled to hear the Hon Desmond Guinness and Jacqueline O'Brien talking about Dublin's Georgian architecture. They were promoting an excellent and lavish book on Dublin's interiors. The whole 'do' sponsored by Dan and Mary Hardy, Minnesota's Irish Georgians. Desmond and Jacqueline both very giddy and full of good humoured mischief. For part of the talk the slides were shown upside down. 'Oh, go on, they're only ceilings,' Desmond Guinness replied in a wicked, tipsy voice when someone pointed out the error. I left early, worried about the route home.

November 20th Yesterday, an early morning flight to Milwaukee to read to James Liddy's group during an Irish Festival. Marvellous crowd, terrific response. Liddy an angel.

November 27th Sunday after Thanksgiving. Snow began to fall this morning. I drove up St Clair in the falling snow to SuperAmerica to buy *The New York Times* and the *Pioneer Press*. I came back covered in snow, but as happy and enervated as Minnesotans are by the first serious sight of winter. Each resident of Minnesota, Irish or African-American, Korean or Hmong, becomes Scandinavian and serious for the duration of the snow.

But today's snow was entirely personal. Kate and Neil are wild with excitement. They can't believe that the snow goes on and on. After a few hours I began to clear the path and steps to the house. I was the only adult outdoors. Dorothy, our neighbour, came to her door to give me an important lesson on the etiquette of snow. 'Did you not listen to the weather forecast, dear? There's no point clearing the snow away. This will go on for another twelve hours.'

December 9th While I was in my office a phone call from the Hungry Mind Bookstore to let me know that the copies of *Dubliners* had come into stock for next semester's seminar. I went down after class to collect my desk copy. Took it back to the student grill where I had a coffee and read Terence Brown's Introduction.

December 10th Looking at the calendar for next year. Spring break is March 18-26. The mid-term grades are due March 29th. All classes end by May 12th, with Commencement on May 20th. My appointment ends officially in the middle of June, after which time we will be trespassing on American soil.

December 12th My last Poetry Workshop, ended at 10.20 p.m. Walked home on a very cold night, exhausted and perplexed. Did they get anything out of this workshop? I don't think I dominated it enough, or encouraged my own style of exchange: I let them engage with each other in the way they were used to. I should have created a greater spark. I should have demanded much, much more from them. I should have pulled and strained and dominated the discussions, instead of allowing the hours to drift by in silence as if we were all at a Quaker meeting. If ever I do a workshop with such senior students again I'll absolutely dominate the floor, I'll not be passive. I have left them disappointed and this saddens me. I don't think I inspired ambition in a single student. This depresses me enormously tonight.

December 13th A reception at Michael Keenan's house on Ashland Avenue. Michael, Chair of the English Department, and his wife, Susan, are retiring soon. They've already bought a house in New Mexico, in a beautiful, burned landscape that looks like Spain or the Greek islands.

December 31st Catherine has gone with Kate Inez and Neil to see the old Vanderbilt farm near Sherbourne on Lake Champlain. I've been reading another book on the Twin Cities, *French Lessons* by Alice Kaplan, a Professor of French at Duke University. Wonderful descriptions of upper middle-class life in the Midwest.

Spent hours with this book, the same kind of hours I spent with Patricia Hampl's memoirs.

Back in my office at Macalester are all the jumbled chapters of the third and final Party novel. It is difficult to work on the third one when the other two have been remaindered. I feel utterly betrayed by that act. But I'm determined that 1995 will see the completion, however flawed and however unsung, of my Waterford Trilogy.

1995

January 18th When I use words to describe history whose words do I use? Truth is, I don't wish to decide upon one Irish world only — I've been close enough to each world to want to hold on to elements of each. But my unwillingness to exclude the world of the Brigadier, for instance, really annoys some people, even Cathy, even my brother Kevin, who wish well for my work. They see these competing loyalties as a barrier that prevents me from breaking through to the 'mainstream' of the dominant literary critics — a literary viewpoint now dominated by the Ulster poets. But because of the Brigadier in the life of my early adulthood, and W E D Allen and Molly Keane, I've inherited this duality of memory. I can see the Protestant viewpoint in Irish history as clearly as the light of day. I've become awkward, politically ambiguous. I've crossed over the barriers in the middle of a conflict.

January 23rd Rose Fitzgerald Kennedy has died from pneumonia at the age of 104. Of all the Irish mothers in America she was the most famous. In that life she embodied the three most powerful elements in Irish Catholic civilization: Family, Politics and the Church. Rose lost four children, two in accidents and two assassinated. Few American mothers were ever called upon to suffer so much. But this continuing mix of Church and Politics was even more graphically illustrated by the death, another Irish-American death, that occurred three weeks ago in Boston. On this day of Rose Kennedy's funeral I still think of the death of young Shannon Lowney, a 1991 graduate of Boston College, singer, piano-player, women's rights activist, who was murdered in an attack on a Planned

Parenthood clinic in Brookline. In her early twenties, she worked as a counsellor. When I think of those two Boston women, the first an embodiment of long-suffering, patriotic Catholic womanhood and the latter an educated, Irish-American Liberal who believed that women should have full authority over their own lives, I wonder which life was more heroically lived? Both lives, I guess. Both lives.

March 3rd Catherine has just finished an excellent short story, 'Everybody's Heard of Michelangelo', a work of at least 12,000 words. It's a terrific achievement: the fulfilment of an idea she had months and months ago. She thinks it may not be as good as 'The Rat and the Flamingo' or 'Rembrandt and Escher' but I think it's her most professional work. It's an extensive piece of fiction, not just a lyrical moment. With this story she has entered through the narrow gate of serious fiction.

May 8th The interesting thing about the Ulster conflict is that it wasn't the vocabulary of the conflict that entered the language through poetry of the last ten years — it was more the vocabulary of our revisionist response. If one looks at the 1970s one sees the 'Triptych' of Heaney in *Field Work*, then the anti-IRA poems of Durcan, the anti-Dev poem that I wrote (by far the most popular of my poems among anthologists precisely because it coincides with an accepted revisionist outlook). Despite this political vacuum, though, the IRA never produced a good Irish Republican poet. Fiction writers, yes, but no poet? Why? Was it because poets are more easily frightened off subject matter by opinion? What is wrong with Ireland that it has never produced a political writer of the calibre of Achebe or Ngũgĩ wa Thiong'o? Have we allowed others to rob us of the meaning of our history?

May 16th A letter from Jacqueline Simms of Oxford saying that, on reflection, she can't publish *The Lost Province*. I just don't think she could poach me from Peter Jay's list. She just couldn't do it; emotionally, I mean. Her personal links with Peter run too deep and I admire her for that loyalty. But I'm the one who is damaged by her withdrawal, even if her reasons are personal. I should tell Greg Delanty and Theo about this because there is now a vacancy at Oxford for a Southern Irish poet — or at least there's a vacancy in Jacqueline Simms' mind that can only be filled by another Irishman or Irishwoman, and probably a poet from the South.

May 25th Reading Wallace Fowlie's *Mallarmé*, a beautiful book, with line drawings by Matisse. This description of Mallarmé really struck me: 'There is a kind of mildness which succeeds in exerting a deeper influence than belligerency can. This was Mallarmé's mildness which, because it was inflexible, was also penetrating.' That's a very West Waterford trait, that penetrating mildness: Dervla Murphy has it, and Pádraig J Daly. Arland Ussher had it too; indeed he was famous for his intransigent mildness. It's a trait that would never be understood in Cork, for example, or any part of Belfast. But it is a very strong thing, a distinctly Waterford strength, and it is constantly misinterpreted as weakness. It is not weak. In me it is an implacably Cappoquin thing, an attitude that you can find in all the Frahers and the Powers of the Blackwater Valley but hardly ever in my own family. This arrogant mildness must have come to me from the air and the soil of Cappoquin.

June 21st I'm sitting on a wooden deck that goes right out over the waters of Lake Superior, a giant inland sea. A flight of ducks just went by, and a few loons. Neil found the trail of a moose in a cave by the rocks where the Manitou River falls into Lake Superior. The only access to this cave is by boat. This shore is beautiful but so isolated, desolate. The Minnesota wilderness really *is* a wilderness. But Neil and

Kate fished and fished, casting and spinning. What a joy this has been for them. What a way to say goodbye to America.

August 2nd Nearly a month back home in Ireland. Psychologically I feel that we've arrived home only in the last few days. Coming back was a kind of nervous breakdown.

August 7th Last Thursday the poet Seán Dunne died. He was only 39. We buried him in St Gobnait's Cemetry in Ballyvourney, the resting place of Seán Ó Ríordáin and Ó Riada. Seán died in his sleep, of heart failure, although he had been in the best of health recently. He leaves behind three children, motherless since Sara left them, and now fatherless. Because of the bad feelings that Seán created between us we had seen very little of him, or his family, in the last six years. Fr Kevin of Mount Melleray Abbey took the funeral, along with Fr Tom Hayes of The Lough parish. I thought that Pádraig J Daly, the Dungarvan priest-poet, might be there, but he wasn't. All of Seán's friends (indeed, all the people he systematically turned against me) were there: Dan Mulhall, Aengus Collins, Barra Ó Seaghdha, editor of *Graph* magazine, Pat Cooke from Waterford and Peter Fallon, the publisher. John Montague gave a marvellous short eulogy after the Communion service. At the graveside twelve friends and poets read a poem of his: we buried him as a poet should be buried, we covered him with his own poems.

After the funeral Trish, his belovèd, took me aside. 'I need to say something to you,' she said, and she took my hands in hers. I sat or rather knelt beside her as she spoke. 'You know, Seán spoke about you a lot before he died. Just this month he said, 'Tom has really drifted away from me. When I was twenty-five we were like brothers.'

Her words made me desperately sad, but they confirmed everything that I'd suspected for years. When I look at the pattern of his friendships and literary relationships I see therein a dark side, the downside.

Ironically, Seán went to Mount Melleray and read Thomas Merton at my urging. I remember giving him copies of Merton's books. But both Melleray and Merton were his own unique developments: the way they happened within him, that is. In them he found his own personal myth. He found a new dialect, an imaginative escape from me. In *The Road to Silence* he found a balm. In this way, therefore, he was at the very beginning of his real literary career. He died at the very beginning. This is cruel in its hardness. Death is the most cruel and envious thing that awaits us all.

August 8th I've just been reading an essay 'The Uncertainty of the Poet' by Michael Heller in *American Poetry Review*. In his concluding remarks he says 'The poet needs, it would seem, to cultivate, at a minimum, a hypersensitivity to the "mythologies" of poetic craft, including those narcotics we call beauty, harmony, symmetry. In this sense, the poet can not afford to be merely a literary figure. His field of activity is the entire language production of the available culture.'

When I think of literary envy, especially poetic envy in Ireland, I'm reminded that this envy occurs only within that very narrow range defined by Heller, the range of 'the literary figure'. Of course this is a cultural thing as well: for to be a 'literary figure' in Ireland is to be *Somebody*.

August 18th Tonight I finished working on the translations of the Romanian poet, Daniela Crăsnaru. This is for an anthology of Romanian poets translated by Irish poets to be published by Bloodaxe Books next Spring. A reciprocal publication of ten Irish poets will come out in Romania in due course.

September 9th Seán Dunne's death has affected me now, much more than in the first weeks after his death. I looked at his photographs in the paper today and thought: 'Friend-poet, how cruel death is. How it serves its own purposes. You were just at the beginning, just at the beginning of discovering your own strength, and death came to plunge a knife in your back.' His death reminds me that there is so little time. Will I, for example, ever live to write the work that I've carried in my head for twenty years, *The Last Geraldine Officer*?

October 3rd Tonight the launch of John Montague's *Collected Poems*. I went directly from work at the library lending-desk to Pierre's restaurant in French Church Street. It was raining yet again, so I arrived at the empty café looking like a drowned rat. After fifteen minutes Tina Neylon of the Firkin Crane Centre arrived, looking very young and elegant. She had dressed up for the occasion: Montague would notice this and it would please that strong social part of his nature. We ordered a bottle of wine and waited. After another fifteen minutes Peter Fallon of The Gallery Press arrived carrying two copies of the new book. A rather stern-looking John on the cover, but a beautiful cover.

Montague and Elizabeth finally arrived at 6.25, leaving us with little more than an hour for the meal. It was John's first glimpse of his *Collected* so we all raised our glasses in salute. I mentioned to Peter Fallon that I'd met a Professor from Deerfield at a Macalester College Board meeting. Peter was able to put a name on him. The waiter interrupted our banter about poets and poetry with the news that the American, O J Simpson, had been found not guilty at his murder trial. Disbelief and anger from both women at the table. That man will now make millions — in a world where name recognition is everything his name will become stronger than that of Nixon or Lindberg. After that news we had no stomach for dessert: we wolfed our coffees and left.

By the time we arrived at the Firkin Crane in Shandon the heavens had opened. The rain was coming down in bucketfuls, as only October rain in Cork does. We raced indoors. I was reassured when I saw Donnchadh Ó Corráin's benign and mischievous face. Then I saw Fidelma Ó Corráin, then

Mary Ahern. Thank God, I thought, Montague's UCC friends haven't deserted him. A decent crowd in the Musgrave Theatre; nothing like the great crowds of Cork poetry's heyday in the UCC 1970s. A good crowd, nevertheless: after all, this launch was taking place during the week of the International Film Festival and the Firkin Crane Centre's Robbie McDonald was in the middle of projection difficulties with Corman's *Boxcar Bertha*. As usual Robbie didn't bat an eyelid so that Montague could have believed that the centre might have been specially built for the launch of his book. I gave a short speech, puffy, unstructured, useless. Then I read the poem 'Crossing'. Patrick Cotter then followed by reading 'Sibyl's Morning' about John's daughter. I was glad to see both Oonagh and Sibyl in the audience, both looking wonderful. Pat Cotter was followed by the UCC scholar Valerie Coogan, a long-time friend of John and Evelyn, followed by Gerry Murphy and Trish Edelstein, Seán D's grieving belovèd. The actor Eamon Maguire then stepped forward and read a chunk of *The Rough Field*. Then Peter Fallon gave a brief talk about the editing and collating process. 'Well, here it is!' he exclaimed, holding the *Collected Poems* aloft. 'I plead not guilty!'

Then John stood up. Quite nervously and quietly he read 'The Trout', 'Like Dolmens Round My Childhood' and two other poems. I was surprised by his choice of poems because in the restaurant he'd said to me — after I'd said that I wanted to read 'All Legendary Obstacles' — 'Ah, leave all that old stuff behind! Read "Border Sick Call" or something from *Time in Armagh*.' He said that love was his abiding thing, *an tír-grá*, patriotism, or in Montague's precise phrase 'landscape love'. While he was reading there were several cracks of thunder. The lights dimmed twice: an appropriate intrusion of the elements. Afterwards, a terrific reception upstairs. Long discussion with Donnchadh and Fidelma about the scandals in the Church. Donnchadh says that it's quite awe-inspiring to see another major historical institution being destroyed before our eyes — so soon after the collapse of the Soviet Communist Party.

Also, met Sally Keane and George Phipps, as well as the ever-present Charlie Hennessy. Hanna O'Sullivan, the City Librarian, was there. I shouted hello to her several times but she ignored me. Hanna hates my guts: God help her. We just hit it off badly from the moment she became City Librarian. Spoke to the two poets of the O'Donoghue clan, Gregory and Liz. And to Debbie Dawson, the artist. Pat Cotter always had the most marvellous luck with very special women, his success due no doubt to his dark, brooding looks and his fluency in German. With Heine on your tongue you could win any woman.

Came home early in the driving rain. Arrived back at the house in a deluge. Ran straight upstairs to check the leaks in Kate's ceiling. Four new wet patches. Our house will fall down if we don't do something soon.

October 4th In the *Guardian* a report that a security firm in Warwickshire has developed a car alarm that emits Rev Ian Paisley's voice at 120 decibels. The director of the firm said that they'd tried many voices but found that Paisley's voice was by far the most terrifying.

Today in the library, a woman looking for the *Paris Review* interview with Robert Frost. Another woman looking for *The Prophet* by Kahlil Gibran. I persuaded her to take Tagore's poetry instead. Tagore was a real artist, whereas Gibran was a chancer and a fool. Just before we closed a man came in looking for a history of the toilet bowl. Somehow it seemed an appropriate end to the day.

October 5th An extraordinary day, a truly extraordinary day in our lives. The Swedish Academy has awarded the Nobel Prize to Seamus Heaney. This is sensational. Everything about that man is sensational; like Gabriel García Márquez he seems to have been born for fame. From the December day in the mid 1960s when the *New Statesman* published a group of his poems fame has stalked him, sought him out, disturbed his peace and challenged his gifts. The wonderful thing is that, like Márquez, he has withstood all the poisonous narcotics of success. Fame just washes over him and he merely shakes himself dry after every encounter.

It was lunchtime in the library when Stephen O'Brien, who ran down from the Reference Library in excitement, said, 'Did you hear about Heaney?' I couldn't believe the news. I phoned home to check with Catherine but she was out. I phoned our neighbour, Nora Stack, Paul Durcan's cousin from County Mayo, but she hadn't been listening to the radio. I went downstairs to the Lending Section to look at his books — sure enough, we had *Death of a Naturalist, North, Seeing Things, Station Island* and *Wintering Out* on the shelves. I placed them all on a display shelf after Bernard Cotter from the Tory Top Road Library phoned to confirm the brilliant news. I phoned Pat Cotter at Waterstone's. He was as jubilant as myself, and as disbelieving, 'Are you sure? Are you sure?'

'Yes.'

'Jesus.'

The first person I could share the news with at the Front Desk was Eamon Corcoran, the old Republican activist, who walked into the library at 2.15. 'Did you hear about Heaney?'

'Dear God, not another dead poet. So soon after Seán Dunne?'

'No, no! It's Heaney, Heaney. He's won the Nobel Prize!'

Eamon was stunned. Tears of Irish Republican pride welled up in his eyes and began to roll down his cheeks. He took off his trilby and bowed to me in admiration of all poets. 'It's a great day for Ireland,' he said, filled with emotion. 'A great day. God bless dem Swedes.' I was overcome and began to cry with Eamon. Library customers looked on in pity. We didn't care. It was a great day for Ireland, it was a joy to be alive on such a day. Thank God we'd lived long enough to see this happen, seventy years after Yeats's Nobel. But Yeats was one of the gentry, today an ordinary Irishman no better than ourselves has won the great Prize. Robert in the Reference Library admitted that it was as exciting, and nearly as important, as Stephen Roche's win in the Tour de France.

And the day went on like that. We all walked on air. My God, Heaney is still in his fifties, yet he has joined the august company of Neruda, Aleixandre, Elytis and Seferis. When Catherine walked into the library I told her. She was thrilled. We decided to buy a bottle of wine on the way home to celebrate. An expensive, good Rioja. When we came home we were glued to the TV. It was the lead story on the 6 o'clock News, pushing paedophile priests and the Bosnian war to one side. For a few minutes the news programmes had turned their eyes to the materials of paradise.

And where was Heaney? Absent. On a walking holiday in Greece. Out of contact. So the media, TV, radio, was forced to use old clips, old footage, old tapes. I thought of what Heaney said when he won the Duff Cooper Award for *North* in 1975: 'During the past few years there has been considerable expectation that poets from Northern Ireland should say something about "the situation", but in the end they will be worth listening to if they are saying something about and to themselves.'

October 7th Bought *USA Today* in a shop on Grand Parade. A photograph of Heaney in the *Headline* feature of its front page. The international nature of his achievement is so palpable in the story credits — the Associated Press provides the text while the photograph is taken from Agence France Press files. The papers mention John Ashbery and Bei Dao as possible contenders. Indeed, I hope that Ashbery gets the Prize soon: too few American poets have won it. Someday, perhaps, Carolyn Forché will win the Nobel Prize. She certainly combines an exquisite lyric gift with a strong, campaigning belief in the redemptive nature of poems. I bought copies of all the Irish papers to send to Tom Redshaw at the University of St Thomas and John Bernstein at Macalester College. Bernstein will be thrilled beyond words. He's been teaching Heaney at Macalester College since *North* in 1975, even possessing early BBC film reels of Heaney that he's kept in his own study at home for fear of the tapes going missing. In St Paul it's been Montague at St Thomas and Heaney at Macalester. It was through one of his Heaney researches that John came across my *Seven Winters in Paris* and bought it — so it was indirectly through Heaney that we all ended up with our joyful family year at Macalester College. I said to John on the phone to America last night that we minor luminaries will probably be using the currency of Heaney in America from now on, the way Padraic Colum and Louis MacNeice floated across America on a Yeatsian carpet in the 1940s and '50s. But at the moment we are all in a state of poetic euphoria. This Heaney fame is a narcotic.

October 8th Last night was a night of poetry and film. Went to Waterstone's at 7 p.m. to take part in a reading of Pablo Neruda's poems. The occasion was a visit by Michael Radford, the British director of *Il Postino*, a film about the poet Neruda's stay in Italy in the '50s (the actual scenes are transferred from Chile to Italy). Most of the poets of the South were there: Theo Dorgan, Paddy Galvin, Gerry Murphy, Liz O'Donoghue. I read 'Being Born in the Woods' from my battered Iowa International Writing Program Delta edition of *Selected Poems*. I said that Neruda was a poet of intimacies and immensities. One dimension that has been lost to all of us is the dimension of communism. The literary world has been deprived of a set of millennial, continental metaphors with the collapse of the Communist East. The great tragedy for poetry in Ireland now is that poets are quickly appropriated by the privileged classes rather than by the oppressed. The rush to embrace our Nobel laureate in recent days is part of that appropriation.

Anyway, all of these thoughts flowed through my mind as I sat with Michael Radford in a box at the Opera House. Looking up at me this night people would see me as a privileged creature. After all I spent the whole evening with the Film Director, an affable, polite and highly polished Englishman who has an E M Forster-like feel for Italy and Italian culture and landscape. A lovely man, certainly. But we do belong to a world of privilege, compared to the struggling world.

October 9th Dropped the kids to school, Catherine to work. We talked and talked about Heaney. I find myself wanting to talk about Heaney all the time — his Prize is such a wondrous thing and so *real* precisely because Heaney is so personable and familiar. What surprised us both, though, was the revelation that he had never been to Greece before.

October 10th Lunch with Gregory O'Donoghue in the Café Mexicana. Gregory showed me a brilliant poem about the funeral of his uncle, the painter John O'Donoghue. Much talk about Heaney, and talk about Montague: the complete absence of media coverage of his *Collected Poems*. Before lunch Desmond O'Grady called into the library to look for a book, *Poets in the Landscape*. I couldn't find it. Instead Desmond went away with my own collection *Seven Winters in Paris*. 'Anything will do,' he said, 'I just want to kill two hours while I wait for the bus to Kinsale.' So he took my book. No mention of Heaney or Nobel Prizes.

October 12th A copy of *Fortnight* came in the post. My Seán Dunne obituary.

October 16th On the midnight train from Dublin after a Poetry Ireland Board meeting. A general feeling of triumph and relief, hope and challenge. Heaney's Nobel Prize has turned on all the lights.

October 21st Yesterday an American woman came into the library to search our records for books by Padraic Colum. I went into the back-store for Colum's 1917 book, *Wild Earth,* and for Mary Colum's *Life and the Dream.* The American woman was thrilled to hold the actual original editions in her hands. She had travelled 6,000 miles from San Francisco State University and now stood in a library that stocks twenty-seven Padraic Colum books. The early collection included 'The Drover' and 'The Old Woman of the Roads', the two poems upon which Colum's immortality is secure. I recited a few stanzas of The Old Woman poem: this made the American scholar's day, I think.

On Thursday a rather sickly-looking youth, with the starved face of a James Joyce, came into the library, looking for Thomas MacGreevy's *Poems.* In this time of the Nobel Prize's white heat of fame it's good to see the obscure talents still sought after by the lonely scholar from across the ocean or the stressed-out intellectual youth from his flat in Wellington Road. Poetry is for them; it's written precisely for them. For them poets release those human parts that are truly desolate. We write for ourselves, or for that part of ourselves that is desolate. All poetry is created in an atmosphere of *Humboldt's Gift.* There was never a poet that didn't feel that he or she was down on her luck. As Heaney stands before the King of Norway some part of him will feel that. He has met with and coped with demons before — that poem 'Exposure' in *North* is the point at which he pulled the poet's sword from the stone. He waited, as all of us wait, for the Comet Kohoutek, wondering what poetry was for: 'For the ear? For the people? / For what is said behind-backs?' So that poems also wait for us, their desolate readers, after they've been written and cast aside by their poets. The awaiting reader is that observer of the night sky. Padraic Colum, the fading comet, found his astronomer yesterday in the form of a San Francisco scholar.

October 25th Yesterday, collected The Brigadier at the airport. Appalling rain. I was soaked to the skin and, as the heater was broken in the car, I felt that I was sitting in a puddle of water all the way to the airport. The Brigadier very tired after his trip to London. He wanted to know if I'd written to the woman in Nijmegen from whose house he'd taken the copy of *The Collected Poems of William Carlos Williams* during the Allied advance through Holland in 1944. I said I'd write to her this week and include a copy of my poem 'Survivors of War' from *The Sorrow Garden*.

On the avenue to Glenshelane House we had to pull up suddenly because a New Age Travellers' truck had broken down. A long wait before we could proceed. A young woman emerged from the back of the truck carrying an infant. 'Is your child not damp?' I asked. 'Oh, aye,' she said in an English accent. 'This is a damp, cold place.'

And just at that moment the place did seem damp, cold and forbidding. Leaves dripping everywhere and drenched animals passing by. The roar of the Glenshelane River in full spate. I think the roar of the river frightened the mother more than anything: there is such murderous power in a swift flow of flood water. Although it was only 6 p.m. it was dark. The scene was like a picture taken from my own life when I was seventeen or eighteen. That dripping, cold darkness of a West Waterford adolescence. And the appalling desolation I felt at having been born poor. Even the wet trees seemed to be stacked up against me at that time. I felt sorry for the New Age mother, but even more sorry for the little baby who couldn't have chosen the circumstances of its birth.

November 7th Yet again on the bleak midnight train from Dublin. The countryside rattles by quickly, all the homes of Kildare, Laois and Tipperary preserved in the purple aspic of the night. Today, a reading at the Writers' Centre in Parnell Square to launch the Irish edition of *Poetry* (Chicago). A terrific crowd, poets, editors, publishers, John F Deane, Fallon,

Montague, Richard Murphy, Michael Hartnett and Nuala Ní Dhomhnaill (hadn't seen either of them for years), Dennis O'Driscoll, eloquent as usual, Julie O'Callaghan, confident but quiet; too quiet, I think. No Theo or Paula. Theo said yesterday that he would boycott this evening because Paula had been ignored by Chris Agee, the Belfast-based guest editor. It is a foolish thing to do, but I do admire his great loyalty.

But the evening was made worthwhile, even special, for me by the presence of two women, Máire Mhac an tSaoi and Jean Kennedy Smith. Máire and I chatted for a few fugitive minutes. When I meet her I feel that I am in the presence of Anna Akhmatova: immense learning, wisdom, grace and easeful social privilege, each aspect of her character set beautifully in place so that when one steps back to look one sees a brilliantly patterned mosaic. Máire Mhac an tSaoi is a woman I could spend a whole day, a whole year, a lifetime, listening to and watching. Jean Kennedy Smith has the same kind of power and grace: a small impeccably dressed woman (well, she is an Ambassador), but full of energy, a coiled spring. We chatted briefly about Lismore (wasn't it her sister 'Kick' Kennedy that was married to a Devonshire?) and about Minnesota, especially Macalester College. I told her I was in Boston when Rose Fitzgerald Kennedy was buried. She was surprised by that. A skilful woman, resourceful, brilliant, without doubt; and one of the lynchpins of the current IRA ceasefire. But giving nothing away — I mean no personal space or personal ground — rather like a princess. Her demeanour very like that of Lady Keane of Cappoquin House, friendly, but a paced, measured giving of the self, a real Boston Brahmin.

Afterwards a group gathered on the steps of the Writers' Centre: Montague, Hartnett, Murphy, Peter Sirr, John F Deane and Nuala. I would like to have gone to the Teachers' Club for a drink but I had to speed away in yet another taxi for Heuston Station. I seem to spend my life speeding away from places where people are about to have fun.

November 8th I've had a chance to look at Pat Crotty's Blackstaff anthology and the special issue of *Poetry*. What kind of picture do they draw of Irish poetry? What do they tell the disinterested reader? I try to imagine both as anthologies of Greek poetry: that I know nothing except a few poems of Seferis and Cavafy, so I am totally dependent on these publications to tell me about Greek poetry. And then I think of the reality of poets *on the ground* in Ireland, so to speak. How does this picture of Irish poetry differ from the reality on the ground? Who is excluded? Who is championed? And what would a Greek reader make of Irish poetry from these two publications?

The conclusions: Patrick Galvin is absent. That's a disgrace. Why put in minor poets, yet exclude a real talent like Galvin? Crotty's anthology contains Iremonger and Seán Dunne. How can they be 'in' while Galvin is excluded? And Greg Delanty is missing from both publications — he should certainly be in. Paula Meehan is missing from *Poetry*, and Rita Ann Higgins is missing from both; that's not just. I could go on, but I'd only annoy myself with endless interior arguments. I have the original typescript of the selection of poets that Pat sent to Blackstaff ages ago. It differs substantially from this published anthology. Here, yet again, the editing has been 'Ulsterized'.

November 22nd Terrible days in Ireland. The forces that have always oppressed this land have surfaced again as part of the Divorce Referendum. The Catholic Hierarchy has now stated that priests should withhold the Sacraments, including the Sacrament of the Sick and the Dying, Extreme Unction, from divorced persons. Today the Pope in Rome has publicly intervened in our National referendum by urging all good Catholics to defeat the Bill. This is a repeat of 1984 and 1985 and poor Garret FitzGerald's brave attempt to modernize our miserable country. It is also a replay of the Mother and Child tyrannies of the 1950s. Living in Ireland now is like living inside an anthology of Austin Clarke's poems.

What is truly disgraceful is the deafening silence of the intellectuals. We need a Yeats or a George Bernard Shaw. But one thing is wonderful, yes, wonderful. The Irish Labour Party has shown its true James Connolly colours. In a crisis as raw and vicious as the Divorce Debate parties do expose their true principles and Labour under Dick Spring, Mervyn Taylor, Michael D and Ruairi Quinn has represented solidly Republican and Liberal values.

November 23rd A letter from Aosdána saying that I've been nominated for membership by Anthony Cronin and Patrick Galvin. Nomination is only a preliminary round. At this stage Aosdána is becoming like The French Academy, a kind of obstacle race.

November 25th Last night at UCC, a reading by Seamus and Marie Heaney and Seán Ó Tuama, to launch Seán Ó Tuama's collection of essays. Ó Tuama witty and self-deprecating, and looking like Seán Ó Ríordáin. Heaney read his versions of *Midnight Court*, a cheeky version, I thought. But he then read his fine poem 'Exposure' from *North*, a work that established his claim to greatness. It pains me to think that he wrote it when he was only thirty-five. I shook hands with him and exchanged a few words of congratulations. When I recited a few lines of 'Exposure' behind his back he swung round and clasped my hand. His hair wispy and snow-white, his voice nearly gone from all the talking since he was awarded the Nobel Prize. It probably won't be possible to have a real conversation with him for two years or more — until the white heat of international fame has cooled. Because of fame he is not really in full possession of himself: the distracted and distrusting world owns him. The look of exhaustion in his eyes, a collapse of the face, was quite frightening to see. But this is fame: what every desolate poet dreams of having. The problem is this: fame is not an optional state, it will not go away when one's need for it is satiated. His face and eyes had the look of a great library that had been ransacked already by vicious thieves and vandals.

December 27th Yesterday, my mother-in-law Kitty Coakley said to me that she needed a new coat. But then she added: 'I'll see what Dr Murphy says first. I have an appointment next week.' Her doctor will report to her on the X-rays taken to track her recurring cancer of the lung. It is typical of Kitty's no-nonsense approach to life that she wouldn't buy a coat if the doctor told her that she had only a few months to live. She would consider it immoral to waste money on herself. I've never met a lovelier woman than Kitty. I can't imagine our lives without her. Catherine has inherited all her qualities, including that great physical elegance.

December 31st In a year-end review on the radio just now, Bill Clinton recited lines by Seamus Heaney: 'Believe in miracles, / And cures and healing wells.' It was perfect. And, afterwards, Heaney's voice from October saying, 'I don't know what the Nobel means. I just want my poems to inhere into the language, to be a part of the language.'

And that seems as fine a way as any to end a year in one's life: 1995, a year that forever belongs to Seamus Heaney.

1996

January 4th Long conversation with Peter Jay about *The Lost Province of Alsace*. I suggested that we postpone the book until the autumn because new collections are due from the dead Seán Dunne and the very alive Seamus Heaney, names that would swamp my own book both North and South. Peter didn't agree. He says we shouldn't delay the book by more than a month. He felt that I needed a new book on the shelves, and sooner rather than later.

Then the conversation turned to the design of the cover. Peter thought the title too ponderous and too limiting. He said that *The Lost Province* would be a neater title, even 'sexier' — he used the word 'sexier', an uncharacteristically commercial word for Peter to use. So we settled on the notion of a May-time launch date and a shorter title *The Lost Province*.

January 31st Joseph Brodsky, the great Russian poet, has died. There's a brilliant obituary in Monday's *Guardian*, written by W L Webb. On St Valentine's Day, 1964, Brodsky was charged with 'social parasitism' since he wasn't licensed to be a poet (Writers' Union membership being the official licence). His trial included this important exchange, published in full in the *Guardian* obituary:

Judge: What is your occupation?

Brodsky: I am a poet.

Judge: Who recognized you as a poet? Who gave you the authority to call yourself poet?

Brodsky: No one. Who gave me the authority to enter the human race?

Judge: Have you studied for it?

Brodsky: For what?

Judge: To become a poet. Why didn't you take further education at school where they prepare you, where you can learn?

Brodsky: I didn't think a poet was a matter of learning.

Judge: What is it then?

Brodsky: I think it is (with evident embarrassment) . . . a gift from God.

Brodsky was sentenced to five years' hard labour.

March 19th Odysseus Elytis has died in Athens. A truly great poet, probably the greatest poet of the Second World War or, rather, the poet of the wars of the 1940s. His *Heroic and Elegiac Song for the Lost Second Lieutenant of the Albania Campaign* and *The Axion Esti* will endure as the great poetic survivors of the mid-century wars. It is possible that he may be the only great war poet of Europe in the '40s. People emphasize the Aegean, the sunlight, Crete etc, rather like people emphasizing the Aran Islands in O'Flaherty and Ó Díreáin. But Elytis has as much to give our own Atlantic as the Aegean. He understood Occupation, Fascism, Civil War; the very things that tear family-nations apart. I return to *The Axion Esti* regularly, not just for the Hellenic stories within it, but because it speaks to me as a poet and it offers itself as an inspiration and a model. It is a document of World civilization. He was over 84-years-old, a great life. They buried him in Athens. Some day I'd like to visit his grave.

March 26th This morning a phone call to the library from Paddy Galvin to say that I'd been elected to membership of Aosdána. Wonderful news, tempered only by the bitter news that Seán Ó Tuama has failed to get elected. In the matter of Academies it's true that there's as much grace to be obtained from exclusion as inclusion. In the year of his death the great Sikelianos failed to get elected to the Athens Academy. And Gide, one of my heroes, was an outsider among French intellectuals all of his life. But the blow to Ó Tuama is bitter.

He is getting old and being elected to Aosdána would have meant the world to him. He will never make it now.

April 19th Night and morning in Galway at the Cúirt Filíochta.

April 28th Molly Keane, one of my first Cappoquin friends in writing, died on Monday. Her stoicism during long years of obscurity was an inspiration and an example to every Waterford writer. She was 92; a long, busy, fretting and creative life. She was the last of that great line of Mandarin stylists produced by Anglo-Ireland — Somerville and Ross, Elizabeth Bowen, Anita Leslie. But even more than that, she was the last Irishwoman from the golden parish of rich women: all twentieth-century ethically 'rich' women artists like Joan Jameson, Evie Hone, Sarah Purser, Mainie Jellett and Estella Solomons. What joy they brought into the world, those wonderful women. What courage they had in the face of sexist and financial trials, and what a deep layer of moral authority they have laid down for every gifted Irishwoman of the future to follow. No gifted Irishwoman, writer or artist, need ever travel outside Ireland to find mentors and an inspiring ancestry — Molly Keane, Elizabeth Bowen, Evie Hone or Sarah Purser are magnificent exemplars.

Molly ('Mrs Bobby' and 'Mrs Keane' to us ordinary Cappoquin folk) was buried on Thursday beside the little church of St James in Ardmore. I spoke at the funeral service, attended mainly by the old and aristocratic survivors of the Blackwater Anglo-Irish. No writers at the funeral, with the exception of myself and Mary Leland who was covering the funeral for *The Cork Examiner*, but mainly the old and frail; Sir Richard and Lady Keane, the Sands of Ballyduff, and old Wexford and Canadian Skrines. We went back to the house in Dysert, Ardmore, after the funeral. Many locals from Ardmore, including the artist Mary Lincoln and Michael O'Reilly, a brilliantly intelligent Ardmore native who comes from landed Catholic gentry of Old Ardmore. Met Gina Pollinger briefly at Molly's house and thanked her for her opinions on my novel. A lively, intelligent, enthusiastic woman.

Wonderful obituaries of Molly in all the English papers — by far the most brilliant one is in *The Daily Telegraph*, full of telling, almost unknown, family detail. Was it written, I wonder, by Mark Bence-Jones or by Hugh Montgomery-Massingberd?

May 29th Final, final proofs of *The Lost Province* from Anvil Press. It looks good, although the print is very small. A note accompanying the proofs from Bill Swainson calls the collection 'wonderful'. High praise from such a man.

Today a phone call from Paul Durcan to say that Francis Stuart has been put forward for the position of *Saoi* in Aosdána. Paul said he'd met Bill Swainson in London who spoke about my new collection, saying it was the best book I'd done. Praise is a mighty tonic, particularly praise from a poetry expert like Swainson. But Stuart's nomination will cause trouble — he is seen as a Nazi collaborator by many in Aosdána because of his broadcasts from Berlin during the Emergency. Paul, who has a heart of gold and adores him, doesn't see the implications of this serious moral complication.

June 13th Last night a reading at the Firkin Crane Centre in 'Homage to John Montague'. I thought it an absurd idea. How many times do we have to pay homage to Montague (or, rather, to Montague's ego)? It is all part of a pathetic national effort to help him cope with Heaney's Nobel. But the evening was actually a huge success. Paddy Galvin, Gregory O'Donoghue (for whom I have a growing admiration), Liz O'Donoghue and Patrick Cotter and I read poems by Montague and poems by ourselves. I noticed that Paddy Galvin, like myself, read only translations (I read my translations of Cathal Ó Searcaigh and Daniela Crăsnaru). Afterwards Mary Johnson, Paddy's wife and a shrewd Ulsterwoman,

said to me, 'I notice that you and Paddy read only trans-
lations, not your own poetry. Do I detect an agenda here?
Am I to read into this a certain reticence to pay homage?'
What a clever woman!

On Tuesday night I collected the Brigadier from the airport.
He'd spent two weeks in London. I waited at the Arrivals gate
for ages — he was the last to emerge from the baggage area. I
was growing frantic, thinking that he'd collapsed at Heathrow or died in a London cab without anyone knowing. I
thought: this is how it will end. Some day I will wait for him
at the Arrivals gate and he won't come out. He had been
delayed because a kitchen knife had been confiscated from
him by baggage handlers at Heathrow. He'd bought it for
Anne. Usually such misadventures would have left him tired
and depressed. But he was still buoyed up from his luncheon
with the Queen Mother at the home of the Duchess of Rox-
burghe. He said the Queen Mother chatted with him for
nearly an hour about Ireland. 'She adores Ireland,' said he.
'She says she still dreams of being able to come over here, to
meet the people, but especially to see the horses and the stud
farms.' The Queen Mother is now 95. What a great life that
woman has had: beautiful when young, ebullient, cheerful
and slightly drunk in old age. An almost perfect life.

July 7th On the Great Blasket Island today. Desolation.
Ruins. Cold summer weather. Heavy swell on the sea. On
top of that, universal sadness at the decline in tourism. There
are fewer visitors to Kerry this year. I stood by the ruined
homes of Peig Sayers and An tOileánach, Tomás Ó Criomh-
thain. How sweet a place this must have been on a glorious
summer's day when one hundred and fifty people lived here.
Now two New Age hippy families live here, the only permanent inhabitants of this desolate place. There's a café here
during the summer, but no toilet facilities that I can see. Not
a happy place: even the sheep that wander the hills are unhappy and shaggy. There's hardly enough grazing. Despite

all the talk of 'natural beauty' etc it is human life that gives meaning to this world — the sound of human voices in the distance is the best kind of loneliness. How useless is beauty when it can't be shared. What is interesting about Alexander Selkirk is not his life on the island, but his memoir of it. It was Selkirk who made the island interesting, not the other way round. People forget that.

When the Great Blasket was abandoned in 1953 only twenty-two inhabitants lived there. Síle Ní Ghormain of Bally-david, in whose house we're staying, says that two old women from America who were born on the island come home each summer. They never take the fateful boat journey to the island, but sit on the high ground above Dunquin Pier for days and days and just watch the island from a distance. It is as if they return in the manner of all who grow old merely to contemplate the place of their birth. It occurred to me that they were right not to cross over the Blasket Sound. They understand something very deep about the nature of places, and the nature of homecomings. When I stood on the ground above An tOileánach's house I thought what a disappointment a place can be when compared to the literature that has arisen from it. (Perhaps Byron's Venice and Yeats's Sligo are the exceptions.) How flat and uninteresting the Blaskets are when compared to the memory of them in *The Islandman* and *Twenty Years A-Growing*. To know the Blaskets fully — I mean to understand the profound impact they've had on the educated Irish mind for three generations — one must read those books. But one should also understand the dynamics of translation, the foreign scholars who came here at the beginning of the century, Englishmen like Robin Flower and George Thompson and the Norwegian, Marstrander. For it wasn't just the Blasket islanders who produced these books, but the creative collision of two cultures: one primitive, the other highly developed. In many ways the Blasket myth was formed in the childhoods of Flower and Thompson as well as in the childhoods of Peig Sayers and Muiris Ó

Súilleabháin. What an interesting project it would be to explore the childhoods of these foreign scholars, to discover which elements of Blasket island life were already present in their British and Scandinavian childhoods. In studying thus we would learn something not only about the complex interdependent nature of translation, but something about the emotional, anthropological impulses that create social narratives like the books of the Blasket Islanders.

August 28th Working on 'The Musician's Love-Nest' about 6 Sidney Place, memories of Seán Dunne and Sara, of Jan Cap and his belovèd, and of Catherine and me soaking it all up.

August 31st Went to the Triskel Arts Centre last night to see Ibsen's *A Doll's House*. A packed house, every available space taken and a terrific air of expectation. In many ways it was an end-of-summer crowd, the hedonism of sea and sand in West Cork now beyond them — an orientation of the mind towards autumnal and winterish things. A brilliant second act, with Catherine Montague of Feedback Theatre Company making Nora her very own: all the anguish, pride and pain of a woman finding her soul. Watching Ibsen performed one can see the birth of Joyce; one can see Molly Bloom's soliloquy in Nora's powerful closing speech (of course, there's more uncompromising Lutheran wisdom in Ibsen's Nora than in Joyce's Molly.) After all, Nora has to find the personal strength to say 'No' to her inadequate husband. Molly Bloom was the invented character who said 'Yes'. Ibsen accepted a woman as equal, absolutely, whose centre of gravity in this world is as valid as a man's. With Joyce there is always that final Irish Catholic failure of nerve in personal relationships — in both Molly Bloom and Gretta Conroy. They are both passive beings, or reflexive at best: ultimately they reflect the nobility or tragedy of the *men* in their lives. What is so wonderful about the clear character of Ibsen's Nora is that her tragedy is *entirely* her own. In owning her own existential crisis in its entirety she seizes the day for herself as a sentient being. In the presence of Ibsen's Nora one suddenly knows what the experience of Liberation means. Men still haven't learned to let go of that power, the heroic Shackleton-like power of being liberated.

September 9th Phone call from Peter Jay to say that copies of *The Lost Province* will be available in early October. We set November 2nd as a tentative date for a publishing party in Cork. It occurs to me that this is the weekend of Catherine's birthday, not a good weekend to have a book launch. The focus should be on her that weekend. But it will be good to see *The Lost Province*. It has hung over me like a Sword of Damocles. Despite Peter Jay's and Bill Swainson's words of encouragement I think the book will receive negative reviews. We'll see. My attention is now focused on the possibility of a *Selected Poems* for 1998.

September 30th *The Last Geraldine Officer*: I think of a novel in verse, a combination of poems/letters/prose/poems, with versions in Irish in italics. But also a dramatized version of the same, with actor in full uniform and a constant projected image, reading italicized texts, interlocking with myself reading the poems, a full piece for theatre.

October 21st Phone call from a Japanese poet, Nobiaki Toshigi, who is in Trinity College. He wants to interview me for a journal in Japan. God bless him. I arranged to meet him on the steps of the NCH after the Aosdána meeting. There goes my free time in Dublin.

Later, a longer phone call from Dennis O'Driscoll. He'd just received a copy of *The Lost Province* from Anvil. He was ecstatic about the collection, saying that the individual music, the rhythms and off rhymes, as well as 'the unique personal politics' of the thing, made it my best book. 'It's ages, ages, since a good Irish collection has been published!' he exclaimed, then

added, 'Oh, months, at least.' I suppose this is the difference
between Dennis and myself. For me 'ages' would be a decade,
certainly several years. But Dennis receives so much information, reads so many books, meets so many poets, that even a
month is an 'age'. I was delighted by his response, though.
This is in marked contrast to Theo's silence. Has Theo bothered
to read the book at all? Later, a phone call from Liam de Bhál
(or Bill Wall) the poet, saying that the launch of his book,
The Mathematician, has had to be postponed. He has lost the
Lord Mayor. Now he wants me to launch it in Waterstone's
on November 15th.

November 7th A good reading yesterday in Firkin Crane by
three visiting Faber poets, Maurice Riordan, Fergus Allen
and Christopher Reid. Reid, the Faber Poetry Editor, an
interesting man, phlegmatic, quiet, civilized, interested in
curiosities, especially Irish anecdotes. He asked many searching questions about Seán Ó Ríordáin. He said that Seamus
Heaney had sent him some poems by Ó Ríordáin. I encouraged him to pursue the idea of a translated edition of our
greatest Munster poet by our greatest Ulster poet. So much
that was interesting about this Faber visit to Cork, and so
little time to record our marvellous conversations, especially
with Reid who is curious about every aspect of Irish life. He
asked so many questions I felt that he was intensely fact-
checking on every aspect of Ireland — checking the facts on
the ground, as it were, against the 'facts' he has heard from
Seamus Heaney and Mossy Riordan over the years. A warm,
intelligent Englishman: talking to him is like talking to Sir Philip
de Zulueta or to the Arnold Bennett of Bennett's *Journals*.

November 19th Today three packages of books arrived from
England via Securicor. Copies of *The Lost Province* for our
launch on Friday.

The other day in the library a woman said to me, 'You
should buy yourself a goose for Christmas. Now's the time

to think about it.' I thought she was trying to say something profound, something metaphorical, but she was only talking about dinner. I said that I was happy enough with turkey. 'Turkey!' she replied indignantly. 'Jesus, boy, turkey meat is as dry as Parnell!' As dry as Parnell: I wonder where that expression came from. Probably from someone in Tim Healy's Bantry gang at Westminster.

November 28th The launch of *The Lost Province* has come and gone. A very modest crowd in Dublin, about 30 people, and of that 30 at least 20 had personal connections with me or Theo or Peter Sirr. Sold a few copies of the book. I have no audience in Dublin, or almost no following. There is really no point in having any kind of 'book launch' in the capital, unless the launch is part of a general literary festival where a crowd is guaranteed. It is difficult to persuade either the publisher or the bookshops of this reality — bookshops, God bless them, still hope against hope for a crowd. I hate to disappoint them, it is unbearable. But at this stage nearly half of my print run has been pre-sold, between Eason's, the Firkin Crane launch (over 120 people), Kennys of Galway and the Hungry Mind Bookstore in the US. It will be interesting to see the Anvil sales figures in March. The book has yet to hit the bookstores in Cork, which will mean a sale of 100+ copies. If I sell 600+ copies I will have earned my advance — a miracle, surely, for a Southern Irish poet.

1997

January 17th Tom Redshaw from St Thomas University arrived yesterday. He's spent an exhausting three days in Dublin in the company of Theo and Micheál Ó Siadhail. He's in Ireland to promote his new journal *New Hibernia Review* and the rejuvenated Center for Irish Studies at St Thomas.

After the social rigours of Dublin he will find my part of Cork very dull. There are other Corks, certainly, that are full of life and late-night parties. But the Cork that Cathy and I have created is a family-centred place. It's a narrow enough bourgeois Cork that we've created as a growing medium for our children, rather than a bohemian College Road or Glasheen Cork. Dear Tom, he will just have to make do. The Gerald Murphys of the Riviera we ain't. From a visiting American's point of view our life is so quiet that it must seem un-Irish.

January 18th On Tuesday I picked up a seed catalogue at Munster Seeds in Maylor Street. The young man there (old Mr Rice is gone) said that the first seed potatoes would be in stock within a week. It's January, but already the long arm of Spring reaches down to us in our winter darkness.

March 19th Back in the library after a week in America. I gave a reading at the Weyerhaeuser Chapel in Macalester College, sponsored by the Hungry Mind Bookstore, plus a lecture on Eavan Boland and the languages of literature. I quoted from June Levine's *Sisters* and Nuala O'Faolain's *Are You Somebody?* Both are vital books in the study of the struggle of Irish women to have a personal life. The students at the University of St Thomas, a great Catholic institution, were truly astounded by June Levine's description of 'the contraceptive train' from Dublin to Belfast and other extraordinary incidents in the Irish war of women's liberation. Boland is visiting the Twin Cities this week, so my talk and subsequent interview about her work with Leslie Miller of St Thomas may bring out some of the punters. In another class I spoke about Nuala Ní Dhomhnaill and Máire Mhac an tSaoi. After ten years or so of talking about them I've begun to feel like a John the Baptist vis-à-vis these women writers. I love to speak about them in public not just because they are women writers, but because they have made a new kind of poetry that's so rich and challenging. I feel challenged by their work and I am grateful for that challenge. The wonderful thing about these women is that they are not just good poets, but they have extended the meaning of the words 'Irish poet'. One thing I am certain of: because I've engaged in a ten-year internal conversation with these poets my own work has changed and matured, both structurally and emotionally. They have enriched everything in my life. Apart from Seferis and, to a lesser extent, Roethke, no poet has effected me as deeply as Máire Mhac an tSaoi. Technically I couldn't follow Ní Dhomhnaill or Mhac an tSaoi because their methods are unique, but they have taught me the moral power of a high technical ambition. Poetically, to try to make poetry new is to see it being reborn. The other day a commentator on the radio said, 'It's not that men deliberately exclude women writers, it's just that they don't count them in.' The fact is, by counting women in, I've enriched my own work. It's as selfish as that.

Holy Thursday Yesterday, two hilarious encounters in the library. An American scholar from the University of California breezed in to become a member. He was wearing a 'dousing crystal' on a leather thong. I asked him what he was doing with this. He replied that the magic crystal was leading him to the books he needed on 'ancient' Irish folkways. I told him that he could check the catalogue instead. He thought that my remark was very funny. Later, when he was leaving the library — and after everyone had been making fun of this student of the 'auld sod' — he stunned the entire company by speaking to us in torrents of fluent Ballyvourney Irish.

Later in the day, a young woman, perhaps eighteen or nineteen, brought back two Mills & Boon romances. She handed them to me. I noticed the bulge of a forgotten bookmark in one of the novels, opened the book and called her back. Her Mills & Boon bookmark was a foil of contraceptive pills. The poor woman went scarlet with embarrassment (there was a queue at the desk, all looking on). I thought this day encapsulates our contemporary Irish reality; an educated American in search of our peasant ways and a young, sexually active Irish woman still searching for romance through middle-aged colonial heroines of Mills & Boon. But why would a beautiful young woman with an active sex life want to read cheap romance? What is it in her life that's missing? For me her contraceptive pills are a true catalogue whereas Mills & Boon novels are as unreliable as dousing crystals.

March 20th Phoned John Bernstein. He said that on St Patrick's Day Garrison Keillor recited my poem 'Sunday Morning' on his *Prairie Home Companion*. This must have been part of the slot called 'The Writer's Almanac'. It is lovely to think of Keillor, a soft voice loaded with irony, reciting my direct and very simple poem of love. It's a dreadful poem, though. I only wrote it to test a Máire Mhac an tSaoi rhyming and alliteration scheme. I wanted to make a poem with its self-referencing internal music. I got the music right, but the poem, as poem, is a sentimental embarrassment.

April 8th Frank McCourt has won the Pulitzer Prize for his memoir *Angela's Ashes*, a harrowing account of his poor Limerick childhood and an angry indictment of the disgusting Catholic 'respectable' classes of that city. He is in his mid-sixties. His success fills me with glee. With his heroic childhood endurance, his redemption through theatre work, even his stint in the Army, he reminds me of Patrick Galvin, of Galvin's *Song for a Poor Boy*. Like me McCourt has a keenly polished chip on his shoulder because of a bitterly difficult childhood. But he doesn't have Patrick Galvin's deep sense of socialism, internationalism and class solidarity. Galvin makes me feel ashamed of my own lack of belief in a broad Left, in revolution, in Cuba, in an international Popular Front. McCourt is just a lone trader in literature like me, a corner-shop owner, a small proprietor of his own home-grown miseries: a man alone. Paddy Galvin will never feel alone: he is loved instinctively, universally, by all the socialist young of Ireland. I envy Galvin that blessing, but it's a blessing he has earned through a fervent, undiminished political belief in the ultimate victory of the working poor.

May 10th A terrible, terrible day. Young Thomas, Baron Offalie, grandson of the Duke of Leinster, has died in a car crash in Cashel, County Tipperary. He was on his way home to England via the Dun Laoghaire Ferry. The Brigadier (his 'minder' in Ireland) phoned me at work. He was devastated, heartbroken. It is a devastating, morale-destroying blow to the Geraldines. He was a handsome, even beautiful, young man. He'd trained as a chef with Myrtle Allen at Ballymaloe House, and he had worked for my neighbour, Michael Ryan of Isaacs and the Arbutus Lodge. He was full of life and laughter. We joked that some day he might move to Dublin and open a restaurant in Lord Edward Street or Thomas Street — and call it after himself, 'Soufflé Thomas'. Now it's the future that's been ruined, as always happens when a child dies. I felt very, very sad for the Brigadier, who was barely able to speak with the grief. It's a terrible day for all living Geraldines. But it's more than a personal tragedy: an historic genealogical map of Irish life is altered forever. Yet again a heartbreak in the house of Leinster.

July 19th Tonight Catherine rang from Mallow at 11 o' clock
to say that our belovèd Kitty, her mother, had died. Today
was her 76th birthday: a most serene and peaceful death of a
sublimely beautiful woman. She lived a truly duty-filled and
honour-driven life. I loved her as much as I loved my own
mother, and as my love for Catherine deepened over the
years so did my love for Kitty. Last night I was with Catherine in Mallow. Then Kitty rallied at around 9 o'clock, after
her sister, Mary Corbett, a nun in Liverpool, came home.
Kitty said, 'Hello Tom' to me when I walked into the room.
She was that alert, at such a late stage of dying. She com-
mented to one member of the family: 'I suppose I should be
sad but I suppose it'll hit me tomorrow.' The supreme irony
and aptness of the comment are typical of Kitty's best 'bon
mots'. She was an absolute master of the understatement. Her
death marks the end of an era in our lives. There will be no
more long family Sundays in her kitchen, no card sessions at
Christmas, no shopping trips to Roches and Cashs with
Cathy. Her living presence was one of the greatest bulwarks
against loneliness. I feel that Catherine in particular will feel
the overwhelming loneliness of her loss.

Leaving eight strong, educated middle-class children behind, what triumph she must have felt as she departed this
world and sensed them around her. What unimaginable
power such an Irish mother must feel, even in the face of
death. And death was pathetic in the face of her, as she had
already won 8-1 in the game of life. I always sensed that
power in her, a kind of silent authority that dominated a huge
household with a quiet, elegant decisiveness about when to
withhold or offer praise. She carried her Irish mother's
power-of-praise around like a small purse of diamonds,
distributing praise rarely, or withholding it with devastating
effect. I often saw her seemingly ebullient, even aggressive,
hopelessly sentimental husband, Tim, reduced to pulp by her
refusal to offer him instant praise. An elegant, powerful,
bourgeois mother. It is always a great mistake to think that

the person creating the most fuss in a household is the one who's most powerful. I don't think her children could ever see how she operated within the family, how she assembled and held power adroitly like a French-speaking Reverend Mother. The Coakley household, her household, was Kitty's 'Presentation Parlour'.

July 22nd Our 15th wedding anniversary. This year it is over-shadowed by Kitty's death, as it should be. Rang Catherine at lunchtime from work to find her alone in the house. Too soon for her to be alone, I think, this day after Kitty's burial. I longed to rush home and hold her. Today we were alone in the world together.

September 16th The 18th century: Barry, Grattan, Swift, the Protestant Ascendancy and the Catholic merchants. Nobody except Corkery has tried to reconstruct the highly influential Catholic nation of the 18th century. In *The Hidden Ireland* Corkery took the poets — and believed them entirely. This was his great mistake. Literature is utterly unreliable as a witness of history — look at how the influence of James Joyce has distorted our view of the vain and capricious Charles Stuart Parnell. In order to see Parnell for what he really was we'd have to eliminate the works of Joyce from our imaginations, now an impossible task. The witness documents around Parnell condemn him. After his great funeral all of Irish national memoir became a form of special pleading. James Joyce, then the Joyce scholars, then the Joyce actors and film directors, compounded the inaccuracies so that the vain Parnell became a demi-god or a saint. Yet the witnesses who saw him burning his unopened constituency correspondence in the fireplace of the Irish Parliamentary Party's committee room — to show his complete contempt for his 'mere' constituents — these witnesses are never quoted now. Such an insolent act of indif-ference describes Parnell more than anything else in his life. We forget Tim Healy's witness and Tim Healy's memoirs.

October 9th Lar Cassidy of the Arts Council has died. The funeral in Dublin on Saturday. Lar, a marvellous man, a great socialist and supporter of Dick Spring. He could never understand what lay behind Fianna Fáil. 'The Party' was beyond him. But he was a great figure, a true friend of poets. He is a real friend lost to poetry — as most writers, today, are without friends. Theo had an amazing relationship with him, an immediate understanding and simultaneous reading of the world, a real socialist bond. He was always a little bit suspicious of me, because of the Fianna Fáil material, not realizing that it was tightly defined literary material with me. Probably seriously misinformed about me by Seán Dunne as well, in that understated but treacherous way Seán had of convincing people that I'd just had dinner with some Fianna Fáil Himmler or Goebbels.

Letter yesterday from Seamus Heaney who promises to come to Cork to read for Triskel. Also, a meeting with Liz McAvoy of Triskel today about the future of *The Cork Review*. It looks as if it will continue to be supported by Triskel but only on condition that I edit it! When Gerry Wrixon — that Machiavelli of UCC — asked me to chair the '*Cork Review* sub-committee' of the Triskel Board I did smell a rat. So I am to be that rat.

December 8th Alan, my sister's son, has died in Bristol. She phoned last night with the terrible news. Mary and her husband, Martin, have taken care of him, a Down Syndrome child, for over fifteen years. He was their only child. It is impossible to exaggerate the gap, that sense of emptiness, that his death will leave in their lives. Alan died in Mary's arms just after she'd read him a story.

December 17th At Bristol Airport, waiting for my flight, delayed by snow that fell all night over England. This morning when we woke up we found the ground covered with snow, still falling heavily. Mawe went to Alan's grave and took photographs of the flowers in the snow. This afternoon she collected the photos from a one-hour shop. It was the first act of her coming to terms with his death. A time of incredible sadness.

1998

April 5th Reading at the Lambert Puppet Theatre for the Poetry Now festival. Clíodhna Shaffrey, Arts Officer.

April 14th Campus radio interview, Dennehy's pub.

April 19th The Poets' House, Falcarragh, County Donegal. Damn blast it: I have just been invited to lunch with Anthony Barton, of the great Léoville vineyard, at Brian Cronin's Blue Haven Hotel in Kinsale. I can't believe that I'm going to miss meeting this wonderful member of the immortal Bartons of Saint-Julien. Damn it.

May 19th Marvin Bell read at Tig Filí. A tiny, humiliating audience: humiliating both for Marvin and for Cork. What kind of an impression does this emptiness of interest make upon a distinguished visitor like Marvin Bell.

May 25th Grand re-opening of Triskel Arts Centre.

May 28th On this day, in 1866, the mortal remains of the immortal Father Prout were received at St Patrick's Church, in our very own parish. I was thinking of Prout and his Loyalism, or, rather, his Royalism, today as I read Annabel Patterson's wonderful book *Reading Holinshed's Chronicles*, published last year by University of Chicago Press. It makes me think, also, of the underlying structure of Irish national-ism — its historiography. Southern Irish nationalist writers, from Thomas Davis to Fintan O'Toole, have never quite appreciated how indebted they are to a structure of thought that is essentially Protestant. The idea of a 'national narrative' is really a Protestant idea. Patterson really illuminates this in her work. She quotes the ex-Carmelite turned Protestant zealot John Bale: 'I would wyshe some learned Englyshe man . . . set forth the inglish chronicles in their right shappe, as certain other lands hath done afore them al affections set a part. I can not think a more necessarye thing be laboured to the honour of God, bewty of the realme, erudicion of the people and commodite of other landes, next the sacred scripturs, than that work wold be.'

Bale worked to establish such a new historiography in a line that would lead to the *Chronicles*, first compiled and edited by Raphael Holinshed and augmented and re-edited by Abraham Fleming. It was the first full reality of Englishness, a Tudor reality that became more and more 'real' through the reigns of four Tudor monarchs. Holinshed's text was a kind of secular Bible, an encyclopedia of English historic consciousness. As John Rawls in his *Theory of Justice and Political Liberalism* had asked: 'How is it possible that there may exist over time a stable and just society of free and equal citizens profoundly divided by reasonable religious, philosophical and moral doctrines? . . . Of course Christianity already made possible the conquest of people, not simply for their land or wealth . . . but to save their souls. The Reformation turned this possibility inward upon itself.'

What Yeats, and to a lesser extent Lady Gregory, knew was that a full and fulsome retelling of history could create a providential view of national destiny. They took their cue from a Protestant ability to reread the past in the light of Enlightenment. The English as embodiment of Reformation carried a providential view of their own destiny. English nationalism is a brave and fearsome thing, and Irish nationalists constantly underestimate the force of this feeling, this providence. What Yeats wanted to do in his work and his propaganda was to make a vast new narrative for Ireland, to give ordinary Irish people a providential sense of themselves as a people of destiny. The cruel irony in all of this is that the 'martyrs' of the 1916 Rising took that sense of national being unto their narrow selves. But it was Yeats, first and foremost, who built upon the structures of Thomas Davis, that Mallow Protestant. The Irish people may be essentially a Catholic people but all the fundamental structures of our national being are overwhelmingly Protestant, and are derived from Protestant thought.

June 26th Dinner at Ballymaloe House with Whitman College English Department and President. Afterwards, talk to Whitman College group.

July 7th Final proofs of *Gardens of Remembrance* arrived at the library today. Last week New Island sent me a copy of the cover with Joan Jameson's beautiful portrait of her son, Shane. I spoke with Andrea last week — she was delighted to confirm permission for use of the picture.

July 31st An excellent month of Nathaniel poems. I am ashamed when I think how conservative this project is: I mean there are urgent themes to write about in Ireland, the Glencree standoff, the plight of refugees arriving in Ireland — forty-seven Romanians arrived in a goods truck from the French ferry this week. It is like the influx of Huguenots from France during the 17th century.

August 8th This week my father-in-law Tim Coakley died. He has been unwell for years, never recovering from a stroke of eight years ago. He took a complete nose-dive when Kitty died last summer. Without Kitty his world lost its meaning, his reason for being alive ceased. Indeed, without Kitty, he could never really be sure that he was still alive.

September 18th In Waterstone's today to talk with Pat Cotter. Professor Gerry Wrixon of the National Microelectronics Centre and Triskel Board came in looking for a copy of

Gardens of Remembrance. I signed the book for him. Gerry is heading off to Italy to do some hillwalking. He says he'll bring the book with him. Last night Theo rang. He'd received a copy of the book. He was moved by my essay on himself, but also by the fact that I remembered his father. A truly gentle and lovely man, he was, and — far more important in the Annals of Cork — he was a founder-member of the great Na Piarsaigh Hurling and Football Club.

Saturday I was in Cappoquin with a brilliant film crew from RTÉ Waterford, directed by Michael Bance. They were doing a 'Newsnight' feature on a poet returning to his native place (myself). We strolled through Cappoquin, stopped at Olden's shop and at Lonergan's Tailors. We visited Glenshelane where they filmed me walking in the garden among the trees and shrubs that the Brigadier and I planted over twenty years ago. We stopped at the very kitsch IRA monument with its floating plaster statue of the Blessèd Virgin. What an unfortunate confluence of iconography that miserable-looking monument is: a sycamore tree planted in remembrance would have been more perfect in its neutrality. But, anyway, it is an image from a moment in the 1960s, that surge of pride and gratitude felt by the whole nation during the Golden Jubilee celebrations of 1916.

The RTÉ men and I struggled through the derelict shell of McCarthy's Desmond Cinema, now used as a workshop space by Coffey's Garage. The camera crew spotted a corner of the cinema, a high wall with plasterwork designs that could only be from a cinema of the 1940s. Sure enough a beam of light was created and as the light crossed to and fro the camera went to work, picking up what might have been the flickering of the cinema walls during a picture show of the post-War years. The whole intention was so artistic, and all of this artistry employed by a full crew who were shooting what was, in effect, a twelve minute slot in a regional news round-up to follow the evening news. The care and attention to detail of the RTÉ crew were really astounding. I'm sure we spent eight solid hours filming before they were happy that they could extract twelve good minutes for broadcast. There were takes and retakes, walks and double-back walks, recitations and repeat recitations, until Michael Bance and the crew were happy that they'd got the pictures they wanted. I suppose what I witnessed was media professionalism at work, serious high standards that just wouldn't be compromised. It's a pity that people don't understand just how much work can go into the simplest few minutes of broadcast television.

Last night I gave a reading at the Arts Centre in Dromroe, Cappoquin. An excellent crowd. I sold twenty books and could have sold forty. This was all Susie Wingfield's doing, Susie of Salterbridge House who became my agent for three happy weeks of intense local publicity.

October 18th *Without Memory,* my constantly abandoned third (and last) novel. The final chapter: Eamon drives through Cappoquin after his visit to his Uncle Gerald (a refusal to be reconciled), the bitterness of the past, the decision to stay put at Steinberg Hayes and to manage the small software group — rather than move to San Diego.

October 30th Catherine rang me at work in the library to tell me that Ted Hughes has died. I met Roz Cowman, the poet, at the library door and told her. She was more shocked than I. I took home *Birthday Letters* to read. Now that Hughes is dead these poems recover their damaged integrity. A wonderful poet, completely original. Yet he was limited in some peculiar way. When I look at his work I am amazed by the absence of politics — politics in the broad sense of 'being in this world'. Plath was a genius too, and they had perhaps four astonishing, happy creative years. To have lived those four astonishing years would be enough for any 'normal' couple. Plath outdid Roethke in many ways — as a poet she had more pace and patience than the grumpy Saginaw poet — but Hughes was a Northern powerhouse, a blast of Pennine wind with a powerful Pentecostal streak: in Hughes there is always the distant rumbling of a colliery brass band. His poems are all the better for this distant rumbling, its promise of a colliery crescendo as it approaches us.

November 15th Last night, an excellent TV feature on myself in Cappoquin, a 'Michael Bance of RTÉ' triumph. Beautiful shots of the Brigadier and me at Glenshelane House, walking in the garden and talking together. And, today, an extremely decent review of *Gardens of Remembrance* in *The Examiner.* (It is the paper's 'Book of the Week'.) This evening there was a repeat broadcast of the TV programme on the Irish-language channel. I must admit that I hate to look at myself on television. I am not impressive physically, I am only impressive when I am five minutes into an argument or a remembrance. But this is precisely why I became a writer: to capture that vital five minutes from a disinterested reader. It is Larry the Lorry Dineen who must speak for this part of my life. Larry will speak for my father's class, my father's blood. In a sense Eamon Glenville, Dr Glenville, does speak for the kind of person I am now. Eamon Glenville is my educated self, but Larry Dineen is my childhood. I mentioned the *third* Glenville novel yet again in the television programme. Now I will have to write it.

1999

January 12th Reading Byron's *Childe Harold*. Spent yesterday and today reading and rereading Cantos The First and The Second. What's shocking when you study the life of Byron is the self-serving dishonesty of people like Shelley, Trelawny, Southey (a scumbag of a Poet Laureate, if ever there was one) and a host of scribblers who benefited from Byron's generosity. Tom Moore was one of the few who truly valued him. Most people tend to see him as a revolutionary, a wild left-winger. But it is best to come upon Byron mentally as a bold Scottish laird. He spoke in the Lords on behalf of English Catholics and he wrote a sonnet from Bologna when King George restored the property of Lord Edward FitzGerald to his widow, Pamela de Genlis FitzGerald. Byron owned too much property and too much position to remain as a *mere sans-culottes* on the barricades. He was wise enough to contain contradictions: he admired the Turks above all for their racial and religious tolerance, yet he died while organizing a regiment that would fight for the liberation of Greece. A truly great poet and, ultimately, a good and patriotic Englishman. Boy, how he could write! He finished whole cantos, even whole books, in ten days. He was nervous on a horse, yet he wrote like a man galloping on horseback. He was a poet of high seriousness, a poet of Yeatsian calibre. I can see why Yeats was enthralled by him.

And one can also see why our minor poet J J Callanan was enthralled by him. The death of a British poet who died in the Mediterranean impinged deeply upon our own Cork poet walking alone on Inchidoney beach. Callanan's indolence and charm had something of Byron within. Even Callanan's death — alone, aboard ship on the Tagus — has something of

Byronic closure about it. Was Callanan in pursuit of something in *Childe Harold* when he went off to Lisbon and Sintra to become a tutor to the children of the Hickey-De Souza family? What is important here is Byron's stamina. Callanan was breathless, while Byron swam across the Tagus.

Looking at the contents of the Crofton Croker correspondence in the library the other day: I held the actual handwritten letters in my own hands. The letters of Daniel Maclise and Rev Francis Mahony most interested me. I intend to make copies of them this week.

Jan 16th Last night, reading Canto The Second of *Childe Harold* — made infinitely more interesting by the copious footnotes in the American edition (probably 19th-century) that I'm using. I have a different edition at work, so I am reading *Childe Harold* as a treble text.

I've worked out the scheme of *Without Memory* on a single page. The thing is now narrowed down to two crises: the fear of Larry Dineen's disgrace and Eamon's fear of losing Kathleen/Grace. I must decide now: it must be Grace, not Kathleen. Grace Kaufman.

January 22nd Is it possible to imagine *anything* too terrible in an Irish political novel? Thirty years ago we had the illegal import of arms by Government Ministers and the creation of the Provos, then the banking scandals and near collapse of all financial systems, then the Beef Tribunal — all that treachery, embezzlement and theft of EC money — and a few years ago a Dáil Deputy arrested for picking up boy prostitutes in the Phoenix Park. And this week more large sums of money, £30,000-£50,000 in various 'plain brown envelopes', given to Fianna Fáil Ministers. There is absolutely no point in putting all this into a political novel. It is truth, but it is journalistic truth. In my Waterford Glenville trilogy I want something more, something about origins and class, something about motivation and the survival of personal shame. I want to know more about Eamon and more about Grace and her Kaufman sisters, Marilyn and Sophia. What makes their lives bearable in Ireland in 1992, the Ireland of my novel? I should never publish this, or I should publish it indifferently thirty years from now, when the toxins have ebbed from the material.

February 11th Today the *Guardian* had a feature on Carol Ann Duffy. They think she may become the new Poet Laureate of England. It would certainly be great for my own publisher, Anvil Press Poetry, which happens to publish everything by her.

February 16th Yesterday I took the Brigadier home from the Bons Secours Hospital. He had a double eye operation on Monday, but he bullied the surgeon, Mr Cleary, into allowing him home after only twenty-four hours. The immense power of an aristocratic Eton accent over the Irish upper middle-class has to be witnessed to be believed. He was chirpy if unsteady and in great form all the way home. He was delighted with the Haughey scandals and the Tribunals because he loves the working out of intrigues. But when we arrived at Glenshelane House he said to Anne, in a pathetic tone, 'I feel ghastly! Oh, terrible! Terrible!' It was an effort to win Anne's sympathy. She took one look at him and said, 'You'll be grand, grand. Sure, you're not dead yet!' She was annoyed that he came home so soon; she had been looking forward to a relaxing few days in the kitchen when she'd be able to make and freeze several dinners.

After lunch he recovered his composure. When we came back into the kitchen from the dining room he tried to regale Anne with stories. He spoke about one nurse, 'a ravishing beauty', who wore a pearl choker and pearl earrings. 'It's a wonder you didn't bring her home with you,' said Anne caustically. But he had been entranced by this vision of beauty. 'Of course, the Bons Secours Hospital does get the best-connected nurses, socially,' he explained to a sceptical Anne.

'One shouldn't be surprised to find a beautiful woman working there. The best Irish Catholic families do produce the most lovely girls. In the 1920s one always saw them riding out with their fathers at the Kildare Hunt.' Anne threw her eyes up to heaven. I half-expected her to come back into the kitchen with a set of rosary beads, to warn the old Brigadier that he should be saying his prayers for an easy death rather than enjoying the sight of these 'ravishing' young nurses.

At 87 his love of human beauty is undiminished. But, then, he loves beautiful things in an aristocratic 1920s way — beauty is what he has always responded to, in dogs, horses, flowers, men and women. One tends to forget that he grew into manhood on the high tide of Capri, Ascot, Baden-Baden and the ski slopes of Cortina. Beauty was the one absolutely negotiable currency in his aristocratic boyhood and youth. That was the era of Yeats and Lady Cunard, of Noel Coward and Lady Diana Cooper.

Yesterday a former Assistant County Manager of Dublin was arrested at Dublin Airport. He was carrying £300,000 in cash and bank drafts that he'd withdrawn that day from banks in the Isle of Man.

March 12th The despair I feel, some days, that none of the most important ideas that come into my mind ever get written down. This is why I admire my fellow Waterford man, Arland Ussher. Everything in his journals seems essential, every thought seems like the essence of a day's work. It astonishes me still to think that the four writers I admire most in the world, Dervla Murphy, Arland Ussher, W E D Allen and Molly Keane, all lived and wrote within a four mile radius of Cappoquin, my hometown.

March 14th The other day Paddy Galvin came into the library to tell me about a meeting he had with the Corporation and the Arts Council about a Writer-in-Residence for the Munster Literature Centre and the City Library. He said my name had been put forward as a possible Writer-in-Residence. He asked me if I'd put my name forward if the post were advertised. I said I would.

March 18th Today a photo in the *International Herald Tribune* of Prince Edward wearing a bunch of shamrock as he celebrates St Patrick's Day with the Irish Guards in Germany. I showed the photograph to a colleague at work thinking she'd be pleased. 'The bastard!' she exclaimed. 'Imagine that bastard appropriating our nation's symbol! No other nation would tolerate it.' I do walk on very thin ice with all my contradictory friendships and loyalties. Yesterday I went to Glenshelane to see the Brigadier. Sunshine really effects his mood. In sunlight he beams with hope. He was proud of his greenhouses, showing Catherine (who'd come with me) his geraniums and tomato plants already sprouting. She was appropriately impressed. The house, though, is beginning to take on the Anglo-Irish pallor of neglect. This saddens me. Glenshelane was always an impeccably maintained house, but now it has begun to fade for want of money being invested in it.

May 8th Frantic phone call from Peter Jay. He wants to do a *Selected* in the autumn. 'You must mean Autumn, 2000,' I say. 'No! This autumn! Let's get cracking!' I've never seen Peter in such haste. Still, all of my books, except *The Non-Aligned Storyteller*, are out of print. To be back in print would be good. I feel embarrassed sometimes when I give public readings and I have no books to sell.

May 11th Sent an email and letter to Peter Jay asking him to consider a hardback version of the *Selected*. Having a HB edition does send a signal to the reading/critical public: it's a flag of seriousness. Phone call from Bob Welch at Coleraine. He wants me to talk about Anthony Cronin's *Irish Times* journalism at a seminar in County Mayo in July. I said yes, although I'll be at the John Hewitt Summer School the following weekend.

May 17th A report in today's London *Times* that Paul Muldoon has been elected to the Chair of Poetry at Oxford to succeed Seamus Heaney. He was elected unopposed in a candidature managed by Tom Paulin. Another astonishing victory for Ulster poetry.

May 26th To Glenshelane last Monday. A glorious day, the roads bursting with life, even animal life — a young deer broke cover on the road between Lismore and Cappoquin.

The Brigadier in much better form. It was good to spend the entire day with him, chatting and arguing and planning for the future of the garden, the future of Glenshelane, the future of his library and paintings.

August 4th Yesterday, a letter from the Department of Foreign Affairs inviting me to a Poetry Festival in Moscow. I wonder which important poet has pulled out? I mean why has this invitation filtered down to my level?

August 23rd Home from our poetry readings in Sweden. A wonderful journey, via Amsterdam and Copenhagen. At a poetry festival at Nässjö in southern Sweden, superb Swedish poets, including Jan Östergren and Marie Silkeberg. I learned that Tomas Tranströmer has had a stroke. Long conversations with Paul Durcan and John F Deane. Paul full of wicked stories and willing to listen to wicked stories in return. Sweden itself: a quiet land, utterly at peace, but a slight sense of having been bypassed by the business of the world. Brilliant public transport and a superb Public Library at Nässjö. Everywhere that clean, unhurried spiritual ease and sense of common purpose, that triumph of Swedish social-ism. A terrific belief in democracy; a quiet confidence in the ordinary people as they walk about purposefully. I think I'd like to move to Sweden. If I got a large advance to write a novel I would rent a house by the lake at Jönköping and write and write. It is the pervasive humanity, the assertive belief in the common dignity of all citizens, that makes Sweden better than any other European country. It's true, though, that most Irishmen, after a few months of this humanist peace, would want to cause trouble, or at least create a public disturbance. As Irishmen we have our limits, and Swedish life would provoke us.

September 5th A cocktail party at Molly Keane's house on Saturday evening, hosted by Desmond FitzGerald, the Knight of Glin. A beautiful evening. The usual Munster Anglo-Irish gang. Desmond and his terrific wife, Olda, and his even more vivacious daughters — both of whom were reading my *Gardens of Remembrance*. They both recalled my descriptions of my grandmother, and of the Cappoquin drunk I met in the Irish Club in London. They thought his reference to Sir Richard Keane as 'the *fokine* Major' was hilarious. Sir Richard himself and Lady Keane there. The Brigadier looking superb in a tailor-made jacket with Geraldine buttons (made by Petie Cahill of Cappoquin; Petie, trained in Saville Row and tailor to most of the Blackwater Fine Gael families). Molly's two daughters, Sally and Virginia, were there too. The two of them are the friendliest intellectuals ever born in West Waterford. We listened to Mainie Jellett's nephew, a hilarious character who spoke about the family's embarrassment when Bruce Arnold came to the house looking for Mainie's paintings. The family used to throw them out with the house rubbish after every Christmas. Angie Shaw, the brilliant Angela Lansbury, was in terrific form as well, looking as beautiful as the most glamorous thirty-year-old. She must be seventy if she's a day. We had a great chat together about architecture, slates, light, and the sea at Ballycotton. She is particularly proud of the new house that Stephen Pearce has designed for her.

October 13th A phone call from Theo in Dublin. Michael Hartnett, the best Munster poet after Ó Ríordáin, has died. He died of liver failure at 8 a.m. this morning. Theo was really heartbroken, but also bitter and angry about the way Hartnett was treated by the 'Poetical Powers' in Dublin. But what are these powers supposed to do, and who are they? With Hartnett, a troubled genius, very little could be done.

November 12th In Moscow. Days of wonder. Punch drunk from new sights and sounds — the beauty of Moscow's churches, the spectral sacredness of Novodevichy Cemetery where I visited the graves of Chekhov and Shostakovich, the snowy twilight of the Arbat, the cathedral-like immensity of the Moscow Metro. So many poets, courteous diplomats and wonderful dinners — caviar and champagne twice in one week. An image I'll carry to the end of my days: the Third Secretary and First Secretary of the Irish Embassy and I rushing up the steps of the Bolshoi Theatre in the snow. I read my poems in a literary café, Coffee Bean, with Frank Ormsby and Tom Paulin, then to The State Tretyakov Gallery. At 7 p.m. a reading at the DOM Club, Bolshaya Ovchinnikovskaya Street, where we read with Lev Rubinstein, Dmitri Prigov, Viktor Koval, Sergey Gandlevsky, Timur Kibirov and Yuli Gugolev. On Monday, a reading at the Anglia Bookshop with Ormsby, Montague and Ní Dhomhnaill and another on Tuesday at Rossiski Fond Kultury.

December 2nd Massive discusson in the library staff room today about the signing away of our Thirty-Two County Republic. Today the Taoiseach Bertie Ahern signed away Articles Two and Three of the Irish Constitution. The Dáil, therefore, has rescinded all claims that the six counties of Northern Ireland form part of our National territory. It is as if Greece ceded authority over Cyprus to an Executive controlled by Turks. This decision is momentous. I'm not sure if such a constitutional change should have been made so quickly. Only time will tell if the sacrifice of such a cherished national aspiration was worth it. Last night I listened to the new Unionist Minister of Culture, McGimpsey, on radio. He said that he wasn't hostile to the Irish language, but he wished to remind everyone that 'Cantonese' is the second language of Ulster. It is extraordinary the lengths to which Unionist politicians like him go to avoid contact with Irishness, or any aspect of Irish culture. The problem is: every time you compromise with Unionism it is seen by their leadership as a sign of weakness, rather than a signal of generosity or strength. Giving away our constitutional claim to our complete national territory, the thirty-two counties of Ireland, may be a concession too far, something we will regret in years to come. Surely this will effect our ability to speak for Ulster in the corridors of power in Brussels? Who will speak for Catholic Ulster in Europe? London certainly won't speak for them, it never has, even in the days of the Attlee and Wilson governments. But this is what Ireland has just signed away. We have suffered a Pyrrhic defeat. Hopefully, the enemies of Irish interest have achieved only a Pyrrhic victory.

December 31st A perfectly beautiful Christmas, our first in our own home. With Tim and Kitty Coakley now gone the great Coakley hearth of Cork Road, Mallow, has come to an end. Those were two friendly, crowded decades of my life, and Cork Road, Mallow, was a place where I was welcomed openly as Catherine's husband.

2000

January 5th I can't think of a better way to start the new century than to paste a few paintings of Daniel Maclise into my notebook. Maclise reminds me that art of the first order can be produced in Cork City, and writing of the first order as well. A young Cork artist or writer has only to think of five or six great local works in order to see the standard that has to be achieved: I'm thinking of Barry's 'Escape from the Cave of Polyphemus', Maclise's 'The Marriage of Strongbow and Aoife', Elizabeth Bowen's *The Death of the Heart*, Seán Ó Ríordáin's 'Adhlacadh Mo Mháthar', Corkery's 'The Cobbler's Den' and Frank O'Connor's 'The Long Road to Ummera'. A young Cork writer or visual artist could spend an entire lifetime trying to make a work of art, a poem, story or novel, as sublime as any of these works. But wouldn't the making of even *one* such work be a lifetime well spent? Cork may give us a provincial life but this need not lead to a provincial work. I would love to give a set of six lectures at UCC on these six works. Of course, to these six works you could easily add six more, by Ó Faoláin, Paddy Galvin, Mary Leland, Mrs Victor Rickard, Seán Ó Tuama and Robert Gibbings.

February 1st Today *The Irish Independent* quotes Dev's grandson, Éamon Ó Cuív, as he attacks both Fianna Fáil and the new Michael Collins film. He says that Fianna Fáil is now a Party of the 'haves' and it is devoid of values. Well, well. At last, there's a Jeremiah in the Party. I'm not the sole Jeremiah.

March 9th Wonderful interview by Eileen Battersby with Michael Longley in *The Irish Times* today. It marks the publication of *The Weather in Japan*. Of Belfast he says, 'It is also one of the most interesting, if heartbreaking, places in the world. It's like living in three places at once; Ulster is a province of Ireland, it's a province of the UK and it's its own awkward self.'

March 22nd In less than two weeks I must begin the final story of the Glenvilles. This year will be the year that answers the question: Do I have any writing muscle left?

April 21st Good Friday Today, reached 11,000 words on the final version of *Without Memory*. This is a cracking pace for me — the best ten days of writing since 1981 or '82. I've tapped a rich vein, working simultaneously on Chapters 1, 2 and 3. Now, the question is: Can I repeat this Trollope-like pace in May?

A letter from Nobi in Japan. He is translating six of my poems, all political ones, into Japanese for an anthology of Irish Poetry. I can't imagine what a Japanese reader would make of all that Fianna Fáil angst.

May 6th At this stage I've written about 18,000 words of *Without Memory*. This novel and its chattering subject matter has filled my days. I hate to do anything else except write, write, write. Even my ten minute tea breaks at work are used to rework one or two sentences. How I would love three months off. If I had just three months I could write the entire novel. But this is not possible, not financially, in our present circumstances.

May 20th A review of *Mr Dineen's Careful Parade* in the *TLS*. A negative view of my work, but not insulting — in fact 'my effort' at poetry is treated with respect. And published with a photograph, a first for me in the *TLS*. Yesterday I was on the phone to Bob Welch at Coleraine. He had seen the review and was furious with the reviewer. He thought that the critic didn't understand my purpose at all. Bob put it rather well: 'Only a South American critic would understand your work, the way you communicate truths with your dream-like Fianna Fáil sequences.' That was a clever and generous perception, although I would use the word 'cinematic' rather than 'dreamlike'. *Without Memory*, now at 40,000 words. More than half way. In this, at least, I have remained faithful to my own promises and committed to my own ambitions.

July 8th Yesterday at Glenshelane. A beautiful summer's day, the sun blazing down on the garden. The Brigadier and I had both lunch and tea on the far lawn, in a bower between a heavily pruned beech and a catalpa. He is wonderfully healthy — as he always seems to be when the sun shines.

July 20th Good review of *Mr Dineen* in this month's *PN Review*. The reviewer is only negative about my impression-istic pieces on Cork. I have reservations about them myself.

July 28th Met the poet Robert O'Donoghue on the street outside the library. I was rushing to get back to work but there was no getting away. We chatted about Seán Ó Riada — one of Ó Riada's earliest compositions was incidental music for Bobby's programme on Cork local radio in the early '50s. Bobby said that by the time their collaboration ended he and Ó Riada weren't on speaking terms. Later when Ó Riada (or 'Jack Reidy' as Bobby calls him) came back from his first visit to Paris he told Bobby that he had 'returned to the faith'. Bobby, as a socialist, couldn't believe this. Then Ó Riada explained that he had had a visionary experience in Paris. He had a sudden urge to attend Mass at the Sacre Coeur early one morning. A young Redemptorist priest was saying Mass. The young priest climbed the pulpit and exclaimed, 'Mon Dieu est mort.' With that he slit his own throat, committing suicide on the spot in the middle of his own Mass. Ó Riada was sitting beneath the pulpit and was

spattered with the young dying priest's blood. 'I was annointed by that Redemptorist blood,' he said to Bobby, 'so I
am a practising Catholic again.'

'I was dumbfounded,' Bobby said to me. 'A man of such
European intelligence, a committed socialist, to embrace the
Church just because he was spattered by blood!' Then he took
his leave of me at the corner of Coburg Street and Leitrim
Street. Paddy Galvin claims that Bobby has a mistress hidden
away in this part of the city, but my guess is that he's visiting
a physiotherapist or an eye specialist on nearby Patrick's Hill.

September 11th Today Catherine had a very funny encounter
with a prison officer. The officer was in her office reading
death notices in the newspaper. He said to Catherine, 'I once
read a book and it had a character in it who always read death
notices. He was called Condolences. He was a gas man, a
Fianna Fáil-er. I can't think now what the novel was called,
but it was by a guy called McCarthy.'

'It's *Without Power* by Thomas McCarthy,' said Cathy.

'Isn't that gas, you've read it?'

'I did. I know the author,' said Cathy.

'No way.'

'He's my husband,' said Cathy.

September 13th This evening, a phone call from the City
Librarian. She wants me to serve on a City Hall committee
that will fight for the nomination of Cork as European City
of Culture for 2008. It will be a hard fight between Limerick,
Galway, Waterford, Kilkenny and Cork. Cork really deserves
this more than any other Irish city. Now we shall see how
Cork is seen by the Government in Dublin. It will be Síle de
Valera's call, unfortunately.

October 8th At home writing the Proposal document for the
City of Culture.

October 22nd End of two-and-a-half fractious weeks. Mark Mulqueen, the City Arts Officer, Noreen Mulcahy, a Senior Staff Officer from the Lord Mayor's Office, and I have spent all of this time trying to pull together a programme for Cork during a possible year of European City of Culture. Endless phone calls, faxes, writing, re-writing, arguing, compromising. This world of Arts politics is so absorbing one could easily get sucked in! So I must be very careful, very careful indeed.

2001

January 6th A time for work: today I began to look at Chapters 8 and 9 of *Without Memory*.

January 10th Bad news by phone and email yesterday. John Bernstein, one of my best friends in America, has been told that his throat cancer has returned. 'This time,' said John on the phone, 'it's a terminal visit, I'm afraid.' It's devastating news for Cathy and myself. Catherine, especially, is devoted to Cindy and John. For Kate Inez and Cathy Cindy is a kind of benchmark of elegance and sophistication while John is a great scholar and critic, a gourmand and wine lover. The idea that this beautiful American couple has been visited by cancer is just unbearable. Unbearable.

January 20th Phone call from Kent Bales of the English Department at the University of Minnesota. John Bernstein is behind this, I've no doubt. Kent wants me to visit the U of Minnesota for a series of readings and workshops. I said I'd love to visit, but I need to talk to Cathy. It's inconceivable that I'd go to the Twin Cities on my own: so much of Cathy's sense of wellbeing is linked to our experience of the Twin Cities that travelling without her would be a kind of theft. We'll see. It would be lovely to see John and Cindy although we will see them in London in ten days.

February 6th One of the highlights of our London visit was the time I spent in Room 24 of the National Portrait Gallery. In the corner of this room I found Daniel Maclise's wonderful portrait of Charles Dickens. Dickens, in a letter of 28th June, 1839, says, 'Maclise has made another face of me, which all people say is astonishing.'

The Maclise portrait shares a corner of the room with a group portrait of the Brontë sisters. People were sitting and staring and whispering in this corner, at the Brontës that is, while Maclise's Dickens was ignored. The portrait of Dickens is truly an astonishing work, a full-length side view of Dickens sitting confidently, even cockily, and looking away to the right, his huge grey eyes lost to the horizon beyond the world of here and now. Dickens' left hand rests on a manuscript, but no pen appears. There's an incredible sense of freshness from every aspect of Dickens; even his clothes look fresh; so do the folds of the curtain that crawls around his chair. This is not the exhausted Dickens of later years, old and broken, but a curly-haired unblemished young buck who has hardly ever suffered from love, never mind poverty. It is this Dickens who best represents the freshness and vitality of Maclise's own mind. The Dickens portrait is really the portrait of a fresh and hope-filled set of relationships. What Dickens and Maclise had in abundance (and this probably applies to all of the Frasers group) was a genius for friendship, that incredible richness of mutual support that one finds so rarely in my own generation.

May 27th At the launch of Desmond O'Grady's *The Wandering Celt* last night. Desmond was in ebullient and professorial form. After I'd finished introducing him he said to the audience: 'I admire Thomas McCarthy's work so much. I've always admired it. He is one of the Twelve Apostles at the table of Irish Poetry.' Desmond takes poetry so seriously he doesn't hand out laurels that easily. The audience in Tig Filí was intrigued by these words, and at the end of his reading people kept coming up to me, repeating the words. One woman in the audience handed me an old copy of *Seven Winters in Paris* and asked if I'd sign it 'To Siobhán, from the Apostle McCarthy'. I was happy to oblige.

At Glenshelane for several hours. The garden looking

beautiful, the Brigadier in good humour, despite pain from a trapped nerve in his leg. The countryside beautiful.

June 9th The CIA is currently reading a 160-page romantic Iraqi novel (*Zabibah and the King*), believing that it is the work of Saddam Hussein. The London newspaper, *Asharq Al-Awsat*, has identified Saddam as the writer of this book. There is no doubt but that Western intelligence has gone to the dogs completely. There is no end to the gormless stupidity of people involved in that vacuous activity called 'National Security'. I often wonder could these people really secure anything, even a donkey at the crossroads?

June 27th In Dublin for the announcement of the Ireland Funds Annual Literary Awards. Long chat with Nuala Ní Dhomhnaill: a wonderful woman, and one of the most brilliant poets now writing in Ireland. Brief chat with Kennelly and Heaney. Heaney talking a lot about Seferis. He's giving a talk on Seferis at Princeton. A delightful conjunction of voices. Shook hands with the newly knighted Tony O'Reilly, now Sir Anthony O'Reilly. A real charmer, but a shameless scoundrel nonetheless. Also, met that wonderful benefactor, Loretta Brennan Glucksman, a real treasure of a woman who has given millions upon millions to Ireland. She and her husband and a circle of rich friends have contributed money to build the new library at Limerick University as well as the restored Ireland House at NYU. She is one of those amazing Americans, just like John Quinn of New York in Yeats's day. I hope Ireland renews itself and enhances its culture enough to repay the million kindnesses of all these American people. There are days when I think this country doesn't deserve such kindness. I'm sure there are days when American donors have the same thought.

July 27th Met John Montague and his partner, the novelist Elizabeth Wassell, at Proby's Bistro. John had gone to

Proby's when he discovered that they sold cheap Lebanese wine before 7 p.m. We had a good gossip about Seán Lucy. John mentioned a very peculiar incident at UCC when he came up for a permanent Lectureship. Seán 'informed' the College President that Montague's marriage was not legally valid, i.e. that Montague was living in sin. This was completely untrue but, quite apart from that, it was a truly outrageous intrusion into J M's personal freedom; the kind of thing that Seán himself would rail against in lectures and in print (Frank O'Connor's treatment at the hands of the Devotional mafia, the Catholic Sodality, in RTÉ of the 1940s, for example). It's quite probable that Seán wanted to get rid of Montague at that stage and informing on his junior colleague's marital status may have been a ruse to get rid of a rival poet in the English Department. In middle age, frustrated, ambitious, panicking, academics are capable of the most sublime treacheries against each other. I've no doubt that Seán was excited to get Montague as a Guest Lecturer in the early '70s, but at the end of the day there's room for only one dominant poet in any territory: that territory could be a College campus, a workplace, even an entire city! Montague was such a prodigious egotist that Seán (or indeed, the UCC wives' club, which was always so influential in academic advancement) must have known that his own locally praised and sustained talent would be asphyxiated by the Montague.

But John also wanted to talk about my theory of 'Ulsterization' in Irish Writing, both commentary and anthologizing. While I spoke about Ulster's dominance he took notes. I couldn't believe this. I wanted to laugh. John's brain is gone, I think. What he has left is a marvellous social presence. Now he believes he can start a campaign against Ulster, but it's really a campaign against Heaney and, without doubt, Edna and Michael Longley. It's idiotic, but it has the added effect of making John look churlish and ungrateful. John sees the 'Ulsterization' of Irish writing as a rhetorical turn that needs to be challenged, but I see it as just a technical matter, a technical adjustment in perspective on Ireland. Perspective on Ireland and values in Irish writing are constantly changing — after all, in the Yeats era all of Irish writing was Dublin-centred. Who knows where the centre of gravity will be in a hundred years: it might even be outside Ireland, among the London-Irish or the American-Irish. Then our conversation turned to the matter of John Carey's (London) *Times* review of John's autobiography. I defended Carey strongly, defending the intelligence of the review, contrasting its trenchant tone with the non-committal nature of Bernard O'Donoghue's review in *The Irish Times*. Then I mentioned Carey's praise of John's descriptive powers. There was silence. Elizabeth turned to John: 'Can I tell him?' she asked. 'Go ahead,' said John, laughing boyishly.

'I wrote that passage, Tom,' said Elizabeth proudly. 'So the praise was for my writing.'

'Now, now,' said John, 'you have to take some blame as well.'

'Well, yes,' admitted Elizabeth, lowering her eyes in that characteristic gesture she has. 'He did attack John's description of his sexual encounter with a Californian student. I'm afraid I wrote that passage also.' And she pouts, like a beautiful, admonished child.

I laughed at this admission. The three of us laughed. John's devotion to Elizabeth is very real, very moving. He really does love her, and he shows this through his immense, very public pride in her writing skills. They have an undeniable bond; their affection for each other clings to the atmosphere of a room long after they've left it. They are like literary twins, true soul companions.

September 3rd We are in Brussels, at the offices of the EU Cultural Directorate. We have just made a 'City of Culture' presentation on behalf of Cork to an International Panel. We were brilliant. I have no hesitation in claiming this: we were simply brilliant and worked tightly, superbly. Our delegation consisted of the new City Manager, Joe Gavin, the City Arts Officer, Liz Meaney, Mary McCarthy (the whizz-kid Director of the National Sculpture Factory) and me. Both our presentation and, more importantly, our handling of questions, went very well. Mary McCarthy, especially, was quick and alert to every question. As we exited from our ordeal we passed the Limerick delegation on the way in to do their bit for their city. I greeted Mícheál Ó Súilleabháin and an elegant-looking Sheila Deegan. A few moments later I could hear the wailing of some strange musical instrument that Mícheál had begun to play. This Limerick wailing followed us down the miserably bare, ill-equipped and impoverished-looking corridors of the Cultural Directorate offices. I could see Joe Gavin giving Liz Meaney a strange look — it was the look of a man who has spent his life dedicated to serious administrative matters and who now finds himself pitching for the ownership of a circus. When we came out of the EU offices and stood on the pavement Joe Gavin turned to me and said, 'Well, Tom, if Cork isn't designated as European City of Culture it won't be our fault. We gave it everything.'

I found the whole process of going to Brussels disgusting. It was like something from the 1960s Soviet Union. We had arrived in Brussels like a delegation from some outlying Soviet Republic to plead with a minor committee of the politburo. Disgusting. The whole EU charade is a matter of disgust. But in the Grand-Place a horde of Scottish supporters playing bagpipes. A timeless Celtic sound. The same sound must have been heard in Brussels on the eve of Waterloo.

On the way home in the plane (we were flying Business Class) both the City Manager and Liz Meaney refused to drink their complimentary bottles of champagne which were served with lunch. I couldn't tolerate this official sobriety. We had worked our butts off for a Cork City that will never know how hard we worked, and without any of us getting a penny extra in wages for all the extra hours we'd put in. God knows how many hours of my own spare time I've used up in writing that bloody Bid Document. And not only the act of writing, but the head space that Cork has occupied, the personal agitation and worry. By the time our flight landed at Cork Airport I'd consumed their two bottles of champagne as well as my own one. I felt dizzy at Arrivals, but full of a drunken belief in Cork's destiny.

September 24th Today I posted sixty-five cards honouring the Brigadier's 90th birthday. I printed ninety copies, one for each year of his life. My hope is that he will get lots of phone calls from friends who receive my card. He always hated his birthday, but when a man reaches ninety he surely deserves some kind of notice and praise.

Yesterday was an extraordinary day in Cork. We hosted a visit from the Capital of Culture Expert Panel — Robert Palmer, the former Director of Glasgow '90, Bernard Faivre d'Arcier, the Director of the Avignon Festival (a highly intelligent and sophisticated Frenchman), Tuula Arkio, the Director of the Helsinki Gallery, Irma Peiponen, a delegate of the EU Committee of the Regions, Franco Bianchini, a *Creative Cities* expert, as well as the Norwegian administrator of the EU Cultural Unit. They had already visited Galway and Limerick. We were worried when word came through from Galway that the Panel had been given a lavish reception at Galway City Hall as well as a free helicopter ride around Connemara. Noreen Mulcahy of City Hall advised me not to mention this to the City Manager as it might force him to make an issue of it if Cork fails to get the nomination. No point in starting a civil war with Galway. The panel had expressed the wish that no time-wasting Civic receptions be held for them and we'd taken them at their word — maybe foolishly. But when we had boarded the bus Mrs Peiponen of the Committee of the Regions, turned to Bob Palmer and said, 'Well, Robert, you have a smile on your face. You have been vindicated by Cork.' At once I felt that this was an indication of how impressed the Panel was by Cork. Cork will win. I feel sure of it.

At the end of the day we were running one-and-a-half hours late. But dinner at Isaacs, Michael and Catherine Ryan's restaurant, was brilliant. Isaacs really pulled out all the stops for Cork. As a result of this visit, and the very serious, searching exchange of views (that Joe Gavin handled adroitly) I'm more confident than ever that Cork will get the designation 'European Capital of Culture 2005'. What a victory for Cork this would be, what an unimaginable joy. And what a kick in the arse for all the nay-sayers and cynics. I'll never forget the scumbag Cork businessman whom we met at the airport as we left for Brussels to put Cork's case. He sidled up to me in his expensive clothes with the confidential air of a greyhound dope-peddler and said, 'I dunno what ye're wastin' taxpayers' money for, ye headin' off to Brussels. I have it on good attoritty from de Govermint dat Galway is ta get dat European title. Ye're wastin' yere time.' What a kick in the arse he'll get. It would be living proof, if such proof were needed, that faith moves mountains and makes new things happen. This year in Cork would be bigger than the Great Exhibitions of 1902 and 1903.

September 29th At Leonardo da Vinci Airport, Rome, after a day of exhausting travel. Around me the sounds of Italy: 'Ciao! Ciao!' everywhere. I am too tired to get into the mood for this blessèd place. At the Baggage Claim area I read this notice: 'Welcome, Pilgrim, to the Eternal City.'

October 4th A phone call to Hollyhill Library from Noreen Mulcahy, the European Officer of Cork Corporation. Great news. Cork has won the nomination as European City of Culture. Noreen can't believe it. I rang Cathy. I rang my brother, Kevin. I rang the City Librarian. Then, when I put the phone down, a call came through from City Hall: 'Hello, Poet McCarthy!' It was the City Manager. 'Hello, Manager of a European City of Culture!' I replied.

What a great day for Cork! What a sweet moment for all of us, Joe Gavin, Mark Mulqueen, Mary McCarthy, Liz Meaney and the faithful, faithful *Evening Echo* that has supported us and urged us on through this Bid process. It's still not official. It may be three or more months before Cork is officially designated by ECOFIN, the Council of Finance Ministers in Europe. But the title now belongs to Cork, city of O'Connor and Ó Faoláin, of Ó Ríordáin and Ó Muirthile, of Corkery, Ó Tuama, James Barry and Daniel Maclise. Cork, the undisputed queen of the South, as Micheál Mac Liammóir once wrote, without irony; Cork, constantly lampooned and misrepresented by comedians; Cork that so deserves this conspicuous fame.

It was the *Irish Times* correspondent, Dick Hogan, who ferreted out the information from Brussels. Hogan contacted Pat Casey of Casey Communications and Pat Casey rang Noreen Mulcahy. *The Irish Times* is going to run with the story tomorrow morning.

October 5th Great excitement at City Hall. The Lord Mayor and the City Manager are both over the moon after Cork's selection was noted in all the papers today. RTÉ's flagship *Morning Ireland* broadcast an interview with me from the archives. Tonight, dinner at Jacques Restaurant as a guest of City Hall. Time now for me to withdraw from all of this; it has become too intense altogether. I can see my peace of mind ruined for the next five years if I become involved in this at any administrative level.

Hints were being dropped left right and centre that I am to be named as one of the Directors of the company that will manage this Capital of Culture. Shit. This kind of thing is just not for me.

October 6th I got a copy of the 'Panel's Recommendation' today. It is signed by Palmer, Faivre D'Arcier, Peiponen, Arkio, Bianchini, one of the EU Council's and one of the EU

Parliament's delegates being absent. It reads:

> *On the basis of an overall evaluation of the applica-*
> *tions from all four cities, the panel finds that Cork*
> *responds best to the objectives and the characteristics*
> *set in Decision 1418/1999/EC of the European Parlia-*
> *ment and the Council. We therefore advise the Insti-*
> *tutions of the European Union that this city hosts the*
> *European Capital of Culture 2005.*

What an historic document in the civic life of Cork City. And what a privilege it was for me to work on this Bid with people like Noreen, Mark, Gerry Barnes, Ted Crosbie and other great names in Cork. Coincidentally *The Irish Times* published my poem 'The Euro' in today's edition. It looked well, and that's the best I could say about it.

December 12th A phone call from the City Manager yesterday. 'Tom, I bought a castle for you!' says he. He'd just bought Blackrock Castle, thereby bringing one of Cork's most famous landmarks back into public ownership. A triumph. Now he is negotiating to purchase St Luke's Church, a magnificent building. It could become an archives institute or an Arts Centre. I told him about Frank O'Connor's house in Douglas Street, that Jim McKeon tells me is on the market. He asked me if I'd look into it and get back to him. I will.

December 16th The head porter in the Hollyhill Shopping Centre was an NCO in the Irish Army for years. During the darkest days of the 1970s he did many tours of duty along the border between Monaghan and Armagh and Tyrone. He had only three weekends of leave in one long double tour of ten months. What he remembers most about that time is his hunger, and the hunger of the soldiers under him. He said that his platoons would have starved to death or died of exposure if it hadn't been for the generosity of the British soldiers, especially the Parachute Regiment. He is one of the few Irish people I've ever heard praising the Paras whose handiwork on Bloody Sunday has made them as vilified as the Black and Tans in West Cork. 'I won't have wan word said agin' them,' warned the porter one day when those murders in Derry were mentioned. The Paras, who sometimes operated within twenty yards of an Irish Army platoon, were sumptuously supplied with food and equipment. They shared everything with the Irish platoons on the Border. The Irish troops had to wait for twelve hours some days for a milk churn of cold soup to arrive from Clones. No food, just cold soup. The British were always supplied with double rations, knowing that their food would be used by the Irish Army across the border.

The porter had a great story about one particular day in the early '70s. A huge helicopter came screaming down the valley from the direction of Crossmaglen. A carpet of smoke bombs was dropped across a small field and the British helicopter circled back over the Irish positions and dropped down into the middle of the smoke. Less than five minutes later the helicopter took off again. When the smoke cleared the Irish soldiers beheld a most incredible sight — a trestle-table complete with a linen tablecloth, place settings, cutlery, bowls, plates, masses of steaming casseroles. The Irish platoon moved forward when they got a signal from a group of Paras hidden in the bushes that straddled the Border. They wondered why such a spectacular show was put on, at such risk to the Paras in this IRA-controlled territory. A young Para officer came over to the Irish position and whispered: 'Her Majesty's Birthday. It's the Queen's Birthday! Enjoy!'

2002

January 8th Bleak and dark weather, a winterish depression over the city as I walked home from work today. The weather matches my dark mood. The fog, ghostly and unexpected, followed me home as if it too wanted to read my copy of Thomas Kinsella's *Collected Poems* that I carried in my satchel. I've always found it difficult to get a 'fix' on Kinsella. His high intelligence is beyond dispute, but it's a dark, regressive intelligence that repels all but the most committed readers of poetry. It's strange how easily we've accepted the tone of Ulster poets like Montague, Heaney, Mahon, yet Kinsella, our Dublin poet, and the most famous chronicler of our capital city since Behan and Beckett, is felt to be beyond us — beyond our empathy, beyond our comprehension. Although his work is full of light, sunlight through windows, sunlight on cobbled streets etc, there's an extraordinary, ungiving darkness in him. It is probably our distinctly Irish Catholicism, that Catholicism-manqué of 1950s Ireland, a sort of Thomist putrefaction, that repels our modern sensibility. He is the inheritor of that paralysed sclerotic Catholicism in George Moore and James Joyce. James Plunkett and Austin Clarke have made interim stabs at the same inert Irish materials, but Kinsella inherits the deepest, most existential point of our Irish Catholic crisis of being. There is a deliberate pointlessness to his poetic soul-searching that no other Irish writer has ever achieved. Even Seán Ó Ríordáin avoided a full frontal assault on the materials attacked by Kinsella. He has also ingested the cruel fatalism of British writing in the 1950s. I mean the writing of early Thom Gunn, William Golding, John Osborne, John Fowles, and he uses their method and attitude when he encounters Irish material: this is what gave his Irish voice such a sense of urgent urbanity in the 1950s. At times, when they approach similar anniversaries or scenarios, the poetry of Kinsella and Geoffrey Hill becomes almost interchangeable. In his entire career Kinsella, like a severe British provincial poet of modest but sure reputation (Basil Bunting, C H Sisson), has never made a single effort to win our sympathy. The reader has to accept this aspect of his character, his mental weather, before tackling the texts. His Dublin is an hermetic space, a place of Guinness workers and desolate civil servants, a space that seems to remain behind the locked gates of St James Brewery. One can never enter this space without an invitation. His territory is forbidden. The only person I ever met who had an immediate rapport with Kinsella's work was the Australian poet, Vincent Buckley. Buckley knew the work intimately and his admiration for Kinsella was total. Interestingly enough, Buckley was a Catholic intellectual, a prince of every kind of 1950s Irish darkness. He could see the fatal cirrhosis of Irish Catholic theology at work in poems like 'Ritual of Departure' — 'saturated / High places traversed by spring sleet, / Thrust up through the thin wind into pounding silence'. Buckley understood 'A sourness in the clay' and the corrosive effect of that sourness on Irishmen of late middle age. Kinsella describes something that we wish to deny within our Irish selves. It is deeper than politics; it is philosophical and a trauma of the soul. Knowing this depth of soul Kinsella has characterized Ulster poetry of the modern era as mere 'journalism' that panders to foreigners in search of a key to the Ulster Troubles. Yet he himself has written such journalism in poetry — I think of *Butcher's Dozen*, his response to the Widgery Tribunal on the Bloody Sunday killings in Derry, or *The Good Fight*, a poem written for the tenth anniversary of John F Kennedy's murder. It's true that Gerry Smyth, another Dublin poet who shares the same urban architecture and who remains passionately loyal to those same St James' cobblestones, also reads Kinsella for the pure pleasure of the work. I spent the whole evening by

the fire reading 'Phoenix Park' with its brooding narrator, its
inevitable exits (Chapelizod, Islandbridge, Knockmaroon),
and thoughts like this:

> *Whatever the ultimate grotesqueries*
> *They'll have to root in more than this sour present.*
> *The ordeal-cup, set at each turn, so far*
> *We have welcomed, sour or sweet.*

I still don't know what that means precisely. What does it
mean? Precisely? In a very real sense Kinsella, in his poetry,
is not making clear statements; rather, he is inviting us to
speculate. I would like to know more. But I think it's too late
for me to try to know. On a night as bleak as this I resist the
temptation to carry yet another 'ordeal-cup'. I refute Kinsella's
dark Irish Catholicism because I was never part of it. Being
sub working class I was never a beneficiary of these Catholic
atmospheres. The liturgy of the streets, the impromptu genius
of my childhood survival, were what sustained me. The
Church that oppressed him intellectually was very far away
from the life I lived in Cappoquin. From my point of view the
1950s anxieties of Kinsella were the crowning privilege of a
bourgeois Irish Catholicism.

Friday At the Sebastian Barry play *White Woman Street* produced by Johnny Hanrahan and Meridian Theatre Company.
An intriguing play, beautifully acted. But an audience of only
20 people — and at vital moments of the play the man beside
me snored loudly.

A phone call from Anne at Glenshelane. The Brigadier has
been confined to bed for a week with severe back and leg
pains. He is very depressed and in great pain. Anne asked me
to ring him to see how he is, to cheer him up.

February 25th Went for coffee at the English Market, then
straight to the library in torrential rain where I spent two

hours reading the two volumes of James Barry papers in the Reference Department. These, edited by Dr Freyer, were published by Cadell & Davies in the Strand, London. If I photocopy from page 57 to 223 I will have the complete correspondence between Burke and Barry for the duration of Barry's sojourn in Rome. After that I will have to get a 'fix' on life in the Irish College in Rome at the same period.

March 10th Today, spent a few hours at Glenshelane with the Brigadier. He has been bed bound with sciatica for three weeks. Long conversation about politics and the abortion referendum, but the sensational news of West Waterford was the double murder at Clashmore and Ardmore: a publican from Clashmore, a respected pillar of the community, whose photograph appeared in *The Examiner* last week when he presented prizes as Captain of the West Waterford Golf Club, has been murdered by an irate young husband.

However, the funniest stories that the Brigadier tells are always about his housekeeper, the devoted Anne. The other day Anne was helping him to walk to the bathroom. She felt that he was slipping from her grasp. 'Will you put your arm around me, Brigadier! Put yer arm around me or you'll fall!' And Denis replied, 'I can't, I can't get my arm around you. You're too wide!' And Anne replied, 'Well, the devil take you. If you're going to be makin' smart-alec remarks about me size I'll let you drop to the floor. You can pick yerself up!'

March 25th Easter Monday Bad news from America. John Bernstein is now very ill; this time it is the cancer, not a virus. The cancer has spread throughout his body. Today I sat on the floor of our bedroom and recorded thirty or so poems of Nathaniel Murphy on an hour-long tape to send to John. John and Cindy were the only persons alive who shared my *Merchant Prince* project from the very beginning. John is the best friend I ever made. His presence has had an enormously buoyant and illuminating effect on our lives over the last ten years. I will miss him greatly, and Cathy will be devastated without his mischievous presence in our lives.

April 17th Still the most glorious weather imaginable. Eight hours of sunshine every day for the last ten days. It creates an extraordinary atmosphere in Cork; it transforms Cork into a Portuguese city.

Reading Stendhal's *Journal* again. His company is compelling, absorbing, precisely because it is so egotistical. Character traits that can make a man obnoxious in person can facilitate a marvellously attractive literary presence. This is one of the ironies of the artistic life.

May 4th 10.30 a.m. Right now I'm sitting in the Bus Terminal at Heathrow Airport. A lovely morning, the sun shining on me and three pigeons fussing at my feet, anticipating that I'll open some food package. Last night I was in Dungarvan for a poetry reading at the Old Market Gallery with the Baile na nGall poet Áine Uí Fhoghlú. Áine, a beautiful poet in the singing tradition of Caitlín Maude. When we read our poems we had one amusing intersection of themes — Portlaoise Prison. I read my political poems from *The Lost Province* and talked about visiting IRA prisoners for poetry workshops.

Later Áine read her poems and said, 'Like Tom, I visited Portlaoise Prison regularly, because my husband was jailed there.' Of course. It occurred to me that Ring, Helvick and Old Parish, that entire Dungarvan Bay area, is an IRA stomping ground. Áine has superb depth and strength of both language and temperament, a strong and wonderful woman. Being the wife of an IRA prisoner she's seen things and endured terrors that no poet should have to endure. But these terrors have made her strong. Certainly, while she continues to write the spirit of Caitlín Maude and Máire Mhac an tSaoi will endure. Very impressive that the Waterford County Manager, Mr Connolly, a very handsome and dapper man, was at this reading. I don't think I've ever seen any Cork City Manager at a poetry reading. It bodes well for a county when its most senior public official is willing to sit through a lengthy reading.

May 10th Yesterday, at the City Hall for another extraordinary Capital of Culture meeting. The designation of Cork as European Capital of Culture 2005 was finally made on Wednesday at the ECOFIN meeting in Brussels. I thought that Mary McCarthy, Liz Meaney, Joe Kennelly and I were being invited into the Manager's office for a glass of champagne — no such luck. It was a serious working session during which the Manager put his cards on the table vis-à-vis a Board of Management for Cork2005 and a job description for the Chief Executive.

May 11th Email from America. John Bernstein is sinking fast, only a few days left. Cindy warns us that if we want to talk to him we'd better phone straight away.

May 15th Spoke with John, who could barely, barely speak. But it was a joy to hear him and an equal joy to be able to say 'I love you' to someone whose friendship has meant so much to me. Armed with that immense quality of his undoubted Jewish ancestry mixed with old Southern Protestant upbringing, John understood my work at once; my poems and the Fianna Fáil novels. He used to say that talking with me about old Fianna Fáil or Fine Gael families was like having a conversation with his father about the old Democrat South.

May 18th A phone call from Minnesota where it is 4 a.m. John Bernstein, scholar, Yeatsian, bon vivant, Macalester Professor, has died. It is the end of an era, an era of such intense friendship. Catherine is devastated. Will we ever again find a friendship to match the friendship that John and Cindy and Catherine and I had between us? Such love between four people will never again happen in our lives. I am devastated, truly heartbroken.

May 25th My last day in the library before I take up my new post as 'Capital of Culture Executive'. An unreal day. I wonder if I'll ever work in the library again? I was hoping to take the No 6 bus from Knocknaheeny to keep this last day as ordinary as possible. It is hard to believe that, on and off, the City Library has been my life for twenty-four years. When I took the job in 1978 I guessed it would be for two or three years until I finished my MA and went off to live and teach poetry in America. But that part of my life never materialized — and I never finished my MA, though I spent a year studying Roethke and nearly another year studying Corkery's fiction.

May 31st Long conversation on the phone with Dr Michael Kuhlemann of the Ruhr-Essen region of Germany. He had contacted me for advice on how best to approach the EU Cultural Unit on behalf of Essen. Dr Kuhleman is chairing a committee to put together a bid for the German European Capital of Culture in 2010. He was very encouraged by our successful Bid as he sees great similarities between Ruhr-Essen and Cork's post-industrial landscapes. He says he will come to visit me in Cork, but in the meantime I'll make up a package of documents for him from our Bid stage.

June 11th Many hours of discussion with Mary Leland. She is now the most distinguished living Cork writer. Mary and I are of the one mind on the need to have a major publishing programme during 2005.

June 17th Phone calls from the Irish Embassy in Paris. Patsy Murphy-Mignot of the Embassy Press Office has been receiving requests for visits to Cork from French journalists. They want to visit soon. I told her I'd show them the sights.

June 18th A major seminar on Cultural Tourism at the Millennium Hall. The City Manager spoke brilliantly, the best public presentation I've ever heard him give. A greater degree of cooperation between the Arts community and Tourist authorities was promised. One practical suggestion: at the beginning of every year a representative of the Arts community would address a meeting of all Tourist Guides.

June 26th We've just had an incredible Midsummer Festival in Cork, with plays by Martin McDonagh and Conor McPherson, a series of play-readings by Corcadorca, a Patrick Scott Retrospective, exhibitions by Martin Gale and William Crozier and a superb series of installations orchestrated by Mary McCarthy of the National Sculpture Factory. The brochure, posters and everything associated with Mary McCarthy and Isabel Vasseur's curating is extraordinary. If we can get Mary to come aboard Cork2005 will be a triumph. This Midsummer Festival is Cork2005 in microcosm.

July 8th Another phone call from Dr Kuhleman of Ruhr-Essen. He wanted to know why the Irish Government had handed over the responsibility of designating a Capital of Culture to Brussels (when the native Government should have made the decision). I couldn't give him a satisfactory answer, but I offered a number of possible scenarios. I told him that this office had no objection to the Selection Criteria as everything had worked out very well for Cork City. At which observation he laughed heartily. Afterwards, I thought: what a lucky day it was for Cork when Síle de Valera decided that she couldn't choose between Limerick and Galway! As Cork shows so often when given a level playing field, it can beat all comers.

July 9th At the opening of Jessica Roth's exhibition in Cashel. The exhibit was opened by Donovan who sang rather than talked. A great event.

July 10th It looks as if a Scottish man got the job as Director of Cork2005.

July 19th Across from my office I can hear a heated argument going on between a group of Housing Officers and their supervisor. There's a real problem to deal with: who shall have a house by tomorrow afternoon and who shall remain homeless. Swamped by high culture one tends to forget that there are *real* social issues decided every day by these City Council officials. I don't envy them. They go past my office door every day to fill their tea kettles at the kitchen sink. They look pale, exhausted, frustrated. Right now they are arguing about a homeless man who has been housed seven times in the last two years. One official reads off the addresses in exasperation: 'Coach Street', 'St Vincent's Terrace', 'Rathmore', 'Leitrim Street'. All of these the names of the most desolate and depressing places where a human could be sent to live in this Capital of Culture. Hearing them, I am reminded of what a privileged world is this world of Art, of Culture, that I live within. I must never forget this. None of us should ever forget this.

September 14th A dreadful week at the Capital of Culture office. Bryan, the Director-designate, came in. A lovely man, quiet-spoken and a terrific listener. Only time will tell if he takes advice. Everything was going well — our own working relationship, our meetings with others in the city, Bryan's dinner at our house (except he is allergic to cats). Then he had a disastrous meeting with the City Manager. What should have been a mere courtesy call, a friendly chat, turned into a frosty exchange about the budget of 2005. Bryan was shaken by this encounter with the Manager, so shaken that he said to me, 'Don't talk, Tom. I need a pint!' I walked with him to The Long Valley where he drank a pint of Beamish. I showed him the lovely print of the Great Cork Exhibition of 1902. I'm afraid this didn't cheer him up. 'I can't believe the Manager's attitude,' he kept saying. 'I can't believe it. Maybe we should embarrass the City Council. I'm talking with *The Examiner* in the morning.' I dissuaded him from this course of action because although we might win a public relations victory over the Council and its Manager — and probably get a *public* guarantee of money — we'd do irreparable damage to our relationship with the Council. It would become impossible to work with them: it would become impossible for them to work with us. In the public service you must be able to trust that people won't run to newspapers when they run into difficulties with you, when the internal going gets tough. I really had to press this fact hard, to ram it home to him.

We met Mary McCarthy of the National Sculpture Factory. She is due to begin working in the Cork2005 office at the end of this month. She was quite sanguine about the Manager's attitude. Like me, she is sure that the Council will release money in due course. She said that the City Manager had promised her a challenge fund of 2.5 million euro. Mary and I had a long chat later. This encounter, and Bryan's fatalistic response to it, makes her very nervous.

We stared into our drinks after Bryan had gone away.

'Oh shit,' said Mary, 'my Sculpture Factory job is advertised in *The Irish Times* today.'

'Shit,' I said. 'I'm so sorry.'

September 17th Lunch with Alf Smiddy, the Managing Director of Beamish & Crawford. He is hugely enthusiastic about Cork2005. Many promises of support, facilities etc.

A visit from the poet Patrick Cotter who has just been appointed Director of the Munster Literature Centre. This visit followed a phone call from Greg Delanty who was worried that Pat Cotter would get the job. Why was he worried? He didn't give me any specific reason, he was just worried. Greg sounds frustrated and angry every time I speak to him; but he is not a malicious person. He is just finding everything that happens to be a worry at the moment. Several other phone calls and visits, including a call from the City Manager who wants to talk to me (about Bryan Beattie, I suppose).

Days of endless exhaustion. Like Seferis, I long for a house by the sea.

September 25th Today an absolutely bizarre phone call from a businessman in Scotland. This man claimed to be a friend of Michael Smurfit, the rich cardboard-box maker. He said that his name was X . . . and that he'd just read that a Scottish fellow had got a big job in Ireland. 'I just read this in the Inverness papers,' said he, 'and I can't believe it. How did he get such a prestigious job? What were ye thinking of?' Then he went on for over half an hour, blackening Bryan's name.

'Well, he's here now,' I replied. 'And we'll support him. We have a great team assembled for him. He has addressed meetings with over a thousand people already. He gets on marvellously with everyone. We'll deliver Cork2005 together.'

Then I decided to be cruel (as this man was being malicious and cruel). 'The contracts are all signed,' I said, 'one hundred thousand a year plus unvouched expenses. Everybody feels that he's worth it, more than worth it.'

'One hundred thousand a year! What! That's half a million over five years! Good God, well, good God. That beats everything!' the man went on, utterly defeated. He hung up in disgust, repeating the huge salary figure: 'one hundred thousand a year'.

The bare-faced Scottish begrudgery of this phone call is astonishing.

Tomorrow I must arrange two desks, two chairs and two phone lines for Bryan and Mary Mac who join the office next week. At last, a Cork2005 team. Not just me and one housing-department phone.

October 8th Disaster at the Capital of Culture office. Bryan Beattie spent three hours at City Hall today trying to come to some contractual agreement with the Manager, Joe Gavin. An appalling personal animosity has developed between the two men. Mary Mac and I spent a few hours with Bryan also.

It is going to be a disaster.

October 9th This morning when I got up I said to Catherine, 'I'm going back to the library. I've had enough of this arts administration shit! I'm telling the Manager this morning.' She said give it one more week. I'm giving it one more week, that's all. Then I'm gone. Gone.

October 10th Bryan Beattie is gone. He took a flight back to Scotland this morning after failing to agree a contract with the Manager. Bryan, a sweet-natured kindly man, was utterly, absolutely decisive about his decision. Last night Mary Mac and I went to dinner with him. Afterwards I walked the streets of Cork with him. The city was buzzing with young people coming from the Film Festival. We talked and talked and talked — about European Culture, about Scottish poetry, about Jack Doyle and the Queen Mother. Bryan was like a man who'd escaped from a terrible fate. Deep down I think he dreaded taking on the task of Director of the European Capital of Culture because he wasn't sure of local support, either political or financial. I don't blame him. I've been here for only two weeks, fielding phone calls, and it's already a total nightmare.

October 26th Visited the Brigadier at Glenshelane. He is much improved. Sitting room was warm, all the Bogdanis lit up. He says that Sir Richard Keane (now 94) has been warned by his housekeeper that he can only have three dinner parties a week or she will leave. What an indomitable spirit.

November 30th Meetings, meetings, meetings. But the week ended well at the Capital of Culture offices. We had a day-long meeting on Thursday with a major international branding company. High stakes.

December 8th and 9th A two-day 'get-together' at the Hayfield Manor Hotel. This was a kind of think-in or reassessment of the Cork2005 Project. It was meant to be an encounter that would inform and empower us. The reverse has happened — we are utterly diminished from the experience and exposed for the fools we are. No answers even to the most basic questions put by a brilliant panel that included Bob Palmer, Franco Bianchini, Patricia Quinn of the Arts Council, Fiach Mac Conghail, the Minister's Arts Advisor, and Doireann Ní Bhriain, the former Director of 'l'Imaginaire Irlandais'. We heard some brilliant phrases from Palmer and Biancini:

'How will Cork understand its own intelligence?'

'How can Cork2005 provoke a mental shift?'

'Culture is what you grow people in.'

December 23rd Lunch yesterday with Louis Marcus, the film-maker. I told him about James Barry and Rev Francis Mahony. Apart from 'The Bells of Shandon' he knew nothing of either writers. We had a long talk, perhaps two hours. Marcus is a gentle man, grey, small neat beard of the mid-century intellectual. When we were parting I promised to send him both of my personal files on Barry and Mahony in the New Year.

December 24th At Glenshelane yesterday evening to see the Brigadier and wish him a Happy Christmas. He was in bed resting as we arrived in the early afternoon. He'd had visitors before lunch (Bill and Joan Roth of San Francisco) who had shared a smoked eel and pink champagne from Corney & Barrow of London. He came down to the kitchen and Cathy and I and he sat by the Aga and talked about champagne, the Iraq crisis and American foreign policy. He was extremely frail but in top form because he had just received a royalty cheque for £72 from the Collins Press. His sister-in-law's book on Lord Kildare has sold nearly 1,500 copies — an extraordinary sale. Again he asked me if I'd talk to Con Collins about publishing Brian FitzGerald's *The Geraldines*, a book first published fifty years ago. I think Con Collins might go for this.

Finished, this week, Molly Keane's *The Rising Tide*. Once again, that war between women, and a whole series of compliant men and horses. I am reminded yet again of the purpose of Art and of that powerful word 'integrity'. There is nothing as powerful as the integrity of a completely imagined world.

2003

January 14th Great excitement in the Capital of Culture office as the Boss and Mary Mac return from Graz in Austria. They came home laden with catalogues, CDs and merchandising, including a cute furry Graz mascot, from this year's European Capital of Culture. All this evidence of very clever branding fills the office with a huge wave of excitement and expectation. The Boss is a changed man: he has been baptized, or anointed rather, by his experiences at Graz.

January 17th Lunch today with Con Collins. We talked about Brian FitzGerald's book, *The Geraldines*. The Brigadier wants me to persuade him to re-publish it. I always have a great laugh with Con. He has terrific stories about authors and I have pieces of gossip from various sources. Con told me that Cork University Press had actually rejected Paddy Galvin's *Song for a Fly Boy*. I reviewed it for *The Irish Times*: sent the review off by email this morning. I promised Con that I'd assemble a file of all my notes and cuttings on Daniel Maclise so that Con could send it to Bruce Arnold — to see if Arnold could be persuaded to write a study of Maclise.

Phone call from Desmond O'Grady who is now in the best of health after two years of surgery and recuperation. Desmond mentioned again those disastrous reading arrangements between Kate O'Brien and Patrick Kavanagh in the 1950s. Desmond was involved in the Spoleto Festival in Italy nearly fifty years ago.

January 28th In the post this morning, a letter from Desmond containing a photograph of 'Two Generations of Hard-Fisted Poets' — a Dan Georgakas photo of Ezra Pound and Desmond at Spoleto in Italy. There are many poets in the world who would give their right arms for such historic proof of a meeting with the maestro, Ezra Pound.

January 29th In Dublin for a meeting of Poetry Ireland in the Bermingham Tower of Dublin Castle. The same dear faces of Frank Downe and Tommy Smith. Michael Longley attended, very quiet and tired; good to see him after so many years. Ronan Sheehan and the effervescent Katie Donovan also present. Katie has left *The Irish Times* and is now studying to be a Reiki healer. Discussions about money, money, money. Why do I agree to be on these Boards? Literature is never discussed. But, ultimately, all voluntary Boards are about money.

Before the meeting I had an hour to spare so I went straight to the National Gallery and stood in front of the four great James Barrys: 'Venus Rising from the Sea' (1770s), 'The Temptation of Adam' (or 'Adam and Eve', but 'Temptation in Paradise' is printed on the gold frame), 'Self-Portrait as Timanthus' — a sublime work that Barry developed over 23 years (from 1780 to 1803) and 'Baptism of the King of Cashel' that was painted in 1801. It's interesting to note that 'Self-Portrait' was purchased in 1934 while the 'Baptism' was purchased in 1966. Even with these four paintings one can see the great expressive power of Barry. How spectacular the great exhibition of all his paintings will be in Cork2005! It will overwhelm people with its majesty.

I spent twenty minutes upstairs looking at Italian paintings. I came upon two incredible marbles, 'Faun with a Goat' and 'Faun with a Kid', made in 1775 by Bartolomeo Cavaceppi (1716-1799). Cavaceppi was a restorer of classical statues (he sculpted the Masters to completion) as well as an antiquarian and a dealer. He had a huge workshop in Rome where all visitors and fellow artists were welcome. The two 'Fauns' stand about one metre tall, perfect, absolutely perfect in their self-possession and finish. They are replicas of much larger

Roman marbles of the second-century AD. They were originally acquired in Italy by the Leesons for their country house, Russborough, in County Wicklow. I could have spent the entire day in the company of Cavaceppi and Barry. As I was leaving the Gallery I noticed, in the distance, the great canvas of Caravaggio's 'The Taking of Christ'. I was tempted to turn back and walk the long corridors down to Carravagio. But I didn't. I felt it would have been an almost unfaithful thing to do — this day belonged to Barry and to Cavaceppi.

January 30th A meeting with Pat Cotter as he prepares his detailed submission to our office on the Cork2005 Translation Series.

Later, excitement in the office. The PR company, Kearney-Melia, sent a photographer to take our photos.

February 5th Yesterday, a successful Aosdána meeting in Dublin. I proposed Julie O'Callaghan for membership and she romped home in the voting. I mentioned the Cork2005 Translation Series to Eiléan Ní Chuilleanáin — she said that she would be very happy to work on the project, saying, also, that she'd love to work with a Romanian poet.

February 27th Paddy Galvin is very ill in the South Infirmary. Today he had a second stroke. He is paralysed down the right side and cannot speak. His poor wife, Mary Johnson, has been flying into a rage with the doctors and nurses. Her wonderful, strong Ulster will power has kept Paddy alive for fifteen years. Paddy has been her obsession and her life's project. She has fought with everyone for Paddy's sake.

March 5th Here at Whitman College in Walla Walla, Washington State. A beautiful place, chic, gentle, wealthy: a place of wheatfields and vineyards. I was invited here by Tom Cronin, the ebullient President of the College. Staying at an expensive and luxury B&B that is run by a descendant of the novelist, John Buchan. Gave two readings and two talks. I gave them good value for my visit, but then they are a generous-hearted people.

Interesting encounters at breakfast: two families, one a wealthy Swiss-educated doctor from San Diego, the other an Italian-American police sergeant and his wife who works as a police-dispatcher, both searching for houses in the Walla Walla valley. Both are tired of life in big cities, both escaping from the stress of the coast and the dangers of terrorist bombs. The doctor's wife told me that she was prepared to spend quarter of a million dollars on a ten-acre vineyard. The police sergeant said he was searching for work as well as looking for houses: he was prepared to do anything, including work as a farmhand in the wheatfields. This is extraordinary, this inner migration of Americans, this flight from the perceived terrors of the coast. Generally the 'coast' is where America encounters the rest of the world, so it is a withdrawal from the world.

March 10th In St Paul at the University of St Thomas where I'm to receive the O'Shaughnessy Prize for Poetry. The Center for Irish Studies, a lively friendly place, all thinking creatively, intelligently, like scholars. Lunch the other day at a St Thomas Alumni 'First Friday'. I sat beside Father Dease, the President, and two mighty old rogues of Minnesota life, Don Regan and Kingsley Murphy. Kingsley owns various radio and TV stations. He founded WCCO, the huge regional broadcaster, and once owned the *Minneapolis Star Tribune*. (As far as I know, that's now owned by Bill Roth's company, McClatchy newspapers.) What is astonishing is that these men, almost Republican to the bone, are totally against the war in Iraq. I was at a dinner party last night at David Lebedoff's house (David, a lawyer, a 'rainmaker', is our only Minsk Irishman, a devout Republican). The entire company at dinner were against the war. Kingsley Murphy's wife, a native of North Carolina, was virulently anti-Bush. She said that it was the first time in history that America was ruled by a complete 'id-eye-ot', as she pronounced it with a great Carolina drawl.

I met Joe Dowling and Siobhán Cleary at David Lebedoff's dinner. Joe was fascinated by Cork's nomination as European Capital of Culture. He said he always found it impossible to do theatre business in Cork. He said the Opera House became so impossible that he stopped trying to put plays into it. An interesting man, not at all opinionated or arrogant. I noticed that he constantly ceded the discussion to others, even on matters of theatre — evidence of a really confident and balanced man. Siobhán Cleary, his wife, is more opinionated, but not unpleasant: a fun-loving creature, in fact. She talked about Nuala O'Faolain whose second book is being promoted on NPR radio all this weekend.

Went to *About Schmidt* with Cindy at the Pavilion at Crossroads; also a terrific play, *Two Trains Running,* by August Wilson at the Penumbra Theatre. Wilson is a playwright of world standards, the Ibsen of African-American life. The depth of his characters, the depth of their humanity and their pain, is simply overwhelming.

March 15th Sitting at Newark Airport. A long layover before I take my flight to Shannon. The last three days were a disaster for me. What should have been the most joyful days were full of fever and exhaustion. At one stage I thought I'd have to go to hospital. Before I gave my last poetry reading last night I took a cold bath for half an hour and this got my temperature down.

April 14th The Boss's great human kindness was revealed to me today. I told him about my visit to the dear Brigadier who has suffered a serious setback to his health. He lies incoherent and disorientated at Ardkeen Hospital in Waterford. JK said to me, 'Tom, if you're in France and the Brigadier dies please use our City of Culture Travel Agents to get you back quickly.' I thought it a lovely gesture, an example of the inate kindness in John Kennedy's character.

The Brigadier had a half-hour blackout last week and nearly died. I visited him at the hospital. He was very disorientated. He thought that the hospital ward was his house and that the nurses and doctors had confiscated his home to set up a Field Hospital. He turned to me, pleading, 'Can you so something, Thomas? Can you contact my solicitors in London and check the deeds of Glenshelane?' Then he turned to one of the nurses and gestured sadly, hopelessly, 'I don't mind them putting up these silly curtains everywhere, but the colour on the walls is frightful, it's not my colour at all! What can I do?' I spoke to the nurses about him. They say he may snap out of his dementia, but that he may have to go into a nursing home for three or four weeks to recover his strength. It was sad to see him struck down so forcibly: a man who has survived wealth and war, the two deadliest enemies of the soul.

Yesterday I visited Paddy Galvin in the South Infirmary. Paddy in an even more serious condition than the Brigadier. He's no longer able to speak properly, nor is he able to eat — he is being fed via a tube. His devoted wife, Mary, and Gráinne his daughter, were in attendance, watching every gesture, every twinkle in Paddy's eye. *Willing* him to get better. Paddy Galvin is the object of so much love and devotion, in contrast to the Brigadier, noble and rich, who is thrown on a miserable gurney in Waterford, alone most of the day and completely at the mercy of strangers. Poets, truly, are blessed.

April 29th Yesterday we went through sixty of the project proposals for 2005. We had all read them already and made notes. By 6 p.m. thirty projects had made it through to the next stage.

May 15th Good week at the Capital of Culture office. We have gone through nearly one hundred proposals, keeping aside about thirty for further discussion and development.

We've spent two days on this. Some truly wonderful ideas — like Jools Gilson-Ellis's 'knitting the city', a huge site-specific idea where an entire community of knitters would knit a tapestry of patterns of traffic in the city (a new meaning to 'knitting pattern'). Or Conal Creedon's simple idea of a huge Céilí, stretching from North Gate Bridge to South Gate Bridge; or the Cork2005 Translation Series; or the Vanbrugh Quartet's idea for a European Festival of Quartets. Yesterday we corresponded with Catherine Sisk of the Department of Culture in Dublin because the office here has never got in touch with the Department. At the same time I sent a 'holding note' to Brit Holtebekk of the Cultural Unit in the Commission at Brussels, just to keep our lines of communication open with Brussels. We need Brussels. They're holding at least 5% of our total budget.

Catherine and I went to see the Brigadier. Incredibly feeble, only barely able to speak. 'I can't complain. I have no pain,' he says, repeating this several times, like a little boy under his blankets. He couldn't attend to the correspondence of the previous week. There are bills and two letters from the British Tax Authorities, but he was incapable of anything. I took cheques from the chequebooks in the kitchen to send to his heir, Adrian, who has power-of-attorney. The cheques are from the Bank of Scotland in Jersey and Lloyds in London, as well as AIB in Lismore. How strange it is, at the end, that so noble and careful an individual as he is ultimately in the hands of strangers: two private nurses and a gardener, a cook and a housekeeper.

May 22nd Days of crisis at the Cork2005 office. Yesterday and today ferociously bad ill-feeling.

This evening, at 7 p.m., a phone call from Emma, the Brigadier's nurse at Glenshelane, who sounded alarmed. He is very poorly. A ball of mucus has settled in his lung and Emma thinks that this may be the beginning of pneumonia. He keeps talking about death, about his mother and about his brother, Brian. At one point he asked Emma: 'Am I dead?' Emma can't get in touch with Adrian. I think he may be in Dublin at a Knights of Malta function. So Emma feels lost. A stranger taking care of a man without family. I spoke to him for a few minutes. Very, very weak.

May 24th Last night, after a day of appalling tension in the Cork2005 office, Cathy and I went to dinner at the Café Mexicana in Carey's Lane.

Just now, another phone call from Emma. The Brigadier is very bad. She wants me to come down to Glenshelane House. I must go.

May 25th Our belovèd Brigadier died today. Catherine and I had just left his bedside at Glenshelane when the nurse rang my mobile. 'He's gone, Thomas,' she said.

Impossible to believe. Impossible.

May 26th I have kept two simple photos. The Brigadier and Peter Fleming, brother of Ian Fleming and Old Etonian, in France, 1930, plus a cutting from *The Tatler and Sketch* of June 17th 1953 of the Brigadier with the Duchess of Rutland and others at the Coronation Ball in the Savoy, London.

May 28th The Brigadier's Death Notice in the (London) *Times* today. 'No letters by request.' That says everything. There is no Geraldine left at Carton, Kilkea or Stansted House who might grieve enough to require a letter.

May 29th We buried the Brigadier today after a beautiful service in Lismore Cathedral. The Marquis of Kildare read the lessons and Sir Richard Keane gave a fine eulogy. I recited five of my poems, written over the years: 'The Leinster Fitz-Geralds', 'Survivors of War', 'Hours Ago, 1973', 'Viburnum Fragrans', 'A Geraldine Officer'. Afterwards we carried the coffin to the graveside — Sir Adrian FitzGerald, Michael my brother and my cousins Anthony and John. So three men of the displaced Munster Eoghanachta and one Geraldine nobleman carried him to his final resting place. Adrian and I, and Michael and Anthony, lowered his coffin into the good earth of Lismore. I said farewell, but I tried not to be too sad — for he had a long and beautiful life, immensely privileged and elegant. He surrounded himself with beauty and friendship all his life, certainly, all his life after the War: Bogdani pictures, Geraldine prints and miniatures, silks, family silver, polished desks and ebony handled cutlery. For most people unconnected with the Anglo-Irish world or European noble families his lifestyle would have seemed unimaginable. It *was* unimaginable in this day and age, that unselfconsciously aristocratic Geraldine life. But it was undeniably noble: to be the grandson of Ireland's premier duke, to be descended directly from both Silken Thomas and Lord Edward Fitz-Gerald, to have had Carton, Kilkea Castle and Johnstown Castle as one's childhood homes. It was a life utterly removed from the life of ordinary Irish people. But he was brave and he absolutely did his duty as a soldier, both in the Norway campaign of 1940 and, later, when he commanded his battalion in the night crossing of the Rhine in 1944. Like many a Kildare Geraldine before him he took part in events that changed history. But he died alone, without family, without wife, son or daughter. That is a great sadness.

I knew him for thirty years and I admit that I basked smugly in the abiding certainty of his praise. I will never again find anyone who will praise me as unreservedly as he did. In a sense his death is truly the end of my long childhood and adolescence. His death forces me into that complete mental isolation known as adulthood. In a very real sense his passing makes my life truly ordinary, and desolate in the ordinary way that most Irish poets' lives are desolate. Knowing the noble old Geraldine, living under his umbrella of praise, allowed me to live a life that constantly denied its ordinariness: no more Geraldine poems, no more Anglo-

Irish drawing rooms where a lyric poet of the South could hide from an oppressive Catholic Irish Free State life. But more than anything it's his brilliant storytelling that I'll miss. I will have to fall back upon my own resources and I dread the desolation of that, my librarian-life that Seamus Deane once described as a study in lower middle-class squalor. Admittedly Deane was referring to Philip Larkin's life at the time.

June 1st Very negative article about Cork and the Capital of Culture in *Magill* magazine. Intelligent, socially aware perceptions, but negative, negative, negative.

June 6th Yet another negative article about Cork2005, this time in *The Evening Echo*. Very unusual for the *Echo* to turn on us, but it's the newspaper that's closest to life on the streets of Cork. It inevitably absorbs that feeling of hatred about Cork2005. Hatred of us everywhere. You can almost feel hatred in the mist that falls from the sky.

June 20th Tonight I gave a poetry reading in the Crawford Art Gallery as part of the Cork Midsummer Festival. A small crowd, about fourteen people. This event clashed with a major reading of Modernist International Poets at the Triskel Arts Centre. Though small my crowd was a very satisfying crowd to read to, including Hugh Lorigan and several other young artists whose work I love.

July 9th Yesterday, a day of absolute joy for me. Kate and I visited Sissinghurst Castle Garden. We took the train from Charing Cross to Staplehurst in Kent and a taxi to the gardens. It was a dream come true for me, a pilgrimage that I first thought of doing nearly thirty years ago. The gardens themselves were stunning beyond belief, beyond anything one could have imagined. All photographs of the gardens are hopelessly inadequate. The 'white garden', a symphonic arrangement of hundreds of white-blossomed and grey-leaved plants, is truly extraordinary. It is the most beautiful garden I have ever seen. We saw it at its best, in early July when roses, buddleias, white lupins etc were all in brilliant luminous blossom. Vita Sackville-West was certainly a poet in her flowers. The garden is the very embodiment of a kind of English dream: it is nature domesticated, beauty become organic.

At Hatchards I bought a copy of PD James' *The Murder Room*, signed by the author. At my favourite bookshop, Gloucester Road Bookshop, I bought a brilliant study of the Swiss artist, Fuseli, and a 1960 Hogarth Press edition of Forster's *Pharos and Pharillon*. I saw a copy of T E Lawrence's *The Arab Revolt* but it was too expensive. I regret not buying it. If I am in London again this year I will go back to that bookshop to see if it's still there.

July 19th Fractious days at Cork2005. I lost an argument over the funding of our Cork2005 Translation Series. The Programming colleagues thought that I had allocated too much money to the Munster Literature Centre for the administrative part of their budget. I was forced to climb down, but my defeat in committee means that we will be giving the Munster Literature Centre € 40,000 less for their needs in 2004 and 2005. I feel humiliated by this defeat, but not half as humiliated as Patrick Cotter will feel when he receives our letter.

August 11th At home for a week on Annual Leave. I spent the day going through old papers. At this stage I feel that every dream I had, every ambition, every hope, for 2005 will go down in flames. I think 2005 will be the final Burning of Cork: we will finish the job that the Black and Tans started in the 1920s. Today a phone call from Adrian FitzGerald in London. It is 100°F in South Kensington. Adrian is coming over next Monday. He'll spend two weeks at Glenshelane. I must go down to sort my books as well as the papers I left behind in my bedroom.

September 4th More disastrous and moral-sapping days at Cork2005. A dreadful Board meeting where the City Manager could barely contain his fury at the incompetence of our 'suits'.

September 14th At Glenshelane yesterday to talk to Adrian. It was dark by the time I arrived at Glenshelane. Adrian was indoors reading papers from his Knights of Malta meeting in Knock. We spent several hours chatting about everything.

September 20th A hectic Cork2005 day on Friday. It was a day of leadership speeches. The most important speaker (in the Conference Centre at the Moran Silversprings Hotel) was Mayor Giuliani of New York who gave a brilliant speech. Giuliani has just become a Director of an Italian winery. We shook hands and spoke briefly about the merits of Italian wines. Bob Palmer, guru of European Capitals of Culture, gave a terrific speech on *Creative Cities*, challenging the six hundred assembled delegates of the MBA Association to support Art and Culture in their own cities.

September 21st Last night I introduced Julia O'Faolain at a reading in the Granary Theatre. I mentioned her *Women in the Wall, No Country for Young Men* and *The Judas Cloth*. But Julia read a very indifferent story about a sexually abusive priest. Afterwards I walked her home to her modest B&B in Western Road. I thought how extraordinary that her reputation has declined so decidedly — all of her novels are now out of print, and the market for intelligent fiction has shrunk completely.

September 22nd A day of misery and depression at the Cork2005 office — relieved only by the visit of Fiach Mac Conghail, the brilliant theatre director and producer who is also the Advisor to the Minister of Culture. He is advising us on theatre matters.

October 2nd Met Ulick O'Connor at the Shelbourne, from where we moved to the Lord Edward for an excellent fish lunch with fine Chardonnay wines. The waiters at the Lord Edward constantly attending to Ulick: 'Are you happy, Mr O'Connor?' 'Have you enough there, Mr O'Connor?' The whole dancing attendance was overdone, but affectionate. Ulick, once the terrible student prince of Dublin's upper crust, now a little down-at-heel and dishevelled. Faded glory. Full of spite and resentment against everyone who has crossed swords with him for forty or more years. While we dined he attacked Anthony Cronin, Louis le Brocquy, Eoghan Harris, RTÉ, *The Irish Times*, British Civilization and Gerald Goldberg (in that order). Ulick has taken to me since I slipped him a note at an Aosdána meeting, praising his journals from John Murray. He is astonished at the number of journals I've read. I brought him the two volumes of Sir John Colville's diaries (Churchill's secretary). He was thrilled by these. He showed me the cover design for the paperback edition of his own journals. I envy him that publisher, John Murray. How wonderful it is to be published by Murray: it pleased Ulick even more when he realized that I *knew* what a coup it was to be accepted by Byron's publisher. But then he went on to attack Dervla Murphy. He always thought her father was English and was astonished to learn that he was an Irish-speaking Sorbonne-educated Republican who sheltered fleeing IRA volunteers even as late as the 1940s. I was delighted to disabuse him on Dervla's background and Ulick was delighted to be so informed. I had to promise him that I'd send his poetry manuscript to Lagan Press in Belfast. Ulick now sees me as his stalking horse, which I am willing to be. At the moment I certainly don't mind playing a part in a minor Dublin literary intrigue. Ulick is a man of intrigues: he sees enemies and conspiracies everywhere. And over time he has been at the centre of most Dublin intrigues.

I had to rush from the Lord Edward to Stephen's Green for the Poetry Ireland meeting. I bumped into Edna Longley in Grafton Street. She had been to the launch by the Taoiseach of the Harry Boland biography at the Mansion House the previous night.

I was sorry to have to rush away from her as I'd have enjoyed half an hour or so of scoffing with her about Free State politics. Like me she is an absolute blackguard when it comes to Southern politicians. We are both dissidents and sceptics of all the grand Irish pieties — I love her for that unrelenting scepticism. She is a real soul mate: one of the few in my literary life.

October 12th Much better days at Cork2005. On Friday we had a very upbeat meeting at UCC.

October 19th Lunch today with Fiona Shaw. Fiona (or Fifi Wilson as she was known at UCC in the 1970s) is brilliant: well-read, astonishingly well-travelled and connected, and hugely interested in working with Cork2005. She talked a great deal about Deborah Warner who has just had a very successful exhibition of 'angels' in New York. Fiona said she would love to collaborate with Warner and Bob Crowley, the designer. She has this incredible sense of Cork as a place asleep, or a place just waking from a long Victorian sleep that has lasted through all of her childhood. A brilliant luncheon. Good things will come of it in 2005.

October 27th Tintoretto, Veronese, Titian, the Accademia, Palazzo Ducale, the Canale Grande, the old and newer church and Basilica S Maria Gloriosa Dei Frari: we did the lot in three wonderful days of excellent but very light meals and mostly Montepulciano wines. Venice is still crowded with visitors, even this late in the season. I wonder if the tourist season ever comes to an end in Venice? Looking at the art what strikes one immediately is the incredible vanity and political credulity of the Venetian Republic. For centuries this immensely wealthy Republic extracted all of the wealth of the Near East — even breaking the power of the Pasha at the Battle of Lepanto with secretly designed warships. But it is the vanity of these Republicans, dedicated entirely to careers of greed, rapacious racism and anti-Semitism, that is everywhere apparent in every canal and waterfront palace. What they made of their wealth was beautiful, utterly beautiful, but it was not used to glorify the grandeur of God in heaven, but to insist that heaven belonged to Venice. Byron encountered Venice at its most touching, at the very nadir of decline; whereas current mass tourism has now extracted a pervasive and wicked vanity from the stench of the Venetian renaissance. Cathy and I were looking at the Palla d'Oro in the Basilica of St Mark and, simultaneously, we both said, 'Disgusting'. We went around like a low-church couple from Bradford, disgusted with Romish opulence.

But there was Titian's glorious painting, 'The Presentation of the Virgin at the Temple', to me by far the most spiritual painting of the Accademia. After all the vanity and self-serving grandiosity of the Doges and their friends (the Saints and God in heaven) to come upon this little girl, the Blessèd Virgin as a child, is to be restored to the original meaning of art, and to be restored to the allegorical meaning and truth of the Catholic Church. When I saw it I stood a long time in awe, and I thanked God for its presence in this revolting sea of merchant vanities.

And I found a panel in the former ghetto, of the two-hundred-and-forty-six citizens of Venice deported to the gas chambers, including names like these: Rosa De Leon, Guisseppi Bora Levi, Corinna Ottolenghi, Elena Corinaldi, Marisa Jesurum, Nina Maestro Russi, Constanza Missano Naccamulli and Beatrice and Ada Kuhn. I stood for a long time and prayed.

October 28th But for Cathy and me this visit was a triumph. This is the other side of Venice, the romantic, artistic side. And it is a genuine aspect of Venice: nobody with an ounce of romance or an ounce of poetry in their blood could fail to be moved by the beauty of Venice. Its buildings are stunning, absolutely beyond belief in the dense baroque urgency of every bridge and balcony. The population itself is very handsome, the product of centuries of financial and agricultural plenty. When we were leaving Venice from Santa Lucia Station last night Cathy said that she'd been looking at a young Venetian woman who had fallen asleep. The young woman, with her perfect chin and nose, her sensuous lips and luxuriant dark hair, her skin as fine as fresh grapes, looked like a young Madonna that Catherine had seen in the Accademia — a face painted by Titian. The sheer physical perfection, the supremely poised sensuousness of Venetians, is what makes time spent in Venice and the Veneto a feast for the soul. No wonder all the cold North Europeans, from Byron to Stravinsky, from Goethe to Joseph Brodsky, fell in love with this city and had an almost sexual relationship with its atmosphere.

Maybe Venice exists at that other end of sexual romance: it lies at that other end of a sensuality we identify with Tahiti or Samoa. I could feel myself wanting to stay several months in Venice, for a whole season like winter or spring, wanting to write a journal of such a sojourn, like Robert Gibbings' 'Islanda'. Even a title like *Winter in Venice* contains a frisson of romance, of poetry, but also of exile.

November 11th More bullshit at the Capital of Culture offices. It is only 2003, but I already despair when I think what a great year 2005 might have been for Cork.

November 27th Today we put together all the main ingredients of our Cork2005 programme. Seeing all the projects together fills me with confidence about the year. I sent a letter of invitation to Gabriel García Márquez via his agent in Barcelona. I wonder if he will ever receive it. I tried to get a contact number for Claudio Magris from the Italian Embassy.

The Board passed a number of projects that I have a special loyalty towards. Three projects for Máire Bradshaw's Cork Women's Poetry Circle — *Cork Literary Review*, €24,000; International Women's Day, €38,000; Eurochild, €69,000.

So I have kept my promise to myself at the beginning of the year. With €131,000 in the bag for them we've made an historical response to the women who run the Tig Filí and Cork Women's Poetry Circle. This is the first time that these women, my heroes since the early 1980s, will have proper budgets to work with. They have never been taken seriously, yet the work Máire Bradshaw has done in literature and society in Cork is the most important literary work of the last half century. Why haven't my male companions ever admitted this achievement? It's as if they'd longed for its failure. I think there are many men, and many literary men, who long to see women fail. I wonder where this attitude comes from; probably from our Catholic upbringing. Crucially, I also got through a fund for Cork University Press, €26,000 to support the *Dictionary of Munster Women Writers, Atlas of Cork History* and *Old World Colony*. These are massively important books in the broad inclusive culture of Cork. The dictionary of Munster women writers, for instance, will restore dozens of important females to the historic record of Cork. Though these may seem like strange, and strangely quiet, projects to our cutting-edge contemporary art teams, they will be more permanent than anything I've encountered in Cork2005. Their audience will be in posterity. A great day, the first day in perhaps a year that I have felt a sense of unmitigated personal triumph. But I am worn out, physically and mentally, from all the committee work that went into getting this funding through. But, damn it, it's been worth it. What Máire Bradshaw has achieved is far more important than my feeling sorry for myself, but all of this stressful manoeuvring in committee has shown me how publishers of poetry feel on days when they must feel sorry for themselves.

December 20th What I regret most about Cork2005 is the loss of affection and prestige that my name will have suffered among people who mean a great deal to me — people like Mary Leland and Paddy Galvin, like Aidan Murphy and Robert O'Donoghue (angry at having been excluded from the Translation Series), publishers like Con Collins and local historians like Jim Fitzpatrick, as well as people like Trish Edelstein. Their high opinion means a great deal to me.

Christmas Eve Yesterday we drove down to Cappoquin to see my sister and her husband in their new house at Coolnagour, Dungarvan, and to visit Glenshelane. Glenshelane House looked bleak in the early winter afternoon, a bloom of algae or moss on the slates of the roof, the windows of the drawing room shuttered and cobwebbed on the outside. My cousin Anthony and his partner were in the smoke-filled annex. The whole place, annex and house, bitterly cold. Everywhere an air of sadness, everything resolutely pushed into the past. I think Anthony misses the Brigadier greatly. He misses the orderly routine of his day, as I would miss it if I still lived at Glenshelane. I spent a few minutes in the booklined sitting room where I had spent so many evenings with the Brigadier. The room incredibly cold. I felt an overwhelming sense of melancholy. A part of my life is gone. In the sitting room, from the shelves above the pile of very cold firewood, I rescued his copy of *Standing Orders of the Brigade of Guards*, that Bible of every commander of a Guards Battalion, that he had promised me so many years ago.

2004

January 1st

> *He realized, more vividly than ever before, that art has two constant, two unending preoccupations; it is always meditating upon death and it is always thereby creating life. He realized this was true of all great and genuine art.*
>
> — Pasternak, *Dr Zhivago*

January 4th Interesting piece in yesterday's *Irish Times* about Cork2005: Mary Leland's writing, no doubt. I hope this piece puts pressure on our sponsorship and corporate side. As usual it leads to a three-way flurry of emails and text messages among the Programming Team. We have really done our bit in terms of programming ideas. We can't do any more, except to protect the budgets of our partners in Cork and ensure they have a steady flow of cash from Cork2005. Met Theo and Paula Meehan with Cathy in The Long Valley yesterday. Theo wants me to leave Anvil Press Poetry and help form a new Irish poetry list with a new publisher. Theo has been in discussion with the owner of New Island Books. He thinks he can leverage money from the Arts Council to set up a five-year publishing programme. It's an interesting idea. I wonder could it work? If Theo and Paula were prepared to direct the Press it could be a new Gallery Books, a new Maunsel, in Dublin. It could work.

January 30th Lengthy conversations today about the 2005 project. We looked over about forty project files and let twenty-five go forward for approval at Wednesday's Board meeting. The financial 'hit' for us of today's decisions: 1.3 million euro. This brings our total commitments to approximately 3.5 million. There are a number of big ticket items to consider soon: including the Paul Mercier idea costing € 300,000 approx or the Edinburgh Festival idea *or* Druid Theatre's brilliant Synge Cycle that would cost us € 300-400,000. Drama is so outrageously expensive. But it keeps many people in employment working upon one creative idea — this is why one can always justify the cost of theatre, from the public purse at any rate. Give € 100,000 to a novelist or artist and one person is kept in employment, give the same amount to a Theatre Company and up to twenty creative people may get work simultaneously. At today's meeting I flagged my own worry that there would be no money left for a Library and Museum programme. The Boss said we'd put aside € 60,000 for the Library.

February 18th Today I wrote the final Project Descriptions and further additions to our general texts of the March 3rd Cork2005 Brochure, *Emerging Shape*. The Communications people showed me a designer's proof of the brochure — actually a booklet of 30-40 pages. It looked absolutely beautiful. I think it will have a wonderful effect on everyone who sees it.

March 2nd Theo and I worked again on the text of the Cork2005 brochure, *Emerging Shape*. It will be a good document.

March 5th The eve of my 50th birthday. Colleagues at work gave me a case of superb wine. All of this was orchestrated by the brilliant and exquisite Anne Cahill. I was taken to lunch at the Star Anise restaurant. These are hectic days. We launched our preliminary brochure at the Millennium Hall to an invited audience of four hundred 'worthies' and artists. Earlier on Wednesday we held a Press Conference for thirty-six journalists in the superb Jacques Restaurant. Two days of really excellent national media coverage, including slots on prime time News at 6 p.m. and 9 p.m. Overall, a wonderful reaction to our plans. Saturation coverage in both *The Examiner* and *Evening Echo*, and a full page in *The Irish Times*. Brilliant editorial in praise of Cork2005 in *The Irish Times* (probably the poet Gerry Smyth's work), and a very decent tribute in *The Examiner* as well.

March 12th A de-briefing meeting with FleishmanHillard, our Dublin public relations people. I thought they'd done a brilliant job, but they weren't completely happy because they use 'metrics' and benchmarks that I don't understand. Their executives are a creative but anxious bunch, never quite satisfied because they are aware of the national (i.e. Dublin) 'latent negativity' about Cork. I worry all the time that Cork people won't change their view of Dublin, but Fleishman-Hillard are aware of that deadly trend in Irish life — the negative thoughts Dublin people have when they think of Cork. Dublin people adore Galway and distrust Cork. I wonder when this negative relationship between Dublin and Cork began? Probably in the early 1600s, as a result of Cork's support of Perkin Warbeck, the Pretender to the English throne, when Cork got the designation as 'Rebel Cork'. It is as old as that and it is just hopeless on my part to believe that Cork2005 could change that — if anything, the intense local chauvinism created by our Capital of Culture designation only irritates those educated Dublin people who should be our best allies. Cork and Dublin should always work together at every level, for the sake of Ireland. But there is this primitive, irritating attitude between the two cities that I can see in action because I am a Waterford man. I am not emotionally involved in it. Cork people's attitude towards Dublin is toxic and unbelievably immature. This attitude leads to a lack of respect from Dublin. What Cork people don't realize is that Limerick City is becoming more and more clever in developing a trusting relationship with Dublin and with central government. Over time Cork's mindless vanity will consume its own advantages. As we walked through the English Market this morning one exasperated Fleishman-Hillard executive said to me, 'If you wanted to kill a brand stone dead in Ireland as a national brand, you'd launch it in Cork. That's what we're up against here in Cork2005.' I understood immediately what he meant and I was in despair as I walked home.

April 2nd Today I told everyone in the office that I intended to resign from Cork2005.

April 5th I demanded — and got — a meeting with the three senior directors, to discuss my wish to resign. I laid down a number of demands that if satisfied would allow me to stay on board. All agreed to all my demands. Of course they would. I think we are all merely going through the motions: the die is cast.

April 25th Reading Mac Liammóir's journals, *Ceo Meala Lá Seaca*, today. Funny to find him, also, enthralled by Kerry. In an entry for June 9th, 1950, at Killarney, he writes: '*Dochreidthe: an áit seo docreidthe: an dath, an solas laoma, na bláthanna, na sléibhte, na locha . . .*' To think that this part of his journal was written fifty years ago. Even after fifty years there's still an unchanging and undiminished magic about County Kerry.

May 1st A momentous day in the life of Europe: seventy-five million people became citizens of the European Union today. Great celebrations in Dublin because Ireland holds the Presidency of the EU right now. Wonderful celebrations in Cork also — we are twinned with Slovakia so tonight we have our Cork2005 Slovakian poet reading with her translator, Bob Welch.

May 12th Sitting in the sunshine of the patio, reading Kinsella's *Notes from the Land of the Dead* and Montague's *The Rough Field*. Kinsella's collection was published by Knopf in 1973 and Montague's book was published by Dolmen in October '72. An absolutely bleak time in Ireland. Nearly thirty years on it is difficult for people to understand just how dreadful those days were, with Ulster falling apart, murderous, lethal, treacherous, ruined, and the Dublin government, post-Arms Trial, barely hanging onto power. Fianna Fáil was at the end of its long hegemony and Stormont was in agony. Both poets, Kinsella and Montague, were literary titans, holding the sky above Ireland aloft. Between 1960 and '67 John Hewitt and Richard Murphy also seemed to be part of something huge, yet their influence dissolved for some reason, some reason difficult to explain. Kinsella, in poems like 'A Hand of Solo', *'All is Emptiness / and I must spin'* or 'Ely Place', and Montague in his audacious rehashing of old 1960s sequences like 'Patriotic Suite' and 'Hymn to the New Omagh Road' into a kind of modernist, interim scrap album of Derricke woodcuts, both made an effort to be intelligent, engaged, cerebral and modern. Montague had his models in the conflict-maestros of France, Malraux, Sartre, Saint-John Perse, but it is difficult to see where Kinsella was getting his energies — probably from American discourse, casualness, and certainly from Beckett. An elliptical phraseology like Beckett drama is in Kinsella (a Dubliner with a Wexford background). In a way John Banville with the same background has picked up the dense Kinsella discourse, a hardness, that 1950s English Movement hardness that must have been England's only linguistic response to French existentialism.

May 20th More crisis, real and imagined, at Cork2005. We were attacked in *The Evening Echo* by our own chairman, the Lord Mayor Burke. But he reflects the desperate ill-will towards us on the streets, in our Board room, and even in the

Arts community. At this stage *The Examiner* and *Evening Echo* has attacked us, the Cork Chamber of Commerce has attacked us, the City Manager has attacked us, the Lord Mayor has attacked us, Neil Prendeville of 96FM has attacked us, Dan Buckley of *The Examiner* has lampooned us, the Head of Cork-Kerry Tourism has attacked us, Alderman Máirín Quill has attacked us, Bride Rosney, the Chairman of RTÉ, has attacked us, Gerry Barnes and Mick Hannigan, key men in local Arts, have attacked us; even our commercial suppliers (who make tons of money from us) have attacked us.

This seems just about right for a European Capital of Culture.

June 15th Another blistering hot day. The garden looks wonderful right now, with *rosa grandiflora* just coming into bloom outside the door. Its effect is offset a little by the rampant *solanum* 'Glasnevin' that has such a nasty smell, like a dung-heap in the distance.

June 22nd One of the good days for Cork2005. Our sponsorship manager, Nigel, told me today that he's landed another big sponsorship — Musgraves, who have promised nearly €400,000 in cash. Brilliant. Also, he has extended the RTÉ deal with us to include a monthly supplement in the *RTÉ Guide*. As the *Guide* is the highest circulation magazine in Ireland this is a terrific coup. In general everything is moving forward.

July 5th Last night the Capital of Culture produced one of its most sublime personal moments yet. I spent five hours at dinner with John Berger, the great writer, critic, Alpine goat-farmer and artist. We walked from the Shandon Court Hotel, down the steps by Lower John Street, along by Pa Johnson's pub, across Patrick's Hill and down MacCurtain Street to Greene's Restaurant. An evening of great food and absolutely brilliant talk. We talked about the '30s in England, about

Picasso — Berger is still smarting from Feltrinelli's refusal to publish his book on Picasso because of the insidious influence of Picasso's communist circles in the '50s and '60s. He signed his copy of that Picasso book for myself and Catherine. But he was mighty proud that Stephen Joyce had phoned him to thank him for a brief essay he wrote on *Ulysses*. He talked a lot about the plight of the Palestinians and the corruption of Arafat and his supporters. When I used the word 'terrorism' he said emphatically that he didn't like the word (we'd been comparing the IRA bombing campaign in England with the new Islamic bombing campaign against the West). But I said I didn't mind the word at all because I see no difference between state terrorism and other forms of terrorism. He smiled and raised his hand in complete agreement. He was absolutely fascinated by the notion that the current Irish Peace Process may have begun when the CIA got a gift of stolen Irish passports from Belfast Republicans. Those passports were Ireland's contribution to the ill-fated Iran-Contra affair with Colonel Oliver North. After the receipt of those gifts — it is said, this is the Irish pub talk — the CIA set up their own liaison unit for Irish terrorism and ceased to rely on British intelligence briefings on Ireland. It was the beginning of real dialogue between the entrenched American interest and the entrenched Irish interest: always a powerful and empowering dialogue when it occurs. And always a danger to British interests, though only to its bilateral interests with Ireland. In terms of world view, of world politics, the Irish interest and the British interest is absolutely the same, despite all the protests of the hyper-nationalists among the English or the Irish.

July 10th 'Venice' — for Catherine —

> *World famous through its reproduction, Venice is*
> *The original of itself, unreal, shunning oil for water.*
> *Only a Doge could turn his back on Europe,*

Resplendent in trade, clothed in a satin sea-water,
Perpetually liquid as a ship of Murano glass.

July 12th Yesterday was a wonderful day at Dungarvan Library where we celebrated the centenary of Molly Keane and the redoubtable Claud Cockburn.

July 18th I worked all day on the poems that my last Geraldine officer must write for his novel. I want to keep the little collection to 17 poems (a magic number, I think). I found the poems on Friday in my notebook for 1992. What a long obsession this novel has been. In truth it's been an obsession since I first met the Brigadier. I've always wanted to create something absolutely sensational and romantic out of the material of his life. I still can't find the earliest notes I made for LGO — *Fuaiscailt na gCathar mBruséil/The Liberation of Brussels*, which is the name I've always wanted to give the LGO's little collection of poems.

Monday 19th Why is the last Geraldine officer's Irish language so crucial to my book? I think of the Irish language as the very core of his being, of his untainted soul, that makes him one with the very soil of West Waterford. The exercise of this language through the making of poems plunges him directly into the powerful territory of his childhood — the neighbourhood of Templemaurice House on the banks of the Déise Blackwater. He writes his poems, at first, because he believes that he will never survive the War. In the cauldron of Normandy, ill-matched against Tiger tanks and 88mm guns, he believes that he will be burned to death, as the Brigadier and his Irish Guards' tank crews believed.

July 20th Today, a wonderful message in my email — from University of California, Irvine. A note from one of the greatest African writers of all time, Ngũgĩ wa Thiong'o, formerly James Ngũgĩ. He has accepted our invitation to read in Cork next February.

August 4th Sad news from America — The Hungry Mind Bookstore, now called Ruminator Books, has closed in St Paul. In its heyday between 1980 and 1995 it was a glorious bookshop right in the heart of the Macalester College campus. Hungry Mind stocked all my books from *The Non-Aligned Storyteller* to *Mr Dineen's Careful Parade*. Yet another American kiosk for Irish poets closes in the world marketplace.

August 17th Yesterday I completed the first draft of our 'Introduction' to the Cork2005 Programme Book.

September 4th A day of glorious sunshine: I take one of the City Library hardback copies of *Dr Zhivago* into the garden to read in the bright sunlight. Giangiacomo Feltrinelli had sold three million copies of this book on the European Continent by 1959, and 800,000 copies had been sold in America. It *must* have disappointed millions who expected what Solzhenitsyn would provide more satisfactorily for the Western journalistic market ten years later. Instead of a Soviet witness-document the reader finds in *Dr Zhivago* a great historical love-poem and Christ-poem; a poem divided into seventeen parts, each part containing between thirty and fifty poetic 'epiphanies'. It is a symphony, written for instrumental parts like a symphony, a masterpiece by a writer whose most formative training was under Scriabin.

October 9th Launch of *City of Making*, the Programme Book of Cork2005. Trying to keep up a cheerful countenance for the sake of poor old betrayed Cork. Over eight-hundred-and-fifty guests at the ritzy launch in the Crawford Gallery; great after-launch party in the Bodega, organized by the brilliant Jay Bourke. Big screens, giant puppets, fire-eaters, *Irish Examiner* Special Supplement, Nationwide Special on

RTÉ1 Television, lunchtime Press conference at the Opera House. Cork2005 has certainly made a splash. Just at this moment, for once, everything comes together for Cork.

October 17th Yesterday's *Irish Times* carried a brilliant review of Theo's book, *Sailing Home*, about his voyage from Antigua to Kinsale. The review page also carries a photo of Mossy Riordan as part of a review of an anthology of Irish poetry. Today *The Sunday Times* credits me with having helped to capture the designation as European Capital of Culture for Cork. Bizarre, but I suppose it's all part of FleishmanHillard's PR hype. Theo was on TV last night and on radio today. This seems to be his moment. He deserves it, certainly.

October 23rd Yet another insane week. Many days I've had six or seven meetings, an average of three of these unscheduled. At the beginning of this month there were only sixty-two meetings scheduled for me, but so far this month I have taken or attended well over one hundred meetings.

October 28th More hectic days. I can't go on living like this. Our schedule complicated by unbelievable floods in Cork City. Patrick Street, Oliver Plunkett Street, the entire Coal Quay and South Mall under water — the worst floods since 1962, and further rainstorms and high tides are forecast. It's not the rain, it's the high tides in an easterly wind that cause chaos in Cork. With global warming the centre of the city will soon be below the level of high tides, whether or not there's the easterly wind.

November 5th A serious problem has occurred as a result of a visit to our Cork2005 office by the British Ambassador, Stewart Eldon. The Ambassador was 'happy', he said, 'to tell us that the Irish Guards Regiment had accepted our invitation to march in the St Patrick's Day parade in 2005'. Alarm bells went off immediately in my head when I heard this.

Having British soldiers marching in Cork in a televised parade is extremely problematic, not just politically, but in terms of security. There are several organizations who would avail of this golden opportunity to shoot at British soldiers. An open parade through the city would be just too easy an opportunity for them to resist. My own political view of this event is quite sanguine, and certainly not nationalistic. But when I mentioned this possibility to a senior official in City Hall, a most respectable middle-class Corkman educated at the exclusive Presentation College, there was a ferociously negative response. He was spitting with nationalist rage.

The Ambassador had just left the Cork2005 office when, after only ten minutes, we had a visit from a Commandant of the Irish Army's Southern Command at Collins Barracks. He had been informed by Irish Army Intelligence that the British Military Attaché had visited the Cork2005 offices. The Irish Army now demanded to be told immediately what was going on. I thought it quite cheeky and presumptuous of him to ask these questions so openly, but he is blunt and honest, and doesn't believe in beating about the bush. The Commandant was outraged when we told him that a member of the festival staff had invited the Irish Guards Regimental Band to march in Cork on St Patrick's Day. He said that no such invitation should ever be issued to foreign military without first informing the commanding officer of the Southern Command, that is, Brigadier Nash. The Irish Army, he explained, would be totally opposed to any British Army presence in a Cork2005 Parade. Such a presence would send confused and dangerous signals to the international media. People in the Arab world watching such reports and pictures from Cork, for instance, would think that the Irish Government approved of the activities of the British Army in the Middle East. The Irish Army had a long tradition of maintaining UN neutrality on Middle Eastern matters, he said, and nothing could be allowed to confuse that position. 'We have old friends of the Irish Defence Forces in Lebanon and

the Golan Heights and we don't want them to begin to con-
fuse the Irish Army with the Irish Guards of the British
Army marching in Cork. This could endanger our sovereign
Irish Army on UN duty in the Middle East.' He spoke about
Lebanon with great affection. The Irish Department of
Foreign Affairs would certainly issue a public reprimand to
Cork2005 and disassociate itself from any such invitation to
a British Regiment or Regimental Band. The Commandant
left us in no doubt that he thought we were a bunch of fools.
But, more than that, a bunch of dangerous fools who would
endanger the hard-won image of Irish neutrality and anti-
Imperialism. The Irish Army was against all Western adven-
turism in the Middle East, he said. 'We support the United
Nations, not NATO forces.' Listening to him I was impressed
at how conditioned in political neutrality Irish Army
Officers really are. They are loyal to three entities only: the
Dáil, the UN and the interests of the Third World. They hate
being confused with NATO Imperialist troops — in fact,
they'd prefer to be identified with Cuba rather than NATO.
That's a fact; it's an emotional conditioning of the Irish military mind; it's a post-colonial thing, a glorious thing. It would
be a huge mistake for any outside observer to confuse Irish
courtesy towards Britain with any kind of fellow-feeling politically. It just isn't there, except in paradigms such as exist
in my own poetry. Politically my published work is incredibly
irresponsible and doesn't give a true picture of commonly
held Irish opinion. I was reminded of this while listening to
the Commandant. If I lived in a tyrannical country I would
be considered a dissident, or a political idiot. I would definitely
be jailed or exiled.

The Commandant also said that the British have been trying
to manoeuvre such invitations to Irish parades for years — but
without success. He said that they would use such a presence
to 'saturate' (his word) the Cork region with Army recruiters
in civvies who'd move among the crowds. Cork City men have
always gone into the Irish Guards while men from coastal

towns, from Youghal to Castletownshend, have always volunteered for the British Navy. But the idea that Cork would be 'saturated' with British Army recruiters seemed highly fanciful to me. This visit has caused consternation. 'Their presence in Cork next year,' said the Commandant, in a kind of withering, withdrawing conclusion, 'would endanger the life of every Irish soldier serving abroad in the neutral blue beret of the United Nations. Do ye want to have the death of an Irish soldier on yere consciences?'

That did it. We were in deep shit. Panic followed. Phone calls, explanations, fudging, people 'not knowing anything' about an invitation etc. The usual cowardice. All the way home I kept thinking of my *Last Geraldine Officer* and what he would think of this encounter. There's no doubt but I've lived a good deal of my life among invented characters.

Sunday I spent the afternoon watching war documentaries on television; a brilliant film on U-boats and another on the German attack on Moscow: the prodigious endurance and bravery of every Russian. Then I had a phone call from another one of our Directors, full of excitement. He has just received a phone call from the British Ambassador informing him that 'HRH' will be coming to Cork next year. I asked 'Which HRH?' and he replied 'The *Big One*, Tom. It's so exciting!' I'm not sure whether he was referring to the Queen or to Prince Charles. Whichever one it is, it will cause unbelievable security problems — and, no doubt, another visit from the Commandant at Collins Barracks. Indeed, the Army may send a Colonel to us to complain about a Buckingham Palace visitor.

December 9th In Dublin yet again; this time to brief the Taoiseach, Bertie Ahern, on our Cork2005 programme. We arrived at Government Buildings at 2 p.m. and were met by John Kennedy, the Taoiseach's 'Commissioner General' as well as by Mr Howlin, Bertie's 'Advisor'. Both men ushered us (the Programme Team) upstairs quickly, through the palatial suite of offices restored by Charlie Haughey. We settled into a small meeting room with cheap, functional furniture and a few nondescript modernist prints, and Bertie Ahern bustled in almost at once. 'How ye lads, how ye lads, great ta see ye. T'anks for comin' in.' His hand is proffered generously to all and sundry. His face beaming with a big smile, but the eyes cold, as if someone else looked out from behind them. We quickly outlined the main elements of the programme and he nodded now and again, courteous at all times. Then, when we came to our page on 'Sport' in 2005, we outlined a plan for a major Open Road Bowling Competition. Well, what a transformation! The Taoiseach practically leapt off his chair with excitement and recounted a great story about the time he himself won £100 on a bowling wager in Phoenix Park when he was Lord Mayor of Dublin. He was thrilled that we were doing bowling 'like I use-ta do myself when I was a young fella in West Cork'. (The fact is: this is not our project, it's merely a listing we've taken on board.)

It was soon time to go. Half an hour. Bertie shuffled away from the table. 'T'anks, lads, t'anks.' He had just come to us from a fractious debriefing on the collapse of the Good Friday talks and he was moving — ten minutes late — to a meeting with EU Ambassadors. I suppose we were just a bizarre interlude in his day, half an hour of fine art. But he gave us an audience — that is important for us. He said he would come down to Cork several times next year, and certainly for the 'Ocean to City' boat race. He can't come to the Opening Ceremony as he is in China in early January. I like Bertie; there's a lot of straight, uncomplicated Dublin decency in him.

On the train coming back to Cork I saw Bishop Buckley, Christ's vicar in Cork and Ross, tall and affable, moving from passenger to passenger talking about hurling non-stop. This country is completely, irremediably, uncontrollably, sports *mad*, from Taoiseach to Bishop. The miracle of it all is that any high art or literature survives in our besotted sports-mad Republic. Why do we even bother trying to promote culture, I mean a fine art culture, when the Irish people really only want Gaelic sports?

Meanwhile, in Cork, rumours everywhere that our Director has been fired. Why would this happen now? We're nearly there. J K's work is almost complete.

December 18th In the hallway and passages of our office cases upon cases of Cork2005 wine and champagne. I asked Nigel if I could have two cases of the wine for the poets who will read during our European Translation series launch on Sunday, January 9th. He was horrified by my request and explained that all of this wine was destined for our 'Corporate Partners' as Christmas presents. I love the corporate world, the way it looks after itself without any sense of embarrassment. I think I would be very happy there. But I would have to join Fine Gael to fit in.

December 26th St Stephen's Day A wonderful Christmas. We had a full house with five of Catherine's brothers and sisters to dinner of turkey, ham, artichokes, olives, Stilton, pudding and Catherine's chocolate roulade. I opened the very last bottle of the Brigadier's Peach Champagne. Catherine gave me Daniel Maclise's *Portrait-Gallery* with notices by William Maginn and Neil gave me a present of Hugh Johnson's *Pocket Wine Guide 2005*.

December 31st The Cork *Evening Echo*, faithful as ever, remembers that it is the bi-centenary of Father Prout/Francis Sylvester Mahony's birth. Mahony, who died in Paris in May 1866, will be forever remembered simply as the author of 'The Bells of Shandon'. *The Evening Echo* in an Editorial says, 'Just a few hours before Cork takes on the mantle of European Capital of Culture, it is fitting to note that today, December 31, 2004, is the 200th anniversary of the birth of one of Cork's notable cultural figures, Francis Sylvester Mahony.' Bravo, *Evening Echo*! Ever, ever faithful to the historic Cork moment.

It is the books that will really endure, as Miłosz puts it in 'And Yet The Books': 'And yet the books will be there on the shelves, separate beings / That appeared once, still wet / As a shining chestnut under a tree in autumn.'

It was Seamus Heaney who sent the above text to me, in a faxed message to the Cork2005 office. Bless him. Bless his good heart.

2005

January 30th Spent yesterday working in the garden. The first cut of grass. While walking in the garden I got the distinct smell of milk chocolate. To my amazement I found that the *azara microphylla* was in full bloom. It was covered in tiny yellow flowers, more like miniature catkins. I took several branches of the plant into the house, so that now the hall smells of chocolate and of Easter at Glenshelane. How powerful that smell is.

February 22nd It has been a hectic fortnight in Cork. Wonderful literary readings and huge crowds. Ngũgĩ wa Thiong'o, the great Gikuyu novelist, read with Nuala Ní Dhomhnaill. It was a glorious reading with an immediate understanding established between the Irish work of Nuala and the Kenyan world of Ngũgĩ . But it was Saturday's reading that was most special to me: Dervla Murphy read with Claudio Magris, the glorious Trieste writer. I took Magris on a walking tour of Cork. We went into the City Library where I took down the Council Book of the Corporation of Cork, edited by Caulfield. Within this we found a description of a ship's manifest, a barque out of Livorno laden with forty tonne of Tuscan wine and twenty tonne of Tuscan olive oil 'for the Corke trade'. This was from 1621, at the height of the Venetian Republic. Magris was utterly fascinated and said, 'Can you take me to where the ocean meets the city?' I took him to the top of Montenotte, to the veranda of the old Murphy mansion, from where we could see Lough Mahon, the inner harbour, the Marina and the city. Magris was enthralled. 'I could live here,' he said, 'I could live in this place and be a writer.' And this Tuesday's post brought a lovely note from him in Trieste.

This Saturday we had a terrific Cork2005 reading from Doris Lessing and Paula Meehan. Paula faced an audience of five hundred in Trinity Church and said, 'I feel that this is my wedding day.' The audience responded with a huge round of applause. Paula was absolutely superb. Doris Lessing, now eighty-six-years-old, stood firmly by the microphone for the entire 45 minutes of her reading.

On Sunday Paul Muldoon read. Brilliant, as always. He lingered in Cork till this morning, in no hurry to return to the burdens of Princeton. He came to dinner last night. Cathy liked him, but says he gives absolutely nothing away. I was surprised at how anti-Republican he is: 'Those murderers want to take over!' he said, bluntly.

Yesterday I took Jeffrey Donaldson, the DUP MP, around Cork. A bizarre experience, especially when we walked along the South Mall. At almost every bank and insurance company doorstep tall and well-dressed men and women came out to shake Jeffrey Donaldson's hand, 'Welcome, Jeffrey, Welcome. Lovely to see you in Cork!' Even Glynnis Casey and the senior management of the old Catholic bank, AIB, ran to the door to greet the DUP man. (How did they know he'd be walking along the South Mall, who alerted them?) It was really the most bizarre thing in the whole world. Are they all Freemasons, I wonder? If Jeffrey Donaldson wanted to switch allegiances he'd certainly be elected to a Dáil seat for Cork. He'd probably top the poll for Fine Gael in Cork South.

March 27th A wonderful night in the annals of Cork2005: a terrific reception at the Glucksman Gallery in UCC for the publication of David Dickson's *Old World Colony*, published by Cork University Press. This is the first of three books published by CUP that our office supported to the tune of €26,000. Absolutely everyone was there, from John A Murphy and Donnchadh Ó Corráin to the UCC President Wrixon and the two ancient Knights of Munster, the Knight of Kerry and the Knight of Glin. Afterwards, Richard Wood of Fota and Carrigrohane House invited Mrs Villiers-Stuart of Dromana (a former Sadler's Wells' ballerina), the two knights and me to have a pizza in Ciao Restaurant in Paul Street. We talked about 'Eddy' Sackville-West, Molly Keane and Elizabeth Bowen — as well as Ambrose Congreve of Mount Congreve in Waterford. Everyone present, the two knights, Richard and Emily, all said that the Congreves are among the most 'difficult' people in Ireland. 'Ambrose is an absolute shit,' said the Knight of Glin, with what I thought was unusual fervour. For a moment it was like being back at Glenshelane House. Adrian's news on the house renovations is still bleak: no kitchen and no end in sight. All the way home I couldn't help thinking of Ambrose Congreve and his unbelievably snobbish wife. What a ménage they created at Mount Congreve, but what a garden they left behind for the nation.

April 1st Yesterday the Indian Ambassador came back to visit us. A lovely man, much talk of Bantry and the *Air India* bombing. Later two German journalists, both very impressed by Cork City and highly approving of our programme. Yesterday, also, the French Ambassador was in town to celebrate the arrival of the Debussy Quartet. He is a fabulous man, a product, of course, of that complex and sophisticated mental training that every representative of the great French Republic receives. Someone remarked recently that French women find only French men really attractive and impressive — all other men are considered second-rate, and for a Frenchwoman to marry a foreigner is always seen as a social failure.

April 3rd Last night, an astonishing concert at UCC — the combined Vanbrugh and ConTempo Quartets playing a terrific Mendelssohn octet to a packed Aula Maxima. Without doubt this was one of the highlights of Cork2005, comparable to the dance of Sol Picó, the readings of Heaney,

Lessing and Claudio Magris, and the beautiful *Fadó* singing of the Portuguese Mariza earlier this week. Though I would also never want to forget that night in January when the Ambassador of Bulgaria and the poet Gregory O'Donoghue shared a reading of the work of Kristin Dimitrova. Nights like last night remind one of the programme that was set in place by all of us, of the integrity and excellence of that programme. Also, Friday, I walked the streets between the Sean Scully exhibition at the Fenton Gallery and the *Ape Opera House* installation at the old ESB sub-station in Caroline Street, behind Brown Thomas. I felt that Cork was alive, pulsing with life and with possibilities for art. I think Cork has an amazing future, a future that hasn't even been revealed to anyone yet. Cork's best years lie ahead: perhaps the second half of the twenty-first century will be Cork's real moment. Now, if only we could encourage more French people to settle in Cork, because it is the encounter with French culture that makes Cork really buzz. Inside the soul of every educated Cork person there's an Irish poet married to a Huguenot silk merchant.

April 17th Last Thursday, the opening of one of our most important exhibitions: *Airgeadóir, 400 Years of Cork Silver and Gold.* Huge crowds at the opening and yesterday, all day, the entire gallery jammed with people. A personal triumph for the property magnate John Bowen who sponsored the entire show. On Friday I got a copy of Theo's translations of Barbara Korun, the young Slovenian poet. Theo dedicates the book to me, a generous, wonderful gesture that embarrasses but pleases me greatly. Only Theo would be bold enough to honour me in public at this moment when I am so unpopular; at this moment when Cork people are still not quite confident that Cork2005 will be a success. It occurred to me recently that the entrenched elites of Cork have treated this European Capital of Culture designation as if it were a disease, an epidemic.

April 25th Yet another weekend of terrific literary activity; this time in honour of World Book Day, a Catalan Festival, all organized by the new City Librarian, Liam Ronayne. Two Catalan poets, Carol Ann Duffy, a wonderful Berlin poet and Gina Moxley all read in a marquee erected on the Grand Parade. At 4 p.m. we launched Theo Dorgan's translations of Barbara Korun. A terrific understanding between both poets, and that fluid, immediate rapport that Theo establishes effortlessly with any person he admires. The Slovenian language sounds beautiful, almost a liquid, olive-y quality. Theo's versions in English are masterful poems. I think Korun understands how powerfully she's been translated and this was the main reason, I think, for her solid confidence as she stood and watched Theo reciting her work. A huge crowd, and the City Library bedecked with Slovenian flags and buntings. Theo's real quality is beyond compare. That he never entered the Dáil is a national tragedy, a national loss: he would have been a David Thornley, a Justin Keating or Conor Cruise O'Brien, but more effective than them, more energetic nationally and able to achieve more. But then again being a poet is the most crucial part of his being. Like me it is through poetry that he wishes to enter into the public realm. He is not interested in any other kind of relationship with his country, only that relationship of poets and poetry. Carol Ann Duffy congratulated me on winning the Literary Prize of the Lannan Foundation. I think she may have been confusing me with the brilliant English novelist, Tom McCarthy. She was really embarrassed about her mistake and kept apologizing. But it was nice of her to think that I deserved it and I told her so.

On Thursday night Colm Tóibín gave a reading: another brilliant, crowded reading. I went to dinner with Colm and an interesting Catalan writer. Much gossip and laughter: Colm has a prodigious and mischievous sense of humour. On Friday a terrific reading from Anthony Cronin to an audience of over one hundred in the City's Reference Library.

Before his reading I showed Cronin the Hayes' *Manuscript Sources for the History of Irish Civilisation*, the great work of an old National Librarian, Dr Richard Hayes. Anthony was thrilled to find therein two-and-a-half columns of entries on himself.

A phone call from Seamus Heaney asking me to take part in an Ireland Funds Literary Awards committee. I agreed. How could I refuse?

April 26th This morning, yet another serious attack on Cork2005 in *The Examiner*. And yet, from afar, there is wonderful news. Colm Tóibín, who read to us on Thursday, has won the *Los Angeles Times* Fiction Prize. What wonderful news! So, what *The Cork Examiner* taketh away the *LA Times* restoreth. Thanks be to God.

April 28th The imagining and the writing of *Merchant Prince* and *The Last Geraldine Officer* constitute a real phase in my life, a really self-contained decade and a half that has almost nothing to do with anything external that happened in Irish life. Both books are part of my profoundly conservative mindset, an anti-demotic streak in my soul that is very much out of tune with the demotic era we live within. I have lived in the wrong era for a person with my temperament. I am a late Victorian person, born into the valley of the Waterford Blackwater where the 19th-century was still very much alive. This Irish Catholic world changed completely between 1964 and 1969; it became contemporary. But my mind has remained glued to the spot where I was born.

May 7th A week of relentless gardening. I feel like someone who has just returned from a war; full of energy and a desire to repair fences. I spent five days on my hands and knees, weeding between the raspberry, blackcurrant and gooseberry bushes.

May 17th In Dublin yesterday at a meeting of the ad-hoc

committee of the Ireland Funds Literary Awards at Foster Place. Before the meeting I met Seamus Heaney who was also killing time in Books Upstairs. He had just come back from a trip to Asturias and Krakow, Poland. What a world traveller. The committee comprised of Seamus Heaney, Senator Maurice Hayes, Terence Brown, Nuala Ní Dhomhnaill and me. There was a very tentative, even unfriendly, atmosphere in the room until we got our bearings. Terence Brown made a very clever suggestion: 'Before we begin why not look at the list of Literature members of Aosdána and the list of past winners of the Ireland Funds Award.' This we did, and noticed only two glaring omissions, William Trevor and Anthony Cronin. Both Terence and I mumbled something about Cronin's recent brilliance and lifelong struggle. Heaney, and more pointedly, Maurice Hayes, expressed alarm that William Trevor was absent from the list of winners. Other names were mentioned. I repeated Cronin's name and added Peter Sirr, surely a poet who deserves a big prize by now. Nuala mentioned Michael Davitt and Cathal Ó Searcaigh. Terence mentioned Harry Clifton and Deirdre Madden — and an obvious absentee, Paul Durcan. I also mentioned Paula Meehan, a poet who *has* to be considered. All the names were bandied about, lists made, names pencilled out or in as someone made a remark or useful observation.

Trevor got it by acclamation. There was no need to vote. We rose from the table, all feeling satisfied that a moral and apt decision had been made. Afterwards Nuala, Seamus and I went for a drink to The Stag's Head. We stayed about one-and-a-half hours, chatting about Seamus's forthcoming *District and Circle* and Nuala's depression and memories of Turkey. I almost missed the 5 p.m. train back to Cork.

June 23rd The shortlist for the Frank O'Connor Prize is announced. In our shortlist we have the Canadian David Bezmozgis, the US writers Alice Hoffman, David Means and Bret Anthony Johnston, and the Chinese-American short-story writer Yiyun Li. Picture in *The Examiner* with myself, Michael O'Flynn of O'Flynn Construction (the brilliant sponsor, an absolutely lovely, mild-mannered businessman) and Pat Cotter.

August 4th Last night, a reception for the Ambassador of Cyprus. It was after midnight when I walked with the Ambassador down along the South Mall to the Clarion Hotel. We talked endlessly of Cyprus, of Seferis and of Elytis.

August 13th Yesterday I had to phone Seamus Heaney because our accountant discovered that Seamus hadn't cashed his not insubstantial cheque, his payment for the 'World Writing Series' readings. When I spoke with Seamus he said, 'Forget it, Tom, let it go. Use the money for someone else.' I asked him three times if he was sure about this, saying that I could have another cheque written etc. But he was adamant. What a heart of gold. This is one of those very rare acts of generosity made towards Cork2005. We chatted for half an hour, about *Merchant Prince* — he restated his admiration for it — and about his own book of poems *District and Circle* that's due to be published in April. He said he felt dubious about the title in view of the London Underground bombings. I said, 'Seamus, history has a way of catching up with your work.' He laughed. Certainly, a man with a plate full of life, a heart of gold.

September 5th Days of complete shock and disbelief. The poet Gregory O'Donoghue has died. He died from septicemia, caused no doubt by liver failure. He had been an alcoholic since his late teens, drinking with Montague and Lucy and the other younger poets of UCC. This is the inevitable progress in an Irish literary family, this great plague of alcoholism that has taken away so many brilliant Irish minds. Gregory was a gifted poet, a gentleman, and a shrewd critic. He will be missed terribly in Cork, especially by the younger poets who learned so much from him in the last ten years. I will miss him. I really liked him and respected him. Meeting him in The Long Valley was always the beginning of a two-hour seminar on Wallace Stevens, Heaney, Akhmatova or Montague. He lived for poetry and only for poetry.

September 15th Further discussions about the Frank O'Connor dinner at the Clarion Hotel. This black-tie dinner has caused a stir, with much jockeying for tickets and great annoyance that partners and spouses were not invited. Unfortunately our number had to be strictly limited to 125-130. This dinner is actually costing € 12,000. An astronomical sum for most organizations in Cork. But it is for Frank O'Connor, and in his native city. I've really put my head on the block for this, but I'm sick of all the tacky, embarrassed, self-conscious occasions associated with literary things in Cork. For once I demand grandeur and formality and I don't apologize to anyone. Now and again literature demands elegance and due deference. A formal dinner is always a memorable thing, and I want O'Connor, the son of a poor Boer War veteran from Harrington Square in Barrackton, to be formally honoured. After all it was O'Connor himself who once said in a BBC interview that Cork was a European city in the era of King Cormac McCarthy.

October 8th I went to an hilarious opening of the William Burges exhibition at the City Museum. It was organized by Richard Wood who has been restoring Fota House and its art collection. The exhibition was opened by the great Led Zeppelin guitarist, Jimmy Page — a lovely man who gave a terrific speech with real insights into Burges. Page lives in Burges' London house. The huge crowd at the Civic Museum consisted of Anglo-Irish gentry, Church of Ireland Bishops and Canons, old 1960s rockers and young 'Goths' with white painted faces, silver jewellery and black clothes. The young and beautiful 'Goths' looked like disciples of William Burges. It was wonderful. And it was terrific to meet Jimmy Page.

October 14th In Athens for several days as part of the European Capital of Culture seminar. I am the sole representative of Cork2005, a sorry state of affairs. There should have been an entire delegation but Cork2005 has now entered penny-pinching mode. The conference was organized by the charismatic Spyros Mercouris, the brother of the great actress and Euro MP, Melina Mercouri. I gave a brief speech to the conference yesterday and made a number of crucial interventions today. The whole thing is pretty heavy going but it is wonderful to talk at this high level for a change. Last evening we attended a lavish reception given by the Mayor of Athens.

It is twenty-one years since I was last in Athens and the place has lost none of its magic. If anything it feels more magical and looks more beautiful and heroic in the October sunlight. It looks even more like a great capital city. I miss Catherine terribly and my joy in this place would be doubled if she were with me. I will definitely come back to Athens with her soon.

Spyros Mercouris took me aside last night at the Athens Town Hall and said, 'Tom, I want to show you something.' He pointed to a wonderful portrait of a distinguished-looking, Victorian man. 'That's my grandfather,' said Spyros, 'He was Mayor of Athens from 1898 to 1916.' I could see that he was immensely proud of him and I could also see the family likeness. What an extraordinary family the Mercouris were. Later Spyros told me the story of how he had had the film treatment of *Never on a Sunday* read to him and his sister. They mortgaged their homes to raise £125,000 but were subsequently told that the film had been sold to United Artists. The memory of losing that film project still hurts Spyros.

15th October This morning we assembled on the hilltop of the Pnyx, the place where Athenians first gathered to form a democratic assembly. We came here to make our 'Pnyx Declaration' on the primacy of culture. We made this declaration in the name of the Mayor of Athens, Dora Bakoyannis, in the name of the European Cultural Networks and in the name of the Mercouri Foundation. It was very moving to watch Spyros Mercouris reading the declaration on our behalf. But it was also very sad because I felt that Spyros expected a bigger occasion with lots of journalists and cameras. I don't think anyone from the media attended (although, yesterday, a journalist from *The Daily Telegraph* appeared incongruously and took copious notes while the Catalan and the German delegates spoke).

October 24th This morning's *Irish Examiner* carries a beautiful photograph of Christine Sheehy standing in the Crawford Gallery beside the Barry painting 'King Lear Weeping over the Dead Body of Cordelia'. It was purchased by the Tate Gallery in 1962 and Tate Britain lent it to us. Will such a painting ever be seen again in Cork in the next five hundred years? The synchronicity of *The Examiner* photo really moves me — it reminds me of how the Barry painting 'The Temptation of Adam and Eve' was first exhibited at the Cork Great Exhibition of 1902, then on loan from the Royal Society of Arts. That painting was subsequently donated by the RSA to the National Gallery of Ireland where it is always exhibited and where I often go to look at it. But for 2005 it is on show in Cork, hanging very close to the 'King Lear . . .' All of these Barry works have become an essential part of the explosive magic of the Capital of Culture. This city has been showered with blessings. But people, especially Cork people, don't appreciate the miracles happening all around them. That they can't see the immensity of what's been achieved in Cork2005 really depresses me.

November 17th These are days of winding down and preliminary closing of files at Cork2005. Yesterday I refused to accept a cultural speaking engagement in Liverpool in April and today I had 'an exchange of words' with JK's PA who wanted me to commit to a lecture on 'Cork2005 and Urban

Regeneration' in Killarney next February. I told her that from mid February next year I was speaking only on my own poetry and on themes of my own choosing. I think this refusal came as a shock in the office. People have got used to me speaking at the drop of a hat. I've been talking about Cork2005 for five long years. I'm worn out from that subject. I've been far too affable and this will have to stop.

November 29th Today President McAleese visited our controversial project, *The Knitting Map*, at St Luke's Church. I greeted her at the door on behalf of the Cork2005 team. Jools Gilson-Ellis, the developer of *The Knitting Map*, the President's husband, Martin, the President and I went on an inspection of the famed *Knitting Map*. The President met the assembled volunteer knitters, thank God.

December 1st This morning, a gift in the post from the Girl Guides of Ireland — their Cork2005 Merit Badge and a silver pin with 'Cork2005' engraved upon it. What an achievement for the Girl Guides in Cork: they created their own cultural programme and a series of cultural tasks for the Guides. This is the kind of thing that nobody in the media notices and no 'contemporary arts practitioner' would care for. But there it is on my desk, something that proves that an extraordinary year has just gone by in Cork: a merit badge and a silver pin.

December 2nd At the Institute of Contemporary Dance in Shandon to take part in Mary Brady's dance seminar. This is part of IDEE, a three year (2005-2008) programme being developed by seven dance houses across Europe: ICD (Cork), Centre National de la Danse (Paris), Dansens Hus (Oslo), Dansens Hus (Stockholm), The Place (London), Tanzquartier (Vienna) and Tanzhaus NRW (Düsseldorf). Mary is brilliant at penetrating such networks. Her European networking experience makes it a pleasure for me just to be with her. She has a holistic and very European understanding of what

'Capital of Culture' means. And, although it's nearly a year since the high oxygen of 'Fête de la Danse', her enthusiasm for Cork2005 hasn't wavered in the least. I really admire her, her integrity, her enthusiasm, her unrelenting courage. I had to participate in the first panel of the day, with a handsome Hungarian intellectual (yet another young man in black) and Johannes Odenthal of the House of World Cultures in Berlin. My talk was called 'Dance as the House of Imagination and Its Human Scale'. When I stopped speaking I determined never to speak on such matters again. The young Hungarian, Boyer, was brilliant in a kind of Jacques Derrida-way (interesting that he invoked Sarat Maharaj). Among the wise things he said were 'contemporary dance is a view of the body' and 'the body is the locus of actualization of experience'. (Mary McCarthy and Tara Byrne would definitely love this guy.) He talked about the modern obsession with the inorganic, prosthetics etc and that this obsession creates 'a new aura which ousts the sacred'.

Aoife told me this afternoon that Tourism Ireland had been monitoring the exposure that Cork is getting as a result of the Capital of Culture designation. They estimate that Cork has got nearly eight million euros in free publicity in European newspapers. This morning, also, a bundle of Hungarian journals arrived with my five-page essay on Cork2005 translated into Hungarian.

December 3rd A message from Kevin today to say that *Merchant Prince* got a good mention in the (London) *Independent*. I looked it up on the internet. Terrific stuff, and one of the Christmas choices for 2005.

A reading with Gerry Smyth and John Wakeman who has just published a new collection with Bradshaw Books. After the reading I took Gerry and Pauline on a hilltop tour of Cork. They were delighted to see the full extent and sheer size of Cork. I brought them for a quick bite to eat — salmon overcooked, ruined apple crumble. Jesus. It was all a terrible rush as I had to drop them to the Everyman to see the last performance of the Neil LaBute *Wrecks*. That particular play is a World Première and a Cork2005 commission. Anyway, like Seamus Heaney and Claudio Magris, Gerry Smyth has seen the real Cork in 2005. That pleases me no end.

December 6th Long morning of discussions at the Cork2005 office: closing ceremonies stuff. It will be very low key, I think, and certainly won't be the kind of 'son et lumière' show that will 'wow' the city into loving us. A Dutch journalist came looking for me — someone in the Tourist Office had given him my name. I went through the Programme Book with him and he was hugely impressed that all of these projects had cost less than ten million euro. He said he had read very positive things about us in Dutch newspapers so he was quite willing to believe me when I said that we'd had a great year in Cork. The fact is: we did have a great year, but we didn't have a 'good' year because that entails positive emotional stuff — that certainly never happened for anyone in Cork2005. How wise young Philip Mackeown was to get out early.

But then I had to rush from the Tig Filí to meet Adrian from Glenshelane, now the new Knight of Kerry, Sir Adrian FitzGerald. He was spending half a day looking at the James Barry exhibition. We had lunch in the Ballymaloe Café. Great talk about Cappoquin, Glenshelane House and James Barry. Peter Murray dropped by and gave Adrian a gift of the Barry catalogue. Adrian was delighted with this.

Still exhausted after last night's terrific openings — Tacita Dean in the South Presentation Convent and John Berger and Marissa Camino at the Vanguard Gallery. Fiona Shaw gave a brilliant speech; speaking without notes she gave an incredible lecture on Berger's aesthetic and politics. Met Mel Mercier and Maura O'Keeffe, two lovebirds who are very much in love: they made us all crazy with jealousy when they told us that they'd bought Finisk Lodge near Affane, Cappoquin. Dinner in the Imperial afterwards with Berger, Tacita

Dean, Tony, Marcella, Mary and the many exquisite creatures of the gallery world. Home in the rain after midnight, tired but happy. Nights like this make the Capital of Culture bearable: and in the morning papers — nothing, as far as I can see. In the newspaper world culture is not News, it is Features.

December 13th A good deal of the day spent hosting an official from the Cultural Ministry in Budapest, Dr Judit Bor. Having briefed her on the Cork2005 programming process I took her to a wonderful Cork Orchestral Society recital by the Greek pianist Magda Nikolaidou, the Athens and Paris-trained pianist playing Rachmaninov, Chopin, Yannis Constantinidis and Manos Hadjidakis. The atmosphere, the extreme heat of the room, and all the while a sense of the presence of those absent Olympians of Cork life, Aloys Fleischman and Sheila Goldberg. How proud they would be of what the Cork Orchestral Society has achieved in this European year — twenty-four recitals by pianists, cellists, violinists and guitarists. They co-ordinated all of these recitals, without our help, with twenty-four embassies in Ireland.

I then went with Dr Judit Bor to lunch at the Ballymaloe Café in the Crawford. After that we went to the English Market, visited St Peter and Paul's Church, designed by Pugin in its High Oxford style, and then returned to the great Barry exhibition. All the while we carried on a long conversation about the Cork2005 experience. When we were walking along Academy Street who should we bump into but Ted Crosbie coming out of his *Examiner* offices. A great beaming, innocent Crosbie smile: 'Ah, Tom! What a wonderful year you've had! You must be very proud!' We chatted in a friendly way for several minutes, noting the highlights of the year etc. Then we walked on.

'Who is that man?' asked Dr Bor.

'He owns the local newspaper group.'

'The ones who have attacked your Capital of Culture?'

'Yes.'

'Then why are you so friendly to him?' she wonders, quite confused.

'Ah, everybody loves Ted Crosbie,' I explain.

'Even if he attacks you?'

'Yes.'

'This aspect of Cork I cannot understand,' she replies. I go on to explain the Crosbies and Cork, and Merchant Princes, and being unconditionally proud of people who embody Cork, its history and its society. 'This is complex politics,' she says, 'I think you are now destined for a life in politics. I expect we will see you in the European Parliament.'

We parted at the door of the Crawford Gallery. Dr Bor is an art historian by profession and she wanted to absorb the James Barry exhibition again. I think she is impressed by the total package that constitutes Cork2005: the beautiful winter city, the energy of Patrick Street, the aromas of the English Market, the burning candles in St Peter and Paul's Church, the John Berger Exhibition, the Programme Book that I saw her flicking through as she listened to Chopin's *Nocturne in D* on Nikolaidou's piano. At such moments, on a bright and very busy winter's day, Cork City makes a deep impression upon an educated stranger. And it is a deeply impressive city.

December 14th A huge night of poetry at the Triskel Arts Centre: the publication of the final book in our Cork2005 European Translation Series, Yilmaz Odabaşi's *Everything But You*. The book was translated by Patrick Galvin and Robert O'Donoghue. Sinéad Mac Aodha launched the book, addressing the crowd first, then, turning to the two translators: 'You have given witness to Odabaşi in this book, you have mended the broken fretwork of the bazooka.' Bobby O'Donoghue, full of immense sorrow for his lost poet-son, stood tensely, looking at the audience as the Turkish translator recited the original texts. Mary Johnson, also, stood quietly to attention. Paddy Galvin in his wheelchair had a rapt look on his face. Obviously this was one of the most serious moments in the public life of poetry in Cork's history. It was the end of a great Munster series; thirteen volumes of poetry translated by fourteen Cork poets in response to the European designation — a cultural and publishing triumph for Patrick Cotter, for which he will get no credit from anyone in this city.

I am so proud of what the poet Cotter has achieved, pulling this entire project together over three years and thirteen European countries. I thanked all the assembled poets on behalf of the European Capital of Culture. The poets of Cork had given over three years of their lives to a deep engagement with Europe; and the result of these thoughts was thirteen volumes of poetry. I also thanked Triskel (what a year Triskel has had!) as well as Heineken for the beer on tap over the entire year. In reciting 'My Sweaty and Handcuffed Children' Mary Johnson allowed the Turkish translator to speak each Turkish name and word. It was very powerful. Having recited his first translation Bobby O'Donoghue explained that the line, 'we were questions who had our answers stolen' ('Stepchildren of God') refers to propagandists and Fascists. Then a brilliant, haunting reading of 'Watermelon Lorries'. Then Mary read portions of the long poem 'Feride', a great ballad. She read with such feeling and intensity that I felt I was listening to a poem of Paddy's — perhaps some violent poem of the Spanish Civil War. There was such a sense of total identification with the foreign poet, a complete sympathy with the moment described. This moment that Mary Johnson created was truly extraordinary, as if the whole of Europe had opened its heart in Cork and shown us all its Eastern pain and suffering. The reading ended with Mary and the Turkish translator reciting 'Letter to a Political Prisoner' by Patrick Galvin. Robert O'Donoghue also read a poem of his own.

I walked home quite early in the night: a cool, crisp December evening in Cork. The city was buzzing with Christmas shoppers. I felt that the city was already folding itself over the voices of all the poets, that revelling, unthinking, generous city. Certainly, this city will close over and enfold the voices of the poets who spoke in 2005. But it will have absorbed everything creative that we have done, and these distant voices out of Europe will enter the generous blood of the place. The blood of Europe is now mingled with the blood of Corkery, Ó Ríordáin, Ó Faoláin, O'Connor. These Cork2005 books will now rest in the 'Cork Collection' of the City Library, becoming part of the story of the place we live in, as real as the ship's manifest out of Livorno in 1620 or the Middle Parish stories told to me by Gerald Goldberg.

December 17th I see that Led Zeppelin's Jimmy Page has been awarded an OBE. He was at Buckingham Palace yesterday and in today's papers there are pictures of him holding his medal. What a charmer he is, and what a sensation he created at the City Museum this year when he came to open the William Burges exhibition. That was a day of pure stairway-to-heaven magic in Cork.

December 18th The library Christmas dinner last night. Everyone brought a gift, but Stephen O'Brien, the last true socialist left in Ireland, a Reference Librarian, gave a colleague a gift of ten Russian cigarettes and a CD of Heavy Metal Japanese music. The Librarian who received the gift complained, 'What the hell are these supposed to mean?' And Stephen explained, without batting an eyelid, 'It's the hundredth anniversary of the Japanese invasion of Russia. For God's sake, do you not know anything!'
 What a pleasure it was to be back among librarians.

December 19th A sense of defeat and decline has overwhelmed the Cork2005 office. The sense of gloom in our office is so complete that it disgusts me.

2006

January 31st We had a lengthy Poetry Ireland meeting at the Royal College of Surgeons. Poetry Ireland, like the Munster Literature Centre, is facing the 'mini crisis' of a budget surplus. This is a bizarre state of affairs for an Irish arts organization, and most certainly a symptom of our buoyant Celtic Tiger economy. I bought Gerald Dawe's two collections at Books Upstairs. *Lake Geneva* is a very fine, very refined work. Dawe is underestimated by everyone; he has done real work in Ulster poetry. But he is a quiet and serious man. He reminds me of Peter Nazareth at Iowa, gentle, brilliant. The quiet men are always overlooked by a cultural media that must search for the weird, the colourful, the unhinged.

Immediately after the PI meeting Gerry Smyth asked me if I'd go for a coffee. We spent the time chatting about Gottfried Benn and Georg Trakl: Smyth loves Trakl and I've just accepted Gottfried Benn as my soul companion while I write *The Last Geraldine Officer*. Gerry then mentioned the *Irish Times* Poetry Prize and how surprised he was that *Merchant Prince* didn't even make the shortlist. I mumbled something about prizes and their unpredictability etc.

Yet I've found my own readers. The other day on Emmet Place a man shouted across the street to me, 'Are you Thomas McCarthy?' I stopped, expecting to be attacked yet again over some Cork2005 matter. But the man had bought and read my *Merchant Prince*. He came across the street to me:

'Was that all imagined?' he asked. 'Did you invent Nathaniel and the Italian poets?'

When I explained that the Italian poets were actually Irish poets, Nulanna Nigonelli is Nuala Ní Dhomhnaill and Count Luigi da Pora is Louis de Paor, he was absolutely thrilled.

'Such a complex book has never before been written by someone in Cork,' he said, adamantly. But I replied that Rev Francis Sylvester Mahony had published such a book in *The Reliques of Father Prout*, as far back as 1836. That that book was the finest book ever written by a Munsterman. But the man said he was going to reread my book in the light of this new information about the 'Italian' poets. He said the book was a masterpiece. I thanked him. Readers like that are a god-send, an absolute godsend.

February 19th Yesterday *The Irish Times* carried the news that Nick Laird has won the Strong Award for his brilliant debut collection. I was the only judge. Giving him this award must seem like gilding the lily, but his book was far-and-away the best collection that the Poetry Now festival sent me. I hope Laird deepens and endures. Certainly in the last ten years a number of brilliant new poets have appeared and then faded from sight. But Laird, I think, is made of strong Ulster stuff: he'll endure and prosper. Then again, many people think I 'disappeared' after winning the Patrick Kavanagh Award in 1977. The only proof that I didn't disappear is in this very journal that I'm writing in today. This diary, though, is my only connection still with my youthful self, with that dreaming prodigious youthful self, fed on a diet of Stendhal's diaries, Arnold Bennett's and Gide's *Journals*. In general Irish people dislike diaries; they are too much like a private betrayal of careless remarks. Even Dennis O'Driscoll, the most literary of men, was taken aback when I told him that I'd accumulated over a quarter of a million words in a private journal since I was twenty years old and that I intended to keep going until my sixtieth year. He was horrified. To this day I still don't understand why he was so horrified by the thought of my having written diaries. He himself is a very serious chronicler of Irish poetry. So why was he horrified? It must be this Irish thing, this love of discretion and forgetting, that makes us want to forget the gossip of the day. Day by day we don't write our poems, as Seferis remarked (in *his* Journal), but day by day we do live. My life has been so bizarre and the people I know are so unexpected, that I need to write down at least a portion of my life into these pages — in the manner of my fellow West Waterford man, Arland Ussher. I wish I'd met Arland Ussher. We would have had great conversations.

February 21st A hectic day of seminars. This morning Luke Gibbons from Notre Dame gave a brilliant talk on the politics of James Barry's paintings, the intrigues of the Royal Academy, the attitude of the King and the murmurings of radicalism and revolution. It was a fine piece of document-study, of hunting after primary sources. Gibbons has discovered an important new link between Barry and the revolutionary Arthur O'Connor. The question is: did this relationship come to the attention of the English King and his circle? Was this the reason that Barry suffered such an accelerated expulsion from the Royal Academy?

February 23rd I am writing this in the Royal Society of Arts Library in the Strand. In London these last two days to conclude our bicentenary celebrations of the death of James Barry, a celebration that was at the heart of the original Cork2005 plans. Excellent seminar in the RSA's Great Room with Barry's mighty Olympian wall paintings looking down on all of us as we spoke and listened. At a reception in the Society's cellars Peter Murray of the Crawford presented me with a 'Barry Medal' in thanks for my five-year-long support of the Barry project. I was thrilled to get this medal as it is the first 'striking' of a design that Barry made, a medallion of Mercury and Minerva, for the RSA in the 1790s. This morning I was at the Fuseli exhibition in the Tate and, right now, in the reading room of the RSA.

February 24th I'm in the café of Waterstone's in Charing Cross:

a fairly decent poetry section; by that I mean there's evidence in the choice of books of someone working here who really knows poetry. No *Merchant Prince*, of course, and no book of mine at all. While this doesn't surprise me it never fails to depress me.

February 28th My last day in the European Capital of Culture office: four long and difficult years come to an end. What a mental strain it has been, what a nightmare of misunderstandings, embarrassments, shattered dreams. But I survived; and indeed my health is no worse than it was in 2002. So, despite all the tension and arguing, cultural stress has been good for my blood pressure. My time at Cork2005 ended as simply and unheroically as it had begun — with a cup of instant Knorr soup and a handshake from the Boss, JK. Back I go to the lending desk in the City Library. Life has suddenly become simpler.

March 12th Last Tuesday I was at the launch of Eibhear Walshe's biography of Kate O'Brien in UCC. A great work of love on his part, and all a part of Eibhear's missionary effort to keep alive the memory of novelists like Kate O'Brien, Elizabeth Bowen and Molly Keane. Molly's daughter, Sally, was there, and George, still surviving both cancer and heart trouble. A huge crowd in UCC's staff dining room — all the professors and lecturers of the English Department. It is many years since I saw them all together, Éamonn Ó Carragáin, Gerry Fitzgibbon, Gwenda Young, Patricia Coughlan (always friendly towards me) and a whole bevy of young English-born lecturers who seemed to know me. The atmosphere was extremely warm, a definite impression of an English Department that works as a unit, a great sense of friendship and ease between them all. It was great to see that, and really unexpected.

When I think of the tension within the UCC English Department when Montague and Lucy ruled the roost I am amazed at the ordinary friendliness of the current teaching team. There's a lot to be said for not having any immortals, or would-be immortals, on your staff.

March 20th And today a reminder of the meanness of bureaucracy — Cork City Council has cut my salary by 30% — I have been immediately dropped down to my Grade 4 library salary. But I earned and accumulated my leave entitlement while acting as Executive Officer, so I should receive the salary of that grade while on leave. But I can't be bothered pursuing this: the meanness of it just depresses me as it depressed poor Seán Ó Ríordáin. After all the work I did for Cork City Council's damn Cork2005 project. Eaten bread is soon forgotten, there's no doubt about that. And no bureaucracy ever gave a damn for a poet — with the possible exception of the Irish Revenue Service that seems to treasure Dennis O'Driscoll. But then again Dennis is a high-ranking official. He is the C H Sisson of the Irish Civil Service. I am no more than a clerk and I've been unceremoniously restored to a clerk's wage by the City Council and treated with the contempt that old bureaucracies reserve for clerks.

March 28th A superb three days in Dublin as part of the Poetry Now festival. On Friday morning — before moving to the Fitzpatrick Castle Hotel — I had a three-hour meeting of the Ireland Funds Literary committee: Heaney, Terence Brown, Maurice Hayes, Nuala Ní Dhomhnaill and I. We had to decide on a winner of the IF Annual Literary Award for 2006. The usual names came up, names we would be happy to see winning this prize: Durcan, Harry Clifton, Brian Friel and then, unexpectedly, Thomas Kinsella. Heaney suggested that Kinsella should be approached to see if he'd accept the award. Perhaps Seamus had been influenced by Pat Crotty's keynote address to the Poetry Now festival on the previous evening. Pat's subject had been Kinsella's fifty years of poetic achievement. 'Would Tom turn us down?' asked Terence nervously, and Nuala, also, expressed the opinion that Kinsella hated and despised all living Irish-language poets. (Can this be true? I doubt it.) A long discussion ensued, but eventually in a roundabout way — our circuit included Clifton, Durcan, Ó Searcaigh, Vona Groarke, Conor O'Callaghan and Peter Sirr etc — we all came back to Kinsella. The prize is his if he wants it. It was an amicable decision.

I then moved on to Dun Laoghaire, a most salubrious and chic town, and now the home of the most important literary event in the Irish calendar. I gave a reading with Alice Oswald, the very fine English poet. She has won the Forward Prize as well as the T S Eliot Prize for her collection, *Dart*. She is very low key, brilliant, and incredibly famous: she has become a female Ted Hughes. Her new book, *Woods etc.*, is superb. It is probably the most important English collection since Craig Raine's *A Martian Sends a Postcard Home*. Her use of language is thrilling and distinctive, the mark of a true genius. Isn't it amazing how England, seemingly indifferent to poetry, blasé, cynical even, suddenly slaps down upon the table a poet to challenge the whole world? It was the same when Craig Raine happened. And Ted Hughes in 1958, just like that. Just like that. Out of thin air; no, not out of thin air, out of a dense impenetrable mist that is the English world.

April 24th Spent part of the day — a day of brilliant sunshine when Munster thrashed Leinster in the Heineken Cup semi-final — reading the two wonderful gifts that dropped through the letter box this week. The first was a little chapbook published in Austin, Texas, written by August Kleinzahler and designed by his Canadian wife, Sarah Kobrinsky. It's called 'I Went to See McCarthy' and it's an account of August's brilliant visit to Cork.

It's an incredible romp of a poem, full of August's New Jersey energy. It's certainly a great honour to me to be the subject of a Kleinzahler poem.

The second gift was from God himself: a copy of *District*

and Circle from Seamus Heaney. It is a real beauty, sure and solid as everything Seamus does. And absolutely sure of its territory, from 'The Turnip-Snedder' to 'The Harrow-Pin', from Wordsworth to Seferis. I've been reading it over and over, for the sheer beauty of it all and that gigantic presence of the Heaney mind, where 'Telluric ash and fire-spores boil away'.

May 7th A 'text message' from Cathy as she boards a British Airways flight to Phoenix, Arizona. What a tremendous journey for her: she is scheduled to give the Keynote Address and two workshops at the Prison Education Annual Conference in Scottsdale, Arizona. I feel abandoned. This is a strange feeling for me as I am usually unaffected by the comings and goings of our household. But I feel abandoned because I feel so close to her these last few months: being apart from her for only one week is unbearable.

For consolation I'm reading Geoffrey Hill's *The Orchards of Syon*, a wonderful work. It's a deeply intellectualized enquiry, but it's Paul Muldoon without the sense of humour. There's neither hollow nor dense laughter in Hill, but still a great, considered gift, with a deep sense of gratitude for thought, for music.

In a sheer effort of will, or 'willed faith', a baptism of desire, Hill pushes his pen towards a kind of divine revelation: 'call him Posthumus / Fortunatus . . . but is not my name.'

Reading Hill reminds me of the conversation I had with Heaney last year: Heaney's very human fear that Hill would win the Nobel Prize. 'Ah, it would spoil the whole thing for me,' said Seamus, with complete sincerity, 'his disciples are frightening people.' I wrote to him today to thank him for his wonderful gift of *District and Circle*.

May 15th An excited phone call from Pat Cotter in San Francisco. He said, 'Have you seen the *London Review of Books*?' My heart leaped with joy as I thought that there must be a good review of *Merchant Prince* therein. But no, it was to tell me that August Kleinzahler's long poem on his stay with me in Cork had been published (in its entirety) across two pages of the *LRB*. What a laugh. What a mischief-maker August is. Of course most people reading it in the *LRB* will think it is a poem about the English novelist, Tom McCarthy. I am about to suffer the same fate as Patrick Kavanagh who was often confused with the English poet P J Kavanagh, or Dublin poet Austin Clarke who was often confused in the British public mind with the Barbados-Canadian novelist of the same name. Nothing can be done about this; we can't change our names, even for the book market.

May 26th Reading Lysaght's biography of Ian Fleming: Fleming's *overwhelming* ambition, his yearning for success. But his negotiations with Hollywood were certainly not as high-powered as Evelyn Waugh's — in 1954 Fleming was offered $500 for a film option and $5,000 for the eventual rights of *Casino Royale*. But six years before that, in 1948, Evelyn Waugh was given $10,000 and a luxury lengthy sojourn on the West Coast , plus a promise of $40,000 if a film was made of *Brideshead Revisited*. Why such a difference in treatment by Hollywood? Was it the differing power of Literary Agents, or was it class differences? Social class often plays a part in the sums offered to English and Irish authors in American negotiations. This is not something that has been properly studied, but my guess is that a very English upper-class author will tend to deal with publishers and film studios at the level of the Board of Directors, at the level of the owners, because upper-class Americans really like to deal personally with upper-class English people, rather than leaving things to more junior staff. (In a publishing house in New York or a studio in Hollywood a class-conscious proprietor would be terrified that an unpolished member of staff would 'let the house down' socially when dealing with an Oxonian or Etonian.) Waugh was indisputably aristocratic in manner and material and I am certain that this put a premium on his commercial value. Fleming, although coming from a family of old Etonians, always operated at the level of Colonels rather than Generals: even his wife didn't admire him socially. Fleming tried too hard all the time and this is never attractive. An Englishman trying too hard always gives the impression that something is missing socially. What upper-class Americans find flabbergasting is the easeful superiority of English ladies or gentlemen. They are simply blown away by it. Fleming was always too anxious to be impressive. In his anxious dealings with Americans he let the English side down. That cost him $35,000.

June 13th In San Francisco with a fund-raising delegation from University College Cork, led by the University Librarian, John FitzGerald. Hectic activity. We carried *The Great Book of Ireland* to San Francisco via Atlanta to a great friend of the project in SF, Joe O'Donoghue. O'Donoghue's a wild and hugely successful chairman of the San Francisco Small Builders' Association. Joe is going to sell his own family's eighteenth-century Irish silver hoard to help raise funds for UCC to purchase *The Great Book*. He arranged a terrific dinner party in his house where I met Jerry Brown, the former Governor of California. He is now Mayor of Oakland and seeking the office of Attorney General of California. In Joe O'Donoghue's sitting room pride of place is given to a huge photograph of Joe with Gerry Adams. Joe is a fervent supporter of Sinn Féin and a determined and unapologetic Anglophobe. But his commitment to the *Great Book* project is astonishing and he's been an extraordinary host. Sinn Féin now own Irish-America and I find that truly disgusting, but Irish-Americans have always made up their own minds about Ireland, even as far back as John Devoy and Judge Cohalan.

Yesterday we drove down the incredible Silicon Valley highway to the world HQ of Palm Computers to meet two Irish executives. A successful meeting. While driving through this Silicon landscape names like San Diego, Dunbarton etc.

brought back the world of Raymond Chandler, the Waterford man who made these valleys his imaginative hinterland. Last night, drinks at O'Reilly's Bar and then dinner. Wonderful Murphy-Goode Cabernet 2002, with the best steak I've eaten in ten years. Magical places. California. A Paradise.

June 18th Home from San Francisco on Thursday. Had to go straight to work from Shannon Airport, then to Lismore where I launched a directory of Waterford writers at the County Library HQ. This book was compiled by Donald Brady, the energetic polymath who is County Librarian.

June 22nd In Dublin for an interview with Andy O'Mahony, the doyen of RTÉ Radio. Andy said he last interviewed me in 1984, a long, long time ago. The interview went well, although I did compare Charles Haughey to a horse fed on oats and Chablis. This will annoy Theo and upset dear Anthony Cronin.

Spent an hour at the National Library looking at the wonderful Yeats exhibition. What a poet Yeats was, what an exemplar: such a careful and studied arrangement of the myths of one life. Such a choreography of elegant things.

July 24th In Kerry, in a beautiful house a stone's throw from Béal Bán beach. The lights of a fully occupied summer Ballyferriter glow in the distance at night. We went for a long walk this morning, but 'rug an fhleath orainn' (the heavy shower overtook us) as they say in *Sean-Chaint na nDéise*.

In the silence interrupted only by rain and the rattle of doors in the wind I think of my *Last Geraldine Officer*, the whole scenario of *The LGO*, that twin catastrophe of war and poetry. What a catastrophe the impulse to make poems has been for me. How ill-equipped I am, not only to make a name for myself but to hold that name once it's been made.

August 4th Sitting in my new tent that I erected at the corner of our Kerry garden, looking out at Smerwick Harbour, a water shimmering in the blazing sunlight. Thinking again of *The LGO*, in particular, about a poem on a Fair Day in Cappoquin in the years after the war.

September 6th This morning I gave a lecture on Father Prout at the Frank O'Connor Library in Mayfield. About eighteen people in attendance, all very attentive and fascinated by the portions of 'Dean Swift's Madness' and 'The Rogueries of Tom Moore' that I read out. I handed out photocopies of Daniel Maclise's etching of the Fraserians as well as a photocopy of a letter that Fr Prout/Mahony wrote to Crofton Croker from Florence.

On Sunday the 90th birthday party for William Matson Roth. I sat between Sir Richard Keane of Cappoquin, now aged 97, and Erica, a printer and partner of Coracle Press. Erica talked about the difficulty of selling poetry pamphlets and she described the wonderful poetry scene in Buffalo, NY. Sir Richard turned to me and said, 'My hearing isn't what it used to be, Thomas. What is that woman saying to you?' It was a great evening with Bill's daughters and grandchildren dancing upon him in devoted attendance. Anna, his daughter who lives in Los Angeles, has become a truly impressive woman. She moved about the house between tables of oysters and tables of champagne, or glided, rather, in a beautiful white dress, fully aware that she was the most beautiful woman abroad in County Tipperary that evening. To still look young, to be beautiful, to be rich — what a great good fortune in any age. Sir Richard, though 97, was hugely impressed by Anna Roth — there was nothing prurient in his being charmed by her; it was merely that the sight of her, confident, willowy, in a beautiful long dress, must have reminded him of young Anglo-Irish women gliding across the Waterford drawing rooms of the 1920s.

September 18th I'm in Clifden, County Galway. The triangular route, Maam Cross-Clifden-Roundstone, is one of the most breathtaking drives in the world. Here in Clifden I had a long conversation with Michael Coady and with Tony Curtis. Tony earns his living from readings in England and Ireland. He was astonished when I told him that I hadn't given a public reading in England for over eight years (actually it may be longer). He gives an average of three readings a week, year round. I met Joan and Joe McBreen, old Galway friends, and Jo Slade, the Limerick poet, an exquisitely beautiful and elegant Limerick woman. Middle-class Limerick women are truly extraordinary; they are like women of the Veneto, fine featured, well-bred, and moving through this world with a sublime social confidence.

September 25th The Frank O'Connor International Prize — a triumphant night for Pat Cotter and the Munster Literature Centre. The previous evening nearly two hundred people assembled at the Millennium Hall to hear Richard Ford reading from his new book. I met Rose Tremain, Samrat Upadhyay and the latest literary star of County Waterford, Philip Ó Ceallaigh. He is fabulously gifted and just at the beginning of what will be a glorious career.

November 2nd Further perfect autumn weather, and that distinctive sense that the year has turned, inexorably, towards Christmas and New Year.

November 12th This morning I came in from the garden where I'd been planting bulbs and sat down to write another prose-poem for *The LGO*.

November 20th The other day I listened to Edith Sitwell reading her poem 'Slow Falls the Rain', an evocative and lyrical war poem about the night raids on London. In the years after the War Dame Edith also wrote a brilliant poem on the atomic bombing of Japan. Sitwell is definitely a presence in the mental landscape of *The LGO*, and in the post-War years her achievement becomes something very important in the lives of both *The LGO* and his beloved.

2007

January 5th New Year dinner at Martin Krasa's and Dr Grace Neville's house in Sunday's Well. Yet again I was attacked for the failures of Cork2005. There's no escape from that year — so many resident artists and cultural operators in Cork were rejected by us — we will never be forgiven. Until they all die, that is, but by then we will be dead as well.

January 18th Jim McKeon in the library. Another Frank O'Connor project. Paul Muldoon at UCC at 3 p.m. Dinner with Muldoon.

January 21st Poetry Ireland meeting in the Royal College of Surgeons. Arts Council briefing at 4 p.m.

February A reading last night with the Israeli poet, Amir Or. We got on famously. He is a gifted man, despairing of the Palestine/Lebanon situation, depressed at the universal rise of anti-Semitism. He laughed when I said that the Jews like the Irish had their best years in the 1950s when Ben Briscoe and La Guardia ruled in Dublin and New York. As I described the atmosphere of welcome within which all Jews operated in the 1950s tears came into his eyes. Those were the golden years as the full horror of the Holocaust was absorbed by the civilized world. They were also the years of Joyce and Yeats Studies, of Brendan Behan and the Clancy Brothers when it was a joy to be Irish or Jewish. I told him about the Goldbergs and the Marcuses of Cork and he was thrilled to hear the strange story of Cork's little Israel. I feel sorry for this Israeli poet, as I feel sorry for myself and all Southern Irish poets. History has no use for us; the intellectual Left does not wish to hear our voices. Before we parted we agreed that one must continue to write even when all seems lost, both politically and personally. I got the sinking feeling that we'll never meet again, and I sensed that he also had this feeling.

And tonight an excellent reading of new fiction by Danny Morrison, the old Provisional IRA man from Belfast. As time goes on his prose becomes deeper and more sophisticated at every level, but especially the level of common humanity. He has become a much better writer than Gerry Adams, for example, because he has discovered the imperative of the personal element in all good writing. Adams doesn't want to know this: his fiction serves a particular revolutionary purpose — and this is the purpose he wants for it.

The truth is that a poem, like a work of fiction, is not a representative viewpoint. There is a whole raft of well-meaning, kind-hearted people who think poetry should advance their cause. The fact is: causes destroy poetry more quickly than almost anything else, more quickly, even, than Fascism or tyrannies of any kind. Dear God, protect us from causes. They are worse than alcoholism in the decline of a poet's mind. Causes, Fascism and tyranny, all belong to the same category of action, the public realm. I'm not saying they're morally equivalent, but they are technically equivalent. In recent days off I've been tidying and culling my library. I've been reading, therefore, a whole sequence of turgid anthologies of poetry, all those beautiful, expensively-bound green anthologies of Irish poetry published from 1848 until, roughly, 1924. Why 1924, I wonder? Ah, yes! Yeats's Nobel Prize and the teaching instrument that was the Nobel Prize in serious Irish literary discourse at that time. It was as if in 1924 a Swedish magnifying glass was held up to Irish poetry, causing the second-rate and the provincial to be burned off. The ballad-makers fell away, those second-rate purveyors of group feeling, and only what was personal, urgent, immortal, came to the forefront. But isn't it amazing how we still canvass poetry as if it should represent us? I have constantly done this, in review after review after review — I can see that I often name a cause or a public purpose in praising some poet when I should have concentrated on the text at hand, the materials inside, the pigments that made the poem. There is no end to it, and I probably won't stop now, at this late stage in my life. When reviewing, you make an effort to canvass support for some poet you admire and wish to see praised more widely, a poet you hope might be 'taken up' by a world of more influential people. We all do this, but it is our inner politician at work. The fact is, the aptness, the excellence, the private greatness we find in really good poems by others is so intimately a personal thing that it can't be advocated on the level at which it's been written. Poems defy the kind of rhetoric we want them to have. Poems represent themselves — it is difficult to see this in the work of Neruda or Seferis for whom public suffering was a kind of private suffering, but you can see it plainly in Pasternak or Sylvia Plath. Poets sometimes become the embodiment of a cause, the voice of a cause or a national movement. But this embodiment is always the result of a conscription drive: the poem has become needed by a public urgency. But the poem was always private before it became public. Hard to make good people, highly motivated people, aware of this. And when you do make them aware of it they think you're being selfish, self-serving, bourgeois. This is why writers don't have this honest conversation with enthusiastic, well-meaning people.

March 4th Ennis is a beautiful town. Although technically in Munster, it really is a Connacht town at heart, a Western town with the feel of the countryside, the atmosphere of the small farm permeates the very cosmopolitan narrow streets; it belongs in a Jack Yeats drawing. It is more like Westport or Clifden than Mallow or Tramore. Once you drive beyond the Shannon, going north, you feel a great sense of relief or escape from the cares of elsewhere. It's difficult to describe it: that sense of being on vacation, of being snatched out of time.

March 8th A Library Council reading at Clonmel Library with Michael Coady.

April 1st The Jan/Feb issue of *American Poetry Review* names four-hundred-and-ninety-four active poets in all of its pages (texts, advertisements, reviews). I was recently reading the Poetry Now-Dun Laoghaire festival website: here, one-hundred-and-twenty-five poets, mainly Irish and British, have been featured over the last ten years. The extraordinary thing is this: I know nearly all of these poets' names and I have an opinion about the work of nearly all of them. Can this be normal, or is this *the* norm? Is it time and time only that is the ultimate editor of all such poetic voices: time that will leave us with ten names, or fewer, from its personal anthology of a century? The fact is nobody has the right to call any one of these poets a minor poet. We just don't know who will be minor and who will be major a century hence. But the one certainty is this: time will sort us all out. In a hundred years, from the pantheon of the present moment, there will be ten poets left, not six-hundred-and-nineteen.

April 20th More than six weeks of extraordinary sunshine and warmth have come to an end today with clouds in the sky. All of the garden is weeded and the plants flowering or budding profusely. Wonderful weather. A false summer. The days have filled me with a profound laziness, a complete inability to get on with the literary task at hand — which is to complete the prose-poems of *The LGO*. Now with the rain coming again maybe I'll get back to work.

April 26th President Yeltsin's funeral. *The Herald Tribune* publishes a marvellous photograph of the funeral procession. A gun carriage carries the body of the 76-year-old President, moving in solemn procession through Moscow to the Novodevichy Cemetery. He reigned for nine tumultuous years. Certainly Russia is too complex a nation and too vast a territory for one man to preside over. It is an awesome task to rule such an amazing land. The picture in the *Tribune* captures something of the immortal nature of Russian life.

Reading Graham Greene's *Congo Journal*, part of his *In Search of a Character*. It's very difficult to make any excuses for Greene and his attitude to Africa despite those novels, *The Heart of the Matter* and *A Burnt-Out Case*. What is so annoying about his writing on Africa is a constant assumption of superiority, an idiotic sense of the white man's burden, and a complete indifference to the integrity of Africa and its right to define its own kinds of freedom. In his writing nowhere is Africa allowed to explain itself. There's also that marauding white sexuality, the alertness to female African beauty, long thighs and firm breasts that might be bargained for with a husband or a father. In this matter he writes like a man of 1759 rather than 1959 — by 1959, almost twenty years after the Holocaust, a writer should know about the dignity of the person, the otherness of others. But Africa is all fair game for Graham Greene; he is dead to its ambitions, achievements and yearnings. If I were an African nationalist, if I were Kenyatta, Mandela or Nyerere, I'd have Greene's balls cut off. And that would be just the start of my dialogue with him. After that one could have a real discussion with him on the meaning of Europe in Africa and one could move on to discuss the purpose of fiction writing and the counter-integrity of African storytelling. Then, after his balls stopped bleeding, I would hand him a copy of Ngūgī wa Thiong'o's *Decolonising the Mind*.

May 24th Today Thomas Kinsella received the Freedom of Dublin, a huge honour.

May 26th Michael Flatley, the dancing star, received the Freedom of Cork. I had to compose and recite a poem for him, something I enjoyed doing. He is an immensely charming man and held everyone spellbound, both in the City Hall and in the Lord Mayor's office. He played the flute brilliantly.

June 18th I gave a talk on Molly Keane's last trilogy, *Good Behavour, Time After Time* and *Loving and Giving* (or *Queen Lear* in America). Already people have begun to forget her, to forget the impact of her enormous late success. Tomorrow there's the launch of the *Irish University Review* with my essay on Eiléan Ní Chuilleanáin.

June 24th Seven extracts from *The LGO* sent to *Poetry Ireland Review.*

July 20th Yesterday *Poetry Review* in London accepted 'Templemaurice House', the four-page lyric that opens *The LGO*. And today I completed the last poem of *The Last Geraldine Officer.* I wrote the first lyrics for this book while I worked in St Mary's Road Branch Library during the bitter Beef Tribunal election of November 1992. So this book has taken fifteen years to complete. I thank God that I lived to complete it. It is one of the main documents of my life.

September 16th In Belfast, waiting for the train to Dublin, and surrounded by hundreds of young Gaelic football supporters travelling to Dublin for the All-Ireland Final.

A wonderful three days at the Louis MacNeice Centenary Celebrations. Last night, a Civic Dinner at Belfast City Hall where we toasted the Queen. Ciaran Carson admonished me for raising my glass, but I explained that as a MacCarthy, a member of one of the oldest royal families of Europe, I couldn't object to toasting an English royal person. He shook his head like the irredentist Ulster Fenian that he is: 'Fuck off, McCarthy,' he said, with real venom. That was our last communication during the entire night. But Ciaran thinks I'm not being serious. Like most Nationalist Ulstermen he underestimates the force of my opinions because they are gently expressed. But I am deadly serious in my opinions: I stand over them. I accept the integrity of Protestant Ulster, I honour its sense of attachment to Britishness. I harbour no wish to defeat it. Its defeat would diminish me and all of Ireland. For people like Ciaran Carson my belief system is despicable. But I will hold my ground, I will say 'No!' with Ulster until that part of Ulster is willing to say 'Yes'. It must be Ulster's choice.

Yesterday we visited MacNeice's grave in Carrowdore Churchyard: a beautiful place, truly idyllic. The ladies of Carrowdore Church had put on a magnificent flower display in response to lines from MacNeice's poetry. The only sour note of the celebrations was struck by Derek Mahon who, when he saw Seamus Heaney arriving to climb aboard our bus accompanied by a BBC television crew, became apoplectic with rage. 'I'm not taking part in this Heaney media circus,' he shouted at me, and then turned away to go back to his hotel. He wasn't going to be part of what he thought was a Heaney media stunt. This was a bitter blow to Michael Longley who'd invested a lot emotionally in the return of Heaney, Mahon and himself to the MacNeice grave after forty years. At the graveside Longley read Mahon's poem: it was a deeply emotional moment.

We visited Carrickfergus, beautiful in the bright blue sunshine — though I noticed several shops shut, a sign of faltering prosperity that makes me nervous for Protestant Ulster. It is vitally important for the new Peace Process that ordinary Protestants can see visible signs of prosperity and wellbeing. Met a huge number of poets and academics, all quite curious about the Fianna Fáil poems I read. Met Simon Armitage and Christopher Reid, both were encouraging and friendly. After the visit to Carrowdore Churchyard I went back to the hotel, the Crescent Town House, to lie down for an hour. Who should I bump into but Derek Mahon who was working on a poem in the upstairs sitting room of the hotel. He looked at me sheepishly and said, 'I'm revising "Carrowdore Churchyard" (his famous, much anthologized poem) and Edna will be furious. She hates revisions.' He didn't seem to regret not going to the MacNeice grave, but said, adamantly, 'I bet it was a circus. A Heaney circus.' I said that indeed there were cameras and he replied, 'Hah! I knew it!' But he was pleased when I gave him a spare copy of the booklet produced by the Carrickfergus Museum, a very handsome publication. What an obdurate, difficult and uncompromising Ulsterman he is. But what a star, what a pure star of Ulster poetry.

November 14th Today *Poetry Ireland Review* sent proof copies of the two *LGO* prose-poems 'February 13th, 1947' and 'May 15th, 1950'. They take up more space on the printed page than I'd imagined. Eiléan Ní Chuilleanáin has given over a page to each poem. But they look good.

November 28th A visit from the New Zealand poet, Bernadette Hall. She has been living with her husband on a visiting residency near Blarney for the last six months. A gentle woman, a former Fellow of the IWP in Iowa: she reminds me a lot of Jane Cooper with that gentle strength but low expectations for her career in the wide world of poetry. All of this modesty will be the death of New Zealand writing. She still doesn't know Pat Cotter of the Munster Literature Centre, for example, and hasn't tried to arrange any public reading of her poems.

2008

January 28th Home again after six days in Japan. I gave a reading and two lectures (on Irish Women Poets and on Frank O'Connor) at Aichi Shukutoku University in Nagoya, three hours east of Tokyo by bullet train — Nagoya is the world HQ of Toyota Motors.

And in the hotel, in my 34th floor apartment, this notice: 'In the event of an earthquake the hotel intends to function normally. Do not use the elevators. There are no stairs.' Ah, Japan.

February 2nd Today a woman came into the library to return a book, *Destiny* by Sally Beauman, a novel of 900 pages. This was the third time she'd read this prodigious book. She said to me, 'I read it first when my daughter was two, then when she was twelve. Now she's twenty.' This novel was published by Bantam in 1987, then reprinted in Time Warner paperback in 2002 and immediately reprinted. Imagine reading a novel of 900 pages three times! When the woman had gone I read the 'Prologue' and first chapter. A stunning opening sequence. A novel of immense maturity and worldliness. Basically, it has love, war, wealth and social glamour, all bound together by very fine cadenced prose. Sally Beauman worked as a journalist for years, with the *New York* magazine and *Vogue*. There's no doubt but a decade spent in journalism is the best training any novelist could wish for.

February 6th I just finished reading two books that couldn't be more different, politically and socially. The first is *Florence and Josephine O'Donoghue's War of Independence* by John Borgonovo, an account of an extraordinary romance between

IRA leader Florence O'Donoghue and a young war-widow, Josephine (who later married O'Donoghue). Josephine's husband had died in the Great War and she found work as the supervisor of the typist's pool at Victoria Barracks in Cork. She supplied the IRA with a copy of every document that passed through her hands, including lists of informers in West Cork and lists of British troop movements and formations. She was by far the most important IRA spy in the British establishment, even more important than Nelligan, the IRA spy in Dublin Castle. God only knows how many West Cork Protestants died because of her spying — almost every British informer in County Cork was murdered because of her efficient work on behalf of the Irish side. The book is extraordinary, a real story of Irish romance and heroism. But the second book — equally compelling and hugely more attractive — is *The Duff Cooper Diaries* by the great British diplomat. His world view is the very antithesis of O'Donoghue's Irish world. The assassination of General Wilson is an incident that connects both books. There are other assassinations in Duff Cooper's *Diaries* such as the murder of the Anglo-Irish Lord Moyne by the Stern Gang in Cairo. Duff Cooper is hugely attractive as a diarist, a lover of life, food, wine, books and mature women. He is a true aristocrat among lovers in that innocence holds no attraction for him. The *Diaries* are absolutely brilliant, vastly superior to Harold Nicolson or Cecil Beaton and easily equal to Evelyn Waugh. They are more like Sir John Colville's *The Fringes of Power,* that is if Colville had been drunk more often. Duff Cooper was connected by temperament, business or marriage to all the great figures of London life. But the greatest work of his life was his astute management of de Gaulle, from the days of the Free French and Casablanca to the collapse of the first post-War Conservative government. He also had a decent relationship with Bevan, the incoming Labour leader. He was a vital bridge between England and France and a brilliant advocate for French interests with the British, while pursuing British interests, always, in Paris. He really was an astonishing diplomat, exemplary in his social instincts and forever positive. He had a great belief in the future of Europe, but a sanguine British attitude to life — refusing, as a matter of education and principle, ever to be discouraged or belittled by events. And what a womanizer! No good-looking wife was quite safe when he turned on his British charm.

February 23rd This weekend the Ulster Troubles finally reached our neighbourhood — nearly eleven years after the IRA ceasefire. When I was leaving for work this morning I saw blood on the footpath outside our gate, enclosed by a white chalked circle of the police Investigation Unit. Last night at around 9 p.m. I heard the almighty blaring of police sirens and our dogs barking wildly. A 'tiger kidnapping' of a wealthy businessman (who lives four doors from us in a detached house) was taking place. Except that the kidnappers had walked into a trap set by the Garda Special Branch and its Emergency Response Unit. On Thursday the Special Branch had informed the businessman that he would be kidnapped on Saturday night. They ordered him to remove his family from the house. Yesterday morning he left his house as usual and members of the Special Branch moved in. When he arrived home after 8 p.m. he was accompanied by other armed guards. As he opened his door he was pounced upon by the kidnappers who were immediately pounced upon by the Special Branch! It was a brilliant piece of work by the Garda anti-terrorist squad. Now the Montenotte neighbourhood is abuzz with excitement and full of the wildest stories.

February 26th Yesterday, an email from Wake Forest University Press in Winston-Salem, North Carolina. They plan to publish forty poems of mine in a new anthology, a kind of *Introductions* anthology. Fair play to Wake Forest. They still haven't lost faith in the Irish world though it can hardly be a lucrative area of publishing nowadays.

February 27th Sure enough yesterday's *Irish Times* carried the names of the alleged men who attempted the kidnapping of our wealthy neighbour.

March 1st This morning *The Irish Times* publishes the short-list for the Poetry Now prize. It is a strong list, a list that makes me thankful that I'm not publishing a book this year. Eamon Grennan, Matthew Sweeney and Dennis O'Driscoll are all on the list, as well as the indisputably brilliant Harry Clifton. I don't know how the judges can decide: Matthew Sweeney's book was already on the T S Eliot Prize list and Harry Clifton was lionized by Derek Mahon in the *TLS* last week. Certainly these books are a reminder of the very high standards now operating among Irish poets of my generation.

March 9th Went to the Everyman Theatre last night to see Red Kettle's production, *Boy Soldier*. It tells the story of John Condon, the Waterford boy who was the youngest British soldier to die in the Great War. This production was directed by Ben Hennessy but it still has all the hallmarks of Pat Kiernan's original direction, lots of shouting, mad running about, many unlinked Brechtian tableaux. Very like an early Corcadorca production, but with Waterford City instead of Cork City accents. It was great to hear placenames like 'Passage', 'John's Park' and 'Ballybricken' uttered on a Cork stage, and the Waterford accent is earthy and superb.

2009

February 27th In Dublin yesterday to sign 200 sheets of a special festschrift for Michael Longley, at the request of Robin Robertson, the young poet-editor at Jonathan Cape. I took the bus in order to save money, a four-and-a-half hour journey through the old Bianconi route of Fermoy-Mitchelstown-Cahir-Cashel-Urlingford-Portlaoise-Dublin. What was truly inspiring about this journey was to see the newness of the country: new roads, bridges, parks, villages, and new houses sitting proudly beside decayed cottages on nearly every farm. Despite the economic downturn the country still looks brand new. All of the European money of the Celtic Tiger years was *not* wasted, despite the current national feeling of despair and betrayal. We have a country that looks (physically, at least) like a bright new penny. Morally, politically, that penny was tarnished by the corruption of bankers, politicians, builders, auctioneers and property journalists.

March 13th In Shanghai for a series of readings at the Shanghai Literary Festival, Fudan University and Shanghai Normal University. Yesterday Pat Cotter and I read at Fudan U: a superb class of undergraduates with a terrific command of English. Two or three students were passionate about Ireland, and one student expressed her dream of going to Trinity College, Dublin, to study Oscar Wilde and Yeats.

Today we visited Tiger Mountain and the prosperous historical region of Suzhou, west of Shanghai.

Gave a reading with Pat at Shanghai Normal University. Not the same atmosphere as at Fudan. But a sincere and enthusiastic scholar has established an Irish Studies Programme. He reminded me of Brendan Flynn of Clifden or

Dr Eoin McKiernan of St Paul: a man working with bound-less energy and limited resources. Dr Durong is obsessed with the notion that he will change the perception of Irish writing all over China. He wants Shaw, Beckett, Yeats and Wilde to be acknowledged as Irish rather than British writers. This is a tall order, I fear, as even American universities, who should know better, treat these writers as part of British Studies. But in the process of discovering the impossibility of his task Dr Durong will learn a great deal about the nature of British cultural power. This power will eventually domi-nate Chinese thinking on Ireland as it dominates the thinking of all upper-class WASPish professors who teach in the top fifty American universities — cultured men and women who fall asleep each night in their lovely campus homes while lis-tening to the BBC broadcasting across the NPR network. In accepting the English language as our cultural instrument Irish writers also accepted this post-colonial hegemony of a great British world. We have learned to live alongside this British behemoth the way certain small birds and animals follow great herds of elephants across the grasslands. Discovering the smallness of Irish interests in this Anglophone world will become part of Dr Durong's hard political education.

Later we visited the Shanghai Writers' Association at its palatial HQ, formerly the residence of the French colonial administrator of the French Concession. Lunch with Zhao Lihong and others in a beautiful restaurant called Lake Garden. We visited the building where the Communist Party of China held its first historic congress. It was the most moving place I've visited in China, a shrine to a single political idea that has delivered both national liberation and pride to the world's greatest country. Five hundred million humans lifted out of poverty in just two generations, the greatest improve-ment in human life in the history of humankind. This is the great achievement of the Chinese Communist Party: it will never be matched in the story of world history. The Chinese themselves are not even aware of this achievement, at least they never speak about it, except in the vaguest possible terms. In the meantime, what has Europe given mankind? Rapacious colonization, Fascism and two world wars that killed about one hundred million people and drained the Third World of almost all its resources. From the viewpoint of a Chinese historian the capitalist West must seem like a jungle of murderous political hypocrites.

March 28th While working in the Reference Store in the Grand Parade Library I came across several copies of *Iris-leabhar na Gaedhilge*, a Gaelic League journal. Interesting to find this wording in a paid advertisement: 'Several Gaelic Leaguers and others have complained to us recently that they were informed we employ Jewish labour . . . ' How extra-ordinary it is that in Dublin in 1909, five years after the mythical Leopold Bloom walked its streets, the seeds of European anti-Semitism were already sown in a hyper-Nationalist Irish journal.

April 28th Trying desperately to finish a brief essay on Paula Meehan for an American journal. I wrote 1700 words over the weekend. I'd like to reach 3,000 words if at all possible by the end of this week. Tonight I have to deliver a talk on 'Daniel Corkery, The Forgotten Genius' to a community history club. I will emphasize the Corkery of the early novel and the short stories — the urban Corkery of 1896-1916 who might have become an Irish Arnold Bennett. This young Corkery is the Corkery who speaks to us, who speaks to our universal experience of living in a city and being belittled by that experience.

April 29th Spent the day working on an exhibition of Robert Gibbings' books. Looking at photographs of Gibbings one could see how charming and handsome he was — one can understand, physically, why he was able to make such an im-pact as a broadcaster and a lover of many women.

May 8th Anvil Press sent on the cover artwork and publicity sheet for *The Last Geraldine Officer*. The cover design looks superb. Publication date has been set for October 10th. The sight of the cover of *The LGO*, after so many years spent attending to the project, has put me in high good spirits.

2010

June 22nd Alone in the universe we invent heavens. But not just the seashore. There has to be another place of integration and imaginative redemption. Perhaps in the city this place is the coffee shop, the place where humans have always sought respite from weariness — the café, the coffee shop, the cafeteria.

September 14th A call from Catherine in Malta — she's just seen two Caravaggios in the cathedral at Valetta: a moment of joy for her. Last night she said that she was thinking of going swimming in the Med. The sea is only a few yards from the hotel where she has to make a speech on Education in Irish Prisons. Of all the delegates, having run a prison education service and edited the *European Journal of Prison Education*, she is now probably the most authoritative and experienced voice in European prison education. This fact would never occur to her. Being Kitty Coakley's daughter she wouldn't allow it to occur to her: it would be too vain. But it occurs to me. Which is why I write it down here.

October 10th At Amsterdam Airport, waiting for my KLM flight to Shanghai. Just had a Baileys and coffee and read a seriously elliptical interview with Chinese Premier, Wen Jiabao. Received a text message from Matthew Sweeney who saw my review of Patrick Crotty's anthology in *The Examiner* in which I'd lamented the absence of both Matthew and Harry Clifton as an exclusion of 'the best poets of our generation'. I think that compliment tickled Matthew. I was telling the truth. They are the best poets of the South.

This week I was in Westport, unquestionably one of the

most beautiful towns on earth. What impressed me was that the town was buzzing, people walking the streets, shopping, and the restaurant where Cathy and I had lunch was packed with diners. It lifted my heart to see business doing so well. On the way home we stopped at Thoor Ballylee and had coffee in a 'New Age' café in Gort. One image on the road between Ballinrobe and Shrule: a hearse driven slowly with a coffin — but piled high in the coffin was the day's shopping, sliced pans, potatoes, carrots, washing powder, all piled on top of the shining cask. It was a homely, rather than a heavenly, image.

At Thoor Ballylee we opened the gate and walked around the beautiful, melancholy tower. Cathy stopped beneath a pear tree and pointed out the little golden-skinned pears that were strewn on the ground. I picked half a dozen of the Yeatsian pears. It comforts me now, as I sit here in a café at Amsterdam Airport, to think of my Yeatsian pears in the freezer, awaiting me. I will make a pear and Cointreau dish, such a dish as Lady ffrench-McGrath brought to Sir Gerald FitzGerald's room. From such imagined worlds the light shines upon me, an Anglo-Irish light. It is a great comfort.

Saturday Shanghai. A glorious day in Shanghai. Bernadette from Kilkenny (whose mother was the ebullient founder of the L'Arche community), now married to a German engineer, took me on a tour of this glorious place. She took me to the People's Park at 7.30 a.m., in time to witness a scene of such intense happiness that its equal cannot be known anywhere else in the world: music everywhere, smiling faces, elderly couples dancing slow foxtrots; in the pools by faded lotus flowers and beneath the weeping willows and ginkgo trees at least three hundred serious but welcoming middle-aged parents share photos of their sons and daughters — this the Shanghai Marriage market. This time of year, early Autumn when all the young return to Shanghai to their universities and those slightly older return to acquire their first jobs, this place of matchmaking is busier than ever. Bernadette reads a notice held up by a mother on behalf of her son 'Born 1984. Tall. A graduate of Western University, currently working as an engineer with 10,000 RMB monthly salary. Would like tall wife, gentle, who dislikes loud music.' And beside the ginkgo tree near the bamboo contemporary art installation a tall and elegant elderly man holds a placard declaring his daughter's eligibility: 'Tall, wishing for a tall husband. She is born in 1988. A University graduate working in an International Bank. Holder of a Shanghai Resident's Permit.' This latter detail is vital. A woman with such a permit qualifies for healthcare as well as guaranteed school places and free education for her unborn children. I look at her photo, held aloft by her chic, elderly father, smoking a very long cigarette. It is an old-fashioned photograph, like a studio portrait of any bourgeois Shanghai girl c.1910 — but these photos, I soon learn, are posed and printed to appeal not to a would-be lover, but to the mothers of lovers. Later, as I walk past, I see these two marriage-brokers in animated conversation. The final stage of the morning's process is underway. The next stage is the exchange of photos and the sharing of a bigger portfolio of pictures so that the parents can choose the images most likely to appeal to a son or daughter. The whole event will turn upon a daughter's first reaction to a photograph: will she like the look of a man or not? Is there something in the look of him that unnerves her or draws her in? An entire lifetime, the begetting of children, the future of China, will turn upon the trained instinct of that Shanghai daughter.

Beyond the ginkgo trees and the lotus flowers, around a pond of giant lilies, dozens of caged birds are hanging from trees and poles, singing wildly, as wildly as the old men who own each cage, who talk and smoke. Each morning elderly men bring their caged birds to the park to hang beside other caged birds. In such company the birds sing wildly and sweetly, the whole sound joined together in a great wave of energy. Sitting here one feels that a burst of Respighi will emerge from the bamboos at any moment. But the birds sing on, hopping from blue and white porcelain water jar to blue and white porcelain grain jar. These caged birds singing, seemingly perfectly contented and excited by the morning companionship of other birds, create a single great metaphor for China and its success — a success based on continuity. China works beautifully, singingly, because of this unwritten but unbroken contract between the Chinese People and their Chinese Communist Party.

Chinese chessplayers, the knot of people around each table, and a more animated knot of people around card players. A young man is playing a saxophone. He accompanies an older woman, perhaps his mother, who sings sharply and precisely in a mezzo voice. She repeats phrases and her son follows her, backtracking and then playing more smoothly. It is now later in the morning, nearly 11.30, and a small number of young couples, lovers devoid of brokers, assemble beneath the clumps of bamboo and spent agapanthus flowers, all listening to the voice and the saxophone. They are silent and impressed in a characteristically Chinese manner. The Chinese love any demonstration of expertise; it reassures them, it integrates Chinese life. At the end of the day that's all that matters in China: to enrich life, to amplify harmony of any kind.

Later, at the Writers' Bureau, I meet again the poet Zhao Lihong. I'm supposed to write an introduction to his poems and I've been reading them for the last few months. A complete absence of politics. I ask Zhao about this. Surely in such a country it can't be possible to avoid politics? To be silent on the subject of politics must in itself be a political act. Zhao disabuses me firmly. He knows exactly what he's doing — politics doesn't interest him. What he loves is nature, history, farms, stones, flowers, the colour yellow. His translators: a delicate, obviously brilliant woman who works as a night editor on the *Shanghai Daily*, a daughter of two parents who are still members of the People's Liberation Army and who has spent her entire childhood and youth in military compounds, and Bivash Mukherjee, her Senior Night Editor, a Bengali producer of a film on the life of Tagore. Bivash and I hit it off immediately when he discovered that I'd met R Parthasarathy and Shrikant Verma many years ago. He says that I am the first person to mention Adil Jussawalla and the Bombay Workshop in his presence in twenty years. He treats me as if I were a follower of Indian cricket. Zhao loves Tagore and has written one of his best poems about him. I state my opinion that Tagore must have nominated Yeats for the Nobel Prize. 'No!' Bivash corrects me. 'The opposite is the case. Your Mr Yeats nominated Tagore.' The mention of that dreaded word 'Nobel' doesn't seem to make anyone feel uncomfortable. No follow-up observation, no expression or praise or outrage. Zhao has no time for politics. He is a man of History. As the Chinese Premier stated recently, when discussing his reading habits with *Time* magazine, there are too many Memoirs being written, but not enough History.

December 21st Astonishing weather, like Minnesota, except without the powerful Minnesotan winter technologies. Last night as I put out the bin it was minus seven. This ice and snow seems to reflect our gloomy national mood. In many ways the weather has created a sense of political calm. It's as if the nation can only deal with one calamity at a time (e.g. Give us the Great Famine, but not the Great Famine *and* the Munster Plantations).

Last night my mood changed suddenly from one of bitter despair to a kind of wistful hopefulness — all because I lit the fire, put on an old video tape of *Brideshead Revisited* and began to read Nancy Mitford's letters. There's no doubt but the company of English aristocrats, their milieu and the sound of their Received Pronounciation, cheers me up enormously. Having been so happy at Glenshelane I think I'll always share the sentiments of an old, doting retainer. This is my mental weather. Though what astonishes me about *BR* is how much it is a treatise on alcoholism — even at that stage Evelyn Waugh knew he was in trouble.

December 30th Just finished reading Nancy Mitford's letters, some of them written from Lismore Castle, the home of her sister, the Duchess of Devonshire. What a joy it was to spend the last four days in Mitford's company — a girl of the 1920s like Molly Keane. Even her mischievous gossiping is so reminiscent of Molly. The book has restored me not only to writing, but to a sense of heightened humanity.

2011

July 14th I've cleared out my study at the top of the house, the biggest clear-out since we moved to Montenotte. I had to part with nearly one and a half thousand books, the accumulation of over thirty years. I am almost back to the library I had in 1984 or '85. But the cleanliness of the room fills me with pleasure; it has been re-painted and re-carpeted. I gave a house painter my 1,500 books in part payment. For the first time my books are also in some kind of order, not in alphabetical order, but in the order within which my mind works: 1. *Irish poets.* 2. *Irish language.* 3. *American poets and essayists.* 4. *English poets.* 5. *English diarists.* 6. *Jewish writers and history.* 7. *Waterford and Cork Local History.* 8. *Reference and literary journals.* 9. *The rest of the known world.*

August 2nd Here in Béal Bán, Ballyferriter, in a house by the beach. Idyllic, as always. My mind is too full of worries and obligations to relax. Even looking over my poems in the last few days I find that it isn't six, but ten, new poems I'd need to write before I can consider publishing a new collection. The way my life is, a life churning with obligations to others, I can't see a clear way ahead into any meadow of ten poems.

August 4th Spent last night in a tent overlooking the sea at Wine Strand. A night of howling wind with occasional heavy pulses of rain; at one point, around 3 a.m., I was sure that water would penetrate such was the force of the rain. But my old *Coleman* tent held fast, the interior remaining bone dry. And this morning glorious sunshine as I fried sausages and boiled my billycan of water. Elemental, perfect. As I ate my breakfast I watched the waves rushing onto the Black Strand.

August 12th Still in Kerry. Torrential rain and constant winds for three days.

August 29th I directed a writing workshop at Molly Keane's house in Ardmore. A lovely group of writers, all women of course: men are just hopeless. I got everyone to start at 7.30 in the morning; a great creative atmosphere and that beautiful atmosphere of Molly everywhere in the house and garden. What a magical presence she was, our own Edith Wharton; what joy knowing her brought into my life. I used excerpts from Elizabeth Bowen's *The Heat of the Day* and Molly's *Time After Time* and *Loving and Giving*. The class was mesmerized by the quality of the writing. I also used Vera Brittain's *On Becoming a Writer*, reading out Brittain's great list of illusions of would-be writers. While I was giving my workshop I learned that the American novelist, Nora Roberts, was at the bottom of the hill in Ardmore, in the Cliff House Hotel, writing. I gave a reading in the evening, with candles, the fire lighting and wine and cake for everyone. After my reading Virginia Brownlow, Molly's daughter, presented me with her mother's silver cocktail shaker. What a sensational gift! Molly bought it for her honeymoon in New York where she brought her young husband, Bobby Keane of Cappoquin, to see her play *Treasure Hunt* that was then showing on Broadway. On the way to the reading Cathy asked two nuns for directions to Molly Keane's house. One nun looked at Cathy with concern and said, 'I think she's dead, my dear.' Earlier a young waiter in the hotel asked Cathy, 'Who's Molly Keane?'

Met Matthew Sweeney for lunch today. He told me that his editor at Jonathan Cape has rejected his latest collection, more or less dropping him from the Cape poetry list. He sent the same collection to Faber but they told him that Faber would now concentrate on 'debutante poets' whose rights they could accumulate over time. That seems to me a reasonable business decision, but of course it wounds Matthew terribly. At least Paul Muldoon has accepted a poem from him for the *New Yorker*. I told him that that was a great achievement, which it is. Matthew is one of the two or three most important Irish poets now living. And it would only take one or two lucky breaks for him to be the number one Irish poet, to become truly famous. But losing Jonathan Cape as publisher is a real tragedy for him. Why did this happen?

August 31st Just got off the phone with Gerry Smyth. He retired today from *The Irish Times* where he was the Managing Editor, a hugely influential presence not just in poetry but in culture generally. For decades he has been the most in-fluential poet at work in the Irish media. Under his guidance *The Irish Times* has become the towering influence in Irish cultural life: he has led and mediated cultural debates in Dublin so that, nowadays, nothing is finally settled in Irish life until *The Irish Times* has issued the last word on it. He has been a great friend to me, and he and Caroline Walsh have been terrific supporters of John Montague as well as the Frank O'Connor Festival in Cork. I remember how worried I was, years ago, when Terence de Vere White left the *IT*, but perhaps there's no need to be so worried: they always seem to find good people in that paper. It attracts the best, rather like the *New Yorker* or the *London Review of Books*. Gerry had just left the offices of the paper in Tara Street when he phoned me. He said that the paper had thrown a huge party on the premises. He sounded very emotional as he walked along, speaking about poets and poetry and newspapermen. We agreed to meet in Dublin very soon.

September 17th I see from the papers that the Knight of Glin, Desmond FitzGerald, has died. He is the last of his line; the end of another Geraldine dynasty. I remember him at Glen-shelane. Last night Cathy and I (relaxing after Cathy's spec-tacular promotion to Principal of the Prison Education Unit) watched a terrific interview/feature on the English writer

Hilary Mantell. It was brilliantly done. But why are all English Catholics completely daft? Mantell could have slipped unnoticed into the drawing room of the Sitwells or the more cracked recesses of a John Betjeman house.

Yesterday, the last meeting of the judging panel for the Frank O'Connor Prize — a not inconsiderable prize with a cheque for £25,000. It's the biggest prize in the world for a collection of short stories. We agreed that really there were only three books left in contention: Yiyun Li's *Gold Boy, Emerald Girl*, Alexander MacLeod's *Light Lifting* and Edna O'Brien's *Saints and Sinners*. I was determined to fight for Edna O'B but we were split three ways. Eventually, I made a statement I'd prepared earlier, 'Look, our choice is ultimately between courage and wisdom. If we are courageous, if we want the more avant-garde to praise us for our boldness, we will choose either Yiyun Li or MacLeod. Their books are brilliant, especially the long opening stories in each collection. But let me say something, a personal thing: I feel a deep affinity with Edna O'Brien, with her long struggle, with her woman's lust for life, her lustfulness and her struggle to survive as a woman in 1950s. I feel that an Olympian, a marathon-runner of Irish literature, has passed beneath my window. I feel I must place a laurel wreath on this great Olympian because I don't think she will be running through our neighbourhood again.'

There was silence, an awkward but important silence.

This is the full statement that I'd prepared:

Edna O'Brien Saints and Sinners

There is something inexplicably faithful, permanent, eternal, in the fiction of Edna O'Brien. As the years pass by we think she has drifted from us, drifted away into a kind of aristocratic Kilburn or haughty Irish Hampstead, and then she does something to rattle the cage: like this new collection of stories,

Saints and Sinners. *Like the character Rafferty who dominates the thought processes of the narrator in 'Shovel Kings'
she warns us about life — '"Mind yourself." Those were the
last words Rafferty said to me. He did not shake hands and,
as on the first morning, he raised his calloused right hand in
a valediction that bespoke courtesy and finality. He had cut
me out, the way he had cut his mother out, and those few who
were dear to him, not from a hardness of heart, but from a
heart that was immeasurably broken.' In 'Shovel Kings' she
encounters an entire history that cannot speak, life below the
gas-tinctured blue clay of 1950s and '60s London, as she waits
to see her own therapist who has moved from a more salubrious
part of London to a cheaper, more Irish, place. The irony is
embodied in the character of Rafferty, her new companion in
the ad hoc waiting room of a pub. This is a long, lyrical, deeply
moving story. In 'Send My Roots Rain' we have Miss Gilhooley,
who might easily have been a passive, one-dimensional siren,
an Austin Clarke 'Martha Blake' or Brian Moore 'Judith
Hearne' — but this is a narrative written by a wise woman
who knows life, who knows the pain of it and the impossi-
bilities. Miss Gilhooley 'turned to poets as she would to God'
after having been rejected by letter, written in both Irish and
English, by a gutless man. She develops an enthusiastic friendship by correspondence with a poet who also fails to become
flesh. It is an old story, but in the pen of Edna O'Brien it is
raised to high and painful art. Love, high love, in the end is as
unreachable as the highest feeling in Gerard Manley Hopkins;
after all it is time's eunuch who cries, 'O thou lord of life, send
my roots rain.' In her deepest lexicon Edna O'Brien knows this.*

*Edna O'Brien's singular gift, her great lustful comfort in
the face of the human condition, is best seen in three of the
shorter works of her new short story collection — I mean the
stories 'Black Flower', 'Sinners' and 'Green Georgette'. In
'Black Flower' we see a remnant of the Troubles, a backwash
from our violent past in which Mona, the volunteer art
teacher, befriends a day-release terrorist, taking him to a*

grand but bleak house for dinner. When Shane decides to make a phone call his fate is sealed: in his death we see the summary execution of History and the powdered remnants of relationships — not quite the portrait of what happened, but the list of possibilities, of what never quite happens, between people. As Mona backs away 'the lambs in their foetal sleep, innocent of slaughter' are all that survive. In 'Sinners' we have a perfect and perfectly understated narrative, a shrewd description of a bourgeois landlady outraged by the sexual behaviour of guests who seemed, at first, to be conventional and respectful. Their contempt for her moral outrage prevents her from upstaging them, forcing her to accept into her mind the sounds of 'something appalling . . . transpiring in there, whispers and tittering and giggles' and making her weep in the realization that 'she had forgotten the little things, the little pleasures, the give and take that is life'. In 'Green Georgette', a story as perfect as anything by William Trevor or Elizabeth Bowen, we have an intense social narrative, subtle and lethal with detail: 'she wore a teddy bear coat that had brown leather buttons with cracks in them. They looked like fallen horse chestnuts . . . She has a butterfly brooch, an amber brooch with a likeness of a beetle, a long-leafed marcasite brooch, and a turquoise wreathed with little seed pearls.' Later, the same woman, a snob, a Bank Manager's wife in the country, will hide a rash, or evidence of something more violent, beneath a georgette scarf. When the scarf loosens an entire social fiction will fall apart.

If you get a chance to buy this collection, now in paperback, please do. You will not be unmoved by it.

September 19th Terrific, positive fallout from the Edna O'Brien prizewinning. A lengthy feature on RTÉ's main news this morning, a very gracious piece by Eileen Battersby in *The Irish Times* and an official word of congratulations from President McAleese to Edna at her hotel. All in all a very positive response. Last night, arms linked, I walked down

MacCurtain Street with the sublime Yiyun Li. She was quite happy to cede the prize to the 81-year-old Edna and Colm Tóibín came up to me and hugged me, saying, 'A wise, wise decision'. Everyone extremely gracious about it. I suppose the young, I mean the provincial young, will be outraged later. But that's fine. There must be at least one unhappy Beckett or Joyce out there, outraged by the Annie M P Smithson/Austin Clarke-like material of Edna.

October 21st Another intense day of library business. I spent the day in O'Mahony's bookshop in Limerick City. I bought nearly three thousand books after a marathon session that exhausted two staff members who followed Ian and me from Cork City Library as we bought all around us for the yet-to-be-built Hollyhill Library.

October 26th Yet another day of intense library purchasing. I spent hours in Waterstone's, buying everything they had on politics, Irish history, local history, including every book published by the three Cork publishers, Collins Press, Mercier Press and Cork University Press. I think I purchased nearly a thousand books, including many luxurious hardbacks that will last at least half a century in the core non-fiction stock of the new Hollyhill Branch Library. It was a terrific feeling — to be able to spend so much money in one bookshop. People may complain that Waterstone's is not an Irish operation but the bookshop in Cork pays huge commercial rates to the council, employs a large number of local graduates and enhances the entire streetscape of Cork. Indeed, if Water-stone's called itself a 'Culture Hub' instead of a 'bookshop' it could justifiably ask for public funds to stay open like any other arts organization. Bookshops are the last remaining cultural centres that don't claim support from the public purse: it's a joy to leave public money in such pivotal busi-nesses. I was glad to see several copies of *The Last Geraldine Officer* in their Irish poetry section, though a recent royalty statement from Anvil Press reminds me that *Merchant Prince* still outsells *The LGO* by a wide margin. *Merchant Prince* is my most successful collection since *The Sorrow Garden* (of thirty years ago). I resisted the temptation to purchase even one copy of my own books with this public money.

December 11th I was mugged last night at 2 a.m. near St Lukes Cross by two young men. I was on my way home, very merry, from the library's Christmas dinner dance. I definitely drank two glasses of red wine more than I can handle and this may have left me vulnerable. Before I knew what was happening I was adroitly pushed into an alleyway near the Cork Chamber of Commerce building on Summerhill North, knocked to the ground and spun around. The muggers made off with my driving licence, my pocket diary, seventy euros in cash and my bank card. More annoying still, my diary was full of little notes, personal numbers and fragments of poems. My knees were cut in the fall but I got off lightly. There was no excessive malice in the youths, they just wanted cash. I phoned Cathy and she came to collect me. I must go to the police and report the loss of my driving licence, a serious matter. The funny thing is that the seventy euros I carried belonged to one of Cathy's prisoners who had sold a piece at the Prisoners' art exhibition in St Peter's Church. A bizarre and slightly embarrassing incident but I came to no great harm. Today I do feel shaken but this is due more to the excess of wine I had consumed rather than the incident itself. I really feel like giving up drink completely. My confidence in nighttime Cork is also shaken, an outcome that depresses me for I always felt extremely safe in Cork.

2012

May 8th Back after three days in Strokestown, County Roscommon. Mary O'Malley and I were judges in the very generous Strokestown International Poetry Prize. A terrific poet from Wexford, Jim Maguire, was the eventual winner. He is a most sensitive, extraordinary individual, a former student of piano and a resident of Korea for fourteen years. He now works for the Vocational Education Committee in Wexford town. (I wonder does the Wexford VEC realize how lucky they are to have someone of his calibre on their staff?) Mary and I had already limited the nearly two thousand poems to a shortlist of ten, a heartbreaking task. But it was far more heartbreaking to narrow that ten down to three winners but we had to do it, and we did. It is extraordinary how attached one becomes to certain poems — we were both seriously attached to Jim's winning poem, but I loved another shortlisted one by a South African poet, Isobel Dixon, another really gifted poet. Anyway, there it is (as Peter Jay might say, sadly). Good to see Merrily Harpur, and James Harpur, the poet, as well as the witty Paddy Bushe and John F Deane sparking off each other. Bushe is a Kerry devil and Deane is a kind of Christ.

May 29th Yet another invitation to read in Edinburgh at the end of August. I will be reading with Alan Gillis, a really fine poet who was born in Belfast. In his collection *Hawks and Doves* he has a poem with the brilliant title 'On a Weekend Break in a Political Vacuum'. And the poem is as good as the title, a great flowing narrative of escape from the world and yet not going anywhere.

June 2nd Very pleased with a poem I wrote today, 'Jerusalem', and the poem I wrote a few months ago, 'A Sound in the Woods'. My next collection must contain at least ten poems of this standard. I had an epiphany the other day about a new book, a collection to be called *Pandemonium* after the house of the Fallen Angels, the Luciferian parliament, in Milton's *Paradise Lost, Book 2.* The word 'pandemonium' has been a recurrent one in a number of my recent poems: this word surfaced of its own volition like a ghost. But Milton is there too, that great English Republican who knew how superstitious, how conniving, how simperingly aristocratic and regressive native Irish life truly is. Milton could have predicted that Irish Catholics, left to their own devices, would create a banking crisis. There is something Bourbon and Romish about our financial crisis — I mean the delusions, the subterfuge, and the bankers acting like a secret Curia. They have brought such shame upon our nation. Absolute shame.

June 11th Spent most of the day at Molly Keane's house in Ardmore, with Virginia her daughter and Lani, their literary advisor. I get such a boost, such a leap of joy, when I walk down those steps to the seaside cottage — expecting at any moment to see Molly's head peek out from behind the blue half-door and to hear Hero's barking. Maybe I'm too attached to these Anglo-Irish people and their houses: it's certainly true that I'm too attached for my own political and literary good. Everything in Irish life now eschews aristocracy and anything that smacks of grace or grandeur. My attachment to Molly Keane or the Brigadier's memory is among the most real emotional strings of my adult life. I have no hope of seeing this attachment reciprocated but that's not what it's about. It's something else, some very deep recognition of universal values that I also associate with a life of writing. For me writers, and especially poets, are born aristocrats — their instincts are value-laden, elitist in a technical sense, and associated with established comfort in that writing requires huge tranches of uninterrupted time the way that the making of a great garden or a great family requires centuries rather than moments of sensation. I am a deeply conservative person. I have been conservative since I was about seven-years-old.

June 30th At the funeral of Aunt Mary in Dungarvan. She was ninety-four years old, dying childless and contented to the very end. Last month she said to my sister Mary (who is named after her), 'You know, Mary, there isn't one day in my life that I'd want to change. If I had my life all over again I would do everything exactly the same.' She meant it. She loved dancing and drinking whiskey, two activities that when combined must surely be the best prescription for a long and happy life. She was a domestic servant all her life, but she was a complete snob. She had tried to prevent my mother from marrying my father, offering my mother money the night before their wedding and a boat-and-train ticket to England if she ran away from him. A fierce Dungarvan chauvinist, she thought people from small towns like Cappoquin were barbarians. She idolized the Palmers of Keating Street, a genteel family, and of course the Baumanns, her employers, an incredibly chic and good-looking middle-class Dungarvan family of master-jewellers with a thriving business in Mary Street. She lived vicariously off the style and social life of the Baumanns, taking sides with them in every detail of life, from deciding which kind of Dungarvan people were 'respectable' to the cut of suits and dresses of people going to Mass. She really basked in the lovely sunlight of the elegant Baumann family as I basked in the sunlight of the Brigadier. She and I had a great deal in common and she admired me above all other persons in the family. In me she recognized a fellow spirit. Even when I was a boy we used to have snobbish conversations about people we didn't admire, most of them my Bray and McCarthy relatives in Cappoquin. She was thrilled with me because I could be wicked and wounding about people, as wicked as she was. Ninety-four years old. What a triumph: Mary Tobin of Keating Street, a great Dungarvan snob.

July 10th A discussion has begun in the library about the coming Years of Remembrance between 2013 and 2023. The City Library should have a major plan for these years, including a schedule of lectures, exhibitions and publications. Today, in Kilmeaden, County Waterford, Christie's and Mealy's auctioneers began to sell off all the furniture, books, wines and general household effects of the late incorrigible snob, Ambrose Congreve of Mount Congreve. Several brilliant books for sale, including Crofton Croker's *Researches in the South of Ireland*, Byron and Samuel Johnson first editions and incredibly rare County Waterford books. There is something sad about all the wine he left behind, Petrus, Léoville Poyferré, Rothschild, all unopened. The catalogue from Mount Congreve is a salutary lesson in the utter uselessness of earthly possessions. That thought consoles me as it would console any penniless poet.

July 12th Today, while shredding old library membership cards, it was interesting to discover a healthy number of what can only be Protestant family names: Kingstons, Kings, Hosfords, Perrotts, Newenhams, Armstrongs, Mathews and Stones, many with characteristic Anglican Christian names like Holly, Heather, Iris, Zoe, George, Stuart and Ivor. The numbers are reassuring as they suggest that Cork, at least, is able to provide a nurturing home for Irishmen and women of the Reformed churches. Cork City Library's membership includes over one-hundred-and-twenty readers called Hosford, a hundred readers called Kingston, seventy Mathews, fifteen Newenhams and twenty-four Armstrongs.

Sadly, of the lively Jewish community who once lived in this city, there's hardly a trace left: only three Marcuses, four Hurwitzes, eight Cohens — and only one Goldberg, and this person had an address at one of the local refugee reception centres so he is a recent arrival from Russia. How ironic that is, given the Lithuanian origins of the original Jewish community in Cork.

July 14th The Irish Times has reported that the Government is seeking at least 4,000 further redundancies in the Public Service. I wonder if this will give me an opportunity to exit the shallow grave of Cork City Council? I cannot believe the number of years I have wasted at the library's lending desk: it's not that my library work is horrible, it certainly is not. What is horrible is that I have squandered over thirty-five of my best years, and the best working hours of those years, to a job that a hundred thousand others could do, when there was another job I should have done, a poet's life among the community of artists (the only proper life). On the margins of my library life I eked out a small literary life. Similar in many ways to Dennis O'Driscoll my life never had the propulsion or energy that Dennis put into the literary part of his existence. But despite everything, despite the absence of an empowering academic career, I think I did produce a body of decent work.

July 24th An incredibly busy few days within which I gave two public lectures and wrote a review of two new poetry books. On Friday I gave a lecture at the Elizabeth Bowen/ William Trevor Summer School in Mitchelstown. A terrific crowd, perhaps ninety people. I talked about 'de Valera, Elizabeth Bowen and the Neutrality of the Dead'. People must have been intrigued by the title: perhaps that's why so many turned out to a lecture that had a ten euro entrance fee. I gave people a picture of Ireland under neutrality, the severe censorship, the determined and really sinister control of Frank Aiken and Connolly, the two hard Ulstermen who controlled everything that moved in the Irish media as firmly as Mike Quill controlled the American Teamsters Union. Compared to them Elizabeth Bowen was a bungling amateur as a spy for Brendan Bracken. I read from 'The Happy

Autumn Fields' and *The Heat of the Day* (her magnificent war novel) as well as from Charles Ritchie's diaries, *The Siren Years*, and from de Valera's brilliant speeches on neutrality. I forgot completely to read from Dan Harvey's history of Collins Barracks which contains that marvellous description of the pro-Treaty and anti-Treaty old Republicans reporting for duty in 1940. They were answering a joint call to arms from Mr Cosgrave and Dev. As Dan Harvey says in his book, the Civil War ended in Collins Barracks in the summer of 1940.

The writer Eoghan Harris introduced me in a terrific opening speech. I was deeply moved.

On Sunday Cathy and I went down to Molly Keane's house where I gave a talk on 'The Integrity of Molly Keane'. Again a packed house of mainly middle-aged middle-class women. (Such a crowd as faced Rilke and Isaac Bashevis Singer in their day, so I cannot complain here.) In Molly's case I mentioned the extraordinary bond between fathers and daughters that Molly covers continuously, as well as the wonderful description of animals and food. I read from *Loving and Giving* that passage when Nicandra loses her baby because she tries to pull a stubborn cork from a wine bottle just after she's discovered that her husband has been having an affair with their mutual friend, Lalage. Virginia, Molly's daughter, was moved to the point of being upset by my reading. Her mother's words went straight to her heart. There's immense power in Molly's writing — every paragraph is emotionally charged in a way that it isn't in Elizabeth Bowen's fiction. It's true that Bowen understood the politics of inanimate things in Anglo-Irish life — Ascendancy interiors, ancestral acres, rooms, furniture — whereas Molly Keane, instinctively, understood the two great animate principals of the same life — adult relationships and the companionship of horses. Bowen, strangely enough, had no instinct for horses, nor did she capture the baroque drama of frustrated Anglo-Irish females. Characters in Bowen are full of thought, but Molly captured their drama — because she herself was dramatic and frustrated.

July 28th Home, and then to Ballyferriter, after two days in Ulster at the John Hewitt Summer School. I read poetry with the young and talented Leanne O'Sullivan. I felt very old as I listened to her introduce and read her work. She is splendid and gifted.

July 30th Monday. In Kerry, in our usual rented house by Béal Bán at Gortadoo. So far I've walked three times across the beach, up through the fields and onto Wine Strand in search of a pitching spot for my tent. All suitable pitches are taken. This is the first year that every suitable tent and caravan pitch at Wine Strand has been occupied. I wandered home across the fields and sand, annoyed as hell.

2013

January 30th For the last two weeks I've been trawling through my poetry files on the computer — collecting every poem I've written since the publication of *The Last Geraldine Officer.* I think I've got more than 150 poems but I'm determined that I won't publish more than 60 — enough to make a poetry book of 72-84 pages. After two physically huge books the last thing I need is another one: 84 pages max. I'm astonished at the unremitting bleakness of the poems. From the evidence in the poems I've certainly come through the seven most bleak years in my life. The title *Pandemonium* is absolutely perfect for such a dark collection. In truth it had been an utterly bleak decade, beginning with the misfortune of my getting involved with the European City of Culture project in 2001 or 2002. My life went downhill for over a decade after that. I was living like someone enslaved, someone chained to desk duties in the library and at the offices of Cork2005, all the while at the beck and call of bosses half my age, having to constantly defend public decisions that were never mine, and being treated with contempt by nearly everyone. It really has been a decade of extraordinary personal humiliations.

February 27th Recently my sister criticized me for not writing more about our family poverty in Cappoquin. She is mystified by my silence upon how much we suffered. She wants to see the evidence of this suffering in my poetry and she doesn't see it. She thinks that its absence is a form of political dishonesty, compounded, no doubt, by my bizarre interest in the Anglo-Irish gentry who surrounded Cappoquin. There's no doubt I was an odd child, and an even more odd youth — my closest friendships were with those Anglo-

Irish as I worked alongside them in their gardens. Those were the sweetest hours of my youth. I had a youth that was like the youth of a 19th-century Church of Ireland curate, being treated with respect and curiosity by the gentry while not having a penny to my name.

May 25th Tom Redshaw from the University of St Thomas in St Paul was here last week. He is still following, like a relentless bloodhound, the now fading Cork trail of John Montague's life. Montague and Dolmen Press are the territories of Redshaw's imagination. Inevitably the Montague trail is going cold. Having to repeat Montague stories has begun to bore me. I live very much in the present moment right now, mindful of the physical things around me, the garden, the pictures, the dogs, the crumbling built environment of Cork. I worry desperately about Cork. Cork is like a child with me. I worry about the future of Cork much more than I've ever worried about the future of Montague.

July 22nd At Molly Keane's house in Ardmore yesterday to give a talk on her three early novels, *Two Days in Aragon*, *Devoted Ladies* and *The Rising Tide*. It's impossible to exaggerate how good these novels are: Molly was a fiendish artist, a genius. She took immense pains over the construction of characters like Jessica in *Devoted Ladies* or Cynthia in *The Rising Tide* or the dark and complex Nan in *Two Days in Aragon*. There were 35-40 prosperous-looking people, a good crowd considering that it was on at four in the afternoon on a day during the summer holiday season when people's thoughts are on sand and ice-cream instead of cerebral, autumnal fictions. I read those parts of *The Rising Tide* when Cynthia on horseback learns of the death of her husband in 1915 and where she arrives, dressed to kill, at the costume party at the end of the novel, as well as the parts of *Devoted Ladies* where Jessica's obsessive attachments to people are revealed, and that part of *Two Days in Aragon* where the house is on

fire and Nan is killed by the Army truck. (This was as if
Molly was taking Elizabeth Bowen's material and reworking
it properly, in a more violent manner.) I think people are always impressed, even astounded, by the quality of Molly's
writing, by the character-driven focus and intensity of it, all
framed by extraordinary descriptions of interiors, flowers,
the countryside and clothes. I think I spoke for over one-
and-a-half hours but nobody left the room. Later, when
everyone had gone, Virginia asked me if I'd stay to supper
and we had pasta and salad, followed by carrageen pudding
and yoghurt. A real Molly Keane meal. Virginia is as great a
gossip as her mother so we gossiped endlessly about the
people of the Blackwater Valley, about Cappoquin and the
Keanes. Sometimes she surprises me with the directness of
her questions about people.

August 22nd Days of indolence and inertia. One thing that
lifted my inertia occured in the Frank O'Connor Library yesterday. A capacity crowd turned up to hear a distinguished
local man, Brendan Goggin, give a lecture on 'Writers of
Montenotte, St Lukes and Dillons Cross'. Early in the morning I'd nervously put out twelve chairs, praying that someone
would show up. With twenty minutes still to go to the start
of the lecture the library was jammed with enthusiastic locals.
It really was an extraordinary atmosphere, electric, enthusiastic, as if Seamus Heaney were expected at any moment. It
was wonderful, and doubly wonderful, that at eleven thirty
in the morning a huge crowd had turned up for a literary talk.
Brendan spoke brilliantly on two completely unknown authors
from Montenotte: Mrs Victor Rickard of 3, Montenotte Road,
author of thirty novels published in London and New York
between 1912 and 1948, and Suzanne Day, author of several
Abbey Theatre plays and the first woman elected to public
office (to the Board of Guardians of the N E Ward) in the
local elections of 1912. Tremendous applause and enthusiasm
— my neighbour, Georgie Walsh, wife of Maurice Walsh's

nephew, took three pages of notes.

This morning Billy O'Callaghan, the short story writer, held his third creative writing workshop: the atmosphere of yesterday continued in some mysterious way so that Billy's workshop was full. So, all is not lost: there is no reason to feel dispirited and inert. The love of literature endures in Cork.

September 4th Another catastrophe has fallen upon us all. Seamus Heaney has died. Kate and I attended his removal at Donnybrook church on Sunday night and the funeral Mass the next day. Before we went into the Mass Paul Muldoon, Paula Meehan, Carol Ann Duffy (now the British Poet Laureate) and I had coffee together. Muldoon gave an extraordinary oration. I didn't travel north to Bellaghy, but a huge contingement of Southern poets did travel north across the border behind the cavalcade. Seamus's death is beyond belief, unreal, tragic. I kissed Marie but as I approached her she blurted out, 'That was a beautiful piece you wrote in *The Examiner*'. I was astonished that she'd read it. She seemed strangely composed, all grief spent by the time I reached her in the long line of poets, journalists, politicians and rock stars who crowded round. His death marks the end of something prodigious in Irish life, a Yeatsian career where Seamus was the matinée idol, a Valentino, a John McCormack or Tom Moore. What a beautiful life he had, and what a beautiful adventure he and Marie had together; an adventure from which we all received postcards and felt included. It is too early to think about the literary meaning of his sudden passing. It will take decades for the full force of his work to be absorbed.

September 12th A phone call from John F Deane, looking for a Heaney poem for *Poetry Ireland Review*; a phone call from a literary group in Youghal who want me to give a talk on Seamus Heaney's life and poetry; an e-mail from Professor

Connolly of the UCC English Department who wants me to read a Seamus Heaney poem at a commemoration at the end of the month. Today a note from Julie O'Callaghan saying that Heaney more or less kept her alive since Dennis O'Driscoll's death. The reverberations created by his death are only beginning. The entire country has experienced a physical wrench. When one learns that over seventy per cent of all books by living poets sold in the UK and Ireland were books by Seamus one begins to understand the sensational dominance of this man, not only as a spiritual leader but as a huge presence in the book trade. What will become of us in this new era of ordinariness?

September 24th We went to Dublin at the weekend to attend Theo's marvellous 60th birthday party in the Sutton Golf Club (itself a monument to the great golfing family of Joe Carr and JD Carr). Terrific night of food and music with the handsome Dorgan family as well as Paula Meehan's relatives and a peppering of luminaries like Brian Maguire the artist and the poet Ciaran Carson. No spark between myself and Ciaran, a pity.

October 6th The Fine Gael Government has been defeated in its opportunistic bid to abolish the Seanad. Both Labour and Sinn Féin, to their eternal shame, supported the Government's efforts. The entire country is shocked by the result — how did all the journalists and professional pollsters get their predictions so wrong? I've been studying a map of the results. It is a social map of Ireland showing the country divided sharply between the Western and Northern country-and-western 'culchies' and the educated, more sophisticated, population of the East Coast around Dublin. The educated and middle-class area of Cork (Douglas, Rochestown and the yachting villages of the harbour) and County Galway's professional, publishing, arts, broadcasting and Irish-speaking elite around Carraroe voted against abolition. Cork's impoverished (and Sinn Féin-dominated) North Central constituency voted for it.

I rang Theo to congratulate him: he was, after all, one of the leading lights of the campaign to save Seanad Éireann. In this he has performed one of the most important duties to his country. I admire him tremendously for his public bravery. This really is one of the crowning moments of his life.

October 14th One of my main sources of drama education was Molly Keane's papers in Ardmore: in particular, the flare-up of Molly's temper when her play *Ducks and Drakes* failed miserably in 1941. The extraordinary correspondence between Molly, John Gielgud and Binkie Beaumont contains illuminating insights into stagecraft, character development, the social limitations of farce, the imperative of conflict and why plays fail. Molly took the failure very badly: she felt that John Gielgud had failed her as director (he certainly had; he would go on to fail her for the next twenty years until he finally killed off her career in the mid 1960s). One of the first reader's reports on the play is damning, 'The play is too long and unfortunately grows less in interest as it progresses. There is nearly a collapse in the last act and I am afraid that this is largely due to the fact that this act depends to such an extent on the recounting of happenings elsewhere, always a bad thing in stagecraft . . . I got very tired of June . . . Racing jargon never goes down extremely well with an audience because a large portion doesn't know what it means . . . I can't see much point in Phyllis's cough.'

Binkie Beaumont's letter to Molly — he was by then virtual owner of H M Tennent operating from The Globe on Shaftesbury Avenue — is a masterpiece. He explained that the War had intervened to ruin upper-class farce. The Blitz audience in London was a new kind of audience that had little patience for upper-class eccentrics. Twenty years later Molly's characters would again be hissed off the stage, by a new blitzed audience of Angry Young Men, an audience inspired by John

Osborne and others.

Another playwriting education was from an unlikely source: The British Council's *The Year's Work in Literature 1950*. Therein Stephen Spender has a brilliant essay on the success of T S Eliot's *The Cocktail Party*, then packing houses in both London and New York. Spender had spotted that there was a remarkable resemblance between Eliot's new play and Shakespeare's *Measure for Measure*. In Shakespeare the Duke of Vienna disappears in order to secretly influence the lives of his subjects; in like manner the character of the psycho-analyst Reilly and his 'assistants' influences the lives of those in *The Cocktail Party*. 'The weakness of Eliot's earlier plays,' writes Spender, 'is that they tended to be monologues, that they scarcely created the personality even of the central character in each, and that the plot was an illustration of a thesis rather than a dramatically conceived story. Their denouements tended to be either an obvious foregone conclusion, as in *Murder in the Cathedral*, or an escape of the main character into a world outside the conditions of his particular drama, as in *The Family Reunion*.'

The marital problems of Edward and Lavinia provide a real plot, real human tension, that bolsters the slightly unreal destiny of another key character, Celia. Edward and Lavinia confront one another, they live out their stage denouement by acting upon each other's lives. Spender puts it brilliantly: 'Here Eliot overcomes a defect which has previously made me doubt whether he was a dramatic writer — a certain congenital disinclination to believe that action is ever significant. A dramatist must surely believe that human problems can be expressed in action, that human beings change and develop in their relationships with one another, are realized or frustrated, made or destroyed by their actions. Being made or developed, being frustrated or destroyed — these are the huge human destinies that need to be felt by a theatre audience on any Friday or Saturday night.'

November 25th It is absolutely crucial that I concentrate completely on theatre writing next year. This thought was in my head for hours today as I cut branches from the beech tree, the old myrtles and several wayward branches of a very old and tired amelanchier.

2014

January 6th Most commentators and anthologists dealing with Irish poetry have missed the most important, the most tectonic, shift in Irish poetry since the death of Yeats. I mean writing by women. In the last half century or more — certainly from 1957 to the present — no shift has been more obvious in Irish writing than the arrival of the female voice at the centre of literary life. And when I look back at the critical part of my life I can see how true this is. I have written the longest and deepest essays on women, from Molly Keane to Eavan Boland to Paula Meehan. Critically I've written almost nothing else of consequence.

February 12th Only a few weeks left before I retire from the City Library. Mentally I have already left the building. My head is full of plans, both for the garden and for my writing. My retirement gratuity is derisory: by the time I cover all my outstanding liabilities I'll have no savings left, not a penny. At the age of sixty, after thirty-seven years of work, this is a disgrace. But there it is. I am a living financial embarrassment. I always have been thus but, also, I do think of the poets before me who reached the age of sixty and had less money — Hartnett, O'Grady, Seán Ó Ríordáin and Patrick Galvin.

February 17th A terrific Munster Literature Centre Spring Poetry Festival has just ended. For the first time in many years I attended most of the readings, so much so that by Saturday night I felt almost physically sick from an excess of poetry.

February 28th Listening, yet again, to a discussion on the mounting crisis of public funding in Northern Ireland on

BBC Ulster. The Tory government is determined to cut funding even further in 2014 and 2015. This will have a devastating effect on Belfast and Derry communities that are only now recovering from the traumatic effects of the Troubles.

March 11th Eudora Welty wrote a lovely letter to Molly after she'd finished reading *Good Behaviour*. I once copied a piece of that letter from Molly's papers. It was written on August 31st, 1981, from Pinehurst Street, Jackson, Mississippi. Here's Eudora Welty writing to Molly: 'I wish I could tell you how extraordinary and how crowning a piece of work I found it. It filled me with pleasure page after page. I felt the kind of admiration for it that's exhilaration, really, something that goes right to the heart of the hope every true lover of fiction feels on opening some longed-for book . . . I knew I had a masterpiece in my hands . . . '

Imagine getting a letter like that from Eudora Welty. Imagine writing a book that deserved such a letter.

April 20th Walking around Gougane this morning after a coffee in Cronin's Café. It was so still and peaceful and ghostly. I thought of those unsaintly ones I love: Robert Gibbings, Eric Cross.

Writing notes, yet again, on the books of W E D Allen of Whitechurch House, Cappoquin. An old obsession, one of the many useless obsessions of my life — useless in the sense that it doesn't fit into any agreed category of knowledge that the scholars teach. I spend my life chasing after obscure moths from history, from Francis Sylvester Mahony ('Father Prout') to Mrs Victor Rickard, from Molly Keane's forgotten novels to Corkery's obscure good stories. I am like a clergyman's widow, placing flowers on the graves of the forgotten of her village on Remembrance Sunday. These obsessions have got me nowhere, but such material fascinates me. It can't be that useless. I've just finished reading the very young W E D Allen's essay 'A Vision: The Lost Garrison', printed in his Macmillan book, *Béled-Es-Siba*, published in 1925 when Allen was only twenty-four-years-old. I'm thinking of writing an essay, or at least preparing a lecture to be called *Prince of Borderlands: The strange journeys of W E D Allen.* I would have to consider all of these books: *The Turks in Europe, Problems of Turkish Power in the Sixteenth Century, A History of the Georgian People, Russian Embassies to the Georgian Kings, The Ukraine, Caucasian Battlefields, Strange Coast* (novel), *David Allens, Béled-Es-Siba, Fascism in Relation to British History and Character* (pamphlet). This is not by any means an exhaustive list of what Bill Allen wrote but it is an indication of his range and brilliance. That essay in *Béled-Es-Siba* begins:

'A rainy day in Omagh — fitful rushing boisterous clouds with sudden whipping showers and occasional half-hourly splashes of the sun . . . Omagh is flagged today and decked with vivid streamers across her muddy High Street — black and blue and orange, they are dripping in the rain — "What we have, we hold", "We stand for King and Empire", "No surrender — 1692", they read in glaring running capitals . . . It is the anniversary of the Siege of Derry, strangely celebrated by these violent historically-minded Ulstermen, yet a matter of some import once, which signified the triumph of Orange William, and may have affected to success the course of that dubious institution — meet for modern explanation and apology, if not for actual and conscientious dissolution — that pirates' coup, the British Empire . . . Under the streamers, in the long and wet and narrow cobbled street, in the early afternoon, they are forming a column. They are marching in a ragged line — that great nuisance of today — the Protestants of Ulster.'

Less than ten years later Allen would write in support of Mosley and British Fascism, taking as his example of the early moral usurpation of Parliament by an efficient band of Fascists, the Ulster Volunteer gunrunning and the Curragh Mutiny. Yet this man, who understood implicitly the fight

for survival of racial groups abandoned in borderlands, became a Unionist MP, an MI6 interrogator, a novelist and great
lover, and one of Soviet Russia's deadliest enemies. Any talk
on his life and work would have to include references to his
career as a Unionist MP, his relationship with Mosley and
Philby, Laurens van der Post's memories of Allen in *Yet Being
Someone Other,* as well as the Natasha Allen *Icons* gift to the
National Gallery, the early encouragement of Dervla Murphy
through an introduction to John Murray and Terence de
Vere White, the building of a great 20,000 volume library of
Slavonic Studies, as well as the creation of a garden at White-
church and his directorship of the family companies, David
Allens.

March 10th Much chat among the Cork poets in the last
few days about the impact, good or ill, of Seamus Heaney's
'career'. That word 'career' is used, as if a poet could set out
to make a 'career' of what is essentially a compulsive, private
accident. Heaney did have a trajectory that looked like a grand
career, in the manner of a great opera singer. Fame attended
him wherever he went; people wanted to be near him in the
way one wants to be near a film star: if not actually at his
table, then at least at a table nearby. Everything he touched
turned to literary gold. Not real gold, but literary gold: that's
the difference. He was always, first and foremost, a scholar
in constant pursuit of even more scholarship — nothing
pleased him more than to hear some new piece of information on a particular poem, an anecdote that might deepen his
understanding of a text. In this he was a born teacher more
than anything else. In a sense he taught us the greatness of
poetry by being a great poet; each of his books was a teaching
instrument. In this he was closest to Yeats, both wanted to
instruct us: Yeats wanted to instruct the nation and Heaney
wanted to instruct his world readership. And it was world
readership he wanted, not world domination. Politically
Heaney was much more passive and modest than Yeats. Yeats

wished to lead his nation into a new history while Heaney wanted to escape the massacre of history, like a humble 'wood-kerne' escaping the massacre of a battlefield. Despite the incredible ambition of his poetry Heaney was utterly devoid of political ambition, as he had written in *North*. He had absolutely no political programme; he just wasn't interested. In this he was completely unlike Yeats and much closer in temperament to someone like Louis MacNeice. Up close one could see an unexpected gentle and genteel streak in Heaney that is so like MacNeice, the MacNeice who mourns a dead cat or notices the pattern of stars. When I think of Heaney's wonderful Glanmore sequences of escape I also think of MacNeice on Achill, following his father's footsteps on the sand at Keel.

But the conversation in recent weeks has turned to the damage Heaney might have done, not to Ireland but to fellow poets. This is a difficult question and it is based upon the assumption that the public has only a limited capacity for attention so that if the same public gave Heaney too much attention it must have meant the starvation of other Irish literary careers. Certainly, over the years, this was Mahon's, Montague's, Cronin's and Kinsella's view. But it is a very subjective view and I don't think it's a correct one. The success of one poet has hardly anything to do with the failure of another. Poets create their own core audience and poets only need the attention of this core audience to carry on writing. Over time most poets create that core audience automatically, moving in a circle of influence from family to colleagues to a local newspaper presence. Fame, when it happens, is essentially an illusion created by the broader book market: it is a cocktail party of public relations, book distribution and display, front rank reviewing and commercially astute media attention. It is an illusion very deliberately created at first by commercial book interests, but it can't be sustained unless a huge audience reacts. This is what happened in Heaney's case: the British audience reacted to something in Heaney, some universal reverberation. This occurred after the publication of *North* in 1975. The Irish, as usual, reacted positively to Heaney's English fame. And within six years of *North*, by switching from Oxford University Press to Farrar, Straus and Giroux in New York, Heaney ignited the same extraordinary reverberation in American audiences.

Such a public response is not a requirement of poetry, or even a common expectation, but it happened in Heaney's case, as it happened to Byron, Thomas Moore, Pasternak and Robert Lowell. It's a huge mistake to think that what happened to Seamus Heaney is the norm. It is not. Poetry is quite an hermetic art: a poet who consistently sells perhaps seven hundred copies of each collection and attracts audiences of forty or fifty people is a poet doing very well indeed. Heaney outsold all other poets combined and addressed audiences of thousands but he, more than anyone else, was aware of the illusion of this. He may have yearned for it at the beginning of his career (up to *North*, 1975, perhaps) but by the time he published *Field Work* in 1979 his fame had become a huge monster, an absolute burden. He was acutely aware of how he had become the servant of his own fame; the work created by this fame exhausted and depressed him, though he loved crowds. He was as famous as George Bernard Shaw, but Shaw had excluding social skills and an adroit skill at repelling unwanted people that Heaney could never avail of. Son of a Catholic cattle dealer and a Gaelic footballer Heaney never once moved to the First Class compartment of society. We would never allow him to escape from Steerage. But I think this illusion of a distinctly Irish kind of fame created by Heaney actually helped other Irish poets. Certainly between 1975 and 2005, those long, fertile thirty years, Irish poets made hay under Heaney's beneficent sunlight. There is no way that American universities would have hired so many Ulster poets if Heaney hadn't been around. Many quite comfortably-off Irish academic poets of today owe their lucrative jobs to that afterglow of Heaney.

They would never admit that, but I am absolutely certain about this. Heaney's fame created the same lucrative afterglow as Yeats — MacNeice, Colum, even Kinsella, first slipped into American academe on the sunbeams created by Yeats's fame. This is all too painful to talk about yet. When it comes to Heaney in certain quarters of Irish poetry there is still a raw feeling of bruised egos. It will be a very long time before his fame is forgiven.

March 17th Just the other day when I read a small selection of my poems to a group of people in the library my instinct about the negativity of FF material was confirmed. A woman came up to me after the reading and said, 'I loved those love poems, the poems for your wife with stones and sea and photographs, and your poems about Brigadier FitzGerald and Molly Keane but, my God, when you mentioned that despicable Party you lost me. I couldn't listen to you.' This educated woman, an English teacher in a first rate Secondary School, was disgusted with me for using such materials in poetry. In talking about Fianna Fáil I lost her affection. This has happened to me throughout my life — I can read poems about love, childen, the sea, the Great War, the Anglo-Irish gentry in West Waterford, even the weather, and I can carry people along with me. But when I mention Fianna Fáil, de Valera, elections, ballot boxes, people are simply disgusted. They literally shrink away from me or from any encounter with me. I have thought hard and long on this matter: in writing about Fianna Fáil I've destroyed any possibility that my work might be taken seriously among educated Irish people. A critical atmosphere is always left-wing and progressive. Knowing Fianna Fáil since my childhood has been the self-destruct button of my poetic 'career'. About once every five years I press this button and the scorn pours in.

October 3rd Yesterday I brought three boxes of my own personal papers from Cork2005 to the City and County

Archives in Gerald Griffin Street. Another three boxes of material had been destroyed while being stored in our garden shed: a pitchfork had penetrated through three heavy-duty plastic bags, destroying all those papers in the downpours of last winter.

October 6th Just ten people in the audience for our Waterstone's reading as we were clashing with a John Banville reading at UCC. But on Saturday I took part in a superb seminar, chaired by Maureen Kennelly of Poetry Ireland, and a short reading at the Dromineer Festival in North Tipperary.

October 12th A nightmare of a month, I mean in terms of reviewing duties. I think I've written nearly eight thousand words since the beginning of this month, a long review of the Derek Mahon biography, published yesterday in *The Examiner* (an embarrassing typo, Emory University is spelled 'Amory', very annoying: I checked my computer file; I had misspelled Emory), another long review of Van Morrison's lyrics, an introductory note on Peter Fallon for Poetry International in Rotterdam and a carefully worded letter of nomination to Aosdána for Enda Wyley.

October 13th A great visit today from Alessandro Gentili of Florence. Tonight we are giving a reading at the Dante Society to celebrate the centenary of Mario Luzi, the great Italian poet who knew Ireland so well. Much news of the Montague with whom Alessandro is in constant touch. Alessandro had an extraordinary story of Montague's behaviour years ago in Florence during a visit to the home of the Florentine poet, Piero Bigongiari.

November 6th Home after a week in Italy: Bologna, Florence and Ravenna. I took part in a reading at the Mario Luzi Conference in Florence where I met Fabrizio Dall'Aglio, the poet-editor at Passigli, Florence, who wants to publish a

Selected Poems of mine in Italian. God bless him, any act that would attach me however tangentially to Italian life would be most welcome. All of this is being pushed by Alessandro Gentili.

November 21st A note last night from Clíona Ní Ríordáin, now a Professor at the Sorbonne. She reports that she's begun teaching *The Last Geraldine Officer* to a post-graduate literature class. In her class are Italians, Moroccans, French and Algerians. She says they are enjoying the book. She will get her reward in heaven. Somewhere in Europe, at least, my work is being read. How ashamed I am of my own lack of respect for scholarship when I was a student at UCC. For years I used to blame Montague and his campus promulgation of the poet as priest (a poet as one of the 'annointed') for this lack of respect for my lecturers and their curriculum. But Montague is not to blame, though I wish Montague had reminded us that he graduated with a Double First from UCD and was just pipped by John Jordan for an Oxford Studentship, and neither is the pernicious influence of Graves' *The White Goddess* that swept through the coterie of poets like *The Thoughts of Chairman Mao*. No. My poor academic experience is entirely my own fault, created by my own early attitudes. From the moment my first poem was published in *The Irish Times* when I was seventeen (and in Fifth Class in St Anne's Secondary School, Cappoquin) my whole attitude to authority and received opinion changed for the worst. I became an intractable romantic and unteachable and I found a willing and enabling disciple in the old Brigadier who, placing me in charge of Glenshelane House and its acres and bank account in his absence, gave me a little kingdom that was independent of family, school and Cappoquin. I colonized Glenshelane, I dominated the Brigadier, I bamboozled myself with a kind of onanistic, determined ambition — the character of which survives to this day and renders me incapable of any sustained sense of belonging to anyone else's projects.

Poetry gave me an alternative world, an imagined and imaginary kingdom; I thrived and I still thrive there, but only in the habitat of my own poetry. Narcissism has huge limitations. It is a regressive quality. It doesn't allow us to cooperate. It makes us reject teamwork.

November 22nd Just finished reviewing Harry Clifton's new Selected, *The Holding Centre*, from Bloodaxe, for Maurice Earls' *Dublin Review of Books*. Clifton is a real master, one of the best, if not the best, of our generation. I complain about him a little bit in my review, but not much. He can be incredibly tiresome and opinionated about others but his gift as a poet is beyond criticism. His narcissism expresses itself constantly in his expressions of resentment at how neglected he is. He is very like Matthew Sweeney in this, whereas my own narcissism has never changed: my narcissism as a poet expresses itself as a quiet self-importance that seems to offend no one. But Clifton really is a genius of a poet, full of intelligence and instinct, and both qualities equally poised to produce an unassailable Irish Auden. Hopefully he'll not become as dull and didactic as Auden in his later years. *The Holding Centre* a beauty of a book.

November 23rd Long phone call from Thomas Dillon Redshaw in St Paul. He is worried about John Montague and his situation in Nice. He says the apartment that John and Elizabeth live in is too small, too difficult to manoeuvre within and located in too dangerous a neighbourhood. Strangely enough I'd been reading Montague's *Smashing the Piano* with its cover by John Shinnors. I loved his birthday poem for Robert Greacen: 'Our gratitude, then, for grafting in a hard time, / to hang in, like Captain Fox, a wily veteran.' But the Robert Graves-like sequence 'Dark Rooms' is also fascinating, written in that voice you hear only now and again from Montague, the Montague of *A Chosen Light* and *Tides*. John is eighty-five years old this year and I agree with Redshaw that he deserves to be living in comfort and elegance, the things he yearned for in his desolate youth. But how can this be arranged when everyone we knew who had money and a love of art is dead? Only an American scholar-poet of limited means like Tom Redshaw can still dream of helping him. Bless him. But Montague's needs are simply overwhelming. If only Montague could be sent to the Park Lane Hotel in NY for the rest of his days like Rafaella, the old Duchess of Leinster, who was sent there by the trustees of the Leinster Estate. There he would be wined and dined, and people like the Irish Consul-General or fellow-Ulsterman Paul Muldoon could call in to see him — it would be adult cocktails in New York after childhood penance in Armagh. This is how his final years should be.

November 26th A long meeting with the historian Tom Dunne about our presentation on James Barry at the National Gallery on Sunday. We spent two hours talking about Barry — Tom is a real expert — and we only stopped talking because Tom had to leave to meet his daughter for lunch in the city centre. We never resolved how we will compress all we want to say into forty-five minutes at the Gallery but, if we bring up even half the issues like Barry's Catholicism, Barry's political support of American Independence, his unhappy relationship with the Royal Academy, his neoclassicism slowly morphing into early nineteenth-century Romanticism, his self-pity, his hopeless attachment to history painting, his financial affairs, the audience in Dublin will have learned something — or will, at least, have moved closer to Barry.

December 1st Home after a hugely successful seminar with Professor Tom Dunne on James Barry at the National Gallery. An excellent Sunday afternoon crowd, perhaps sixty people, including Jennifer Johnston and Clíodhna Ní Anluain of RTÉ. Tom and I went deeply into the James Barry myth; we were like two old friends of Barry, throwing out details and anecdotes, and worrying, like the family of Edmund Burke, about Barry's terrible character. I tried to hammer home a number of key points on Barry's achievement: his absolute belief in the primacy of art as seen through history painting, his anxiety for British imagination, his defence of that imagination against all comers, his dreadful, irascible character that could not cope with dissent from others and, crucially, the deficit of love in his life, a deficit that made him more and more intolerant and more isolated.

December 14th It is a great source of happiness to me, and gives me a great sense of confidence in the future of Irish poetry, when I see gifted creatures like Leanne O'Sullivan and John McAuliffe emerging into the light. Their stars may not reach their zenith until well into the 2020s or even the 2030s. I will be gone by then but poetry — that permanent thing, poetry — will be singing at full voice through them. This is the great, joyful thing about poetry, it renews itself through new voices in every generation.

December 26th Yet again reading more of W E D Allen on Turkey, Russia and Ukraine, as well as the letters and diaries of Charles Ritchie and Elizabeth Bowen. Bowen was in her early forties when she first met the Canadian diplomat. She had been married for eighteen years and was by then the author of six novels — a mature, worldly woman who knew her appetites and knew how to have them satisfied. Emotionally as well as intellectually she was vastly more sophisticated than Molly Keane. It is no wonder that Molly lived in awe of her, and was a little afraid of her, though it was Molly who had led the way in matters of love. After all Molly married her tall and handsome Bobby Keane of Cappoquin who was six years her junior. It was soon after Molly returned from her honeymoon in New York with her handsome Cappoquin Keane that Bowen began her affair with the much younger Ritchie. Was the affair begun as a form of one-upmanship over Molly, I wonder? Such things are possible and do happen. Bowen was competitive, brooding, calculating; certainly not an open person in the way Molly was an open book emotionally. In the bleak years of the mid-forties to the mid-fifties Molly would stay at Bowenscourt, writing in one room while Elizabeth wrote in the other. Bowen, in one letter to Charles Ritchie, remarks on the terrifying power of Molly's cynicism and pessimism. Remaining guarded, in everything, was one of the abiding characteristics of Elizabeth Bowen. Molly was certainly the more Irish of the two, if that really matters, and it probably doesn't. The proof of Molly's Irishness is in *Two Days in Aragon*. Only an Irish countrywoman could have written a book like that. The baroque sensuousness of Molly is pure Bram Stoker or Sheridan Le Fanu.

December 29th In Dublin yesterday at Leopardstown Races. A wonderful day. The day also enjoyed equally by Kate Inez who has inherited my relishing of beautiful atmospheres. It was a day of pure magic. On the way home, our consciences quelled by the knowledge that we'd backed as many winners as losers, Kate described the day brilliantly: 'It's not any one thing about horseracing, it's the whole package, the loveliest, most friendly people imaginable all around, the seriousness of everyone involved with the horses, from the stewards (including, I see in the racecard, a Justice of the High Court as Acting Steward of the day) to the jockeys, and, of course, the gods and goddesses themselves, those stallions and mares bred to be the greatest racing horses in the world.' It is easy to see why the impressionable, competitive and romantic young Molly Keane was so overwhelmed by the atmosphere of horses and horse racing: she fell in love with the atmosphere of the Perry yard of County Tipperary, that combination of comfort, hope and hard work that characterizes every family that is wedded to the Irish turf. The Perrys, the O'Learys, the Magniers, the Meades: may they live as long as Ireland itself. As far as I'm concerned they are immortal families;

their well-bred horses make them nearly as important as a circle of poets.

Neil came home from London with a terrific London-Irish girl, Ciara, librarian daughter of a Portlaoise father and a literary mother with Tipperary connections. In her he seems to have found the love of his life. But he is increasingly depressed about the film industry in London. It is a difficult business, this film business; it is more uncertain than a life in writing. The creative life was ever a precarious one and a journey in the arts is rarely paved with gold; it's not even paved with copper. But I'd still encourage Neil and Kate Inez, and every young person, to write; to persist, to never give up. Don't expect writing to give you a living, but its inability to give you a living is not a judgement upon its importance. As Isaac Bashevis Singer once wrote, a life of writing is the same as a life dedicated to the study of the Talmud — it is its own reward. A life in writing may be endlessly hand-to-mouth, but it is full of life. As Molly Keane used to say — holding a champagne Martini or a Bloody Mary aloft in front of the blazing drawing-room fire at Glenshelane House — to write is hell, but not to write is even worse.

Acknowledgements

The author wishes to express his gratitude to Catherine Coakley for her companionship and support over many of the years covered in these journals.

The author also thanks the Editors of *Irish Pages* (Belfast) and *New Hibernia Review* (Minnesota) who published excerpts from the journals. Excerpts were also published in *Gardens of Remembrance* (New Island Books, 1998).

Gratitude is also extended to Princeton University Library where many of the original manuscript journals are held as part of The Leonard L Milberg Collection of Irish Poetry.

Finally, deep gratitude to Peter, Jean and Suella of The Gallery Press for the hours and hours of exhaustive editing that they put into this book.